The Harp, The Cross, and The Sword

By John Padraig McLiam

Illustrations by Jane R. Washburn

ISBN 0-7414-4467-4

Published by:

1094 New DeHaven Street, Suite 100
West Conshohocken, PA 19428-2713
Info@buybooksontheweb.com
www.buybooksontheweb.com
Toll-free (877) BUY BOOK
Local Phone (610) 941-9999
Fax (610) 941-9959

Printed in the United States of America

Printed on Recycled Paper

Published March 2008

Preface

The story begins with the Neolithic period, at a time when history was sustained by oral tradition; continuing through twenty-four chapters, wherein history was recorded first by the oral poetry of the bards, subsequently by the ballads telling it in song and ultimately by the written word. The story takes the reader to the middle of the twentieth-century, when the republic was recognized by the nations of the world, and on through the power deadlock of the twenty-first century to devolved, power-sharing in northern Ireland. I have made an effort to summarize the domestic policies, and events of the last half-century, in an easily readable style, and to portray the situation in an accurate, yet positive, perspective.

The poetry and the music, has kept their history alive in the collective Irish memory. Little wonder that the Irish people have such a long memory of past injustices.

The Neolithic age describes the early residents of Ireland before the coming of the four Celtic tribes, These are treated rather superficially, as they were pretty much the same as any stone-age society. These people were easily displaced by the Celts, at a later time, as they had developed the use of bronze, and ultimately iron weapons, and tools.

The four Celtic groups, the Formorians, the Firbolgs, the Dannans, and the Milesians, migrated from eastern Europe in four different migratory waves, each playing their separate roles in the development of Celtic Society.

The Celts had their own mythology, which was memorized and told orally, and was only written down after several hundred years. The first cycle, called the Red Branch, covered the first two centuries, and tells of the *Tain Bo Cuailage*, (The Cattle Raid of Cooley), and the super warrior *Cuchilain..* This was followed by what is called the Fenian Cycle, which tells of *King Finn McCool, and his Fenian Warriors.* This legend, resembles the English legend of *King Arthur, and the Knights of the Round Table.*

These earlier cycles were followed by the two "King Cycles," which covered the next three hundred year period, to about 500 AD. These were only myths, not history, but they did describe early Celtic society.

The coming of Christianity, and St Patrick, in the fourth century, had great impact on Celtic culture, and changed Ireland forever. The Viking invasion began near the end of the eighth century, and ended in 1014, when Ireland's, greatest Ard Ri, High King Brian of Boruma, was the first ruler to unite Ireland as a nation, and drive the Vikings out from the island. This was, unfortunately, negated in 1169 with the coming of the English, in what history has called, the Norman Invasion.

The rest of the story relates the events of the following nine-hundred years, telling of Ireland's struggles to be free of English domination, and suppression. I have endeavored to tell this story in an easy to read style, dealing honestly with the more significant events; the Tudor dynasty, the rule of Oliver Cromwell, the role of the church, the persecutions, and the penal laws. Ultimately, came King James, and the Battle of the Boyne, igniting a lasting struggle that persisted to the present time.

All those, of Irish heritage, should know the names of the Irish patriots, such as Theobald Wolfe Tone, Father Michael Murphy, Robert Emmett, Daniel O'Connell, Stewart Parnell, the Fenians, Michael Collins, Eamon deValera, and others. Certain events had major effects on our modern world; the Great Famine, the Act of Union, the Rising of 1916, partition of the North, the Irish Civil War, and the Orange movement.

I do not present *The Harp, The Cross, and the Sword,* as a comprehensive work, but merely a selective chronology of the struggle of a great people. The *Harp* represents the oral tradition, the poetry, and the Irish folk music; from the early bards and traveling minstrels, to the pub "minstrels" of today. The *Cross*, obviously, represents Christianity, which has played a major role in Irish culture, in the past and to the present time. The *Sword*, of course, represents the use of arms, during a two thousand year struggle to be a nation. I have tried to be accurate, and as unbiased as reasonably possible. I hope it will be received in that light. God Bless Ireland!

J.P. McLiam

Table of Contents

Chapter One
Pre-Christian Ireland
7000 B.C.- 400 A.D.

Way Before History, The Development of a Society, The Expanded Family, Tribal Society, The Land, Mesolithic Age, Neolithic Age, The Bronze Age, The Iron Age, The Mythological Cycles, The Formorians, The Firbolgs, The Danaans, The Milesians, Celtic Society, The King, The Poet, The Story Teller, The Warriors, King's Advisors, The Druids, The Judges, The Freeman, The Slaves

Way Before History:

In the times before history, when man first evolved, or was created, the basic social unit was the family. Initially this unit consisted of two humans. One of them was a man. The other one was different from the man, and both of them came to appreciate this difference. After a while they came to notice that every once in a while another small human would emerge from the body of the different one.

Not understanding the cause of this occurrence, they simply accepted it and went on appreciating one another. However, both of these people were different from the other animals that inhabited their world, in-as-much as they both were endowed with free will, and the ability to reason. It wasn't long before they figured out that one plus one results in three. Anyway, it worked out well because human lifespan was short in those days, and child mortality high, due to marauders, disease and wild beasts. It was to their advantage to have as many children as possible, as there was safety in larger numbers.

The Development of a Society:

Because of the difference in their size and strength, and other physiological attributes, it turned out that the man would be the hunter, protector and provider, while the other one, who would come to be called womb-man, (woman), would of course produce and rear the children and keep the cave. This was a good arrangement, and it really caught on. However, this being a hunter-gatherer type of culture, there arose one serious problem; poachers. Times were hard. No cave man wanted to take on the risk and responsibility for protecting and providing for some other man's off-spring.

Consequently, adultery was to be considered a crime. Now in-as-much as the woman, as the receptacle of the seed, was the only one capable of being adulterated, it was determined that adultery would be a crime that only a woman could commit. The male was left free to appreciate as many women as he was capable of appreciating.

While this undoubtedly worked in favor of the process of natural selection, one can hardly make an argument for the fairness, or equality of the system. However, this was the system of nearly every primitive culture, continuing right through the time of Moses, and the resulting Judeo-Christian traditions of modern times. Polygamy bad! Monogamy Good!

The Expanded Family:

The concept of family expanded to include aunts, uncles and cousins, and eventually became a clan. This expanded as different clans intermarried, widening the gene pool and actually resulting in an improvement of the species. As more clans were joined together they became a tribe.

Tribal Society:

Tribes would find hunting together an advantage, and as they progressed from a hunter/gatherer culture to a herding culture, or agrarian culture, they found that they then had property to protect. This of course required property laws of some sort. It also required warriors to protect the property from other tribes. Laws and warriors require some sort of government.

In the times before memory governments were generally autocratic. They consisted primarily of a chieftain and his chosen associates. The criterion, for selecting a chieftain, was quite simple and direct. In-as-much-as the prime directive of those times was, "The fittest survive, " the chieftain would be the fittest and the strongest, or in some way, at least, the most successful warrior in the tribe. In primitive society, there was usually one family in the tribe that was dominant, and the chieftain was generally selected from that family. This resulted in the development of a warrior aristocracy.

The Land:

Let's take a look at how this human condition played out in Ireland. Let's assume that before there were people, there was the land. Ireland is an island, but that was not always true. For that matter, neither was it true in Britain. Geologists tell us that at one time Britain and Ireland were connected to Europe by two land bridges, and it was by these means that the first inhabitants of these isles arrived from Europe.

As the ice age warmed and thawed, the rising sea slowly covered the bridges. Some of these early people, from the continent, apparently moved on to pre-historic Ireland, while others remained on the larger island. Ireland's bridge, from present day Britain, was cut off much earlier than Britain's bridge, from present day Belgium and Netherlands, thus isolating the pre-historic Irish from England, and European influence. It has been estimated that the first immigrants to present day Ireland, may have come as early as 9,000 B.C. **(1)**

Mesolithic Age:

Geologists estimate that the bridge across the Irish Sea was submerged around 6700 B.C., leaving the island cut off from the rest of Europe.**(2)** The earliest human inhabitants must have arrived prior to this time. Very little is known about these first Mesolithic inhabitants of Ireland except that they were a nomadic people who were hunters and gathers. We might assume that their clothing was made of animal skins, and their diet consisted of meat and fruits and berries. They most likely had fire and had learned to cook their food. The earliest human remains from this group was found in Co. Londonderry and dated at approximately 6600 B.C. **(3)**

Neolithic Age:

Neolithic (Later Stone Age) people came to Ireland between 5000 and 3000 B.C. Originating in the Middle East, they were gradually forced to emigrate in search of more farm land, due to increasing population pressure. They moved through the Balkans and gradually worked their way westward along the Mediterranean coast, and then northward.

It is believed they came to Ireland from Spain, Portugal and Brittany in skin covered boats. They were farmers and herders raising food crops and keeping cattle, pigs and sheep. Consequently they did not have to rely on the success of the hunt to ward off starvation.

When they did hunt, they used flint headed arrows and spears. They used polished stone implements with wooden handles, and were accomplished in crafts. They made pottery in which they stored and cooked their food. With the development of spinning and weaving they were able to make wool clothing. Their houses had stone foundations, the buildings being either round or rectangular, with wooden frame walls filled with turf.

The most impressive remains of their culture are the huge stone megaliths and dolmens they constructed for burial chambers around 3000 B.C. In Egypt, at this time, the Great Pyramid had not yet been conceived. In Northern Ireland they were burying their dead in long, open, earth-covered stone galleries, called "court graves, " Later groups, around 2800 B.C., built "passage graves" along the East coast and the Boyne River. These were laid out as a long stone passage leading to a circular burial chamber.

The dead were buried with various artifacts and personal belongings, beads, pottery and tools, indicating that they had a belief in some form of afterlife.(4) Some of the finest examples of passage graves are located at Newgrange, in Co. Meath. It has been suggested that these Neolithic monuments later gave rise to fanciful tales of fairies and leprechauns that became a part of Irish folklore.(5) I have been told that there are still country folk today who will not deny the existence of the "Little people."

The Bronze Age:

Around 2000 B.C. another group of immigrants arrived. They were of a more advanced culture than the earlier inhabitants and brought with them metallurgical skills. The bronze age had arrived in Ireland. Tools and weapons of bronze were far superior to flint spears and stone plows.(6) The newcomers mingled with the earlier residents, who were readily absorbed into the new culture. A peaceful agrarian economy flourished.

This dolman in the burren of County Clare marks
the entrance to a portal tomb.

The newcomers spread throughout the country and began mining metal ores. Everywhere modern-day copper-deposits have been located evidence of pre-historic mining has been uncovered. Gold was also discovered in the Wicklow Mountains. Golden neck ornaments, and other jewelry was fashioned by skilled Irish craftsmen, and even exported to European markets, along with bronze axes and weapons.

The Iron Age:

It is estimated by some historians, and I say estimated because no-one seems to know for sure, that as early as 900 B.C. various Celtic tribes began to migrate westward. They were a large federation of tribes based upon a warrior aristocracy. Originating in the area of the Caspian Sea and having advanced to the iron-age, they easily overcame and dominated the more primitive Germanic people of Central Europe.

Other tribes of Celts moved along the Mediterranean Coast in Southern Europe, fighting sometimes in alliance with the Greeks, or with Alexander the Great. The Celts dominated much of Europe for centuries, and even laid siege to Rome itself, in the seventh and fourth centuries B.C.**(7)** They continued moving northward, through what is now France, Spain, and Britain and finally across the North and Irish Seas.

The Mythological Cycles:

The history of the pre-Christian period is told in the "Mythological Cycles", as illustrated in "The Red Branch Cycle, " covering the first and second centuries A.D. In it, we find tales such as, *The Tain Bo Cuailnge,* (The Cattle Raid of Cooley) and the heroic figure of *Cuchulain,* (a Paul Bunyanesque super-hero).

Then there is the "Fenian Cycle, " covering the third and subsequent centuries, telling us of *Finn McCool and the Fenians.* the Fenians tales were much like those of King Arthur and the Knights of the Round Table.

Finally, The "King Cycle" covers the whole first mellinium. Bear in mind, they are called Mythological Cycles for good reason. They were not written down until hundreds of years later. Consequently, Irish history is still a bit uncertain in this period, as it is for the rest of the world.**(8)**

By 500 B.C. Ireland was completely Celtic. Rome was just a minor city-state on the Italian peninsula. Written language was developing around the Mediterranean, but the rest of Europe was still in a blissful state of illiteracy. The Celts had no written language except Olgham writing. This was used for boundaries and tomb markers, but apparently did not lend itself to literary expression. Memory of historical happenings only survived through oral tradition and the Gaelic Celts had a strong tradition of history, as memorized and retold by their poets (fili) and story-tellers (seanachaihe).**(9)**

The Fomorians:

They told of four separate Celtic tribes that eventually arrived in Ireland, each by a different route, and each at a different time. First came a tribe known as the Fomorians. These were a race of sea faring giants who made their homes in present day Donegal.**(10)**

The Firbolgs:

The second group to arrive in Ireland was the Firbolgs. Both the Fomorians and the Firbolgs came to Ireland by the Mediterranean route, and were described in the Mythological Cycle as being a dark, sinister people, more or less given to evil ways.

The chieftains of the two groups agreed to hold a meeting at a place called Tara. At this meeting they agreed to live peacefully and proceeded to divide Ireland into five separate kingdoms: Ulster, Meath, Leinster, Munster, and Connaught. The peace lasted for thirty-six years until the arrival of the next Celtic tribe, the Danaans.**(11)**

The Danaans:

The Danaans are described as fair skinned people, with light hair and blue eyes, who immigrated from the northern islands. The Danaans were so much more advanced in crafts and learning than the Fomorians and Firbolgs, that they were reputed to have magical powers. Among their treasures was the *"Lia Fail,"* at Tara, a magical standing stone which was alleged to cry out whenever a "true king" was enthroned.

The Danaan King Nuada, made an alliance with the Fomorian King, Balor of the Evil Eye. Balor's daughter, Ethne, was even given in marriage to Cian, a Danaan prince.

The Firbolgs, on the other hand, had no such peaceful intent and were all but defeated in a four-day battle. In negotiations Nuada generously offered them the option to live in peace in one of the five kingdoms. The Firbolgs accepted the offer and chose Connaught as their domain.

In a later conflict between the Fomorians and the Danaans, both Nuada and Balor were slain. The Fomorians were defeated and driven out of Ireland. For a time, the Danaans ruled Ireland in peace, but that is not the end of the story.**(12)**

The Milesians:

From the Red Branch Cycle we next hear of a fourth Celtic tribe, the Milesians. The Milesians are reputed to have come from Spain in thirty ships. Somehow the Danaans were warned of the invasion and, using magic, created a dense fog that prevented the Milesians from landing. They also are alledged to have created a great storm which caused many of the invaders to drown.**(13)**

In spite of all this magic, the invaders managed to land at Tara, and defeat the Danaans. So badly were the Danaans beaten, that it is said they were driven into caves to live underground. According to legend, they still live in their underground kingdom as fairies and leprechauns, working their magic on mankind.

Celtic Society:

The Celts of Ireland, the Gaels, lived in a highly structured warrior society, which had three social levels: an aristocracy, freemen, and slaves. Celtic tribes had a common language, religion, and culture, but no sense of national identity. Tribal Chieftains fought each other for supremacy of the provincial Kingdoms: (Ulster, Meath, Leinster, Munster, and Connaught)

Ultimately, the five Kings vied to see who would be the Ard Ri (High King). Tara, originally the Celtic religous center, became the seat for the Ard Ri. The common threads that held Celtic society together were the Gaelic language, the Druid religion, and the Brehon Law.

The King:

At the top of the aristocracy was the king, (ri) Unlike kings of later societies, primogeniture played no part in selecting the king. The oldest son of the king did not automatically succeed his father. Any candidate, however, had to be a member of the royal, or primary, family of the tribe. (tuath) Any of the king's sons, regardless of seniority, or his brother, uncles, cousins, or nephews were eligible to become king.

The king may have been chosen for his skill as a warrior, or as a leader. Or, he may have been selected for his knowledge, wisdom, compassion, charisma, or any number of traits. What made the process singular was the fact that the king was always elected by the freemen of the tuath.

The Poet:

The court poet (fili) was always the most honored of men, except for the King himself, and his place at the table was always next to the King. Poets were actually very learned men. It usually required at least twenty years of study for a poet to prepare. They were so revered it was considered one of the most serious offenses for anyone, even for the King, to insult a poet.

The Storyteller:

The historian, or story teller (seanachaihe) as the repository of the tribe's history and tradition was also accorded a place of honor at the table, and his stories not only entertained his listeners, informed as well. In order to preserve history as accurately as possible, the seanchaihe had to memorize each story word for word.

The fili and seanachaihe had amazing memorys, along with a good sense of showmanship, coupled with fanciful imaginations. Supposedly, the original teller of the tale stuck to the facts of the event. From that point on, all subsequent tellers of the tale were to maintain the story, word for word. At this point we must consider the fine distinction between hard "fact, " and "minor embellishment, " for dramatic effect. If we are to believe this early history, we must assume that the seanachaihes made that distinction.

The Warriors:

The warriors (flathi) were a major part of the aristocracy. These men were qualified by virtue of their size, strength, and bravery in battle. In as much as, the various tuatha were constantly fighting with someone, this was not always a good career choice. Even if you were at the top of your profession, the retirement plan left a lot to be desired.

King's Advisors:

The King's advisors (aos dana) had better prospects. Their job was to help the king in planning feasts for special occasions.

The Celts liked a good party, so there were many special occasions. This kept the advisors busy, so they were not called upon to do battle, and they always had a good place at the banquet table.

The Druids:

The Druids (draoi) were the religious leaders, or priests. Their job was to advise the king on supernatural matters and to interpret omens and such. The draoi were trained from childhood to fulfill this sacred task.

The Judges:

The judges (brehon) played a most vital role in Celtic society. Brehon Law governed the Celts in every conceivable interaction among humans. Even the King himself was subject to Brehon rulings. These laws had evolved over a period of hundreds of years, and were the real fabric that held Celtic society together. As there was no written language, Brehon law had to be committed to memory. It generally required half a lifetime, for a student to become a Brehon.

The Freeman:

In the middle level of Celtic society was the freeman. These were the farmers, craftsmen, and merchants, and they made up the major portion of the population. They had a somewhat client relationship with the king, paying him rent for protection. A man's wealth was measured in the number of cows that he owned. Freemen were not generally called upon as warriors.

The Slaves:

Actually they had very few slaves. Most of these were members of other tribes who had been captured in battle. Some were non-Celtic captives taken on raids. Saint Patrick was himself a Briton who was taken captive from his father's home at the age of sixteen, during such a raid. He was held for six years in Ireland, during which time he served as a shepherd for a tribal king. He was well treated and grew to love his captors. Still longing for his home, he ultimately escaped and made his way back to Britain. He returned to Ireland many years later as a Christian Bishop, and changed Irish society forever.

Brehon Law:

The Brehon law applied to everyone, slave or aristocrat, King or shepherd, male or female. It included civil law, criminal law, and martial law. Every aspect of tribal life, of every level of society was subject to the law of the Brehons.

Capital Punishment:

Only on the rarest occasion did a crime call for capital punishment. In its place was an elaborate system of compensation for the victims survivors. In a case of murder, the circumstances of the act would be carefully weighed. What was the reason for the killing? Did the victim provoke his killer? What were the social levels of the principals? Was it a fair fight? Was the murder malicious? Etc.

Lesser Penalties:

The perpetrator, if convicted, could be ordered to pay a substantial amount of cattle to the victim's family, depending upon their social levels. If the killer could not, or would not pay the fine, his family would be held responsible. If his family refused to pay the fine, the offender would then be turned over to the victim's family, who would have the option to either sell him as a slave, or then, and only then put him to death.

Adultery:

The crime of adultery was a serious offense, for the wife. If found guilty, she could be burned alive. On the other hand, divorce was an easy matter and could be granted simply by mutual consent. By and large, women had equal protection under the law, with the one aforementioned exception.

Oldest Law:

The Irish are very proud of their Celtic ancestor's cultural achievements. Consider, a time before recorded history, when Europe was populated with uncivilized, barbarian tribes without structure or morality. Of a time before memory, when the pyramids were new, and the Roman Empire was yet to be dreamed of, the Celts had the Brehon Law.

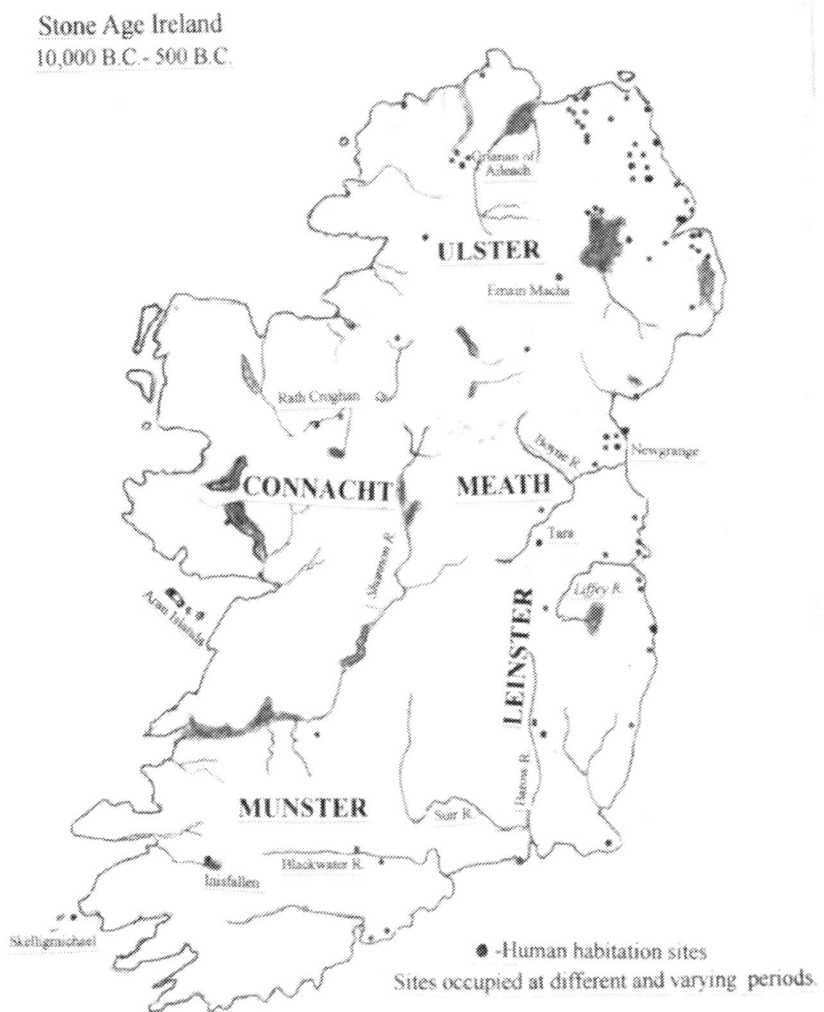

Stone Age Ireland
10,000 B.C. - 500 B.C.
ULSTER
Emain Macha
CONNACHT
Rath Croghan
MEATH
Newgrange
Tara
LEINSTER
MUNSTER
Skellig Michael
Innisfallen
Blackwater R.
Suir R.
Liffey R.
● -Human habitation sites
Sites occupied at different and varying periods.

Chapter Two
The Land of Saints and Scholars
400-795

Irish Raiders, The Captive Slave, The Escape, A Calling, The Mission of Paladius, Bishop Paricus, The High King at Tara, Sacred Lorca Faed Fiada, Faith vs. Magic, Patrick's Mission, Sleive Croagh Patrick, The Church in Ireland, St. Columcille, The Purloined Psalter, St. Brendan, St. Brigid

They Made History:

Niall of the Nine Hostages: *King in pre-Christian I reland. Abductor of Maewyn Succat.*
Maewyn Succat: *St. Patrick as a youth*
Paladius: *An early Chrsitain missionary to Ireland, before Patrick.*
St. Patrick:: *An early Christian Bishop. Patron Saint of Ireland.*
King Laoghaire: *Ard Ri (High King) of pe-Christian Ireland.*
St. Columcille: *Founder of monasteries. A revered Irish Saint.*
St. Brendan. *The navigator monk. First to Sail to the New World. A revered Saint*
St Brigid: *Founder of convents, revered Irish Saint. (female).*

Irish Raiders:

Niall of the Nine Hostages was an early High King of Ireland (Ard Ri), and without doubt the greatest Ard Ri of the early Christian period. With few interruptions, his descendants for the next six centuries continued to hold the throne at Tara as Ard Righs. The dynasty came to be called, "Of Niall, "or Ui Neill, finally O'Neill.

Niall's conquests were many, as he spread fear of Ireland to the foreign shores of Britain, and Gaul (France). His raids into these Roman controlled lands yielded much booty, and many captives. The captives were destined to be sold as slave labor to the various Irish tribal chieftains.

The early fifth century, unfortunately, was not a safe time to be a Britain under Roman protection. The Empire was in decline and the Roman legions were being pulled back from outlying territories. The Romans were no longer able to protect the coast of Britain from pagan Hibernian sea raiders.(1)

The Captive Slave:

On one of Niall's raids, in 406 AD, on the district of Cumbria, in Britain, a sixteen year old youth named Maewyn Succat was taken captive from the home of his father, Calpurnius, a tax collector for the Romans.(2) Maewyn's family were devote Christians, and his grandfather was a Christian monk. In the early days of Christianity, monks, priests and bishops were permitted to marry and have families. Maewyn was carried off to Ireland and sold, according to one account, into slavery in Antrim, to a local chieftain named Milcho. He was assigned duties tending Milcho's flocks of sheep, on Slemish Mountain. Here he met other Christians and began to participate in their masses on the mountain. These masses were a closely guarded secret, for Christianity was not accepted in pagan Ireland.

For six years he lived the isolated life of a shepherd, tending his flock, and spending many hours of each day in prayer, and many more hours during the night. He learned the Irish language and customs. With the passage of time, he came to love this land in which he was a captive. While he was happy on Slemish Mountain, he still longed for his home, and his family in Britian.

The Escape:

From time to time he had the duty of caring for Milcho's hunting dogs. He had a natural manner with animals, and he very quickly became a skilled handler. This new skill would serve him well. In 412 AD he seized upon an opportunity to escape. Even though he had come to love Ireland, a slave is still a slave. His isolated duties afforded him the opportunity to slip away. He worked his way to the coast and asked to gain passage on an outbound merchant ship. The captain refused to take him aboard.

Then fortune took a turn. A cargo of several Irish wolf-hounds, was bound to Britain in a French ship. Their dog handler apparently had met with an accident, leaving the captain shorthanded. Patrick announced that he was an experienced dog handler, and wolf hounds, being what they were, the captain was glad to take him aboard as part of the crew.

Following a three day passage to a remote part of Britain and a twenty-eight day walk Maewyn at last found his way home, the exact location of which is uncertain. His family was overjoyed to see him again. They thought, after six years, that he was gone forever.

They listened to his story about the Irish people, of his years on Slemish Mountain, how he had learned the Irish language, and became a shepherd. They made him promise that he would never leave home again, and for the moment he had no intention of doing so.

A Calling:

However, Maewyn, during his years in captivity, had become increasingly devout. It is not surprising then, that after a few years he felt a calling to a vocation. He left home again, traveling to the south of France, where he entered a monastery near Tours. Here he spent the next few years training for the priesthood.

After being ordained, Maewyn was sent to Italy, where he served for several years, traveling to various islands in the Mediterranean. During this period he had a vision, in a dream, in which he felt he was being called back to Ireland.(3) Consequently, Maewyn, made a request to his superior that he be sent to Ireland as a missionary. The next year he was called to Rome where he met with Pope Celestine.

The Mission of Paladius:

It seems that the previous year, in 430, Paladius, an Irish priest, had been appointed as a bishop by Pope Celestine to go to Ireland, and nourish the spiritual life of the Irish, "believing in Christ." Maewyn's request had been granted and he would travel to Ireland, to assist Paladius.

Maewyn traveled to northern France where he would embark on a ship. It was here that he received word of the death of Paladius, and the failure of his mission. Maewyn returned to Rome for instructions. Pope Celestine immediately consecrated him as a bishop, giving him the name *Patricus,* meaning "well born." and again was sent on his way to Ireland.(4)

Bishop Patricus:

It might seem surprising that a young priest would be so soon appointed a bishop, but it suggests that Patrick was already recognized for his sanctity, and that there was already a considerable Christian population in Ireland. This would require that Rome send a bishop, in order to ordain additional priests to serve the needs of Irish Christians.

Patrick arrived in Ireland in 432, ten years after his departure from that country. He landed in Wicklow with twenty-four followers. From there they made their way to Tara, the seat of High King Laoghaire, who was the son of High King Niall, of the Nine Hostages.(5)

The High King at Tara:

On Easter eve Patrick's party arrived at Slaine, across the Boyne River from Tara. They set up camp and lit a roaring fire for warmth. Coincidentally, across the River at Tara, the Kings's Druid's were about to light a large fire to commence a special Druid festival. When they saw the fire of the Christian's they were astounded and outraged. It was forbidden by law and long custom, for anyone to light a fire prior to the lighting of the king's fire at Tara.

King Laoghaire demanded of his druids, "Who is this upstart?" Now, in-as-much-as Druids were very wise, they had a ready answer. "Obviously, " They said, "It is the fulfillment of an old prophecy, of one who has come to replace the King and rule Erinn, unless his fire was extinguished this very night."

The King immediately ordered that this trespasser be dragged before the court. The King's soldiers quickly set out to comply with this order. The Druids, meanwhile, set up an ambush to kill these intruders on the way back.

Sacred Lorca, Faed Fiada:

The Christians offered no resistance, and proceeded, under guard, in procession order, led by Patrick, to Tara. As they proceeded they chanted the sacred lorca, *"Faed Fiada"* (Deer Cry).

Tradition claims that the Druids, waiting in ambush, never saw the procession pass by, but saw only a harmless herd of deer wandering.(6) A less miraculous explanation may be that the procession simply may have taken a different route than the one staked out by the Druids. In any event, Patrick and his party arrived at Tara unscathed. Laoghaire, not knowing what to expect of the stranger, had forbidden the members of his court to display any sign of respect for him.

Faith vs. Magic

However, so impressive did Patrick and his followers appear in their vestments that the King's poet and one nobleman stood in respect for Patrick, in spite of the warning. Then the Druids challenged Patrick in a contest of wills, eloquence, and Druid magic, against Christian miracles. The legend is that Patrick prevailed and delivered a strong sermon on Christianity as well.

The Legend of the Shamrock:

It is reputed to be on this occasion that Patrick explained the holy trinity, by using the shamrock as an illustration of how three persons can be one. This resulted in the conversion of several members of the court, including the Queen, to the new faith, and while Laoghaire himself was not converted, he was so completely won over by Patrick, the man, that he accorded him the right to preach Christianity throughout Ireland.(7)

Patrick's Mission:

Most of Patrick's work was accomplished in the present day provinces of Ulster, Leinster, and Connacht. Most of the religious establishments that claim St. Patrick as their founder are located in these areas. After twelve years, he was finally able to build his first church, in Ireland, at Armagh, which became his apostolic see. Armagh became, and remains, the center of the Christian faith in Ireland.

Patrick's mission in Ireland continued for approximately thirty years, traveling over much of Ireland, baptizing new converts, founding abbeys and monasteries, ordaining priests, and consecrating new bishops. Patrick baptized thousands of new converts to the faith, not by condemning their Celtic laws and customs, but by adapting them to fit the new faith. Halloween, a Celtic Pagan holiday, became The Feast of All Saints to the newly converted Christians. A few early Christian Saints may have found their names changed to that of some early Celtic heroes of legend.

Sleive Croagh Patrick:

On the summit of Sleive Croagh Patrick, in Co. Mayo, St. Patrick is alleged to have driven all of the snakes out of Ireland. This is an interesting bit of folklore, and the Gaels do love to embellish on a good story. But there were no snakes in Ireland to be driven out.The land bridge that once connected Ireland to Britain and the European continent was submerged, by the melting of the polar ice cap, long before the climate became warm enough to support any reptile population.

One thing is certain, however. Before the coming of Patrick, Ireland was a land of superstition, influenced by Druids, and pagan ritual. It has been suggested that the snakes were merely a metaphor for this superstition.(8) Obviously, leprechauns and fairies were not included in the metaphor, for even today, many well educated Irishmen will not disturb an apparent fairy ring, and everyone knows that the *"little people"* can become very irate at times.

The Church in Ireland:

The church organization envisioned by St. Patrick was modeled after the Roman episcopal system, as he knew it in Gaul and Britain. Bishoprics would consist of various diocese located at towns or cities. Each diocese would consist of a number of parishes, overseen by a local priest. The priests would be responsible to the bishop.

Early Christian Ireland, however, was not suited to this model. The countryside was still very densely forested. Roads did not exist and travel between tribal kingdoms was dangerous, to say the least. There were no towns and communication was extremely limited. Consequently the episcopal system was replaced by monasticism. Abbeys and monasteries were established in the shadow of the forts and raths of the Gaelic kings.

A monastery or abbey was under the charge of an abbot and was usually the property of the ruling family. A church would be associated with these, and served by one or more priests. Occasionally an abbey would also shelter a convent. Monks recorded old legends and epics, in the old Irish and Latin. They wrote religious and legal poems, and actually recorded much of Brehon Law in writing. They illuminated *The Book of Darrow,* and *The Book of Kells.*

Bishops, priests and abbots were permitted to marry and in those times have families. Frequently the title of abbot was passed down from father to son, and the abbey became a family business. Rarely was an abbot consecrated as a bishop. His function was to teach and manage the abbey. If a bishop were associated with a monastery, he was generally subordinate to the abbot. His function was to teach and ordain priests.(9)

All religious life was centered about the abbeys and monasteries that were established by Patrick, and the other missionaries who came after him. One of the singular features in the conversion of the Irish to Christianity was the extreme love of knowledge on the part of the people themselves. Gaelic society reserved its most honored positions for men of learning, such as the *seanachaihe* and the *fili* (historians and poets) and the *bards* and *Brehon*, (writers and judges). All of these were highly learned men. With the collapse of Roman society in the 6th century, and the decline of the Celtic kings during the same period, these scholarly men found their places in the abbeys and the monasteries of St. Patrick's Ireland.

St. Colmcille

One of these scholarly men was born at Gartan, Co. Donegal in 521 to the Northern Ui Neill clan, a descendant of the line of High King Niall, of the Nine Hostages. Niall has been considered by many as the greatest high king Ireland had in the early Christian period. This was the same Niall who was the captor of Maewyn, a.k.a. Patrick, some sixty years earlier. You will recall that in Celtic society provincial kings were chosen in election by the freemen of the clan. As a member of the royal line this young man was eligible for election to the kingship.

The Kylemore Abbey, in Connacht, survives intact, from the early days.

This young man was named Crimthann, and he was raised with a strong devotion to the faith. He spent so much time in church that his boyhood friends gave him the name Colmcille (Dove of the Church). Little is known of his early years except that he studied at various monastic schools. He was ordained as a priest and in 546 he founded a church and monastery at Derry. As was the custom, the monastery belonged to the family and Colmcille became its first abbot.

The Purloined Psalter:

He studied, for a time, with Finnian, the Abbot of Moville. In the course of his study he made a copy of a psalter which belonged to his teacher. When Finnian was informed of the copy, he demanded that Colmcille return it. The demand was refused and the matter was taken to High King Diarmait, of the Southern Ui Neill, for judgment. The King's ruling went against Colmcille, and may very well be the first decision in history regarding copyright infringement. It stated, "To every cow belongs its calf, to every book its copy."

Colmcille defied the King's ruling and his Donnegal kinsmen, the Northern Ui Neill, came to his defense. In 561, a great battle was fought at Cul Dremna by the two branches of Ui Neill clan. This may have been in defense of Colmcille, or it may have simply been an excuse for the Northern Ui Neill to attack the Southern Ui Neill and seize the high kingship. In any event over 3,000 died in the battle, Dairmait lost his throne, and Colmcille kept the purloined psalter.

A church synod was held in 563 to determine the Fate of Colmcille.(10) The ruling of the synod may have been that he would be exiled from Ireland forever, and that may well have happened had it not been for passionate defense put on by one of Colmcille's associates, Brendan. Regardless, Colmcille was so guilt ridden at the loss of life at Cul Dremna that he decided on a self imposed exile, and that he must convert as many souls to the faith as had been killed in the battle.

Colmcille and twelve of his followers set sail for the island of Iona, which was in the Kingdom of the Dal Riada. This kingdom later became Scotland. The Dal Riada were Irish Celts, closely associated with the Northern Ui Neill. This hardly amounted to an exile, as Colmcille remained in close touch with the Northern Ui Neill, in the realm of politics, even returning to Ireland occasionally, founding monasteries at Swords, Durrow, and Kells.

His monastery at Iona became his home site for the launching of numerous other monasteries in Scotland and Britain. St. Columba, as he was called in Iona, is credited by most historians as being responsible for bringing Christianity to those two countries. St. Columba, or St.Colmcille, is one of the most revered saints in Ireland today, second only to St. Patrick.

St. Brendan:

Brendan was another of St.Finnian's "Twelve Apostles of Ireland, " and the founder of the monastery at Clonfert. Brendan is best known for his reputed voyage across the Atlantic Ocean in a wood framed, leather covered "coracle" in the mid-sixth century. Legend tells us that Brendan and his monks encountered sea monsters "as big as an island, " fire-flinging demons, and a column of floating crystal. In all probability they encounter a pod of whales impersonating sea monsters, "demons" threw the fire from inside a volcano, and the column of floating crystal was merely an iceberg.(11)

In the course of his seven year voyage, Brendan and his followers are believed to have spent time in Iceland, and then sailed on further west, possibly to Newfoundland. Brendan was convinced of a great paradise beyond the great ocean. Perhaps he did discover America, seven hundred years before Columbus, perhaps not. There are no hard facts, in as much as the tale was not recorded until the ninth century. He is often referred to as "St. Brendan, The Navigator, " and is today revered as the patron saint of County Kerry.

St. Brigid:

Most of what we know of St. Brigid is mixed with early folklore, except that she was born in 452 and died in 526. This makes her a contemporary of St. Patrick. Brigid may, or may not have been, her given name. There was a pre-Christian Celtic goddess named Brigid who was both goddess of fertility, and of the harvest. The young virgin, who was made the Abbess of Kildare, may have been named after the goddess by her mother, or by someone else, or she may have taken the name herself.

What we do know about her is that she was a very pious, and spiritual woman, who devoted her life to prayer, and serving Christ. She lived a saintly life, and was endowed with the title St. Brigid. According to tradition, St. Brigid, who is patron saint of the harvest, made a cross out of rushes, to protect the harvest from the evil work of the devil. The cross represents the crucifixion, a Christian symbol, and the four arms of the cross represent the rays of the sun, an ancient Celtic symbol. St. Brigid crosses hang in homes, all over the country, and she is the third most revered saint in Ireland. Saint Patrick often mixed the old pagan religion with the new Christianity, in order to make it more understandable and acceptable to the converts. I feel certain that Patrick knew of Brigid's spiritual nature and piety. Did he, or someone else endow St. Brigid with the attributes of the goddess of the harvest? The feast day of the harvest goddess and the feast day of St. Brigid are both on February 1st.

Chapter Three
The Viking Invasion
795-1014

The Norsemen, The Irish Defenders, The Round Towers, From Raiding to Invading, Irish vs. Irish vs. Vikings, Brian of Boruma, King Mahon of Thomond, The Sacking of Limerick, Brian Becomes King and Seeks Vengeance, Two High Kings, A Nation At Last, The Grand Tour, The Battle of Clontarf, Mac Laig's Tribute, Kinkora

They Made History:

High King Cormac : 9th Century, --Early 10th Century, Of the Eoganachta, (Egan clan), High King (Ard Righ), Killed in 908 at the Battle of Ballaghmoon.

King Mahon of Munster- (968-976) Mid 10th Century, of the Dal Cais tribe. Older brother of Brian Boru, a.k.a., Mahon Cennedi, Murdered in 976 by rival King Malloy and the Viking King Ivar.

King Brian Boru (976-1014) Mid 10th Century, Early 11th Century, Of the Dal Cais tribe. King of Munster in 976, following Mahon. High King in 1002. a.k.a., Brian MacCennedi, Boru-Killed at the Battle of Clontarf 1014.

High King Malachy II (980-1002) (1014-1022) of Meath, Mid 10th Century, Early 11th a.k.a., Malacky Mael Sechnaill, Malacky Mor, Malachy the Great, second husband of Gormlaith, Ally to Brian. Became High King again following Brian's death. Died in 1022.

Mac Liag Court poet and confidant to Ard Righ, Brian Boru.

The Norsemen:

The present day Scandinavian countries of Norway, and Denmark were far to the north, consequently the growing season was short and not especially conducive to agriculture. An abundance of trees for shipbuilding and an extensive, irregular coastline turned the Norsemen to the sea and the men of the north became superb seamen, and fearless navigators.

The primary Norse gods, Odin and Thor, were gods of war, so violence was a built-in part of their culture, and pillage and plunder became a way of life. It was considered normal and proper for a Viking to take for himself whatever he could, from foreigners, but not from another Viking, ; unless, of course, he was able to. Not only was it considered a right for a Viking to plunder, but it was also a duty. Might was right and only the strong survived in the world of the Norseman.

The Viking invasion of Ireland began with a Norwegian raid on the island monastery of Iona, where they desecrated the grave of St. Colmcille. They also raided the northeast coast of Ireland in the year 795, sacking and plundering other monasteries.**(1)**

The battle tactics of the Vikings were both vicious and bloody. Their huge battleaxes could cleave a man in half, and they displayed no reluctance to use them. A special type of warrior, the "berserkers" swept all before them, killing without mercy, and totally terrorizing the few who survived. Any young men and women, who were spared, were carried off to be sold into slavery.

At first these raids usually involved only one dragon ship attacking an area close to the coast. As time went on groups of ships would sail further inland. In 837 fleets as large as sixty, or more, dragon ships reached far inland on both the Boyne, and Liffey Rivers.**(2)**

The Irish Defenders:

There were, as yet, no cities in Ireland, so the only centers of population were the many Christian monasteries that had been established throughout the countryside. The monks were highly skilled in the crafting of gold ands silver ornamentation, and they produced quantities of vessels, and other art objects for their altars and shrines. These treasures made the Irish monasteries prime targets for the Scandinavian sea-raiders in their dragon ships.

The Irish tribal chieftains and their warriors usually had little opportunity to protect their subjects from the surprise, hit and run attacks. Some of the "warrior" monks made brave attempts to defend their monasteries, but this could have been little more than a futile gesture. It is likely that few ever survived the attempt.

The Round Towers:

By the middle of the ninth century, the Irish monks had built over one hundred round towers as a means of passive protection from the raiding Vikings. The towers were generally wider at the base, up to seventeen feet, than they were at the top. The access door was twelve to fifteen feet above ground level, and could only be reached by means of a ladder. There were up to four levels inside, some fifteen to twenty-five feet apart. Each level had its own ladder.

When the alarm was sounded by the lookout at the top, warning of an attack, the monks would take refuge in the tower, bringing all the valuables with them. Once inside, the access ladder was taken up. Food and water cached inside, enabled the monks to easily await the departure of the frustrated Norsemen, who were left screaming threats and shaking their weapons at the stone wall. The attackers could neither gain entrance to the tower, nor did they have the ability to destroy it. Many of these beautiful spires are still standing today, after thirteen hundred years.

From Raiding to Invading:

It wasn't long before the invaders began to establish permanent bases at port locations, where they could moor their fleets. They constructed fortifications and other buildings. In 841 a Norwegian King founded the city of Dublin at the mouth of the Liffey River. This was the first Viking settlement to be established in Ireland and was soon followed by another Viking port at Drogheda, just north of Dublin.**(3)**

These established locations gave the Vikings the advantage of bases from which to operate, and brisk trade was established. Looted Irish treasure was soon available in many of the ports of Britain and northern Europe as the Viking raids continued.

There was another result of fixed bases that the Vikings had not foreseen. The war-like Irish chieftains now had places where they could attack the Vikings. Retaliatory attacks on the Viking settlements soon followed, and the Irish found that Vikings can bleed just like Irishmen can. No doubt that the local Irish kings could have driven the Vikings out of Ireland, if they only had the ability to unite with their kinsmen and fight together. Unfortunately, this was not to be, for the man who was to unite Ireland was not to be born for another hundred years.

Irish vs. Irish vs. Vikings:

Meanwhile, throughout the ninth century the kings of two rival clans, the Ui Neill and the Eoganachta, were fighting each other for the High Kingship of all Ireland. The situation ebbed and flowed back and forth, in a continual state of warfare. Gradually the Vikings were drawn into local politics and changing alliances. It seemed that everyone was fighting everyone else.

The Vikings had their own differences and it became a contest of Norwegians vs. Danes. In 851, the Norwegians were defeated by the Danes and driven out of Dublin.**(4)** The change provided no respite for the Irish, merely a different set of foes.

The Ui'Neill clan defeated the Vikings in the Northern part of Ireland, but Dublin remained strongly Dane. This was due to an alliance with the King of Leinster, who, himself, was not a contender, but did represent a threat. This enabled the Danes to resist the efforts of both the major clans, who promptly resumed fighting each other. The other local kings were likewise so busy fighting one another that they could not unite to fight the Vikings under one command. Not one of them was powerful enough to truly be the Irish King.

In 908, King Cormac, of the Eoganachta, was killed in the Battle of Ballaghmoon. The Ui'Neills became dominant and the Eoganachta never recovered their former status. Before the Ui Neills could assert their position the Viking incursion increased.**(5)**

In 914, a major Viking incursion in the south established a strong Viking settlement at Waterford. By 920, other Viking settlements were firmly established at Wexford, Cork, and Limerick. The Irish farmers and the monasteries were at the mercy of the Vikings.**(6)**

Brian of Boruma:

In the year 941, Brian Mac Cennedi was born in a spot known as Beal Boru, or Borumain the province of Thomond, near the mouth of the Shannon River, This is near the present day village of Killaloe. His family name was Cennedi, (pronounced *kennedi)* of the Dal Cais Tribe.

He was the fourth son of the King of the Dal Cais. Brian did not grow up under the burden of being a royal heir however, as primogeniture played no part in the selection of kings. According to Brehon Law, kings were elected by the free men of the tribe. They were selected from members of the ruling family. Brothers, cousins, uncles, and sons were all eligible.**(7)**

King Mahon of Thomond:

Upon the death of Brian's father, in 951, his older brother Mahon, was elected King of the Dal Cais. Brian and Mahon were very close. Brian was sent to the monastery at Clonnmacnois for schooling. He learned to read both Latin and Greek, studied philosophy and religion, and read of the military campaigns of Caesar and Hannibal. After growing to manhood, he joined his brother in 961 as a warrior against the Vikings of Limerick.**(8)**

Brian had become a giant of a man; and a natural warrior. He turned out to be a bold tactician and became Mahon's right hand, and second in command. Together, they would defeat the Vikings in Limerick

The Sacking of Limerick:

Brian's campaign against the Vikings in 962, drove them out of Thomond and across the Shannon River. In 968 Brian and Mahon attacked the city of Limerick and plundered it. Ivar, the Viking King of Limerick, and his ally an Irish tribal king named Malloy were forced to flee in a dragon ship. Brian and Mahon took home rich booty of jewels, gold, silver, and silk goods.**(9)**

This attack on the strongest of the Viking strongholds, in Limerick, did not go unnoticed by the other kings of Munster. That same year, Donogh of the Owenenachts, who had been recently crowned King of Munster, died of natural causes, apparently appendicitis. Donogh had no male heirs, so the throne of Munster was not contested. Mahon, of the Dal Cais, King of Thomond, asserted his claim to the kingship and was crowned unopposed.**(10)**

In the following years, petty jealousies by the lesser Munster Chieftains, especially the Owenachts, were the source of minor conflicts. In 976 Mahon was invited to a banquet by his enemy King Malloy, ostensibly to form friendship and future alliances. It was a trap. Aided by Ivar of Limerick, Mahon was taken prisoner and treacherously murdered.

Brian Becomes King and Seeks Vengeance:

Brian, who was now called Brian of Boruma, placed the crown of Munster on his own head and swore vengeance on Malloy and Ivar. He became King of Munster unopposed. He plundered Limerick again in 977. King Ivar took shelter in the church, but Brian sought him out and slew him, and his two sons.**(11)**

He allowed the Vikings to remain in Limerick in return for annual tribute of imported wine. Brian continued his quest for vengeance on King Malloy, and met him the following year at the Battle of Belach Lecta. Malloy did not survive the encounter.

Two High Kings:

In 985 Brian came into contention with High King Malachy Mael Schnell of Meath, or Malachy Mor, (*The Great*) as he was called. Instead of doing the traditional thing and going to war, they were wise enough to resort to diplomacy. The two kings came to an agreement. Malachy would rule supreme in the North and Brian would rule in the South.**(12)**

This caused the chieftains, in Leinster, to revolt and ally themselves with the Danes in Dublin. Brian and Malachy united their forces and put down the rebellion. After defeating the Danes of Dublin, Brian made a visit to Armaugh and restored it to ecclesiastical primacy, thus re-establishing it as the principal seat of Christianity in Ireland. Carrol, royal scribe to Ard Ri Brian, recording the event in the Book of Armaugh, referred to Brian as *Imperator Scottorum, or* "Emperor of the Irish."

A Nation At Last:

In 1002, Brian defeated the O'Neills, who were strong contenders for the High Kingship and opposed to the dual monarchy. King Malachy II, Brian's ally, and co-ruler, acknowledged Brian as the sole High King, while he, himself, retained the provincial crown of Meath. All Irish Kings were united as a nation, with Brian Boru as the Ard Ri (High King of all Ireland.)**(13)**

Brian turned out to be a wise, strong, and just King. Christianity, education and rule of law flourished during his rein. He ruled from Cashel, but later restored the family castle at Kincora, making it a beautiful luxury palace on the Shannon River.

The Grand Tour :

Brian made a grand tour of northern provinces to solidify his position as High King. Starting at Kincora he traveled north through Connaught, clockwise through Ulster then south through Meath, Dublin and Leinster, back to Cashel. He was accompanied by royalty from Connaught, Leinster and his Viking Allies from Dublin. All of the provincial Kings along the way pledged fealty to the High King.

The Ui Eoganacht, of Leinster, had traditionally opposed the Ui Neill dynasty of Ulster for the High Kingship and lost. They did not want to be subservient to this upstart from Thomond. Their Dublin Viking allies did not think Brian best served their interests in trade and commerce with the Normans in Britain. Over the years, both groups became equally unhappy with the new High King and wished to be rid of him. Toward this end, the Leinster King Mael Morda sent envoys to enlist the support of the Ui Neill in a revolt against Brian.

The Battle of Clontarf:

At the Battle of Clontarf, in 1014 the Danes were thoroughly defeated, ending the Viking incursions, their power broken forever. Brian, then in his seventies, was too old to engage in personal combat. While his guards and attendants were pursuing fleeing Vikings, they briefly left him unguarded. A straggling Viking captain, named Brodir, discovered Brian at prayer in his tent. Brian died with a sword in his hand, but he was no match for the younger man. But the principle of Irish nationhood had been established under his rule.**(14)**

Mac Laig's Tribute:

Much of Ireland's history is, traditionally, preserved in poetry. It was fitting that Brian's Court Poet, MacLaig, should pay tribute to Ireland's greatest king in verse. (Translated from The Gaelic) **(15)**

KINCORA

Oh, where, Kincora is Brian the Great?
And where is the beauty that once was thine?
Oh, where are the princes and nobles that sate
At the feast in thy halls, and drank the red wine/
Where, oh, Kincora?
Oh, where, Kincora! Are thy valorous lords?
Oh, whither, thou Hospitable! are they gone?
Oh, where are the Dalcassians of the Golden Swords?
And where are the warriors Brian led on?
Where, oh, Kincora?
And where is Murrough, the descendant of Kings-
The defeater of a hundred- the daringly brave-
Who set but slight store by jewels and rings-
Who swam down the torrent and laughed at its wave?
Where, oh, Kincora?
And where is Donough, King Brian's worthy son?
And where is Conaing, the Beaautiful Chief?
And Kian, and Corc? Alas! They are gone-
They have left me this night alone with my grief,
Left me, Kincora!
And where are the chiefs with whom Brian went forth?
The ne'er vanquished sons of Erin the Brave,
The great king of Onaght, renowned for his worth,
And the hosts of Baskinn, from the western wave?

Where, oh, Kincora?
Oh, where is Duvlann of the swift footed Steeds?
And where is Clan, who was son of Molloy?
And where is King Lonergan, the fame of whose deeds,
In the red battle-field no time can destroy?
Where, oh, Kincora?
And where is that youth of majestic height,
The faith-keeping Prince of the Scots—Even he
As wide as his fame was, as great as his might,
Was tributary, oh, Kincora, to thee!
Thee, oh, Kincora!
They are gone, those heroes of royal birth,
Who plundered no churches, and broke no trust,
"Tis weary for me to be living on earth
While they, oh, Kincora, lie low in the dust!
Low, oh, Kincora
Oh, never again will Princes appear,
To rival the Dalcassians of cleaving swords!
I can ne'er dream of meeting afar or anear,
In the east or the west, such heroes and lords!
Never, Kincora
Oh, dear are the images my memory calls up
Of Brian Boru! how he would never miss,
To give me at the banquet the first bright cup!
And why did he heap on me honor like this?
Why, oh, Kincora?
I am MacLiag, and my home is on the lake;
Thither often, to that palace whose beauty is fled
Came Brian to ask me, and I went for his sake,
Oh, my grief! That I should live, and Brian be dead!
Dead, oh, Kincora

IRELAND AND THE
VIKING INVASION
1000 A.D.
TIRCONAILL
TIREOGAIN
ULIDA
Derry
Glen Columcille
SUB
KINGDOM
OF BREFNI
Craeve Macha
Armagh
KINGDOM
OF ORIEL
Mayo
KINGDOM OF
CONNACHT
Kells
KINGDOM
OF
MEATH
Cong
Tuam
Clonmacnoise
Nore
Tara
KINGDOM
OF
LEINSTER
NORSE CITY OF DUBLIN
Killaloe
Kildare
THOMOND
Norse City of
Limerick
Castel
Ferns
KINGDOM
OF MUNSTER
Lismore
Norse City
Wexford
Cork
Norse City of
of Waterford
Norse City
of Cork

Chapter Four
The Norman Invasion
1014-1270

Needed: One Irish High King, Malachy Mor, Donough O'Brien, Turough O'Brien, The Queen of Breffni "Abducted, " The Razing of Kincora, Turlough O'Connor, Changes in the Irish Church, Murichertach MacLochlainn, The Last Ard Ri, TheBeginning of the Troubles, Invasion, More Normans, The Siege of Waterford, Dermot Keeps a Promise and Makes a Threat, Exit Dermot, A Norman King of Leinster, A Grosse Mistake, The Normans Learn New Tricks, The Lord of Ireland The Death of Strongbow, John deCourcy, Prince John, the Royal Idiot, , Dominus Hibernaie, Prince John Offends the Iirish Chieftans, Ireland's Last Great Hope. Everybody Fought Everybody Else, King Richard (The Lion Hearted), "It Would be Good to be the 'King'" The Lions Last Roar, Bad for John, Good for Ireland, The "Good Ould Days In Ireland, The Fly in the Ointment, The Magna Carta, Henry III, The " Ard R"of Connaught, The Gallowglasses, The Battle of Downpatrick, The Turning of the Tide,

They Made History:

High King Malachy II: of Meath, I(980-1002) (1014-1022) Mid 10th century, .Became High King again following Brian's death in 1014.

High King Donough O'Brien: (1022-1033) a.k.a. Donnchadh, 2nd High King after death of Boru.Had his own brother, Teige, murdered.

High King Turlough O'Brien: (1033-1101) 3rd High King after death of Boru. Avenged the murder of his father, by defeating his uncle in 1033.

High King Muirchertach O'Brien: (1101-1114) 4th High King after death of Brian Boru.

High King Turlough O'Connor: of Connaught, (1119-1156) 5th High King after Boru, Son of Hugh O'Connor, who razed Kincora to spite the O'Briens.

High King Muirchertach MacLochlainn: of Ulster, (1162-1166) 6th High King after death of Boru. Gained the throne through treachery.

Dermot MacMurrough: King of Ui Chennselaig (Ferns) a.k.a.Diarmait MacMurrough. The abductor of Dervorgilla, and general trouble maker.

Tiernan O'Rourke: Husband of Dervorgilla, bitter enemy of MacMurrough

Pope Adrian IV: (1155) The only English Pope. Alleged author of Papal Bull conferring the title "Lord of Ireland" upon King Henry II.

King Henry II: Late 12th Century. French speaking ruler of England and Normandy.

Strongbow: Later 12th Century. Norman adventurer, opportunist and usurper. a.k.a., Earl of Pembroke. Leader of the Norman Invasion.

Raymond le Gros: One of Strongbow's Norman commanders. a.k.a.-Fat Raymond

Donal More O'Brien: King of Thomond. Victor at Battle of Thurls.

John deCourcy: The Norman knight who conquered Ulster, and ruled it for 27 years.

High King Cathal O'Connor: (1199-1224) Ineffective Ard Ri. Chaos prevailed.

King Richard I : (1189-1199) Left John in charge. a.k.a. Richard the Lionhearted

King John : (1199-1216) Idiot prince. Foul-up. As king he signed the Magna Carta in 1215

King Henry III : (1216-1272) Built Irish commerce. Gave Ireland to Prince Edward.

High King Brian O'Neill: (1258-1260) The " Ard Ri of Connaught".

Hugh O'Connor: Defeated the Normans at The Battle of Ath-an-Chip.

Needed: One Irish High King:

Brian's son, Murchadh, was also lost at Clontarf, leaving no heir apparent to the High Kingship. His younger son, Donnchadh, lacked his father's, and his late brother's ability to lead, and their political awareness. This left Brian's two grandsons, Donough and Turlough, neither of whom were up to the job at the time.

Malachy Mor:

In 1015, Malachy II led his army against the discontents in Dublin and suppressed the last efforts of the Danes to regain control. Malachy II then again assumed the high kingship as the last unopposed Ard Ri, and ruled Ireland until his death in 1022. Following Malachy, the Irish provincial kings resumed vying for high kingship, and fighting among themselves. For the next 144 years the Ui Neills of Ulster, The O'Briens of Thomond and the O'Connors of Connaght would engage in bitter feuding. **(1)**

Donough O'Brien:

In 1022 Donough O'Brien, then felt that he was up to the job, but unfortunately his brother Teige stood in his way. He solved that little problem by having his brother murdered, made good his claim to the High Kingship. He ruled from Kincora for eleven years. **(2)**

Turlough O'Brien:

In 1033 Turlough O'Brien, the son of the murdered Teige, avenged his father by defeating his uncle Donough in battle. In the process he became the third Ard Ri after Brian. He ruled, for sixty-eight years, in relative, but not total, peace. There was still a power struggle and minor skirmishes between the O'Connors of Connaght, and the O'Briens, or the O'Connors and the Dubliners and Leinstermen, High King Turlough and the Leinstermen.

The Queen of Breffni "Abducted":

In 1051, Dermot McMurrough, the King of Ui Chennselaig (Ferns), in Leinster, abducted Queen Dervorgilla of Breffni, while her husband, King Tighearnan O'Rourke, was off fighting some other minor king. O'Rourke, of course was a neighbor and ally of the O'Connors, who had ruled Connaught for generations. Now practically everyone was at odds with Leinster, except the Dubliners.

There was, and is, considerable doubt, as to the nature of this abduction. Dervorgilla was, in fact, carried off on horseback, kicking and screaming for help; but it is also a fact that she managed to take her money, and all of her furniture with her. That seems like a pretty good trick, and raises considerable question regarding the virtue of the queen and suggests her possible complicity. It is possible that she found the dashingly handsome Dermot more to her liking than one-eyed O'Rourke.(3)

One year later, Dervorgilla was returned to her husband. Tierrnan was not a forgiving man. A year after that she moved out again, this time taking up residence in a convent, and again taking all her furniture with her. Dermot, of course, was obviously not an honorable man, in fact, he was totally without principle, morals, or conscience. He further proved this by refusing to compensate O'Rourke for his loss, according to Brehon law. "After all, he reasoned, O'Rourke got his property back unharmed. Didn't he?" O'Rourke never forgave Dermot for this affront and swore revenge.

The Razing of Kincora:

In 1061 King of Connaught, Hugh O'Connor, vented his anger at the Ard Ri, who was now an old man, and against the O'Briens in general. He destroyed the beautiful castle at Kincora that was built by Brian Boru. Now it was O'Briens vs O'Connors. Turlough O'Brien died of natural causes within a year, and his son Muirchertach succeeded to the high kingship as the last Ard Ri of the line of Brian Boru. He ruled for the next stormy thirteen years, in constant conflict with the O'Connors. After his death the high kingship was fiercely contested for the next five years. **(4)**

Turlough O'Connor:

It was Turlough O'Connor who finally prevailed and became High King in 1119. In that same year, the newly crowned High King plundered Munster, as an act of revenge against the O'Briens. While he was at it, Turlough finished razing what was left of Kincora, by having his men throw all its stones and timbers into the Shannon River, thus completing the job his father had started fifty-eight years earlier. To add further insult to injury, he then made a lunch of the two royal salmon from the fountain of former High King Muirchertach O'Brien.(5)

Changes in the Irish Church:

The Irish church had evolved into a system, or rather a lack of system, comprised of abbeys and monasteries, to serve the spiritual needs of the people. From the time of St. Patrick until the Norman invasion there had been no written communication between the Irish Church and the Pope. The Irish monks and abbots did not recognize the authority of the Pope. The Irish took no part in the Crusades, and the reformation, taking place in Europe, had little, or no, effect in Ireland. It wasn't until the Synod of Kells, in 1152, that the Irish Church recognized Papal authority. **(6)**

In 1155 Pope Adrian IV published the Papal Bull, "Laudabiliter, " wherein he granted King Henry II, of England the title of Lord of Ireland. This, of course, became the basis for an English claim to Ireland. Adrian IV, incidentally, was the first and only Englishman in history to become Pope, but that probably had nothing to do with "Laudabiliter." One wonders, however, why it was called "Bull."

Murichertach MacLochlainn:

Ard Ri Turlough O'Connor died in 1156, and a bitter six year struggle for the throne followed. The first to vie for the job was a scoundrel from Ulster, Muirchertach MacLochlainn, who did not even have the support of his own subjects, or the other provincial kings. The only support he had was the King of Dublin, and, not surprisingly, the scoundrel King of Ui Chennselaig, Dermot McMurrough, who was his strongest supporter. MacLochlainn did succeed in gaining the high kingship through the vicious use of force and treachery, not the least of which was the blinding of the King of Ulidia, even after he had been defeated, and submitted. This unnecessary blinding was done to flaw him, and render him ineligible to be a king. According to Brehon law, the king must be unblemished.

Yet, the biggest trouble maker of them all was to be McMurrough. If Muirchertach MacLochlainn had been the devil, then Dermot would have been his disciple. Dermot had also gained the throne of Ui Chennselaig through treachery and murder. He had killed two princes and blinded another in order to gain his purpose. He had earned the hatred of nearly all of his countrymen by supporting MacLochlainn, as well as his role in the Dervorgilla affair.

The Last Ard Ri:

King of Connaught, Rory O'Connor did not give up the fight. In 1166, aided by the other Connaught Chieftains, and especially Tigehearnan O'Rourke. MacLochlainn was finally defeated, and killed in battle. **(7)** Rory O'Connor became the last, and quite possibly the most effective Ard Ri since Brian Boru, but the Leinstermen, and the Dubliners, remained resistant to rule from Connaght. To the misfortune of Ireland, the new Ard Ri was destined to loose in the end.

The Beginning of the Troubles:

With the death of MacLochlainn, Dermot McMurrough had lost his strongest and only ally. Tigehearnan O'Rourke had waited for this day, and he lost no time in gathering support from the sub-kings and chieftains of Leinster; in defeating McMurrough, and depriving him of the minor kingship of Ui Chennselaig. Dermot McMurrough was an outcast in Ireland, so he left the country to seek help elsewhere. He traveled to Lismore, in England, where he consulted with the Papal representative. It was likely here that he learned of the 1155 Papal Bull Laudabiliter. **(8)**

Dermot lost no time in going to Normandy, to look for an ally in King Henry. He found the King in Acquitaine, defending his claims in France. Henry, a warrior and a conqueror, in the Norman tradition, was up to his elbows in hostile Frenchmen. He was interested in what Dermot had to say, especially when he was reminded of Laudabiliter, and the title"Lord of Ireland." Unfortunately, he was fully committed, at this point, in trying to hold on to Normandy. He told Dermot that even though he was sympathetic to his plight, he could not give him the support he needed to regain the throne of Ui Chennsilaige. He did, however, give Dermot a letter authorizing him to enlist the support of some of Henry's noblemen in England. This was a "no loose" deal for Henry II. If one of his nobles should assist McMurrough, and they were defeated, Henry, himself, would have lost nothing. If, on the other hand, they were successful, Henry would be the Lord of those properties, in fact, as well as by Papal title.

Upon returning to England, Dermot made the rounds of the available nobles. Most of them declined his offer. Finally in Wales he met the Earl of Pembroke, Richard FitzGilbert de Clare, commonly known as Strongbow. Dermot offered him the hand of his pretty daughter, Aoife, in marriage, as well as being his heir to the kingship of Leinster, a title Dermot had no actual claim to. The Earl, being generally un-propertied, was immediately interested in such an opportunity to gain wealth and position.**(9)**

Dermot McMurrough returned to Ireland in 1167, with a few mercenaries, and re-established himself at Ferns. No-one took much notice of this, and Dermot maintained a low profile for the next two years, as he awaited the arrival of the promised support from Strongbow.

Invasion:

The Norman invasion was launched on May 1st 1169 with 500 men landing unopposed at Brannow, and capturing Wexford. This was a small, but well disciplined army under the command of two of Strongbow's kinsmen; his uncle Herve de Mont Maurice, and his cousin Maurice de Predergast. Upon hearing of their arrival, Dermot hurried to join them with five hundred Leinstermen. Their combined forces had little difficulty in capturing Wexford, and its garrison of two thousand. McMurrough promptly inducted the captives into his own army, and declared himself the King of Leinster.

Dermot's first victim, in his campaign to make good this claim, was the King of Ossory. The Ossory men fought well, but in the end they were forced to surrender. Following this capitulation, the remaining Leinster Chieftains submitted to Dermot, one by one, with only two holdouts. McMurrough and his Normans attacked the two holdout Leinster chieftains, decimating their armies. To teach them a lesson he laid waste to their lands. Not a very smart thing for a king to do to his own prospective subjects!

Meanwhile, the other provincial kings, and Ard Ri O'Connor, who was still trying to secure his claim to the High Kingship, paid scant attention to what was going on in Leinster. After all, it was not uncommon practice for one Irish king to import mercenaries from abroad to help him wage war on another Irish king. However, they eventually began to feel that Dermot had crossed the line. They finally marched against Dermot to put him in his place, but the Ard Righ was actually prepared to compromise with him.

Maurice Predergast, commanding about one third of the Norman Army, struck a deal with Ard Ri O'Connor, and in good Norman fashion, defected. This enabled O'Connor to defeat Dermot at Ferns and force him to negotiate. Dermot submitted to O'Connor and agreed that the Norman mercenaries would embark at once for Britain. In return, O'Connor recognized Dermot's claim as King of Leinster. Rory O'Connor returned to Connaught thinking the uprising settled, and the situation well in hand.**(10)**

More Normans:

Dermot McMurrough, however, had no intention that his Norman allies would embark for anywhere at all. For that matter, he had no ability to compel them to do anything. Instead, he wrote to Strongbow for reinforcements. Back in Britain, Strongbow had not yet received specific approval from King Henry for the venture. Consequently, he was unable to go to Dermot's aid himself. He did, however, send Raymond le Gros with ten knights, seventy archers and a herd of cattle. The invaders landed in May, 1170 at Baginbu near Wexford and were met by two thousand angry men from Waterford. The Irish defenders were caught by surprise; when the Normans stampeded the cattle and charged at them, killing a few hundred and capturing about seventy of them in the confusion. The prisoners, were all cruelly slain by the victors, first by having their limbs broken, and then flung off the cliffs into the sea. In this fashion, the Irish were given an introduction to Norman chivalry.**(11)**

The Siege of Waterford:

In August, Strongbow, having secured the blessings of King Henry, landed near Waterford with two hundred knights and one thousand soldiers. He was joined by Le Gros and Mont Maurice and lay siege to Waterford. They made several assaults on the city, being stopped by an impregnable stone wall. Ultimately, they discovered a house built into a corner of the wall, supported by heavy timbers. They cut out the timbers, the house fell, and the wall was breached. The Normans poured into the city, slaughtering its inhabitants, and its Danish rulers. More Norman chivalry!**(12)**

Dermot Keeps a Promise and Makes a Threat:

Upon word of this victory, Dermot hurried to Waterford with his daughter, the fair Aoife (Eva), in tow. As promised, her marriage to Strongbow took place promptly, amid the carnage of Waterford. Also as promised, by virtue of this marriage, (if virtue is the right word) Strongbow became heir apparent to the throne of Leinster. McMurrough was feeling pretty cocky at this point, so he set out to punish his arch enemy O'Rourke, by rampaging through Meath and Breffni.

This, of course, upset Ard Ri Rory O'Connor, who sent a warning to McMurrough to desist immediately. In reply, McMurrough sent back an insulting threat, to the effect that when he was finished with O'Rourke, he would be coming to Connaught to pay the High King a similar visit.

McMurrough plundered on, and by the end of September he and Strongbow had captured Dublin and gained control of all of Leinster. The Irish, with no armor, and using light swords, battleaxes and spears, were no match for Norman weaponry and tactics. Dermot may even have been entertaining thoughts of gaining the high kingship for himself.

Exit Dermot:

Any dream of Dermot MacMurough's, to become Ireland's High King, came to an end during the winter of 1171, when he died at Ferns of natural causes. Nature accomplished what Rory O'Connor had been unable to do. There was little mourning among the Irish, or the Normans.

A Norman King of Leinster:

Contrary to Brehon Law and Irish custom, Strongbow assumed the throne of Leinster, but his claim was shaky. In order to strengthen his position he pledged fealty to Henry II and thus allied himself with the English Crown.

High King Rory O'Connor continued to press his attack to drive out the invader and usurper. The siege went on and appeared to be a standoff. Strongbow proposed a treaty, offering to pledge fealty to the High King, and to hold Leinster for him. O'Connor refused the offer, being unwilling to give up Leinster.

Had he accepted Strongbow's offer, Irish history may have taken a whole different course. Instead, in a counter offer, he proposed that Strongbow hold only the towns of Dublin, Waterford, and Wexford. The deadlock continued, but ultimately the balance tipped in favor of the Normans. Rory O'Connor's army was routed and the Normans gained total control of all Leinster. **(13)**

A Grosse Mistake:

Strongbow rewarded Raymond le Gros, (also known as "Fat Raymond") for his assistance to McMurrough and to himself, by giving him the city of Carlow. It seems, however, that that was not enough for le Gros. He decided he wanted Cork as well, and proceeded to take it. His plans backfired on him, in 1172, by the intervention of the King of Thomond, Donal More O'Brien, another Irish King from the line of Boru. O'Brien's forces whipped the Normans royally at the battle of Thurles, decimating them and driving them from the field in disarray.

The Normans Learn New Tricks:

The Normans learned from Thurles that the warlike Irish Kings could still give them plenty of trouble. In Norman fashion they embarked on a path of treachery and deceit. They began eliminating Irish chiftans one by one with Norman trickery. In one incident, of many, King Tienan O'Rourke was murdered by Hugh deLacy, while attending a peace parley.

The Lord of Ireland:

King Henry of England, meanwhile, was beginning to think that Strongbow could be getting ideas of grandeur. Consequently, Strongbow received a summons from the King, one he dare not put off. He returned to Henry's Court and presented his cities and his territories to his monarch. He pleaded to be Henry's right hand in Leinster. Henry consented.

On October 17th, 1172, to protect his own interest, and demonstrate who was boss, King Henry landed at Waterford, with a large army; large enough, in any case to intimidate Strongbow, and make a lasting impression on the Irish. Henry proceeded to Dublin where all of the sub kings and chieftains of Munster and Leinster were assembled to pay him homage. By this time most all of the Irish bishops and kings had submitted. The Pope, Alexander III, conferred upon Henry II, the title of "Lord of Ireland."**(14)**

The Death of Strongbow:

Strongbow's reign as King of Leinster was of relatively short duration, for he was to die three years later of blood poisoning, from an ulceration on his foot. In that same year, 1175, High King, Rory O'Connor, of Connaught, traveled to Windsor, England to conclude a treaty with Henry. He swore allegiance to Henry II, and Henry granted him Kingship of those parts of Ireland that were not yet under Norman control.

This was a promise Henry was in no position to keep. He was unable to control his, now Irish-Norman, subjects, as they continued to seize more and more Irish land.

John deCourcy:

In 1177, a fierce young knight named John deCourcy was more given to the direct approach. In Dublin, he recruited his own army of about 300 Norman soldiers, and a number of idle Irish warriors. Marching north, they invaded Ulida (Ulster) and assaulted the strongly defended town of Downpatrick, the capital. By a remarkable feat of arms, even for Normans, they defeaed King MacDunlevy, who retired from the field.

MacDunlevy, enlisted the aid of his neighbor King MacLochlain. Together, they returned to Downpatrick, with their combined armies and attacked deCourcy. They were both soundly defeated by the Normans, and young deCourcy proclaimed himself to be the Lord of Ulida. He built castles at Carlingford, Carrickfergus, Coleraine, Downpatrick, Dundrum and Newry. Around these castles abbeys and towns developed, and the area prospered. John deCourcy ruled this part of Ulster for the next twenty-seven years. He did all of this without any charter from the King. **(15)**

Prince John, the Royal Idiot:

King Henry II, had enough problems in Europe to keep him busy and apparently lost interest in Ireland. In 1177 he gave the country to his youngest son, Prince John, his father's favorite was not what one might call a bright light. To say that John was slow would be about the best thing one could say of him. The fact is that the young prince was pampered, spoiled, and not too bright.

Dominus Hibernaie:

In 1177 Prince John was given the title, "Dominus Hibernaie" or Lord of Ireland. It would seem that Henry must have had a sense of humor, after all. Ireland became John's plaything. He wanted it to make money for him, so he established Anglo-Irish dynasties in Ireland in 1185, intending to people the country with Anglos.

Prince John Offends Irish Chieftains:

In 1185, when he was nineteen years old, Prince John visited Ireland to examine his new holdings. Accompanying him was a crowd of drunken, over-privileged, over-bearing young royalty, who comprised his court. With very little effort, they managed to offend just about everyone, Irish and Norman alike, by insulting and mocking those Irish chieftains who had come to pay homage. **(16)**

After getting off on the wrong foot with just about everyone, Prince John decided that he would have to change things in his little empire if he was going to hold control. He may have been an idiot, but he was smart enough to know that loyalty could be bought, if the price is right.

Ireland's Last Great Hope:

This was, however, a bad time for the Normans in Ireland. They suffered a major setback trying to conquer Connaught, their army being nearly annihilated by the forces of young Connor of

Maenmagh, the son of Ard Ri Rory O'Connor. The other major Irish princes, under his leadership, had formed an alliance and were on the verge of driving the English out of Ireland when fate intervened. Young Connor was slain in battle and the alliance fell apart.

High King, Rory O'Connor was at the cross road of Irish history. He might have changed things forever, but he came up short again and failed to provide the strong leadership the situation required. The opportunity was lost and the English barely managed to hold on to Ireland, but hold on they did. Rory O'Connor lost Connaught, lost his throne, and lost Ireland. He abdicated, became a monk, and entered the Abbey at Cong. He remained there until his death in 1188. **(17)**

Everybody Fought Everybody Else:

Following the death of High King Rory O'Connor at Cong in 1188, he was succeeded by his brother, Cathal O'Connor, as High King of Ireland, but it remained an empty title. He had no control over the other Irish Kings or Chieftains. They each did their own thing fighting the Normans, or fighting each other. In any event, Connaught remained virually unconquered until after his death in 1224. Henry II shamelessly dolled out other parts of Ulster and Munster to his barons. No central government existed, and there was no overall plan. The Normans merely took with force, whatever was given them by their master. This resulted in a state of constant warfare with the unconquered Irish Kings and Chieftains.

King Richard, (The Lion Hearted):

In England, Henry II went to his reward of natural causes in 1189. His son Richard (Coeur de Lion) ascended to the throne. Richard had other things on his mind, however, and after six months departed for the Crusades.**(18)** He left his slow witted brother, Prince John, to rule in his absence. In Palestine, Richard made many enemies among other crusading nobles and royal princes. On the way back to England, in the guise of an ordinary knight, Richard fell into the hands of an old enemy, Leopold, Duke of Austria. He was thrown into a dungeon and held for ransom.

"It Would be Good to be the King":

When Prince John received word of the King's imprisonment, he simply left him to languish in that Teutonic jail, and usurped the throne. John may have been an idiot, but not idiot enough to bail out Richard. After all, John thought "It would be good to be the King."

Under pressure from his nobles, however, John finally relented, and King Richard was ultimately ransomed. Upon returning to England in March 1194, Richard generously forgave John for his eagerness, and promptly set off again, this time for Aquitaine, to wage war against The King of France.

The Lion's Last Roar:

King Richard, being older and wiser now, left the throne in the charge of his justicare, Herbert Walter. After fighting in Normandy for five years, he was ultimately mortally wounded in battle.

At last, in 1199, Price John finally had become King, in his own right. As King, however, John had little time for Ireland. Not being much of a manager, he suffered a number of setbacks, such as loosing all of the provinces he owned in France, including Normandy. He lost the crown jewels, by accident, in a river, and he offended Pope Innocent III, in a disagreement over the Archbishop of Canterbury, which resulted in his excommunication from the Church.**(19)**

Bad for John, Good for Ireland:

King John, who was generally incompetent, did manage, however, to do at least a few things that had positive results. He organized some form of Anglo-Irish government. He introduced coinage in Ireland and he encouraged the development of Irish commerce. Towns and villages grew, and an Irish middle class of tradesmen and merchants evolved.

The "Good Ould Days" in Ireland:

Ireland was left pretty much alone for the time being. The barons and earls continued to rule, but had little authority beyond the immediate surrounding area of their castles. They fought among themselves, just as the Irish tribal chieftains had done for centuries. In fact, the Irish chieftains fought each other, the Norman barons, and the earls. It was like the "good ould days, a time of chaos. The Gaelic people were not dispossessed with the exception of the Irish nobles. The farmers were encouraged to stay and work the farm, as before, only as tenants, on what had been their own land. No large influx of Anglo settlers occurred. Many of the English nobles simply abandoned their castles and returned to England. The Norman barons and earls became more and more Irish, and the native Irish again had some control over their own destinies.

The Fly in the Ointment:

Ireland continued to prosper, but for one major drawback. With the exception of those Irish, who fought for the Normans and the Anglo-Irish, the rest of the native population had no rights in an English, or Anglo-Irish court. There was absolutely no penalty, under the law, for killing a Gaelic person. **(20)**

The Magna Carta:

John became aloof and abusive to his subjects. He attempted, time after time, to override the law, believing that the King could do no wrong. He was wrong about that. Ultimately, his nobles rebelled and forced him to sign the Magna Carta, in 1215, thus establishing Parliament and guaranteeing certain rights to all Englishmen. This act greatly diminished his own powers, and those of all future monarchs.

Henry III:

In 1216 King John died, and his son Henry became King Henry III.**(21)** As with his grandfather, Henry also seemed to care little what happened in Ireland. He soon gave it to his fourteen year old son, Edward, who grew up to be a handsome, young royal fop, with expensive tastes, and little sense. Fortunately for Edward, his father had encouraged an import/export trade with Ireland that had been beneficial to both countries.

Ireland, being agricultural, exported smoked salmon, corn, cowhides, and wool, as well as fast Irish horses, for which she was famous. In return she imported English linen, salt and beer, as well as English iron goods. Ireland had prospered. Edward had, indeed, been given a goose that lays golden eggs.

The "Ard Ri" of Connaught:

In 1258 Brian O'Neill, the King of the powerful O'Neill clan proclaimed himself to be Ard Ri, the High King of all Ireland. This was acknowledged by the O'Connor clan of Connaught, and the O'Brien clan of Thomond.

The Gallowglasses:

In this same year, some of the Ulster kings and chieftains began to employ the services of Scottish-Norse mercenaries in their battles with the Normans. These tall warriors, skilled in European military tactics, wore protective helmets and coats of mail. Their weapon of choice was a nearly six foot battle-axe. The Irish referred to them as "gall-o-glaigh", (*gaul-oh-gla*) meaning foreign warrior. The Anglo-Irish and Normans found them formidable foes, and unlike the Irish soldier, who though brave enough, but clad in cotton tunic with a short sword, was no match for Norman armor and arrows.

The galloglasses were to play a major role in Irish history for the next two hundred years, and would fight in every corner of Ireland. Within a few years no Irish King, or chieftain would be found without his company of Scottish warriors. It was unfortunate, that recently proclaimed Ard Ri, Brian O'Neill, had no *gall-o-glaigh* with him in 1260. It seems King Henry III was rather put out at Brian's claim, in as much as his grandfather, Henry II, had already been proclaimed "Lord of Ireland" way back in 1172, as per Papal "Bull Laudabiliter."

The Battle of Downpatrick:

Henry sent an overwhelming force of Anglo-Irish troops north from Dublin to register his ire. Ard Ri O'Neill was defeated, with heavy losses, at the Battle of Downpatrick. Brian, himself, was taken prisoner. As was a common practice at the time, he was decapitated and his head was sent to Henry, in England, to be displayed on a pike pole. He was the last Irish King to claim the title of Ard Ri.**(22)**

The Turning of the Tide

In 1270 the Normans met their greatest defeat at the hand of Hugh O'Connor in the Battle at the ford of Ath-an-Chip. They were routed and fled the field, leaving arms and suits of mail behind. The galloglasses, protected by mail, and swinging long, deadly battle-axes, demonstrated that the Irish now had an effective answer to Norman military superiority. This marked the failure of the Norman plan of conquest. There was left no central authority, no high king. The local Irish kings remained strong, and continued with their minor feuds. The Normans continued to be "Gaelicised" in language and custom. The extent of the Norman failure would become more obvious nearly one hundred years later with the enactment of the Statute of Kilkenny.

TIR CONAILL
Donegal
TIR EOGAIN
Derry
EARLDOM OF ULSTER
Belfast
FERMANAGH
Enniskillen
ARMAGH
Monaghan
Newry
ORIEL
Dundrum
BREFNI
Cavan
KINGDOM OF CONNACHT
Tuam
Cong
Galway
Clonmacnoise
Athenry
DE LACY EARLDOM OF MEATH
Kells
Trim
Kinlory
Tara
Athlone
Drogheda
Dublin
STRONGBOW'S LAND OF LEINSTER
County of Dublin
Wicklow
KINGDOM OF
Killaloe
Ennis
Arklow
ORMOND
Cashel
LIMERICK OR THOMOND
Limerick
Ferns
Enniscorthy
Tralee
Waterford
Wexford
Killorglin
Killarney
DECIES
KINGDOM OF CORK OR DESMOND
Cork
Youghal
Kinsale
Ireland
After the Norman Invasion
1216

Chapter Five
The Resurgence
1270-1509

Edward The "Conqueror", A Gift For a Prince, England's Parliament-More Power to It, Parliament in Ireland, No Irish Need Apply, It's Tough Being Gaelic, Edward II, The Bruce Invasion, "King" By Proxy, They Created a Monster, Edward Bruce Must Go, Served and Serviced, The Black Death, The Statutes of Kilkenny, , The Return of the Gaelic Kings, Art MacMurrough Rules Leinster, Richard II. First Visit to Ireland, The Birth of The Pale, Ah! Those Legal Loopholes, Richard II Second Visit to Ireland, Henry In-Richard Out, Irish Kings Rule Ireland, The Earl of Ormonde, The Normans Become More Irish, Earl of Desmond Appointed Governor, Desmond Killed By "The Butcher, " "The Butcher" is Butchered, The Earl of Kildare, Poynings Law, The Great Earl Rules Ireland.

They Made History:

King Edward I: 1272-1307 Self-indulgent. Fancied himself a conqueror,
King Edward II: 1307-1327 Cuckolded King. Murdered by the queen.
Robert Bruce: Gaelic King of Scotland. Drove the English out of Scotland.
Edward Bruce: Brother of Robert Bruce. Would-be king of Ireland .by proxy.
Roger Mortimer: Lord Lieutenant of Ireland under Edward II. Fancied to the Queen.
Queen Isabella: Child bride of Edward II. Fancied Mortimer. Murdered the King.
Art Mac Murrough: Pugnacious King of Leinster who plagued King Richard II
King Richard II: 1330-1377 Tried to tame Ireland. Deposed by cousin Henry IV.
James Butler: Fourth Earl of Ormonde. Briefly Governor of Ireland.
Thomas FitzGerald: Eighth Earl of Desmonde. Chief Governor, Executed by Tiptoft
Sir John Tiptoft: Replaced Desmonde as Governor. a.k.a. "The Butcher"
Garret More FitzGerald: Eighth Earl of Kildare, Chief Governor. a.k.a. The Great Earl,
Sir Edward Poynings Chief Governor. Framer of Poynings Law. Recalled by Henry VII.

Edward I, "The "Conqueror":

King Henry III died in 1272, after a reign of fifty-six years. He succeeded by his son, King Edward I. Edward lived an extravagant and self-indulgent life style, believing strongly in his own divine right to rule. He fancied himself a conqueror, so he sent his troops out to conquer for him. Unfortunately this was an expensive hobby. It cost money to arm and maintain an army, not to mention building castles, fortifications and ships. As Edward's resources dried up he had to find money elsewhere. Edward again called upon the resources of his "golden goose, " only to wring her neck. It wasn't long before he had depleted whatever prosperity Ireland had developed.

A Gift For a Prince:

Edward I had little further interest in Ireland, once it ceased to lay the golden eggs. As his grandfather had done before him, he gave it to his son, Prince Edward, when the boy was fourteen years old. Young Edward was the lord of a down and out

Ireland. He grew up to be a handsome, self-indulgent young man with expensive tastes, and an eye for the ladies.

England's Parliament- More Power to It:

Since his grandfather signed the Magna Carta, it had been the Parliament who controlled the royal purse strings. Every time Edward went to the Parliament for more money he had to bargain away specified powers. It was by this means that the English nobles gained more and more individual rights, and control of the government. This worked out well for the English, but it didn't help the Irish one little bit.

Parliament in Ireland- No Irish Need Apply:

In 1297 the Normans established a British type of Parliament for Ireland, but not for the Irish. Norman-Irish representatives were chosen from every part of Ireland, except western Connaught and western Ulster, which were still not under Norman control. By the year 1300, towns and cities also had representation. In reality this was a Norman parliament and only the ruling class was represented. The native Irish had no right to vote for representatives. The fact is, they had no rights at all. This was a parliament of the ruling class only.

It's Tough Being Gaelic:

One early law, passed by this assembly made it unlawful for the Norman-Irish to wear Gaelic dress because it made it difficult to tell Anglo-Irish from Gaelic-Irish. This was especially confusing when it came to killing Gaels. Anglo-Irish were protected by law, but it was open season on Gaels. Irish people could be killed without penalty, perhaps just because they were Irish, or perhaps if a Norman wanted his property.(1)

Edward II:

Edward I died in 1307. His son, Edward II, succeeded on the throne. Edward was an ineffective king, and did not make much of an impact on the political scene. He had, however, married a French princess, Isabella, who was only seven years old, when he was the young Prince of Wales. Isabella was the strong one.

The Norman conquest of Ireland would continue in decline. Events in England and France pretty well demanded Edward's attention, so he had little time for Irish affairs. Things were settling down in Ireland. The Norman culture was dominant only in the areas under Norman control, mostly in the towns. In the rural areas the, Norman settlers were slowly, but steadily, being assimilated by the native Irish.

The Bruce Invasion:

In 1314 Robert Bruce was proclaimed King of Scotland. This rather irritated Edward II, of England, who was under the impression that he owned Scotland. Edward sent an army to Scotland to teach Robert a lesson in humility. Instead, it was Edward who learned the lesson, at the Battle of Bannockburn. The Scots whipped the English troops badly.

When word of Bruce's victory reached Ireland, the Irish chieftains were impressed. They sent word to the Scottish King that he would be welcomed, if he wanted to cause more trouble for Edward II on Irish soil.

Robert Bruce saw this as a great opportunity. He reasoned that the Irish and the Scots were pretty much the same people, and they had a common enemy. If he could keep the English busy in Ireland, it would take some pressure off of Scotland.

"King" By Proxy:

Robert did not feel that it would be a good idea for he, himself, to leave Scotland at that time, but he had a younger brother, Edward, who was a capable military leader, and a man of ambition. He also had a few thousand warriors who weren't doing anything in particular at the moment. Thus it was that Edward Bruce, with a fleet of two hundred ships and 6, 000 seasoned, mail clad warriors, landed in Ireland in 1315.(2)

The Scots were joined by the forces of several Irish chieftains, and their combined forces were unstoppable, as they swept through Antrim, Meath and Leinster. There was a general resurgence, and more and more Irish joined the Scots. Edward was informally proclaimed by an over-enthusiastic crowd as the "King of Erin." It seems that Edward took the crowd's enthusiasm seriously.

They Created a Monster:

Edward seemed to change from liberator to conqueror. Robert Bruce joined Edward for a short term, hoping to strengthen his position in Ireland. Edward became intent on collecting tributes and forcing the Irish to submit to his authority. Most of the Irish chieftains became disenchanted with their "liberator".

The "final straw" was provided by the conduct of some of Edward's men. They treated the Irish with contempt, raided their crops, took what they wanted, insulted the Irish women and even set a few fires. The Irish, who had been plundered by experts, didn't want any of it from the Scots. Edward's local support evaporated.(3)

Edward Bruce Must Go:

King Edward II was aware that Ireland had, long since been "milked dry, " and he long ago proclaimed that whatever revenues Ireland might produce should be spent, in Ireland, to preserve the peace. Now he saw that preserving the peace meant getting rid of Edward Bruce.

To this end, in 1317 Edward made a young Anglo-Irishman, Roger Mortimer, his Lord Lieutenant of Ireland, and gave him the job of rousing the English barons to take military action against Edward Bruce.

Mortimer sent a strong force, under John deBermingham to go after the usurper. Bruce retired to Ulster, being pressed by a superior force of Norman-Irish, led by deBermingham. The two sides met at Faughart, near Dundalk in 1318. Edward Bruce was killed, and his forces driven from the field and dispersed. His fleeing warriors were left to make their own way home to Scotland.(4)

Served and Serviced:

Roger Mortimer had served his king well, and continued to do so for the next nine years. He became Edward's right hand, performing many of the king's routine duties, and more. He not only served the king well, but he also serviced the young Queen Isabella.

In fact, Roger performed his duty so well that the Queen decided that they didn't need Edward any longer. In 1327 Isabella and Roger ambushed the King in Berkley Castle, put him in chains, and tortured him to death.

Strangely enough, they almost got away with it. As the Royal Lieutenant, Roger, and the Queen-Mother Isabella, ruled England for the next three years. However, in 1330, Edward's son, Prince Edward, overthrew Roger and became King Edward III.

The king's mother was not implicated, but alas, poor Roger Mortimer was hung. Or was it hanged?(5)

The Black Death:

In the mid-fourteenth century a major disaster struck Europe, In Ireland, the Black Plague first appeared in Drogheda and Howth in early August 1348. This pestilence, more properly called the bubonic plague, was carried by lice on black rats, and decimated the population of Europe. In Ireland it carried off about one third of the population during a two year period. It affected the Irish in the rural areas to a lesser degree, but was devastating to the population in the Norman towns and cities. For the time being, the English conquest of Ireland was at a standstill.

Small outbreaks of the Black Plague returned periodically for the next fifty years, mostly affecting the very young. The overall death toll, combined with a decreased birth rate, reduced Europe's population by fifty percent by the end of the century. Ireland faired slightly better than that because of its isolated location.

In the English Parliament the Irish were frequently referred to as savages, barbarians, and the term "enemy" was even applied to them. They were considered, by most proper Englishmen, to be outlaws in their own land. The Norman landlords, meanwhile, were becoming more and more Irish in language, custom and dress. In fact, it has been said that the English/Normans were "Becoming more Irish than the Irish themselves." This would not be the first time that Irish culture had more appeal to an invader, than had their own. Legal affairs were even managed according to Brehon Law, rather than the Norman system.

The Statutes of Kilkenny:

In 1366 the Anglo-Irish Parliament met in Kilkenny and passed a series of statutes designed to put an end to the conversion of the Normans to Irish. The "Statutes of Kilkenny" specifically forbade, under penalty of death, the Norman/English to have any formal contact with the barbarian Irish. This included taking an Irish wife, or concubine, as well as adoption of any Irish person. They were forbidden to trade with the Irish. They were required to ride only a saddled horse, as bareback riding was considered savage. They could no longer engage in the sport of hurling, as that was an Irish sport. They were restrained from hiring, or keeping any Irish musician, singer, or poet. The frosting on the cake was the banning of the ancient code of Brehon law. Only English law would be recognized.(6)

An interesting, and surprising outcome of the Statutes of Kilkenny, turned out to be, that in spite of the severe penalty for violation, just about everyone ignored them. They were virtually unenforceable, except in small areas in and around the towns that were under Norman control. The Norman/English landlords continued to live as Irish.

The Return of the Gaelic Kings:

The times had been relatively peaceful, as various Irish chieftains, the MacMurroughs, MacCarthys, O'Neills, O'Connors O'Briens, O'Byrnes, O'Tooles, and Kavanaghs, jockeyed for position, and supremacy in Leinster, Munster and Connaught. The conflicts were minor, and the Gaels seemed to have things pretty much their own way.

This, of course, was somewhat alarming to the Anglo earls of Kildare, Desmond, and Ormond. They apprised the King of the situation, and in 1367 the "Irish" Parliament recommended that the absentee earls return to Ireland and defend their holdings, or forfeit them.

Art MacMurrough Rules Leinster:

The next nine years saw various exchanges of hostilities between the Irish Chieftains and the English land owners. This resulted in a stronger federation of the Irish, and inauguration of Art MacMurrough as King of Leinster, in 1376

King MacMurrough summoned all the old kings and chiefs of Leinster, then ravaged and plundered the English lands of Leinster. The Irish now embarked on a program of building up their local and provincial kingships in Leinster, Munster and Connaught. Following the Norman model, the Irish built castles and attempted to establish a royal line of succession by inheritance. As you might well guess, this led to bitter and destructive wars among themselves.

Richard II. First Visit to Ireland:

By 1394 King Richard II decided to take a hand in the matter himself and bring these wild Irish into submission. In 1394 he landed in Waterford at the head of an army of 30,000 men. He marched northward through Leinster to subdue King Art

MacMurrough, whom he considered to be his greatest threat. MacMurrough reacted by burning New Ross and retreating into the wilds of Wicklow.

The Birth of The Pale:

Richard moved on to Dublin. The plan was to invite the Irish Kings, with the exception of MacMurrough, to an honorable submission and negotiation. Several of the Irish kings had planned a stiff resistance to the English King, but they were persuaded to submit peaceably. There were four policies that King Richard and the Irish kings agreed to:

1. King Art MacMurrough, who was still at large, must give up the lands of Leinster.
2. The Irish kings would surrender the lands they had taken from the English colonists, and swear fealty to the King, and obedience to the Norman earls to whom they owed homage. They, in turn, would be confirmed to the lands they had always held, (This did not apply to Art MacMurrough)
3. On the east coast an English reserve was established from Dundalk to Waterford. This was referred to as The Pale.
4. The rebel " English" were to be pardoned and restored to their properties.

Ah! Those Legal Loopholes:

Richard, having completed his purpose of bringing the Irish under control, returned to Waterford and departed for England, confident that he had achieved a magnificent triumph. It is interesting to consider a few fine points regarding this triumph. First, the Irish Kings swore their oaths in Gaelic, not English or French. Second, King Richard never took the trouble to have the Dublin Parliament ratify, or approve the proceedings. Third, the Statutes of Kilkenny were not repealed, hence the Gaels had no legal rights under the Statutes, and Gaelic was not a recognized language.(7)

One may well wonder how these "homages, " that were paid Richard and his barons, could be considered binding. In any event, Art MacMurrouogh never surrendered a single field of Leinster, and the Irish kings never returned a square foot of the "English lands" that they allegedly "usurped."

Richard II- Second Visit to Ireland:

Richard was furious at the reneging of the Irish kings, especially that of Art MacMurrough, and considered it to be a heinous breach of faith. He vowed to take strong measures, and mounted a second expedition to Ireland. He landed at Waterford in June of 1399, with an even larger army than before. He marched north, intending to burn MacMurrough out of the woods. Many flocked to MacMurroough's banner, hoping to drive the foreigner out of Ireland.

Henry In-Richard Out:

While chasing MacMurrough, Richard received word that his arch enemy, cousin Henry Bolingbroke, of Lancaster, had landed in England and seized the throne. Richard returned to England, but was forced to abdicate by cousin Henry, who now was called King Henry IV. Richard died in prison.**(8)**

Irish Kings Rule Ireland:

Henry IV and his successors were to be kept busy for most of the fifteenth century with the Hundred Year War against France and the War of the Roses, between the House of York, and the House of Lancaster. This left them little time to meddle in Irish affairs. The English Pale was reduced to about a thirty mile diameter around Dublin, and no other English monarch, until the seventeenth century, attempted to assert his claim to the title of "Lord of Ireland."

During the early part of the fifteenth century Anglo-Norman control was limited to a few small areas, principally within the Pale. Outside of that area the Gaelic chieftains pretty much ran the country according to Gaelic laws and traditions. An area extending generally from Dublin, southeast to Cork was controlled by three powerful Anglo-Irish families, descended from the Normans. Their chieftains, who were now called earls, pretty well controlled the rest of the country. They were the Butlers of Ormond, and the Fitzgeralds of Desmond and Kildare. Art MacMurrough reclaimed his Kingdom of Leinster. Other Irish kings followed his lead and formed a federation. The Irish had learned well from the Normans, and the galloglaighs. The English no longer enjoyed a military tactical advantage.

The Earl of Ormond:

The fourth Earl of Ormond, Sir James Butler, was appointed Chief Governor of Ireland by being respected more for his tact and diplomacy, than his military prowess. His rule brought a period of peace to Ireland that was welcome, but took some getting used to. Unfortunately, his son married an Englishwoman and Butler, a Lancastrian sympathizer, lost influence by allying himself with the crown.

The Normans Become More Irish:

Some of the Anglo-Irish were now hard to distinguish from the Gaelic-Irish, in dress, custom or language, in spite of the Statutes of Kilkenny. Thomas Fitzgerald, descended from one of Strongbow's Norman Barons. The son of the Seventh Earl of Desmond was one of these. A strong Yorkist supporter, he defeated the forces of Sir John Butler, a Lancastrian supporter, at the Battle of Pilltown in 1462.

Earl of Desmond Appointed Governor:

After Thomas succeeded his father in 1463, as the Eight Earl of Desmond, Edward the IV, a Yorkist, appointed him Chief Governor of Ireland. He ruled like the old Gaelic Chieftains, consequently, both the Anglo-Irish rulers and the native Irish chiefs followed him. After four years, his Gaelic ways incurred the wrath of the English Bishop of Meath. He was accused of violating the Statutes of Kilkenny, as if that was not a common practice.

Desmond Killed By "The Butcher:"

In any event, King Edward gave into pressure from the Pale and decided to replace Desmond. In 1467 Sir John Tiptoft arrived to replace the earl. Tiptoft was known as a ruthless man, totally without mercy when it came to capital punishment for the King's enemies. His methods had earned him the title of "the butcher." When Desmond went to Drogheda to answer the charges against him, Tiptoft wasted no time in summarily beheading him.(9)

"The Butcher" is Butchered:

This caused shock and anger among both the Gaelic and Anglo-Irish earls and they reacted violently. Tiptof was recalled to England, and Garret More FitzGerald, the Eighth Earl of Kildare, was prevailed upon by Edward IV to use his influence with the earls to maintain the peace. "The Great Earl, " as he came to be called, was then appointed Chief Governor, replacing the ruthless Tiptoft. In England, during a brief restoration of the Lancasters, Tiptoft was sentenced to be executed. The execution had to be delayed for one day, due to a riotous mob who tried to lynch "the butcher."

The Earl of Kildare:

The Eighth Earl of Kildare had six daughters who married into leading families, both Anglo-Irish and Gaelic-Irish, thus having family ties in both groups. Garret was a well known scholar of Irish culture, and spoke and wrote poetry in Gaelic. He supported the Yorkist cause and clearly represented a potential threat to English rule in Ireland. When Henry VII, a Tudor of the house of Lancaster, came to the throne in 1485 he felt the need to replace The Great Earl. He appointed Sir Edward Poyning, who had a reputation as a soldier and an administrator. Poyning was charged with the task of reducing Ireland to "whole and perfect obedience." Kildare even warned his own followers that Poynings was not, "a man to be trifled with."

Poynings Law:

The new Chief Governor called a meeting of the Irish Parliament in Drogheda in December of 1494. The legislation that he called for reinstated the Statues of Kilkenny, with the exception that it did not forbid the speaking of the Irish language. The native language had become so wide spread, even in the towns and the Pale, that routine daily intercourse and business could not be conducted without it.

Poynings Law did make one very significant change. Irish Parliament could no longer assemble without the permission of the English King. Furthermore, the king and his council must first approve of any business the Parliament proposed to discuss and/or enact.

The Great Earl Rules Ireland:

Garret More FitzGerald was arrested by Poynings, under suspicion of treasonable alliances with Irish chiefs in the North, and supporting the Yorkist cause. This caused a great furor throughout the country and Henry VII was wise enough to read the writing on the wall, so to speak. He said, *"Since all Ireland cannot rule this man, he shall rule all Ireland.*" Henry relieved Poyning and restored the Great Earl as Chief Governor. The Earl of Kildare, no longer a Yorkist supporter, served King Henry VII loyally. He continued to serve, even after Henry VIII came to the throne in 1509. The Great Earl, often referred to as *"the King of Ireland, in all-but-name"* ruled Ireland wisely, and justly as Chief Governor, until his death in 1513.**(10)**

TIR CONNAIL
EARLDOM OF ULSTER
TIR LOCHAIN
FERMANAGH
IRISH ORIEL
DE BURGO LORDSHIP OF CONNACHT
BREFNI
THE KING'S CANTREDS
ENGLISH ORIEL
MEATH
HYMANY
OFFALY
EARLDOM OF KILDARE
LORDSHIP OF THOMOND
LIBERTY OF LEIX
COUNTY OF DUBLIN
PALATINE EARLDOM OF ORMOND
LIBERTY OF KILKENNY
LIBERTY OF CARLOW
LIBERTY OF WEXFORD
EARLDOM OF DESMOND
COUNTY WATERFORD
MacCarthy Country
IRELAND 1330
Under the
Anglo-Norman Lordships

Chapter Six
The Protestant Assumption
1509-1570

They Made History:

Henry VII, King of England: (1485-1509) The first Tudor King, Father of Henry VIII.

Henry VIII, King of England: (1509-1547), Founded the Church of England in order to divorce Catherine of Aragon.

Cardinal Thomas Wolsey: Chief Advisor to Henry VIII. Very powerful.

Catherine of Aragon: Henry's first wife and mother of Queen Mary.

Ann Boleyn: Henry's second wife and mother of Queen Elizabeth.

Garret Oge FitzGerald: Ninth earl of Kildare, Chief Governor of Ireland, Father of

Thomas FitzGerald, Son of Garet Fitzgerald, Earl of Offaly,

Sir William Skeffington: Henry's Commander at the massacre of Maynooth

Conn O'Neill: First Earl of Tyrone, Father of Shane O'Neill.

Edward IV, King of England (1547-1553) Sickly son of Henry VIII.

Mary I, Queen of England, (1553-1558) a.k.a. Mary, Queen of Scots, Bloody Mary.

Elizabeth I, Queen of England (1558-1603) Most powerful of the Tudors. Her navy defeated the Spanish Armada.

Shane O'Neill: King of the Ulster Chieftains, Powerful Gaelic rebel, . a.k.a The O'Neill,

Sir James FitzMaurice: Cousin of Earl of Desmond and Leader of the Munster rebellion.

Philip II: King of Spain, and Queen Elizabeth's natural enemy.

"The King is Dead, Long Live the King:"

Henry VII died in 1509, bringing his eighteen year old son, Prince Henry, to the throne. He was a large, handsome young man, with a hearty, good humored nature. He was well liked by the court and his subjects. Henry VIII, according to his late father's wishes, had married his brother's widow, the Spanish princess, Catherine of Aragon. This formed an alliance between England and Spain which resulted in England becoming involved in European conflicts, particularly against France.

The new king's policy toward Ireland remained pretty much, "hands off" initially. In fact, during the early years of his reign, Henry was pretty much a "hands off, " monarch, leaving matters of state in the hands of able ministers, with Cardinal Thomas Wolsey as his chief advisor. Garret Oge FitzGerald, the Ninth Earl of Kildare, was retained as Chief Governor of Ireland, and continued to serve the Tudor King. **(1)**

A New World Power:

In 1519, Henry VIII, and Cardinal Wolsey, decided to take a more active role in Irish affairs. The strong and willful Henry felt that Ireland was a flaw in the English armor, especially with regard to Spain. Even though he was married to a Spanish princess, Henry was concerned about Spain's growth as a world power. Since Columbus had discovered the new world in 1492, Spain was becoming a threat, as well as an ally. He felt that the disorder in Ireland might render it susceptible to foreign incursion

Surry's "Good Order:"

In 1519, Kildare, a known nationalist, was summoned to London to answer charges of possible treason. He was lodged in the Tower of London. Henry then sent the Earl of Surry, an English nobleman, to Ireland with a small force of soldiers, with orders to reduce the country to "Good order and obedience."

Surry found it impossible to reduce the Anglo-Irish earls and Gaelic Chieftains to anything resembling "good order and obedience" in the English sense of the phrase. Surry understood neither the customs nor the language of the Irish, and his small force of troops was totally inadequate. He reported to Henry that it would require at least a force of 6,000 men, supported by artillery, and extensive fortifications. Henry realized that this alone wouldn't solve the problem. It would also require a sizable English population of settlers to be imported and occupy the Irish lands. **(2)**

Surry also attempted to Anglicize the Irish church, and unify it with the English church under Cardinal Wolsey. The English bishops, which Wolsey appointed to oversee the Gaelic Irish dioceses, were usually absentees. Those few who did reside in the Irish diocese failed to understand either the traditions, or the language of their parishes. The obstacles proved insurmountable, and Henry ultimately decided that none of it would be worth the effort and the cost. Henry recalled Surry to England in 1522, and reinstated Kildare as Governor.

The disorder and friction between the Gaelic Chiefs and colonists continued, especially around the Pale. Governor Garret Oge FitzGerald was called to London again in 1527, but as before, was found blameless.

The King Has a Fling:

Meanwhile, King Henry, who had been having a fling with one of the ladies of the court, Anne Boleyn, decided he should have a male heir. The Pope refused to annul his marriage to Catherine, so in 1533 Henry nullified it himself, claiming that Church law forbade a man marrying his own brother's widow. That same year he married Anne Boleyn. This also marked the end of Cardinal Wolsey's influence with Henry, in-as–much as Wolsey had failed in his assignment to persuade the Pope to grant Henry a divorce from Catherine. He was replaced as chief advisor to the king, by a clever politician, one Thomas Cromwell.

Henry's New Title:

In 1534, Henry VIII, having been excommunicated from the Catholic Church, decided to create a church of his own and established the Church of England. The Act of Supremacy, passed by Parliament named Henry as "The supreme head on earth of the Church of England."

Kildare in Trouble:

In that same year The Ninth Earl of Kildare, Garret Oge FitzGerald was called to London for the last time. Before leaving, in February, he appointed his son, Thomas, a young man of twenty, as acting Governor of Ireland. This time FitzGerald was found guilty of treason and confined in the Tower of London. In spite of his father's warning to be guided by the advice of his elders, young Thomas was easily duped by the intrigue of English enemies in Dublin Castle. A false rumor was spread that the Earl had been beheaded in the Tower of London.

The Rebellion of Silken Thomas:

Upon hearing, and believing the rumor, young Thomas FitzGerald, Earl of Offaly galloped into Dublin at the head of one hundred and forty armed men, in coats of mail. Each one of the band wore a silken fringe on his jacket, as Lord Offaly was also known as "Silken Thomas." He stormed into the council chamber of St. Mary's Abbey, glared at the councilors, and flung down the sword of state to the floor, proclaiming, "I am not Henry's deputy. I am his foe." (3)

The rebellion of Silken Thomas had little military significance. He attempted to storm Dublin Castle, but was turned back. Henry sent Sir William Skeffington to Ireland, at the head of the largest army Ireland had seen at this time. Skeffington occupied Dublin and proclaimed Silken Thomas a traitor.

The "Maynooth Pardon:"

Thomas and his followers retreated to the FitzGerald stronghold, Maynooth Castle. Skeffington followed, and in March 1535 began a two week siege. Skeffington moved in his artillery, for what would be the first use of artillery in Ireland. Ruthlessly, he pounded Maynooth Castle to rubble, killing two thirds of the Irish defenders, and forcing Thomas to surrender the garrison.

The English commander, then, did something that had never happened in the Irish wars before. It was an atrocity that has gone down in Irish history, as the "Maynooth Pardon. He executed every one of the survivors. This was to be an example to all others who opposed the rule of the English crown. It had its effect. It could also have been read as a preview of what was yet to come. When Garret Oge FitzGerald, still in the Tower of London, heard the news of his son's rebellion, his health failed, and he died in his grief. (4)

The End of Kildare:

Silken Thomas was spared the Maynooth Pardon. In August of 1535 he was sent to England, for a miserable two year imprisonment in the Tower of London. Ultimately, he was hanged, drawn, and quartered. Also executed with him were his five uncles, who were brothers of his father. This marked the end of the House of Kildare. It also marked the end of Irish governorships. From that day forward, until 1922, all viceroys would be proper Englishmen, and there would be an English army in Dublin.

Another New Title for Henry:

In 1536 Parliament stirred the Irish pot by passing the Irish Supremacy Act, which for the first time declared the English monarch to be the King of Ireland This also made Henry, "The only Supreme Head on Earth of the whole Church of Ireland." This, however, caused no real problem in Henry's time, as the Irish continued their religious practice without change.(5) The Gaelic-Irish culture was harshly impacted by the forbidding of the Gaelic language and dress, as well as the banning and persecution of the brehons, poets, seanachaihes, and harpists.

Henry's "Irish Enemies, "

One of Henry's deputies reported to him that in Ireland there were over sixty regions, of disparate size, inhabited by "Irish enemies, " and ruled by Gaelic chieftains, who call themselves Kings, princes, or dukes. There were also thirty regions of Anglo-Irish subjects, ruled by barons and earls. All of these rulers assume the right to make war on their own, without the King's authority. In the midst of this, Henry's Lord Deputies Grey and St. Leger were demonstrating the resolve of England with a series of military actions, which more properly should be called raids; destroying cathedrals, looting monasteries, abbeys, and desecrating relics. All of this, while Henry was still pursuing a path of "good and discrete persuasions" with his Anglo-Irish earls and Gaelic chieftains.

Henry the Diplomat:

It was Henry's policy that persuaded the Earl of Desmond, and O'Brien of Thomond to submit, followed by MacWilliam Burke of Galway. In 1541, the Great Conn O'Neill, of Ulster finally went to Henry and swore fealty, in Gaelic. These last three were ennobled by Henry in 1542, O'Brien as the Earl of Thomond, Burke as Earl of Clanrickard, and O'Neill as the Earl of Tyrone.

These earls agreed to abandon the old ways, and dress and speak English. Henry wanted to create a single class of Irishman by Anglicizing the Anglo-Irish and the Gaelic- Irish into one class of king's subjects, Englishmen. In the coming centuries, the common Irish farmers were to suffer from poverty and starvation. In Gaelic society they had benefited from the common wealth of their tribe. Under the plantation system this was not the case. They found themselves to be tenants on their own land, paying rent to the new landlords. (6)

Edward VI:

In 1547 the reign of King Henry VIII came to an end. Prince Edward, even though his two half-sisters, Mary and Elizabeth were older, was named heir to the throne by Henry, as males were preferred rulers. He became Edward VI, when he was only ten years old. Edward was a sickly child, and a weak king. His reign lasted only six years. Edward was "advised" by his uncle, the Duke of Somerset, and later by the Duke of

Northumberland. These two men made England strongly Protestant, initiating many changes. In 1549, without even consulting Parliament, the mass was banned, crucifixes were forbidden, and new prayer books were printed.

"Bloody Mary:"

When Edward died Protestant interests tried, unsuccessfully, to keep Catholic Mary Tudor, from the throne. Mary had a stormy five year reign. She executed so many Protestants, that she was commonly called, "Bloody Mary." Even though she was a Catholic she did not let that interfere with politics and economics. She confiscated lands in Laois and Offaly, renaming them "Queensland" for herself and "Kingsland" in honor of her Spanish husband. Here she established a strong plantation system by importing English landlords, to displace the original Irish occupants. (7)

The Virgin Queen:

Mary died in 1558, her half-sister Elizabeth ascended to the throne. Elizabeth turned out to be the strongest ruler of all the Tudors, as well as the last. She was strongly Protestant, and sought to secure that faith throughout her dominion. In 1560 the Irish Parliament, which represented only the Anglicized parts of Ireland, tried to legislate Protestantism for the entire country. The whole thing backfired on Elizabeth. The act proved to be a strong unifying force for the Gaelic Irish, who would have no part of it. Stronger resistance to England was the natural outcome. Queen Elizabeth, like her father, hoped to achieve her purposes with persuasion and negotiation.

The Population of Ireland Divided:

Ireland had evolved into a land with three distinct populations. First, there were the Gaelic Irish, who were descended from the Celts of pre-Christian times, and the Viking invaders. Their language was Gaelic. They were mostly the poor farmers, who were Catholics and tenants on their own land. Second, there were the Old English-Irish, who came with the Norman invasion. These people originally spoke French, and later English. Many of the old English adopted Gaelic ways and the Gaelic language. They were mostly the land owners, and part of the ruling class. Many were loyal to the crown, but some had divided loyalty. Some were Protestant, and some were Catholic, but all were Irish. Finally, came the New English-Irish during the Tudor reign and plantation era. They spoke only English and were the major portion of the ruling class. The New English-Irish were first of all English, and their loyalty was to the crown, Most were land owners, and Protestant.

These groups did not live in harmony. The Gaelic-Irish somewhat mistrusted the Old English-Irish, but the two groups were mutually dependent, and they got along together. Both the Gaelic-Irish and the Old English-Irish distrusted and hated the New English-Irish. This mix provided a fertile ground for future conflict and revolution, involving economic, political, and religious issues.

The First Earl of Tyrone:

Conn O'Neill, had surrendered his property, renounced his claim as an Irish King, in return for which Henry had made him the Earl of Tyrone for life. He had sworn fealty as a king's loyal subject. After Conn died in 1599, his son Mathew was his heir under English law.

The O'Neill:

Another son, Shane O'Neill, claimed the title, stating that the land that Conn had surrendered did not belong to him, according to the system upon which all Gaelic lordships rested, but rather to the clan. Therefore, Conn had no estate to surrender, hence the earldom was not valid. Shane claimed the lordship.

A Command Performance:

Elizabeth, by "royal invitation" commanded Shane to make an appearance in her court. Shane O'Neill stated his case before the Queen in 1562, in company with an escort of two-hundred wolf-skin attired "Gallowglasses, " armed with six-foot battleaxes. The O'Neill prostrated himself before the Queen, and then howled like a wolf. He spoke to the Queen in Gaelic, presenting himself to her highness as an equal. After all, he controlled three entire counties in Ulster, as well as the vassalage of numerous chieftains, including the McGuire, the MacMahon, and the O'Reilly. The Queen was somewhat taken aback, but she was fascinated by him, as she was by all handsome men.

To gain a perceived political advantage Elizabeth negotiated with Shane through an interpreter. Shane was not at a disadvantage. He was an astute politician, with a charming sense of humor, and a natural eloquence. She was impressed with him and sought to win him by persuasion, and make him an ally. Shane was honored as a Gaelic chieftain and sent home, after five months, to rule his earldom in Irish fashion. At least in Ulster, Anglicization was for the moment, reversed. **(8)**

"The Lord of Tyrone:"

Shane O'Neill was recognized, unofficially, by the crown, as the Lord of Tyrone, and the major power in Ulster. In less than a year Shane the Proud, The O'Neill, was again in rebellion against that same crown. Shane was willing to recognize Elizabeth as sovereign, as long as he was allowed to rule in Ulster. Ireland as a nation, or Ireland as Catholic, were of less concern to him than O'Neill as "King " of Ulster. Sir Henry Sidney, the Queens Lieutenant in Ireland, recognized O'Neill as the most powerful man in Ireland, but tended to tolerate him, as he kept the MacDonnell Scots of Antrim and the O'Donnell of Donegal in check. In 1565 the O'Neill defeated the forces of James MacDonnell, chief of the Antrim Scots at Glenshesk. James was killed in the battle.

The O'Neill's Fatal Error:

Shane then turned his attention to the O'Donnells. Initially he was successful, but by 1566 the government was supporting the O'Donnells. At the battle of Farsetmore, in 1567, Shane was completely defeated, his army decimated by Hugh Duv O'Donnell. Shane escaped and sought refuge with his old defeated enemies, the Antrim Scots, MacDonnell.

This was not the smartest thing that Shane ever did; in fact, it was probably the dumbest. Sorely Boy MacDonnell gave Shane sanctuary, but at a banquet of hospitality, old wounds festered. In a drunken brawl, Shane the Proud, the greatest O'Neill of the old Gaels, lost his life. His head, on a pike, was displayed at Dublin Castle. **(9)**

A New Landlord in Tyrone:

The Queen took possession of Shane's three Ulster counties while Shane's successor, Turlogh Luineach O'Neill, grandson of Conn More O'Neill, became the new landlord of Tyrone. He was a loyal Queen's man, and posed no problem to the crown. He would continue in this capacity for the next two decades. As far as Elizabeth was concerned, Ulster was secure.

Another O'Neill:

Meanwhile, another grandson of Conn, Hugh O"Neill, was made the Earl of Dungannon in 1568. He had been a young boy when Shane came to power, had been raised as a Protestant from age nine. He was educated in England, and had grown up under the care of Sir Henry Sidney, a loyal Queen's man, who would become the Queen's deputy in 1575.

At 18, young Hugh returned to Ireland, having been educated as a proper English gentleman. In 1569, the Earl of Dungannon commanded a troop of Queen's Horse and would help to suppress the Munster uprising. It was here that the young earl gained his early military training and experience in leadership.(10)

Queen Elizabeth VS. Pope Gregory XIII:

In 1570 Pope Gregory XIII declared that Queen Elizabeth was an illegitimate child of Henry VIII and excommunicated her. I doubt that this bothered her much in the spiritual sense. Her father was excommunicated and formed the Church of England when he had married her mother, Ann Boleyn, so Elizabeth was not a Catholic to begin with. However, it represented a challenge to her right to rule, and thus placed her at odds with all the other royal houses of Europe. Viewing Ireland as a potential entry point for foreign incursion, Elizabeth now became determined to make Ireland Protestant.

Chapter Seven
A Period of Revolution
1570-1603

Munster Rebels, The Smerwick Expedition, Fitzmaurice Killed, Desmond's Fate, Rebellion in Leinster, The Earl of Tyrone, Perrot Started Something, The Armada, The Best Laid Plans..., An Opportunity Lost, Red Hugh Escapes, Briefly, The Killing of O'Rourke, Red Hugh Escapes Again, , A New Alliance, The O'Donnell, O'Neill Prepares, O'Neill Charged With Treason, "The O'Neill, " The Ulster Rebellion, The Battle of Yellow Ford, Earl of Essex, ODonnell Abu, Lord Mountjoy, Aid From Spain, The Battle of Kinsale, The Spanish Give It Up, The End of the Gaelic Lordships

They Made History:

Elizabeth I, Queen of England (1558-1603): Most powerful of the Tudors. Defeated Spanish Armada.

Hugh O'Neill: Earl of Tyrone, nephew to Shane, Grandson of Conn, a.k.a. The O'Neill.

Sir Henry Bagnal: Hugh O'Neill's brother -in-law. Looked, when he should have ducked.

Hugh Roe O'Donnell: Kidnapped as a young man by Dublin Officials. Held in Dublin Castle. Escaped with aid of Hugh O'Neill., a.k.a., The O'Donnell

Sir Robert Devereux: Second Earl of Essex. Queen's Deputy. Made truce with O'Neill.

Sir Charles Blount: Lord Mountjoy. Queens Deputy. Defeated O'Neill at Kinsale.

Sir James Fitzmaurice: Cousin of 14th Earl of Desmond. Leader of the rebellion, in 1579.

Gerald FitzGerald: Fourteenth Earldom of Desmond in 1558. Finally joined the Munster Rebellion in 1583. Died in Kerry.

Sir Walter Raleigh: An English adventurer, and favorite of Queen Elizabeth. Massacred the surrendered garrison at Fort del Ore.

Fiach MacHugh O'Byrne: Irish rebel and successful guerilla leader in the Wicklows.

Sir Henry Sidney: Queen's Deputy of Ireland, Fostered young Hugh O'Neill.

Hugh O'Niell: The Earl of Tyrone

Sir Robert Devereux: 2nd Earl of Essex

Gerald Fitzgerald: 14th Earl of Desmond.

Col. Sebastian SanJose: Leader of Spanish forces at Kinsale.

Lord Grey deWilton: Defeated at the Battle of Glenmalure

Sir John Perrot: Queen's deputy in Ireland

Red Hugh O'Donnell: Nephew of Hugh O'Donnell

Captain John Hawkins: Captain of the "Sea Hawks" who fought off he Armada.

Captain Francis Drake: Captain of the "Sea Hawks" who fought off he Armada

Brian O'Rourke: *A Gaelic chieftain.*

Art and Henry O'Niell: Sons of Shane O'Niell. Escaped with Red Hugh.

Comac O'Niell: Routed the English at Battle of Ford-of-the-Biscuits.

Turlough Luinach O'Niell: "The O'Niell" who stepped down for Hugh., "The O'Niell".

Phelim O'Byrne: Son of Fiach, and a guerilla leader.

Rory O.Donnell : Brother of Red Hugh, the Earl of Tyrconnell.

King Philip II: King of Spain

Viscount Baltinglass: Led a revolt in Lienster.

Munster Rebels:

The renewal of the reformation did not sit well in Ireland. In 1572 rebellion broke out in Munster, led by Sir James Fitzmaurice, the cousin of Gerald, the fourteenth Earl of Desmond. Fitzmaurice sought support from King Philip II, of Spain. This was a logical thing to do. Spain, being a Catholic country, was greatly favored by the Irish. In fact, the Gaelic Irish believed that their forbearers came from Spain. The port cities of Munster had offered aid to Fitzmaurice on several occasions, not to mention that he was Elizabeth's bitter enemy.

The Smerwick Expedition:

King Philip, of Spain, promised support to Fitzmaurice, but due to Spanish problems elsewhere in Europe, the promised aid failed to materialize. The rising was easily put down and Fitzmaurice fled to the continent and sought aid from Henry III, of France and then from Don John of Austria, both of whom refused him. In Rome he obtained a document from Pope Gregory XII, a Papal Bull, urging Catholics to condemn Queen Elizabeth's reign and calling upon all Irish Catholics to resist Protestant incursion. **(1)**

A small supporting force was fitted out, and paid for by the Pope. King Philip was responsible to maintain the expedition. Sir James Fitzmaurice returned to Ireland, landing at Smerwick Harbor in Dingle, County Kerry, on July 18, 1579. He was accompanied by 700 Spanish soldiers, and armed with the Papal Bull. The Spanish soldiers garrisoned at Fort del Ore, and strengthened its defenses. The fort was on a small island, (Golden Island) connected to the Dingle Peninsula by a narrow neck of land, and considered impregnable.

Fitzmaurice Killed:

A fatal blow to the rebellion occurred a month later, when Fitzmaurice was killed, at Castleconnell, in a family dispute with two of his Burke kinsmen. John Geraldine, a brother of the Earl of Desmond, then took command of the expedition. The small force remained in Fort del Ore, untouchable. The Earl of Desmond was not present, and tried to distance himself from Fitzmaurice and Geraldine. He was under suspicion, but was not apprehended.

A second expedition, fitted out by Philip, arrived the next year in September 1580, commanded by a Colonel Sebastian San Jose. The fort was strengthened, and the insurrection was revived. It wasn't too long, however, before the Lord Deputy Grey de Wilton arrived to lay siege, both by land, and from the sea. The Spanish commander, San Jose, negotiated a treaty with the Lord Deputy, making conditions for only the Spaniards. The fort was surrendered and six hundred Irish defenders were then massacred by the English troops led by the Queen's favorite, Sir Walter Raleigh.(2)

Desmond's Fate:

The Earl of Desmond was found complicit in the rebellion, even though he was not present at the battle. As a gift from the Queen, some forty-thousand acres of Desmond's lands were confiscated, and later colonized by the Sir Walter Raleigh syndicate. The lands, belonging to the other rebels, were to be given to English colonists. At this point Elizabeth gave up her policy of negotiation all together. She was no longer interested in mere control, or conversion of the Irish Catholics. She wanted to be rid of them. (3) The Earl of Desmond, who had finally rebelled openly, was declared a traitor to the crown, and his forces were decimated. He, himself, was hunted like an animal, and finally captured in Kerry. Twenty-five of his soldiers were put to the sword. On November 11, 1583 he was executed by decapitation. His head sent to the Queen, impaled on a pike and displayed on London Bridge. (4)

Rebellion in Leinster:

The following year another rebellion, resisting Protestant incursion, led by Viscount Baltinglass, a lord of the Pale, broke out in Leinster. This was culminated in a lonely pass in the Wicklow Mountains. The Irish, under command of the rebel Fiach MacHugh O'Byrne, soundly defeated the forces of Deputy Lord Grey de Wilton, at the battle of Glenmalure. This Irish victory, however, had no apparent effect on the outcome of the rebellion. The results were indecisive. By 1585 England was prospering, as Elizabeth set out to Anglicize the rest of Ireland. Connaught, was more easily organized under English government, but lasting hatred of British rule developed there, as well as in Munster, and Leinster.

The Earl of Tyrone:

In 1582, young Hugh O'Neill, the Earl of Dunganon, had been elevated to be the Earl of Tyrone, and given full title to the O'Neill lands. At the age of 19, he led a troop of the Queen's horse, and helped suppress a rising in Munster. Now, at the age of thirty-two he became a major part of the English administration.

He had also become a cautious and courageous leader, who planned carefully to over come his rivals, the O'Donnells and the MacDonnells, and solidify his power in Tyrone. (5) He had married the daughter of Sir Hugh O'Donnell, so at least one of his rivals was family. He developed love of power, which would soon bring him into conflict with the Queen herself.

Perrot Started Something:

In 1587, Deputy Sir John Perrot unwittingly sparked a major rebellion in Ulster, which up until this time had been pretty much the Queen's own province. However, being fearful of the power of the O'Donnells, he caused the kidnapping of sixteen year old Red Hugh O'Donnell, the son of the Chief of the Tyrconnel O'Donnells, and a nephew of Hugh O'Neill. His intent was to hold him in the Tower of Dublin Castle, as a hostage, in order to assure the clan's good behavior. The Earl of Tyrone, Hugh O'Neill, a loyal Queen's man, took exception to these high handed tactics in dealing with an Ulster Chieftain. He secretly made plans to bring about the escape of Red Hugh from Dublin Castle. This would be his first disloyal act, and quite possibly the birth of an idea of founding an Irish national movement. At any rate, Hugh O'Neill began planning covertly, contrary to the interest of the crown, to achieve the boy's release.

Hugh O'Neill's wife had died, leaving him a widower. In the course of human behavior, Hugh later met, and became smitten with, the lovely sister of Sir Henry Bagnal, a Queen's soldier, of the New English-Irish order. When Sir Henry got word of this new relationship he was indignant. He shipped the lady off to Dublin, to live with her sister and her husband. He did not want his family's blood mixed with the family of a Gaelic Irishman This did not stop the Earl of Tyrone. He arranged for her consensual abduction, after which they were married. Sir Henry, of course, was furious. Simultaneously, he became O'Neill's brother-in-law, and his bitter enemy.

The Armada:

By 1588, England had not heard the last from King Philip II, of Spain, who undoubtedly, even nine years later, still smarted from the slaughter of the Smerwick expedition. Nor had he forgotten how Henry VIII had set aside his sister, Catherine of Aragon, for the mother of illegitimate Elizabeth. Not only that, but Spain was Catholic and England was not. Spain had the wealth of its colonies in the new world and by that had become the greatest naval power in the world. In September, Philip decided to use this power against his natural enemy, Queen Elizabeth. He sent the mightiest Armada the world had ever seen to invade England. All Elizabeth had for defense was a relatively small force of privateers, under the command of Captains John Hawkins and Francis Drake.

The Best Laid Plans….

The British were outgunned, but with smaller, faster, and more maneuverable ships, they were able to stand off the larger, clumsy Spanish galleons. Nature did the rest, when a severe autumn storm drove many galleons ashore in France. The remaining ships fled to the North Sea and westward, then down the west coast of Ireland, where seventy-five more galleons were driven ashore by a North Atlantic storm.

An Opportunity Lost:

Had Spanish troops landed successfully in England, or even in Ireland itself, English and Irish history would undoubtedly have taken a whole different turn at that point. Ireland might even have achieved it's long dreamed of national unity, and independence. But mother nature and human nature ruled otherwise. In spite of these close ties, and political advantage, Spanish survivors were hunted down by misguided Irish chieftains and a population terrorized by tyrannical government. All provincial governors were ordered to execute all Spaniards taken. In Connaught, citizens were warned that anyone harboring survivors for more than twenty-four hours would be proclaimed a traitor, and executed. The slaughter was pitiless. Spanish casualties have been estimated at up to ten thousand, lost at sea, or murdered ashore.(6) A few earls and chieftains in Ulster worked secretly to save as many as they could. Hugh O'Donnell harbored over 3, 000 of the fugitives, and, with the assistance of Hugh O'Neill, got them to safety in Scotland. Brian O'Rourke sheltered another 1, 000, many of them getting safely away. Brian, himself, escaped to Scotland.

Red Hugh Escapes, Briefly:

Meanwhile, Red Hugh O'Donnell had been languishing in the tower of Dublin Castle. In 1590, after three years as a guest of Sir John Perrot, young O'Donnell, escaped. His freedom was short lived, however. He was recaptured a short time later, wandering in the Wicklow Mountains, in search of the camp of the rebel leader, Fiach MacHugh O'Byrne.

The Cliffs of More, where the the Spanish Armada was driven ashore

The Killing of O'Rourke:

Brian O'Rourke, the Gaelic chieftain who had fled to Scotland was unfortunately, captured by James VI and shamefully extradited him to Queen Elizabeth. He had been tried as a common criminal and executed in London in 1591. This was an event that shocked the Gaelic earls and pushed them one step closer to open rebellion. Many believed that this was all part of a conspiracy, favoring a few of O'Rourke's New English-Irish enemies, in order to obtain title to O'Rourke's property. The young chieftan had been very popular, and this increased the bitterness. (7)

Red Hugh Escapes, Again:

On Christmas day, 1591, Red Hugh, covertly aided by Uncle Hugh O'Neill, again escaped from Dublin Castle, this time with two companions, Henry and Art O'Neill, sons of Shane, and cousins to Hugh O'Neill. One might conclude that this was as much a family matter, as it was a political one.

A New Alliance:

Henry was successful in getting back to Ulster on his own. Red Hugh and Art O'Neill became lost in the Wicklow Mountains in the cold of winter. They were found by rebel leader, Fiach

O'Byrne, in a cave. Art was frozen to death, but Red Hugh recovered slowly. He stayed a few weeks with O'Neill at Dungannon Castle, where they agreed to an alliance, thus ending the feud between the two clans. (8) From this point on they would become partners in political intrigue.

The O'Donnell:

Red Hugh O'Donnell was pretty much laid up for the rest of the winter, recovering from his ordeal and frost bite. He had to have his two big toes amputated. When he was sufficiently recovered, the O'Donnell clan was convened. In the usual Gaelic tradition, Red Hugh was elected to the chieftaincy of the clan. Endowed with this new status, he undertook small raids and incursions upon English occupied lands. O'Neill prevailed upon the Lord Deputy to give O'Donnell a full pardon for his escape from Dublin Tower. In the interest of not having a premature rebellion, he also prevailed upon the O'Donnell to curb his activities until the time was ripe.

O'Neill Prepares:

Hugh O'Neill was now, definitely, leading a double life. Publicly he was a Queen's man, and loyal subject. In reality he had, for some time, been secretly assisting rebellious neighbors who had been carrying out small raids and incursions. But O'Neill was an outstanding organizer. By law, as the Earl of Tyrone, he was permitted to keep six hundred men under arms. As Hugh O'Neill, he a had better idea. As his men were trained, they were placed in reserve, and another group would take their place. In this fashion, he trained and equipped an army of over 10, 000 men. (9) His troops were musketeers, cavalrymen, and pikemen. At his expense they were provided ample firearms. They even had uniforms with red jackets. O'Neill purchased a large quantity of lead, ostensibly to repair the roof of Dungannon Castle. The major portion of it however, was used to mold bullets.

It was becoming more and more difficult to maintain his cover. On one occasion it was only by a hair, and a last minute covert contact that he was able to avert battle with a Gaelic-Irish force. On another occasion, at the siege of Enniskillen he was able to send his brother, Cormac O'Neill, who openly routed the English, killing many of them at a battle that was called the "Ford of the Biscuits." The Irish had everything they needed except artillery. However, the guerrilla tactics of ambush, and hit and run were proving quite successful.

O'Neill Charged With Treason:

On August 11, 1594 The O'Neill appeared before the new Deputy Sir William Russell to answer questions of doubt concerning his loyalty. The Deputy seemed favorably impressed, but Hugh's brother-in-law, Sir Henry Bagnal, charged him with treason. In answer to the charge O'Neill challenged Sir Henry to individual combat to settle the question. Sir Henry refused the offer, and the matter was dropped for the time being.

"The O'Neill:"

In 1595, Hugh O'Neill's uncle, Turlogh Luineach O'Neill resigned his position as chieftain of the O'Neill clan, in favor of his nephew. Hugh was recognized as The O'Neill, according to Gaelic custom, and essentially, along with his ally, the O'Donnell, he was now the absolute ruler of Ulster, with possibly the largest and best trained army in Ireland. Now the time was ripe. No more double-life. With the combined armies of The O'Neill and The O'Donnell, they jointly led an open rebellion. O'Neill gave reality to Queen Elizabeth's old fear that Ireland could be a back door to England for her enemies. They invited King Philip, of Spain, to join them.

The Ulster Rebellion:

Various hit and run conflicts, with the Irish in advantage and various cruelties and atrocities, at which the English excelled, continued for the next four years. Both sides were coming closer and closer to open warfare. Finally, on June 7, 1598, the O'Neill laid siege to the Blackwater Fort. The English tried to relieve the siege, but the reinforcements were ambushed en-route at Dungannon, and over four hundred English troops were killed.

The Battle of Yellow Ford:

Sir Henry Bagnal, with a force of over 2,000 set out for Armaugh, to do battle with his despised brother-in-law. He had good troops and was confident of the outcome. On August 14th, they arrived at Yellow Ford, two miles from Armaugh. Here they were attacked by the Irish forces, under the command of O'Neill. Sir Henry was not lacking in valor, but he was a poor tactician. He deployed his men poorly and his army was being torn to pieces.

Sir Henry raised the visor of his helmet to get a better view of the battle around him. Bad move! At that moment a musket ball came his way, and struck him right where his visor had previously been. Sir Henry dropped like a rock. At just that moment an ammunition wagon exploded nearby, and his troops scattered. Panic ensued, and the rout was complete.

About 2,000 survivors reached Armaugh and barricaded themselves in the Cathedral, leaving hundreds of their dead comrades on the field, along with abandoned arms and provisions. Irish losses were about 200 killed and 600 wounded. Word of the Battle of Yellow Ford quickly spread all over Ireland. The name of the Earl of Tyrone was acclaimed throughout the island, and O'Neill's revolt spread into Munster. **(10)**

Earl of Essex:

In April of 1599, Sir Robert Devereux, the second Earl of Essex was sent to Ireland as the Queen's new Deputy. With him, he brought reenforcements of 1,600 foot soldiers and 1,300 mounted. His orders were to directly engage the Earl of Tyrone in battle, and kill, or capture him. This, he was not able to do. He dispatched a portion of his army to the south, where, in the Wicklow Mountains, they were cut off and defeated, at Glenmalure, by the forces of Phelim O'Byrne, the son of Fiach. Through the next few months his forces were gradually reduced, by battle and sickness, to about 4,000 men.

O'Donnell Abu:

Meanwhile Red Hugh O'Donnell had been busy in Connaught, kicking the daylights out of the Queen's royal forces with his tall galloglasses. Essex then moved north, where he met The O'Neill for a parley. A truce was arranged, the terms of which were never revealed. Essex was recalled to England by an angry Elizabeth. Apparently the Queen was not amused, for she referred Essex to her headsman, for permanent retirement. **(11)** The exploits of Red Hugh O'Donnell have been kept in Irish memory by an unknown poet in the ballad, *"O'Donnell Abu."* The title was taken from the Gaelic war cry, which in translation means, "O'Donnell Forward!"

Lord Mountjoy:

It was now clear that the Irish would never accept the Protestant Reformation. There was even speculation that the Irish had won. This, however, proved not to be the case. Sir Charles Blount, Lord Mountjoy, replaced Essex as Deputy, arriving in February of 1600, with a well trained army of 20, 000 troops. He was given wide powers in how to defeat O'Neill, but Elizabeth made it plain no pardon was to be given the traitor. He was either to be killed, or brought to her in chains.

O'Donnell Abu

Proudly the note of the trumpet is sounding,
Loudly the war cries arise on the gale,
Fleetly the steed by Lough Swilly is bounding,
To join the thick squadrons on Saimer's green vale.
On every mountaineer strangers, to fight or fear;
Rush to the standard of dauntless Red Hugh.
Bonnaught and Gallowglass throng from each mountain pass,
Onward for Erin, O' Donnell Abu!
Princely O'Neill to our aid is advancing,
With manly a chieftain and warrior clan,
A thousand proud steed in vangard are prancing,
'Neath the borders brave from the banks of the Bann
Many a heart shall quail, under its coat of mail,
Deeply the merciless foeman shall rue
When on his ear shall ring borne on the breeze's wing,
Tir Connell's dread war cry, "O''Donnell Abu!"

Wildly o'er desmond the war wolf is howling:
fearless the eagle sweeps over the plain.
The fox in the streets of the city is prowling,
And all who would scare them are banished or slain.
On with O'Donnell then, fight the old fight again;
Sons of Tir Connell, are valiant and true.
Make the proud Saxon feel, Erin's avenging steel.
Strike for your country, "O'Donnell Abu!"

Raids and skirmishes continued to annoy Mountjoy, whose strategy was to starve the Irish in Munster by burning their crops, and subduing the chieftains one by one. Ultimately the war turned to the north, where O'Neill still had an army of 4,000 of musketeers, pikemen, and horse. There were several attempts to assassinate The O'Neill in 1601. A bounty of 2,000 pounds was offered for his capture, or 1,000 pounds for his head. There were no takers! **(12)**

Aid From Spain:

Finally, in September, the long awaited aid from Philip of Spain, arrived. A few ships, carrying only 3,500 men sailed into the harbor at Kinsale. Most of the county of Cork had already been subdued by Mountjoy, so they found no friendly troops on the shore to meet them. Mountyjoy, deploying what was left of his army, some 6,500 men, promptly laid siege to the Spanish position from land and sea.

The Battle of Kinsale:

O'Neill and O'Donnell hurried to support the Spaniards, but each was faced with a long forced march to Kinsale. The O'Donnell arrived first, in mid November, and began harassing action at Mountjoy's rear. In early December, reinforcements had arrived from Spain, consisting of fewer than 200 men. Considering losses they had sustained since landing in September, Spanish forces now numbered about 3,000. The O'Neill, marching the full length of Ireland did not arrive until December 21st, at which time he joined O'Donnell in harassing the besiegers from the rear.

With O'Neill's 6,000 foot soldiers and 500 horse, the Irish, fielded a combined army of 12,000, including a number of Spanish troops. The English army had been reduced, due to battle casualties and sickness, to 6,500. Mountjoy was also aided by loyalist Irish troops from the Earl of Clanrickard, the Earl of Thomond, Cormac MacCarthy of Cork, and St. Lawrence, from the Pale. To sum it up, the Irish and Spanish, in the field, besieged the English and the Irish, in the field, who in turn, besieged the Spanish and the Irish, in the fort.

The Irish were unable to use their hit and run tactics, which had worked so well for them, and were forced to face a smaller army, which was equipped with cannon, by maneuvering in large formations. This manner of fighting, in large formations, was unfamiliar to the Irish troops, and confusion developed. The Irish planned a surprise attack, but lost the advantage when their plan was given to the English commander, by a traitor. Lord Mountjoy, having been warned, was able to over-run the Irish divisions, one by one. **(13)**

The Spanish Give It Up:

The Spanish commander, who is said to have been bribed, sought terms for his troops, making no provision for the Irish forces who fought alongside him. O'Neill's and O'Donnell's Irish troops were routed and slain. Their losses were estimated at 2,000, plus 840 out of 900 galloglasses were killed outright. Irish troops, who were taken prisoner, were hanged.

Red Hugh O'Donnell delegated Tyrconnell chieftaincy to his brother, Rory, before sailing for Spain with the Spanish troops. He intended to plead with Philip for further aid. He was graciously received by the King, but soon met his death by poisoning, presumably by English agents. **(14)** Hugh O'Neill and Rory O'Donnell fought back to Ulster, and remained at large, trying to keep the cause alive. They were not actively sought by Lord Mountjoy. Queen Elizabeth's health had been failing, and she died on March 24, 1603, reportedly quite mad. The news was carefully guarded, however, as Hugh O'Neill had not yet surrendered.

The End of The Gaelic Lordships:

Hugh O'Neill, the Earl of Tyrone remained at large for over another year. When Rory O'Donnell received word of his brother's death in Spain, he surrendered. Hugh finally realized that the cause was lost and he surrendered at Mellifont on March 30, 1603. Lord Mountjoy, accepted his surrender with honor, but he was required to renounce title of "The O'Neill, " which was the real source of his power. He surrendered his title as Earl of Tyrone, and his land to Queen Elizabeth, not knowing that she had died six days earlier, on March 24th. Had he known, he would ave undoubtedly held out for better terms from King James. Hugh O'Neill and Rory O'Donnell traveled to London with Lord Mountjoy to be graciously received by recently crowned King James I.

The new king, a Scot, had once been a friend of O'Neill's, and he generously restored the title of Earl of Tyrone to him, along with some of his property. Rory O'Donnell received similar treatment, and was accorded the title of Earl of Tyrconnell. The titles were limited, however, bestowing no real authority on the recipients. With their surrender the age of the Gaelic lordships in Ireland was gone forever.

IRELAND
THE GREAT LORDSHIPS
OF THE
SIXTEENTH CENTURY
TIRCONNELL
SUPREMACY OF O'DONNELL
SUPREMACY OF O'NEILL
THE ROUTE
CLANNEBOY
THE FREEDOM OF ULSTER
LORDSHIP OF O'BRIEN
FERMANAGH
TYRONE
IVEAGH
SUPREMACY OF O'REILLY
O'FARRELL OF ANALY
LIBERTY OF TRIM
THE ENGLISH
CLAN RICKARD BURKE
HY MANY
LIBERTY OF TRIM
THE ENGLISH PALE
THOMOND SUPREMACY OF O'BRIEN
LORDSHIP OF LEIX
EARLDOM OF KILDARE
SUPREMACY OF MacMURROUGH
EARLDOM AND SUPREMACY OF ORMOND
EARLDOM AND SUPREMACY OF DESMOND
WATERFORD
LORDSHIP OF WEXFORD

Chapter Eight
Hard Times and Rebellion
1603-1652

King James I, Divine Right of Kings, Not a "Closet Catholic, " The Act of Oblivion, The Gunpowder Plot, , Forerunner of the Penal Acts, The Flight of the Earls, The Sons of Ireland, Plantation, Plantation, Plantation, The Silent Threat, Charles I and the Counter-Reformation,, The "Graces," Gaelic Culture Survived, The Earl of Stratford, War With Scotland, Charles Concedes More Power, An Old Solution, Troubles in Ireland, The Ulster Revolt, The Portatown Massacre, The Rising of 1641, The Church Supports the Rebellion, Control of the Army Contested, Cavaliers vs. Roundheads, Owen Roe O'Neill, Confederation of Catholics of Ireland, Everybody Has An Army, Oliver Cromwell and the Commonwealth, The King is Dead, Oliver Cromwell, Lord Protector, Lord Protect Us All, Parliament Celebrates the Atrocity, The Death of Owen Roe, Cromwell Outfoxed At Clonmel, ,

They Made History:

King James I, King of England (1603-1625) Son of Queen Mary, was also James VI of Scotland,

King Charles I, King of England (1625-1649) Son of James I, English Civil War, Overthrown by Puritan Parliament.

Charles Wentworth, The Earl of Stratford, Lord Deputy of Ireland under Charles I.

Sir Phelim O'Neill, Another O'Neill, Leader of the Ulster Revolt.

Owen Roe O'Neill, Nephew of the "Great O'Neill," Became an inspiring military leader.

Oliver Cromwell, Lord Protector of England (1649-1660), Dictator, Ruled Puritan Parliament, Butcher of Drogheda.

Charles II, King of England (1660-1685), Extravagant, playboy, Controlled by parliament.

King James I:

Queen Elizabeth, unlike her father, never married and consequently left no heir to the throne. Accordingly, the throne passed to the son of the previous Queen who was Elizabeth's half sister, Mary, who was also the Queen of Scotland. The new king was King James VI of Scotland, who also became King James I, of England.

Divine Right of Kings:

King James I had one particular notion that was to cause much trouble and turmoil in England, and in Ireland as well. He believed in the divine right of Kings. That is to say, that the king can do no wrong. He believed that his right to rule came directly from God, not Parliament, and that he was responsible only to God. He immediately defied Parliament and the Magna Carta by levying his own taxes, illegally.

Not a "Closet Catholic:"

King James, the son of a Catholic Queen, did not have strong anti-Catholic sentiments. This fostered the notion among the Irish that the persecutions of the reformation were over, and Catholics in southern Munster began celebrating the mass openly. They soon discovered that nothing had changed. Many, in England, believed that the King was actually a closet Catholic. James felt he must prove that he was not. To that end, he ordered Lord Mountjoy, with his 20,000 man army, to continued enforcement of the ban on exercising the mass(1).

The Act of Oblivion:

In 1604, a magnanimous Parliament passed the Act of Oblivion, by which terms all previous offenses of the law were forgiven. This applied to Catholics in general, however, it did not apply to fugitive priests, who continued to offend the law by saying mass and giving sacraments. (2)

The Gunpowder Plot:

1605 saw increasing intolerance in England toward Catholics by radical groups. King James was able to do little to appease them. The Puritans, in particular, did not accept the Act of Oblivion. In what came to be called, "The Gunpowder Plot, " the Puritans filled the cellars of Parliament with explosives, planning to blow up the Lords, the Commons, and the King. One of their number, Guy Fawks, was to detonate the package. Fortunately for Westminster the plot was discovered in time to prevent the carnage. (3) But the threat was plain, and parliament got the message.

Forerunner of the Penal Acts:

The next year Parliament passed some severely anti-Catholic laws, which became a model for future legislation. The Catholic clergy was banned. Catholics were required to attend the Protestant Church of Ireland, and non-attendance was heavily fined. The needs of the faithful had to be served in secret, in remote locations, using "Mass rocks" for altars. Priests were to be hunted and persecuted. Actual branding of priests had been proposed, but not passed. On the other hand, it was found acceptable to kill priests who were caught performing mass, or teaching Irish children in one of the "Hedge schools." These laws were most effective in Ulster, which was heavily planted with

English and Scot settlers, but were largely ignored in the four other provinces, where persecution only served to strengthen the Catholic faith.

The Flight of the Earls:

For nearly four years Hugh O'Neil, the Earl of Tyrone, and Rory O'Donnell, the Earl of Tyrconnell lived quietly, but not securely. O'Donnell had been covertly, but vainly trying to obtain Spanish help. Hugh O'Neil had been falsely accused of plotting against the crown, and summoned to London to answer charges. By the summer of 1607 the two had decided that the situation was hopeless.

On September 14th they, and ninety-nine other Gaelic Chieftains and earls, with their families, boarded a ship in Rathmullen harbor, County Donegal, and left Ireland forever. They landed in the Netherlands as fugitives, and settled in the Catholic countries of France, Spain, and Italy. O'Neil and O'Donnell traveled to Rome, where they lived out their lives in quiet exile.

Many remaining Irish lords and chiefs, guilty or not, were accused of treason and conspiracy by a predominantly Protestant Dublin parliament. Resisters were hunted down and slain. Most of the accused were convicted and confined. The end result was that Ireland was left without leaders, and the Gaelic population was at the mercy of a greedy government. **(4)**

The Sons of Ireland:

The sons of the exiled earls, and chiefs had but few choices in life. Most of them entered into the military forces of various European kings, and were outstanding soldiers. Many others entered the priesthood, joining hundreds of other sons, who fled Ireland, and entered one of the twenty-some new seminaries the Church had established, to provide training for Irish clergy, on the continent.

Most of these newly ordained apostles returned to Ireland, where they were hunted and persecuted. The faith, in Ireland, was perpetuated by these fugitive priests, who risked death by performing the mass. Many were martyred, but they kept the faith alive at the mass rocks and in the hedge schools. Ministers of the King's Church of Ireland, on the other hand, had no such zeal. Consequently, English discrimination had an opposite effect than the conquerors had hoped, and the majority of the population became deeply set in Catholicism. To most Irish, the Catholic religion, and Irish national identity, became one and the same cause. **(5)**

Plantation, Plantation, Plantation:

The slow process of anglicizing Ulster was replaced with the plantation system. Confiscation of Irish land in the north went on wholesale. O'Neill and O'Donnell lands were forfeited to the king to become the counties of Armaugh, Cavan, Donegal, Fermanaugh and Tyrone, with a special arrangement for Coleraine, which was given to the trade Guilds of the City of London, as County Londonderry. Initially, some 500, 000 acres of land were taken, and the plan soon encompassed all of Ulster. Twenty-three new towns were planned, each with a central "Diamond, " or town square. By the year 1622, thirteen-thousand new people had been moved in. It was so successful that it spread to other parts of Ireland, where even loyalist earls and land owners were displaced. By the end of the century, this number would rise to one hundred-seventy thousand English and Scottish Protestant settlers.

However, the plantation program was not a complete success. It seems that, without the native Irish Catholics, there were not enough settlers to provide a cheap source of labor, particularly farmers. This resulted in the failure of a number of plantations. Not surprisingly, Irish farmers gradually crept back into the system, to become tenants on the land that was stolen from them.

The Silent Threat:

Even though the native Irish were needed, the Protestant land owners came to regard them as a silent threat. They felt that their smiling, hard working, tenants, might harbor some resentment for the theft of their land. Especially as they were required to pay double the rent that a Protestant tenant paid. The native Irish were considered, by their landlords, to be disloyal and inferior. Consequently, by law, they were allowed to occupy no more than one quarter of the land. One of the worst fears of Protestant settlers was living among a majority of Irish Catholics, who might bear them ill-will for past injustice.

Charles I and the Counter-Reformation:

In 1625 King James went to his divine reward, and his son, Charles I ascended to the throne. Charles, like his father, also believed that the king could do no wrong. Charles dismissed Parliament and ruled without them for the next eleven years. His policies in Ireland were unchanged, and the persecuted Irish stubbornly clung to their faith. Most of the old-English Irish were, by now, Catholic. Unlike the Celtic-Irish, they were still loyal to the crown, and were privileged to own about one third of the land in Ireland. However, they were increasingly concerned that the English government no longer valued their loyalty, nor trusted them. Their concerns were not groundless. The government maintained an appearance of trust, but tended to look upon all Catholics as disloyal.

The "Graces:"

The on-going war with Spain made it necessary for Charles to raise money. As an incentive, he granted concessions to the old English, whose concerns were mostly for their property and titles. The King's approval, or "Graces" accorded special guarantees of their property titles. The King, of course, had no intention of honoring these promises. It was all about money. Huge quarterly installments were extracted from the old-English, in return for these "Graces". When the war ended, the Graces were disavowed.

Gaelic Culture Survived:

Throughout Ireland there was a façade of superficial conformity to English law. It was like a secret Ireland, known only to the native Irish, invisible to the stranger. In the remote, rural areas, Gaelic customs and Brehon law was alive and well. The seanachaihes told their stories and genealogies. The poets composed and recited their verse, and the minstrels sang of the glories of days long past, but not forgotten. Elsewhere, particularly in the towns and cities, English law prevailed.

The Earl of Stratford:

The concerns of the old English were greater than ever. There was much ill will toward the King for his repudiation of the Graces. Charles I dealt with this ill will in 1633, by appointing Charles Wentworth, the Earl of Stratford, as the new Lord Deputy in Ireland. The King had found a deputy whose principles and honor pretty much reflected those of his monarch. Wentworth made no bones about it. He treated the Anglo-Irish and the native Irish the same, and repudiated whatever Graces still existed.. The Anglo-Irish had no more security in their lands, or homes than did the Gaels. One quarter of the Catholic owned land in Connaught was confiscated, and many planters in Ulster were dispossessed for defaulting on their contracts. The City of London Guilds lost their charter in Londonderry, along with a 70,000 pound fine for not meeting all the terms. Wentworth was able to limit the 1634 Dublin Parliament to dealing only with matters which he presented to it. This rendered any opposition to his policies powerless.

War With Scotland:

In 1640 Scotland, not liking an absentee king, whose interests were more English than Scottish, rebelled against Charles. Wentworth fearing that the plantation Scots in Ulster might support their homeland, required the settlers to take the "Black Oath, " by which they had to swear allegiance, and non-resistance to King Charles. He assembled an Irish army of 9,000 men at Carrickfergus, and made plans to move against the rebels. Apparently, his intentions were so extreme that even the king objected to them, . **(6)**

Charles Concedes More Power:

Wars are expensive, so Charles called Parliament into session to raise money, and recruit troops. Parliament wasn't quite ready to give the King what he demanded. Parliament had some demands of its own. To get what he needed, the King had to make concessions. They insisted that in the future Parliament could not be dismissed without its consent. Charles was forced to give in to the demands of Parliament in return for their help. In spite of all the King's efforts and plans, Scotland won its freedom. Charles must have been wondering about the divinity of his crown and his divine right to wear it. He had lost Scotland, and was now faced with a Parliament whose powers were more on a par with his own.

An Old Solution:

The frosting on the cake was that Wentworth's high handed policies had, by now, alienated just about every influential group in the three "Kingdoms, " including the Puritans in the Parliament, and the Guilds of London. Charles was forced to recall Wentworth to England to answer a multitude of complaints. His army of 9,000 was disbanded, and the Earl of Stratford was accused by a host of enemies. He was convicted of treason, and subsequently deprived of his head. (7)

Troubles in Ireland:

In 1641, troubles were coming to a head in Ireland. The broken promises, the persecution of both Catholics and Presbyterians, a Puritan controlled Parliament, the failure of the plantations, and general resentment of Wentworth's government had brought about extreme unrest in all of Ireland, but especially in Ulster, where Catholics were in opposition to the Protestant ascendancy over the disenfranchisement of Irish Catholics, and the increasing seizure of land from the Anglo-Irish.

The Ulster Revolt:

An all Ireland revolt was planned, not against King Charles, but against the Irish Parliament and the government officers. In October, Dublin Castle was to be captured, along with the leading members of the government, concurrent with a general uprising to capture key strong points in Ulster. On the eve of the attack a drunken slip up led to the discovery of the plan, so the attack on Dublin Castle was never carried out. The rising in Ulster, however, proceeded on schedule, under the command of Sir Phelim O'Neill. (8)

The Portatown Massacre:

In the course of the rising, an incident occurred in Portatown in County Armaugh; a massacre of over 2,000, mostly Scot Presbyterians. This was all the more deplorable because the victims were non-combatants, mostly old men, women and children. This was not a matter of O'Neill's policy, but a lack of discipline, and personal vengeance on the part of the Catholic rebels. The Irish commanders sought out, and imposed capital punishment on their own soldiers, who were found to be guilty of the crime.

As deplorable as it was, the magnitude of the incident was greatly exaggerated by the Scots and the Puritans. One Scottish report stated that over 300,000 people had been massacred. This is an incredible loss to a population that never numbered more than 100,000. But the crime was blown all out of proportion by the propagandists of the time, fed by the myth that wholesale extermination of Protestants was the sole purpose of the rebellion.

It's an historical fact that many murders were committed, but not nearly as many as the rebels have been blamed for. The Planters worst fears of being surrounded and outnumbered by silent enemies were falsely confirmed. (9)

The Rising of 1641:

The rising was initially successful, and O'Neill marched south into Leinster, and Meath, where they lay siege to Drogheda. They were joined by the local Anglo-Irish, men who were loyal to the King, but fearful of the all Protestant Dublin Parliament. The combined forces called themselves the "Catholic Army."

The Church Supports the Rebellion:

In March, a synod was held at Kells and the Primate of Ireland declared the Ulster rebellion a just cause in defense of the faith. He declared that all who did not support the rebellion were excommunicated.

Control of the Army Contested:

King Charles perceived the turmoil as an opportunity to gain control of the army, but this new and powerful, Puritan controlled, Parliament was not to be easily managed. Parliament had debated sending reinforcements to Ireland to cope with Sir Phelim O'Neill and his Catholic army. However, at this time, the power struggle between Parliament and King Charles was becoming crucial and taking on greater importance than a mere uprising in Ulster. Parliament was more concerned with controlling the King than it was with controlling the rebellion in Ulster. It was a matter of King vs. Parliament. The rebel cause might well have succeeded, but ultimately, Parliament sent the needed reinforcements to oppose O'Neill. By April the rebel forces had been pushed back into Ulster. Parliament was going to make a fight of it.

Cavaliers vs. Roundheads

The following year, actual fighting broke out between Parliament and the loyalists in England. The Puritans, in control of Parliament, were called "Roundheads, " from their close cropped hair style. Those loyal to King Charles were called "Cavaliers, " from their shoulder length curls. The rebels in Ulster remained loyal to the king, for they had more to loose, if the Parliament were to prevail.

Owen Roe O'Neill:

1642 was also a time when many sons of Ireland, who had not become clergy, began returning to Ireland to lead the Irish forces. These were the exiles who had served in the foreign armies of Europe, and were trained in the art of war. Among them was another O'Neill, a nephew of the Earl of Tyrone, Colonel Owen Roe O'Neill, who then commanded the Irish army. O'Neill was the most inspiring military commander in the country, and all Ireland joined the revolt.**(10)**

Thomas Moore, an early nineteenth century poet, later composed an inspiring verse, immortalizing a traveling minstrel boy.

The Minstrel Boy

The Minstrel boy to the war has gone,
In the ranks of death you'll find him,
His father's sword he has girded on,
And his wild harp slung behind him.
Land of song said the warrior bard,
Tho' all the world betrays thee,
One sword at least thy rights shall guard,
One harp shall ever praise thee.

The minstrel fell, but the foeman's chains,
Could not bring this proud soul under,
The harp he loved never spoke again,
For he tore its cords asunder.
He said, "No chains shall sully thee,
Thou soul of love and liberty,
Thy song were made for the pure and free,
They shall never sound in slavery.

King Charles had hoped to use O'Neill's army against the Roundheads in England, but in June all of the Catholic Members of Parliament were expelled from the Dublin Parliament as rebels, leaving the Anglo-Irish with no voice in government.

Confederation of Catholic Ireland:

The rebels called a representative assembly in KilKenny in October, and formed a Confederation. This was, in effect, an

Irish government, separate from that in Dublin. The Anglo-Irish were willing to fight for the King, provided he agreed to certain conditions. They demanded that Charles repeal Poynings Law, restore confiscated lands, and give full recognition to Catholicism. The King made counter proposals which the Confederation rejected. The situation dragged on.

Everybody Has An Army:

Meanwhile, King Charles kept an army in Ireland, but concentrated his efforts against .the parliamentary army of Roundheads in England. Scotland maintained an army in Ireland, for the protection of their kinsmen planters in Ulster. The English Parliament built up its army in Ireland, but did little to prosecute the war against the Confederate Catholics. In 1646, O'Neill won a resounding victory over the Scot's parliamentary army, inflicting losses, of over 3,000, at the Battle of Benburb. **(11)**

In 1647 the Earl of Ormond, Commanding the King's army in Dublin, surrendered to the Roundheads. In England, things were also not going at all well for the Cavaliers. A brilliant Puritan leader, named Oliver Cromwell, was distinguishing himself in battle, at their expense. Cromwell, was an outstanding soldier, and would soon become the commander of the parliamentary army.

Oliver Cromwell and The Commonwealth:

In 1649, King Charles' forces were defeated by Oliver Cromwell, bringing an end to the civil war. The Roundhead Parliament revolted and declared England a Commonwealth. Oliver Cromwell, the hero, now controlled Parliament, and with title "Lord Protector, " became a virtual dictator.

The King is Dead:

Poor King Charles I, was tried for treason by the Commonwealth, found guilty and executed. His family was able to flee to France, under the protection of the French Court of Louis XIV.

Oliver Cromwell, Lord Protector:

Parliament saw Ireland as a major threat to the new Commonwealth, and Oliver Cromwell, as the Lord Protector must protect the Commonwealth from this Catholic threat. In August of 1649 Cromwell landed in Dublin with a Puritan army of 12,000 men. joining 8,000 more already there. No more Mr. "Nice Guy!" Cromwell meant business, and if that business meant killing Catholics, so much the better. He was there to subdue the entire island and to avenge the Ulster massacre of 1641 at Portatown. **(12)**

Lord Protect Us All:

It was the latter that he seemed to be most obsessed with. In September, his 20,000 man army crushed all resistance in its path, as the Roundhead army advanced on the Royalist stronghold at Drogheda. Sir Arthur Aston, an Anglo-Irish Catholic, in command of the Royalist garrison at the fortified town, felt that the town could withstand the attack. They were successful, at first, and inflicted heavy losses on the Roundhead troops. In the end, however, it was Cromwell's cannons that determined the outcome. The cannons breeched the wall, and 7,000 Roundheads poured into the city. They proceeded to kill everyone in sight. One large crowd was herded into a church, which was then set on fire. Women and children were put to the sword and the Royalist defenders were compelled to surrender.

On Cromwell's order, Aston and the entire surrendered garrison was executed on the spot. The same fate was inflicted upon the entire civilian population of over 3,500 people. Unlike the massacre of Portatown, this was not due to rage and lack of discipline. This was wholesale murder, in compliance with the direct orders of the " Lord Protector." **(13)**

Parliament Celebrates the Atrocity:

October 2nd was designated by the Puritan Parliament as a day of thanksgiving to "celebrate the slaughter at Drogheda, " as an "Act of justice…" The same policy was repeated two weeks later, following the surrender of the town of Wexford. On that occasion, over 2,000 were slaughtered, including 300 women who had gathered at the great Cross in the town square. All were put to the sword, in the name of Puritan justice. The town of New Ross surrendered to Cromwell without resistance. Cromwell made a half-hearted attempt at Waterford, but then passed it by for the easier objective of Cork, "defended" by English Protestants, who easily surrendered the town, for future rewards.**(14)**

Death of Owen Roe:

In November, the Commander of the Irish Army, Owen Roe O'Neill, was stricken and died of an illness in County Cavan.

Rumors were spread that he had been poisoned. Ireland had lost another of its heroic sons. His army was dissolved and distributed among various Irish units.

In January, after a brief rest to re-provision, Cromwell moved on. Next on his list were Fethard, Cashel, and Carrick. In March Kilkenny surrendered without a shot being fired. The Confederation of Catholics of Ireland was dissolved. Cromwell now controlled the Provinces of Munster, Limerick and most of Ulster. The cities of Clonmel, Waterford, Limerick and Galway still held out.

Not even the stone walls of Drogheda could save the population from Oliver Cromwell's wrath.

Cromwell Outfoxed At Clonmel:

Cromwell suffered his one setback on May 9th, when he attacked the city of Clonmel, defended by Hugh O'Neill, (nephew of the late Owen Roe O'Neill,) and his small force of 1, 500 men.

The Roundhead army was allowed to enter the city, unopposed. In the narrow city streets, O'Neill sprang a carefully planned ambush, killing five hundred of the invaders. Cromwell was forced to abandon the city, in a disorderly retreat, and the attack turned into a siege.

Eventually, as the defenders ran out of provisions, O'Neill and his entire army quietly slipped away in the dark of night. The mayor of the city, following O'Neill's instructions, gave them several hours head start, and then offered to surrender the city, with good terms. Cromwell bought the deception and accorded good terms of surrender, not realizing that the city was totally undefended.

Oliver Cromwell returned to England on May 26th, leaving his son-in-law, Ireton, in command. By July the Commonwealth armies controlled most of Ulster and the rest of Ireland, except the province of Connaught.

In October the Irish army in Limerick, under Hugh O'Neill, finally surrendered to Ireton. However, there were still small pockets of resistance in early 1652, as several Irish armies fought on. In May, all resistance finally ended with the surrender of Galway, in Connaught

Chapter Nine
The Treaty of Limerick
1652-1692

The Articles of Kilkenny, Irish Sold Into Slavery, Dublin Parliament Disolved, "To Hell, or Connaught, The Church as a Special Target, Another Form of Slavery, Two Different Cultures, The Death of Oliver Cromwell, The Monarchy Restored, Things Get a Little Better, The Death of Charles II, A Two-Sided Problem William In--James Out, James Seeks Help from Louis XIV, The Apprentice Boys, No Surrender, James Lands at Kinsale, The Siege of Londonderry, The Patriot Parliament, , The Siege is Lifted, Schomberg's Army Decimated, Battle of the Boyne, His Majesty Wins the Race, Williamites in Leinster and Munster, The Earl of Lucan, The Battle of Athlone, The Death of St.Ruth, The Second Siege of Limerick, The Treaty of Limerick, French Aid Too Late, The Wild Geese, Patrick Sarsfield- A True Irish Hero, A Nation Dishonors Itself,

They Made History:

James II, King of England (1685-1688) A Catholic, Controlled by Parliament. Deposed by, Son-in-law, Prince William.

Richard Talbot, Earl of Tyrconnell, first Catholic Lord Deputy of Ireland, under James II. Commander of the Irish Army.

William III (of Orange), King of England (1689-1702) Deposed James II. Victor at the Battle of the Boyne.

Patrick Sarsfield, French trained Irish general, Defender of Limerick, Man of honor, Commanded "The Irish Brigade, "

The Apprentice Boys, Thirteen teenagers who slammed shut the gates of Derry.

Marshall Schomberg, Williamite Dutch General at Battle of the Boyne

General St.Ruth, French General, Commanded Irish Army at Athlo.

Lord Sidney, Lord Deputy of Ireland for King William, 1697.

Queen Anne, Queen of England (1702- 1714) Very anti-Catholic.

The Articles of Kilkenny:

On May 12, 1652 hostilities officially ended with the signing of the Articles of Kilkenny. Thus ended the most inhumane and bitter struggle, against overwhelming odds, that Ireland ever suffered in its long, sad history. In the course of the Cromwellian war approximately one third of the Irish-Catholic population had been killed. One of the articles in the treaty provided that Irish soldiers would be permitted, if they chose, to enlist in the armies of European nations friendly to Britain. This was undoubtedly the best course open to them. About thirty thousand went into the service of Spain. Roughly nine thousand went to other countries, including Poland and France. **(1)**

Irish Sold Into Slavery:

Because the larger portion of Irish casualties in the war were young men, there were few young men left in Ireland. In a spirit of Puritan compassion, Cromwell then allowed the sale of thousands of Gaelic-Irish, young women, between the ages of twelve and forty-five, to be sold into slavery, at a handsome profit, and transported to the West Indies. A lesser number of young men were similarly sold. The numbers of Irish young people, sold in this fashion have been estimated to be between thirty-thousand to eighty thousand. By 1688, as a result of Puritan justice, the population of Ireland had been reduced from 3,000,000 to about 500,000 people. Those were mostly either young children or old men and women. **(2)**

Dublin Parliament Dissolved:

In 1653, Cromwell, now in complete control of parliament, abolished Irish Parliament, and asserted that Ireland was part of Britain. The Irish part of British Parliament was to have thirty members, out of a total of four hundred and sixty. There was not one Catholic in the bunch.

"To Hell, or Connaught:"

All Irish Catholic landowners, who were found guilty of participating in the rebellion were to forfeit their land. Those land owners, not involved in the rebellion were allowed to own land, at least some land, but not the same land. All were to be removed to land west of the Shannon River, in County Clare and Connaught. Native Irish, who were found east of the Shannon River, after May 1,1654, faced death, or transportation to slavery in the West Indies. The more level, fertile land, to the east, over 11,000,000 acres was confiscated and given to 1,000 adventurers, or investors, and 35,000 Cromwellian soldiers, three quarters of whom sold their shares to wealthy Protestant planters. For Irish Catholics it was, "To hell, or Connaught!" (3)

The Church as a Special Target:

Cromwell declared war on the Catholic Church in no uncertain terms. Altars were looted, monasteries and abbeys destroyed, bishops and priests were hunted, with a price on their heads. Catholics were forbidden to participate in the mass. A priest caught saying mass would be decapitated. Cromwell, a staunch Puritan, was convinced that the Catholic faith was the cause of all the evils in Ireland, and that he was doing the work of God.

Another Form of Slavery:

Those who attempted plantation had a major problem. So many young, native Irish had been sold into slavery, there were not enough farmers left to work the land. Consequently, many of the Gaelic Irish were allowed to drift back to work the land as tenants. The result was a two class society. The new planters, and other property owners comprised the upper ruling class. The lower class was the poor, tenant farmers who were very poor indeed. They were kept that way by the greed of the land-owning upper class. If a farmer were successful and productive, the landlord increased his rent. Consequently, tenant-farmers had little incentive to make improvements, to do more than merely subsist.

Two Different Cultures:

The new planters like the Vikings and the Normans before them would gradually morph into Irishmen themselves. Only in the six northern counties, with a strong Scot-Presbyterian influence, did the differences continue. There, where the planters were convinced that the Irish Catholics were evil, vengeful, and not to be trusted, did the cultural distinctions remain. They swore to defend their way of life to the end.

The Death of Oliver Cromwell:

In 1658 Oliver Cromwell went to his reward, wherever, and the title of Lord Protector was passed on to his son, Richard Cromwell. Richard ruled for about one year, before the British people grew tired of a military government. Several leaders in Parliament sent to France for Prince Charles, the son of the overthrown Charles I.

The Monarchy Restored:

Prince Charles returned to England and in 1660 the monarchy was restored, under his reign, as Charles II. The new king was compelled to recognized the power of Parliament, and that his authority to rule came from Parliament and not from the Deity. There would be no more of this divine right nonsense. The army was dissolved and a period of peace and prosperity followed. Charles was an extravagant and pleasure loving king. Many people in England did not approve of his life style, but still preferred it over the stern, joyless Puritan code. Charles was suspected by some of leaning toward the Catholic faith, for his lack of enthusiasm, and his slack enforcement of anti-Catholic measures passed by Parliament. Catholics were frustrated and Protestants were uneasy. **(4)**

Things Get a Little Better:

Some lands were restored to about 500 dispossessed former Catholic landowners, but with only a fraction of their previous holdings. Many were still dissatisfied. Charles' reign was also a period of economic expansion. In spite of English trade restrictions, Ireland prospered as trade for Irish butter, meat and wool, in exchange for English manufactured goods, was brisk. In twenty-five years Ireland's population had recovered to approximately 2, 000, 000.

The Death of Charles II:

Charles II died in 1685 and his younger brother, James succeeded to the throne. James II was Catholic, so Irish Catholics thought that things would go their way at last. James was in no position to buck Parliament on land settlement issues, and the Church of Ireland was well established. No big changes occurred. Richard Talbot, a Catholic and long time friend of James, was appointed as the Earl of Tyrconnell, and commander of the Irish Army. He was soon appointed to replace Lord Clarendon as Lord Lieutenant of Ireland. In this capacity he appointed Catholics to many key government offices. The Protestants now became even more uneasy.

A Two-Sided Problem:

There was another problem that both sides worried about. The King had a daughter, Mary, who of course became the heir presumptive to the throne. Mary was Protestant, and wife to Dutch

Prince William, of Orange. If James had a son, he would be Catholic, and become the new heir presumptive to the throne. The Protestants were afraid that James would have a son; the Catholics were afraid he would not. (5)

William In, James Out:

Finally, in 1688, James second wife delivered him a male heir who would be heir presumptive to the throne. The King's Protestant opponents in Parliament, realizing that Prince William's claim to succeed to the throne no longer existed, contacted Prince William of Orange, and invited him to come to England, ostensibly to confer with King James to join the league which had been formed against Louis XIV of France. Prince William accepted the invitation to visit, but he arrived with a considerably larger personal guard than called for by the occasion. It was large enough for him, with the additional aid of disloyal English forces, to seize the throne of England, forcing his father-in-law to flee for his life. James II fled back to France to seek help from his friend, King Louis XIV. James was still recognized by the Catholics in Ireland, as the lawful English king. (6)

James Seeks Help From Louis XIV:

The dethroned James II was no stranger to the court of Louis XIV of France. He and his brother, Charles had fled there with their father, when he was dethroned by Oliver Cromwell. Now it was James who sought support from the French King, after being deposed by Prince William of Orange. In-as-much as France was at war with England at this time, and France was already harassing English colonies in North America, it was only logical for Louis to seize the opportunity to harass England's colony in Ireland as well. Louis XIV was only too willing to give James financial and military support. (7)

Lord Deputy, Richard Talbot, the Earl of Tyrconnell, was mindful of a disloyal Protestant element in Ulster, particularly in Londonderry, and Enniskillen. Tyrconnell wished to secure Ulster for King James. The Guilds of Londonderry recognized James II as the rightful king, and the general population had agreed to allow the loyalist Irish army to enter the city, even though it was largely comprised of Catholic soldiers.

The Apprentice Boys:

Tyrconnell led the Jacobite army, consisting of Irish Catholics, and the Irish Loyalist troops, to Londonderry, arriving there on December 7, 1688. Then, suddenly, the situation changed dramatically. The defending garrison, consisting of thirteen teenage apprentice boys, made up the minds of the rest of the community. Acting impetuously, as teenagers sometimes do, they slammed the gates closed, shouting, "No surrender!" Tyrconnell's army was locked out. (8)

No Surrender:

The townspeople, were predominantly Protestant, and loyal to the crown because they feared Catholic domination. They also had been somewhat coerced by, the strongly loyalist, Guilds, whose interests were chiefly financial. However, with a largely Catholic army approaching, it didn't take very much to change the minds of the people. The exaggerated stories of the Portatown massacre, nearly a half century ago, was still in their memory. The predominantly Presbyterian population followed the lead of the apprentice boys, and began shouting "No surrender." The phrase quickly caught on, and remains, to this day, a slogan for the Protestant unionists.

James Lands At Kinsale:

James landed at Kinsale in March of 1689, supplied with French money, French arms, ammunition, and four hundred French officers and gunners. He was warmly welcomed by the Lord Deputy, and commander of the Irish army, Tyrconnell. James received great support from both the Irish Catholic army, and the Protestant loyalist army. He was also warmly acclaimed by the general population. Dublin took on a holiday atmosphere, in celebration. (9)

The Siege of Londonderry:

The first thing on James' agenda was to subdue the rebellion in Londonderry. James realized that to attack a walled city of 30,000, mainly loyalist Protestants would be poor politics. It would also destroy valuable English property, which would not be well received by the London Guilds. Besides, the loyalist army was outnumbered, and out gunned. The only option was to starve them out. The siege of Londonderry began in April, and lasted three and a half months. The townspeople faced starvation, and no household pet was safe from ingestion, but the siege went on. James left the matter to Tyrconnell and turned his attention to Parliament in Dublin.

The Patriot Parliament:

Parliament was convened, and was chiefly under the influence of the Old-English Irish. Thirty-five legislative acts were passed, chief among them was the Declaratory Act, which, in essence, stated that Ireland was no longer subject to the rule of English Parliament. The old Land Act of Settlement, which had bestowed Irish Catholic land on Cromwell's veterans, and adventurers was repealed, and the Cromwellians declared rebels. Catholics were no longer required to tithe the Anglican church, rather each group would tithe its own church respectively. Ireland's trade would no longer be controlled by English law, and Irish exports would not have to pass through English ports. James did insist, however, that Poynings Law remain in effect, in the interest of loyalty to the crown. Years later this parliament would be referred to as the "Patriot Parliament." Many wrongs would have been set right, if only James had won the war. **(10)**

The Siege Is Lifted:

Meanwhile, back in Londonderry, the siege was lifted when King William's fleet arrived, breeched the river boom, and relieved the town. This cleared the way for the King's's Dutch Marshal Schomberg to land at Belfast, with 20,000 troops. He captured Carrickfergus after a one week siege, allowing the garrison to leave with honors., and then went into winter camp at Dundalk. **(11)**

Schomberg's Army Decimated:

Schomberg's army was struck by tragedy in the form of a plague, which killed nearly 10,000 of his troops. Had James struck this devastated, and ravaged remnant of an army, the story would undoubtedly have had a different ending, but James failed to take advantage of his foes misfortune. In the spring, Schomberg was re-supplied and reinforced with 7,000 men sent over from England by King William. On June 14, 1690, William himself joined Schomberg at Carrickfergus, with another 19,000 men, bringing their combined forces to 36,000 well equipped, fresh troops. **(12)**

Battle of the Boyne:

On July 1, 1690, they encountered James and Tyrconnell, with their Irish forces of 20,000 less well equipped men, in the Boyne Valley. In a fierce skirmish near the hamlet of Slane, General Schomberg was killed attempting a river crossing. Generally speaking, this was not the hard fought battle it has been reported to have been. James was indecisive, and again failed to take advantages of vital tactical opportunities. The Irish fought bravely and well, but King James seemed indifferent, He seemed to have made up his mind that his cause was already lost, and he was more concerned with making preparation for his own safe withdrawal and departure. **(13)**

He had previously given orders that a ship in Kinsale, be made ready, and waiting, to carry him and his family to France. He, with his 200 man body-guard, were the first to withdraw from the battle, fleeing headlong to Dublin, leaving Tyrconnell to cover his retreat. At the end of the day both sides withdrew in relatively good order. Actually, the battle was more of a forfeit by James, rather than the glorious victory the "Orangemen" have, ever since, claimed it to be.

His Majesty Wins the Race:

Upon reaching Dublin James complained that the Irish had not fought well, and that Tyrconnell had failed to support him. When he mentioned this in front of Lady Tyrconnell, she, replied, with ready wit, "But, it was your Majesty who won the race!" **(14)**

The next morning, before departing, he again berated the Irish, who had risked everything for his cause, blaming them for his defeat. James fled again to France, never to see England, or Ireland again. He died in 1701.

Williamites in Leinster and Munster:

Prince William met little resistance on his way to capture Dublin. Ulster and Leinster were now in his hands, and Munster soon fell with the capture of Cork and Kinsale. Tyrconnell ordered that the Irish armies, each under their own commanders, retreat to Limerick and dig in. William advanced on Limerick, which was stoutly defended by Tyrconnell, and a French trained, Irish general named Patrick Sarsfield. Sarsfield was a brave, aggressive commander, and a man of high principle. William's assault was fierce, but no more so than the defense presented by the Irish. Sarsfield, by a brilliant maneuver, intercepted and destroyed William's artillery train, enroute from Waterford. William sent for more artillery, and began to prepare his emplacements. In spite of harassment by Sarsfield's defenders, the batteries were in place by August 24, 1690 and a murderous fire was poured upon Limerick. On the 27th a breech was made in the walls, and an assault by 10,000 troops was launched. The defense was fierce and culminated by the detonation of a mine that had been prepared. After three hours of bitter combat, the attackers were forced to withdraw. They had lost 2,000 men, and still failed to take the city. On August 31st the siege was raised, and King William returned to England on more pressing business, leaving the Dutch General de Ginkell in command.**(15)**

The Earl of Lucan:

The French forces, meanwhile, had returned to France through the port of Galway, accompanied by Tyrconnell, who went to consult with King James. Tyrconnell returned in January, 1691 with a small amount of money and some provisions. He also brought with him a patent from James, creating Sarsfield, Earl of Lucan.

The Battle at Athlone:

In May a French fleet arrived, bringing provision, and ammunition. It also brought a distinguished French officer, a General St. Ruth, who was to take command of the Jacobite Army. Hostilities were resumed on June 7th. Ballymore Castle in West Meath fell to the Williamites. General Ginkell then attempted to cross the Shannon River at Athlone, with 4,000 men. St. Ruth arrived, on the west side of the river, with 15,000 Irish defenders to oppose him. **(16)**

The Death of St. Ruth:

The English had the advantage of firepower, and the Jacobites received a tremendous barrage of cannon ball and bombs. In the course of the battle, General St. Ruth maneuvered brilliantly and the Irish fought with great valor and daring. Just when it seemed that victory was assured, St. Ruth literally lost his head, when it was removed by an English cannon ball. Total confusion followed the loss of command, and the Irish forces were totally routed. **(17)**

Sarsfield, who had been placed in the rear by a jealous St. Ruth, was remote from the battle, and unable to take command in time to make a difference. He could do little, except pull the remaining force together, and withdraw to Limerick, to help Tyrconnell establish defensive positions. In the disorder and confusion, Tyrconnell died of apoplexy, and the military command was left in the hands of Sarsfield.

The Second Siege of Limerick:

Limerick was once again under siege. A gallant defense was made by the Irish forces, but in the end the situation was hopeless. Sarsfield asked for terms and a truce was called on September 24th. An honorable surrender with favorable terms was agreed upon and Sarsfield surrendered the garrison. the Treaty of Limerick was signed on October 3, 1691.

The Treaty of Limerick:

contained fifty-two articles of surrender. They included:

1. The Irish were to lay down their arms,
2. Irish rights, including the free exercise of their religion were guaranteed,
3. Catholics could participate in government, including election to Parliament,
4. Freedom of trade,
5. Irish land and property would be protected,
6. A general amnesty, and
7. the 15,000 surrendering Irish officers and men were to have a free choice of their own futures.

Some 1,000 chose to enter the Ulster battalion and serve King William III. Another 2,000 were given passes to return home, as free men. The remaining 11,000 were transported to France, to serve in the "Irish Brigade" for King Louis XIV. They joined another 5,000 Irish troops already serving. They came to be called Ireland's "Wild Geese."

French Aid, Too Late:

Two days after the signing of the Treaty, a French fleet sailed up the Shannon, bearing 3,000 soldiers, 200 officers, and 10,000 new rifles. Sarsfield was urged to repudiate the treaty, and resume the conflict. But Patrick Sarsfield was a soldier, and a man of honor. He refused to break faith and dishonor himself and his country. Honorable terms had been given, and the treaty of Limerick would stand.(18)

The Wild Geese:

Due to the custom of primogeniture, only the first born son would inherit the family property and land. Irish sons, who were not first born, lacking property, and fortune, were forced to learn a trade, enter the clergy, become old, hanging on uncles, on the dole, or become soldiers. Consequently, Irish sons flocked to continental armies for generations. In the next forty years over 120,000 Gaelic Irish and old English Irish left Ireland to serve in various European armies. These "Wild Geese, " were renouned as fierce and capable soldiers. Their leaving, left Ireland without leadership and protection from their foreign rulers. Ireland's sons were spent fighting for every cause except Ireland's.

Patrick Sarsfield, a True Irish Hero:

Patrick Sarsfield, one of Ireland's true heros, returned to the service of Louis XIV and became a Field Marshal, commanding the "Wild Geese" brigade. Other Irish Brigades were formed, not only in France, but in all the major armies of Europe.

A Nation Dishonors Itself:

History is witness to the fact that although the Irish lost the war, the British nation lost its honor. The Treaty of Limerick, which was so honorably signed by Patrick Sarsfield, was almost totally ignored by Westminister. The one part that was honored, pertained to the men who had entered the service of King William, and King Louis.

It was the second clause of the treaty that protected Irish property rights. Parliament dealt with that problem quite deftly. They simply omitted it. The two thousand men who chose to return to their homes were to find that nothing had changed for the better.

King William was a Protestant, but he was no bigot. In 1692, he reinserted the omitted clause, in his own hand, before approving it. Parliament, however, was in no hurry to approve the Treaty. They dragged their feet until 1697 before the final ratification. They solved their dilemma by determining that the second clause only applied to the officers and men of the surrendering garrison.

King William, like his predecessor, had discovered that the King could no longer over-ride Parliament. It was the king who needed the approval of Parliament, not the other way around. The document was, in this way, relieved of its "honorable" terms. Parliament had reneged on Catholic rights and property protection, at the expense of English honor.

Chapter Ten
The Penal Laws
1691-1782

The Great Land Theft, Queen Anne, The Penal Laws, Land Ownership Denied, All Civil Rights Denied, Fugitive Priests, The Church of Ireland, Catholic Extirpation, The Real Purpose of the Penal laws, The Hedge Schools, Mass Rocks, Catholic Disqualification, The Tenant "Cottage, " Between a Rock and a Hard Place, Dublin Parliament Disabled, Dissent in Ulster, Clergy Denied, Ulster Rebels, The Catholic Farmers, Crisis and Famine, The "Gombeen" Men, The English Perception of the Irish, Why Eviction? Secret Societies, The Wild Geese, Trouble in the Other Colonies, Resurgence of Irish Nationalism, Volunteerism, Demand for Reforms, Those Revolting Americans, Henry Grattan, Almost Independent .

They Made History:

Lord Sidney: Lord Lieutenant of Ireland in 1697
Queen Anne: Grand-daughter of Charles I. Very Anti-Catholic. "Pope-a-phobic" Queen.
King George III: King 1760-1820. Went slightly mad.
Lord Cornwallis : Surrendered at Yorktown, Became Lord Lieutenant of Ireland.
Henry Grattan: Ascendancy, Member of Parliament, A nationalist advocate.

The Great Land Theft:

Following the second Treaty of Limerick in 1691, Ireland enjoyed a period of relative peace, that was to last for most of the eighteenth century. The land owning Protestants prospered, but it was not a good time to be an Irish-Catholic farmer. The country may have been at peace, but a period of suppression, and persecution would soon follow.

Apparently the British government felt well compensated for the loss of its honor for reneging on the Treaty. In 1697 Lord Sidney, then Lord Lieutenant of Ireland, evicted 4,000 Catholic land owners and seized 1,700,000 acres of Irish land. This was directed primarily at the land owning Anglo-Irish Catholics, in-as-much as most of the poor Gaelic-Irish farmers had long since been deprived of land ownership. William, however, used the influence of the Crown to restore approximately one quarter of the confiscated land to its rightful Anglo-Catholic owners. He then gained the ire of Parliament, by making large grants to some of his Dutch supporters, including the Duchess of Orkney, his former mistress.

In the end, approximately 1,000,000 acres went on the open market. Under the Protestant controlled Parliament, Catholics had been strictly prohibited from purchasing, or leasing any more than two acres. Parliament was determined to keep the size of Catholic estates to the minimum. The Anglo-Irish Protestants had also become very aware that they were an isolated religious minority, living among, what could become, a hostile Catholic majority. Consequently, they had to rely on the military might of "Mother England, " for their protection and prosperity.

Queen Anne:

William III died in March 1702, and was succeeded by his sister-in-law, Anne, who was a grand-daughter of Charles I. It was Ireland's great misfortune, that in addition to an all Protestant Parliament, they now had a protestant Queen with a serious case of Pope-a-phobia.

The Penal Laws:

In 1704, just seven years after the gigantic land theft, the Tory Parliament, with the blessings of the Queen had the shear audacity to enact a series of unprecedented legislative atrocities. These laws were enacted by Westminister over a period of several years. They were designed, primarily, to keep the potentially hostile Catholic population in a state of subjugation. They were referred to as the "popery code, " but were more commonly known as the "Penal Laws." In retrospect, one must wonder what kind of men these were, and what kind of monarch was Queen Anne. By what perverse logic were they able to rationalize this to be even a remote resemblance to morality?

The practice of primogeniture, in Catholic Ireland, whereby the oldest son would inherit the entire family estate, was abolished under the Penal Acts. This would assure that the land would be further subdivided among all the male heirs. This was just another method of assuring the fragmentation of Irish-Catholic estates. This was not aimed at the small farmer, who owned his own land. There were not enough of them to worry about. But the law would have the effect of reducing the size of larger holdings, until there were no parcels that were more than a small garden.

Land Ownership Denied:

It wasn't long before Parliament made the issue of primogeniture a moot point, as they enacted another law making it illegal for a Catholic to buy, sell, lease, or even own land in the first place. This was the one measure that most assured Catholic subjugation. The Irish-Catholic farmer was forced to become a tenant, on land that he had previously owned. This, more than anything else, worked the greatest hardship on the Irish farmer.

All Civil Rights Denied:

Catholics were also denied the right to vote, and to hold a public office. They were excluded from all professions and scientific field work. Catholics were also forbidden to live in any corporate town or city, or within five miles of one. They were forbidden to own a horse worth more than five pounds, and if offered five pounds for a horse, they were compelled to sell. (1)

Fugitive Priests:

The vocation of the priesthood was denied them, because bishops and priests had been banned. Furthermore, any priest caught entering the country was to be hanged. The law was even tougher on Bishops. They could be disemboweled, drawn and quartered, or both. Catholic clergymen were hunted like animals by the government, and sheltered, fed and hidden by the faithful, at the risk of their own lives.

The Church of Ireland:

The Church of Ireland (Anglican) was the official state religion. The non-conformist Presbyterians, and Catholics, were forced to tithe to the state church, or be fined. The government even tried to deny Catholics their very faith. Catholics were required to attend Protestant worship, and forbidden to attend mass, or any form of Catholic worship, which of course, couldn't be done, legally anyway, as there were no priests, or bishops, permitted in the country. Without clergy, it would also have made it impossible for a Catholic to marry another Catholic.

Then there was still another law forbidding them to marry a Protestant. In addition, there were many other new laws, that were strictly anti-Catholic. Catholic schools were forbidden, and it was illegal to educate a Catholic. If a child was sent out of the country to school, that child could not inherit any property, either in Ireland, or England. The logic of that restriction escapes me, as the offspring wouldn't have been allowed to own property, even if they could have inherited it.

Catholic Extirpation:

One is left to wonder, exactly how, in Ireland, a Catholic was supposed to exist, or what kind of work he was permitted to do. Those tenants who had not yet been evicted it seems, were the only ones legally permitted. There were a few who converted to the Church of Ireland in order to retain their property, and other rights, but they were the rare exceptions, mostly barristers. Those who remained true to their faith could not own property, or practice any profession. They could hardly even be a tradesman, as they were not permitted to live in, or near a town. They couldn't even be a successful highwayman, as they were also forbidden to carry, or own a weapon of any kind.

The Real Purpose of the Penal Laws:

It appears that the only real purposes of the Penal Laws had to be the complete collapse of Catholicism in Ireland. The Irish were legally denied the practice of their faith. They were denied their civil, and economic liberty, and even their dignity. They were condemned to ignorance and denied access to cities and towns. Their language and culture were threatened with extinction. What did English Parliament intend for the Irish Catholics, but their ultimate, and total extirpation?

For that purpose, however, the government didn't even come close. Dr. Arthur Colahan made reference to the suppression of Irish culture in his sentimental ballad *Galway Bay,* which became very popular among the Irish people, and is still sung in the pubs to this day.

Galway Bay

If you ever go across the sea to Ireland,
Then maybe at the closing of your day,
You will sit and watch the moon rise over Claddagh,
And see the sun go down on Galway Bay.

Just to hear again the ripple of the trout stream,
The women in the meadow making hay,
And to sit beside the turf fire in the cabin,
And watch the barefoot gossans at their play.

For the breezes blowing o'ere the sea from Ireland,
Are perfumed by the heather as they blow,
And the women in the uplands diggin' praties,
Speak a language that the stranger does not know.

For the strangers came and tried to teach us their ways,
And they scorned us just for being what we are,
But they might as well go chasin' after moonbeams,
Or light a penny candle from a star.

The Hedge Schools:

Because of the Penal laws forbidding the education of Irish children, these so called "hedge schools" thrived in Ireland through most of the 1700's, until the repeal of the Penal Laws in 1782. The priests, the seanachaihes, the bards, the poets and minstrels, at the risk of their lives, carried on an undercover educational system, using remote locations in the woods and behind the hedges. It may be stretching it a bit, to refer to it as a "system, " but standards were high, and Irish literature and culture survived. The children, the future bards and poets, learned not only literature, poetry, and history, but they were also well versed in such subjects as mathematics and astronomy. The Irish-Catholics were subjugated, but never conquered. Their history, and the language were preserved. **(2)**

Mass Rocks:

In much the same way, fugitive priests kept the faith alive by holding mass in the pastures, behind the hedges, and in the mountains. This was much the same way it was done when Christianity first came to pagan Ireland. Today, there are still large, flat topped boulders, that served as altars, in remote sites. They are reverently referred to as "mass rocks."

Catholic Disqualification:

Many aspects of the Penal laws were absolutely unenforceable. As we have seen, education still thrived behind the hedges. Mass was still performed in secret places. The Irish language was still spoken, and the Gaelic culture survived. The only laws that were effectively enforced, besides the bar to land ownership, were those which barred Irish-Catholics from sitting in Parliament, holding government office, practicing the legal profession, or from holding commissioned rank in the army or the navy. This was achieved automatically, simply by requiring, of these offices, an oath which denied the basic tenets of the Catholic faith. There were only a few Irish who took the oath. Those who did so were mostly lawyers, and a few property owners who did so in order to retain their land.**(3)**

Still, in the absence of war, the Irish-Catholic population increased greatly. This was due in large part to the doctrine of the Church regarding birth control. The ultimate effect, however, was to lower their standard of living still further. This was due to the greater number of people to be supported, from a limited agricultural resource, and because primogeniture was forbidden, the sub-dividing of the tenancies, among all of the male heirs, made the farm plots smaller and smaller with each generation.

The Tenant "Cottage:"

The tenant farmer's cottage was, generally, nothing more than a crude shelter, made of dried-mud walls, and a roof of thatch. When it rained, and in Ireland that is often, the roof probably leaked, and the walls might return to the wet-mud state. The shelter was heated by a single fire, which also served as a place where the wife could boil potatoes. There was no chimney, just a hole in the roof, or in the wall, to let the smoke out. (4) There was a small plot of land, usually less than five acres, but they could scratch out a subsistence from it. Their diet was, for the most part, potatoes and milk. This was a rather mundane diet, but the potato proved to be the perfect nourishment, and the Irish survived in reasonably good health.

Between a Rock and a Hard-place:

The rent that the tenant farmer paid to the landowner was generally two-thirds of the value of the crop he produced. If the farmer had a good year, and produced a larger crop than usual, the landlord would automatically assume that the farmer had previously been less productive than he should have been. Therefore, his rent would be raised commensurate to his current level of production. Any Protestant aware of a tenant willfully withholding more than one third of the value of the crop, could by merely swearing to the fact, take possession of that tenancy. The tenant, would of course, be evicted. If a tenant were industrious, and made repairs on his house, or increased the size of an out building, his rent would likewise be raised, as the property was then more valuable. There was no way for him to get ahead, or improve his condition.(5)

Dublin Parliament Disabled:

In 1720 British Parliament showed it distrusted even the Protestant controlled Irish Parliament, by way of declaring their own exclusive right to legislate for Ireland. This reduced the Ascendancy Parliament in Dublin to the status of a colony of Great Britain, and a rubber stamp. They could only discuss, and legislate on matters approved by Westminister, and were in the best interests of the Crown. Specifically, this assured that Ireland would never compete with England in the field of commerce. The Irish woolen manufacturers were virtually out of business. Even the executive of Ireland, the Lord Lieutenant, was appointed and controlled by Westminster. (6)

Dissent in Ulster:

The Catholics were not the only dissenters from the Anglican Church of Ireland. There was considerable discrimination against the Scotch-Presbyterians in Ulster. They too, were treated as second class citizens by the Penal Laws. Like the Irish-Catholics, they were not eligible to sit in Parliament, and yet, both were required to tithe to the Church of Ireland. Unlike the Irish-Catholics, the Presbyterians were permitted to own property, and their right to own and carry arms was not restricted.

Clergy Denied:

The Presbyterian clergy, though permitted to exist, were not recognized as legally ordained. That, of course meant that couples married by Presbyterian clergymen were not legally married and their children would be considered illegitimate. In effect, in those days, such a child would have virtually no legal rights at all. The situation was the same for Irish-Catholics in Ulster, but this was of little concern, for under the Penal Laws, Catholics had no legal rights in the first place. They didn't even have the status of second class citizens. (7)

Ulster Rebels:

In 1717 the Scotch-Irish, in Ulster, rebelled. They rebelled by emigration. Many of them had achieved considerable success and wealth, and they resented Anglican discrimination. This type of discrimination was not an issue in the American colonies, so the emigration began. What started as a trickle, soon became a flood, with up to 4,000 people leaving Ireland each year, and taking their assets with them. By the 1775's as many as 200,000 Scotch-Irish dissenters had emigrated to the New World.(8) They arrived in time to help build a new nation; one that would become separate from "Mother England."

The Catholic Farmers:

Irish-Catholic farmers did not have the options available to them as did their Presbyterian neighbors. Emigration, at this point was not a choice. They were unable to pay the passage. They had no property rights, and were unable to acquire wealth. They had to rent the land from the propertied Presbyterians, or Anglicans, that may, at one time, have been their own. As tenants, their lives were considerably different than that of their neighbors.

Crisis and Famine:

From 1727 to 1730 there was a major crop failure and economic crisis in the southern counties in Munster. The tenant farmers, who depended solely upon the crop for subsistence suffered severe hardship. Many died of starvation, and many other families were evicted. In 1740 -41 the crops were poor. This time the famine that followed affected the entire country, and the suffering was much more severe and widespread. Again, it was the tenant farmers who suffered most. Many more people died of starvation, or disease. **(9)** Those who were unable to pay the rent were forcibly evicted; a terrible, and heartless process. If the farmer resisted he would be beaten, shot, or hanged, or all three There was no mercy.

The "Gombeen" Men:

There was just no way for the tenant to better himself, and no motivation for him to try to make improvements. If he were ultimately unable to meet his financial obligations, he might resort to borrowing the rent money from the only credit source he had; the "gombeen men." They were actually a bunch of thugs, who readily loaned money, but at impossibly high interest rates. Today, we call them "loan sharks." In most countries today, loan sharking is against the law. In eighteenth century Ireland the loan sharks were in partnership with the landlords, and the law supported the landlords.

In the end, if the tenant could not keep up, he and his family were evicted. The victims were, at best, allowed to remove their few personal belongings, before the invaders set fire to the thatched roof, and smashed what could be smashed. Nothing usable remained. The family was left without shelter, food, or any means of livelihood. They had little more than the cloths upon their backs. There was seldom help from neighbors for most of them were nearly as bad off as the evictees.

The English Perception of the Irish:

The English government's perception of the situation does them little credit. They perceived the Irish as an inferior race. If a tenant farmer could not keep up, it was seen as his own fault. They were considered ignorant, lazy and shiftless. They were viewed as drunkards, and superstitious papists, and were not considered to be worth worrying about.

Why Eviction?

One might wonder what purpose eviction served. The answer was simply plain economics. Ireland's main value, as an English colony, was to produce agricultural crops for export to Britain, just as it was in the American colonies. The tenant farmers, on their small farms, were chiefly engaged in mere subsistence farming. There was little, if any, cash crop. The small rent the farmer was able to pay was not nearly as valuable to the landlord as the land would be for raising cattle and horses, or a cash crop such as wheat, or flax for the linen mills.

Secret Societies:

The government's cruel and repressive policies toward the Catholic farmers caused a festering resentment. The evictions by the landlords and their "gombeens, " caused an underlying hatred to evolve, and grow over the years. Eventually, beginning around 1747, the subjugated, having no legal recourse, turned to illegal methods. Secret societies were formed to right the wrongs. These groups began a campaign of hit and run tactics against those they identified as their oppressors; the landlords and their agents, the tithe collectors, and the sheriffs. One group was called "Whiteboys" because they blackened their faces and wore white smocks over their cloths. Houses were burned, livestock killed, or maimed. Landlords were beaten, or sometimes even killed. The terrorism spread to other parts of the country, with names such as "Hearts of Steel, " or Hearts of Oak." **(10)**

In Ulster, a Protestant society called, "The Peep o'Day Boys, " fearing growing Catholic influence, began beating up Catholics, and attacking property owners. The Catholics retaliated by forming a counter-society called the "Defenders." All of these societies had varying degrees of success and failure, but the underlying problems persisted.

The "Wild Geese:"

By mid-century the English government was beginning to have second thoughts regarding the generous terms accorded Patrick Sarsfield, and the rest of the "Wild Geese, " in the Treaty of Limerick. Since that time their numbers had increased dramatically, with nearly 100,000 Irish warriors at that time, in the service of European armies. The Irish exiles had gained a reputation as skilled and ferocious fighters, and a very large number of Irish soldiers were in the service of the French King, Louis XIV. **(11)**

At this time England and France were at war with one another, off and on, for a period, later to be referred to, as the "Hundred Years War. King George II had cause to regret the loss of their services, when the military skill and daring of the "Wild Geese, " caused him to loose the Battle of Fontenoy to the French in 1745. The English feared that if these "Wild Geese" were used to spearhead an invasion of Ireland, the Catholic population would join them in rebellion. The Penal Laws were enforced to keep this majority group in subjugation.

Trouble in the Other Colonies:

By 1775 Great Britain had other problems, with some of its colonies across the Atlantic. In April, riots in the port of Boston had resulted in armed conflict in the surrounding countryside. By July 4th of the following year, the thirteen colonies, in North America, had united, and declared their independence, and sovereignty from "Mother England." King George III was fit to be tied. Ireland, had suddenly become one of his lesser worries. **(12)**

Resurgence of Irish Nationalism:

The American Revolution had a singular affect on Irish political thought. There were some striking similarities. The American colonies each had their own separate legislatures, just as Ireland had. The British Parliament had declared its right to legislate for the American colonies, just as it had for Ireland's Protestant Parliament. Irishmen, Catholics, Presbyterians, and Anglicans, were all similarly disposed, to identify, and sympathize with the American cause. **(13)** At this point, however, there was an important difference. In America, religion played no part in the political nature of the assemblies, as it did in Ireland. Consequently, the Protestant ruling class, had their own concerns regarding the potential threat represented by the subjugated Catholic majority. The Ascendancy, therefore, felt compelled to support British efforts in America. British troops in Ireland, paid for by the Dublin legislature, were sent overseas to fight against the Americans.

Volunteerism:

This left Ireland deprived of the "protection" of British troops, and wide open to assault by England's traditional rivals, France and Spain. In-as-much as these were both Catholic countries, Irish Protestants felt they had to mobilized to protect Ireland, and their own special interests. It became quite fashionable to volunteer. It seemed everyone was joining one volunteer corps, or another. The men wore smartly tailored uniforms. They drilled and had fine parades, and reviews. Tradesmen and merchants became corporals and sergeants, while landlords and squires became captains and colonels. Everyone was having a grand time. **(14)**

Demand for Reforms:

Irish merchants and industrialists saw the situation as an opportunity to press Westminister for reforms. The gentlemen of the Ascendancy were still disgruntled over the trade restrictions imposed by "Mother England, " under King William. The various Irish volunteer corps became political sounding boards. In 1778 Irish volunteers paraded in Dublin, dragging a canon bearing a placard demanding free trade. In 1779 most of these duties and restrictions were removed by the government. Westminister also came to the realization that with the absence of British military power, the Penal Laws were all but impossible to enforce.

Those Revolting Americans:

In 1781 Lord Cornwallis was forced to surrender his Majesty's forces in America, to General George Washington, at Yorktown, Virginia. The loss of the American colonies pretty well put the "frosting on the cake" for British colonialism. The fear of serious trouble in Ireland became very real to Westminister, and the Whigs prevailed. Prime Minister Lord North's government was voted out. **(15)**

Henry Grattan:

In 1782, Irish Parliament was influenced by the persuasive powers of Henry Grattan, an ascendancy barrister, and member of the Dublin Parliament, who presented strong nationalistic opinions. He was able to prevail upon Westminister to repeal Poynings Law, and to renounce its right to legislate for Ireland. Gratten also campaigned for religious toleration for Catholics and Presbyterian dissenters. The unenforceable Penal Laws were partially repealed. Ultimately, Catholics were permitted to buy land. Presbyterians were given the right to run for political office, a right that was still denied Irish Catholics.

Almost Independent:

Grattan's objective was to achieve Ireland's sovereignty, and independence. Coming from the Ascendancy, he was, of course, loyal to the king. He envisioned two independent countries, sharing the same King. In a sense, he did achieve that purpose, with two small exceptions. One was that the King retained the power to veto Irish legislation. The other was that British Parliament still appointed the Lord Lieutenant of Ireland, who, therefore, was not, accountable to the Irish Parliament. The Lord Lieutenant controlled the executive functions, meaning he also controlled all the patronage. Members of Parliament, and the ascendancy owed their titles and positions to the good offices of the Lord Lieutenant, ergo, England still retained a tremendous control over Ireland's affairs. **(16)**

Chapter Eleven
The United Irishmen
1782-1798

The New Nation, Theobald Wolfe Tone, The French Revolution, Tone vs. Grattan, Society of United Irishmen, Some Are More Equal Than Others The Catholic Committee, Westminster's Plan to Split the Committee, France Declares War, The Convention and Insurrection Acts, United Irish Meet Covertly, Rev. William Jackson, Spy, More Militia, Tone Travels to France, "Battle of the Diamond, " The Orange Society Established in Ulster, Orange Terrorism, The French at Bantry Bay, More Orange Terror, Let's Make It Legal, United Irishmen Gear Up, Military Law Proclaimed in Ulster, Sir Ralph Abercrombie, The Informers, Leinster Directory Arrested, Risings in Dublin, and Naas, Savage Revenge at Prosperous, Honor Dishonored, Orangemen Warfare on Civilians, Boulevouge, Die With a Pike in Your Hand More Revenge, The Death of Father Michael Murphy, Vinegar Hill, The Death of Father John Murphy, Orange Justice, Reprisal, Here Come the French... Again, The Capture of Tone, This is Not the End.

They Made History:

Theobald Wolfe Tone: Organizer and moving force of the United Irishmen.
Henry Grattan: (1746-1820) Of the Ascendancy, Advocate of dominion status for Ireland.
A persuasive leader in Dublin Parliament.
Napper Tandy: Colorful speaker, Political Organizer, Secretary of United Irishmen.
George III: King of England (1760 to 1820)
Rev. William Jackson: Exiled Irish clergyman who became a French Spy.
General Hoche: French General who did not find Bantry Bay.
Sir Ralph Abercrombie: Commander of British forces in Ireland who resigned in disgust.
Lord Edward Fitzgerald: Commander in Chief of United Irishmen.
General Girard Lake: Ruthless torturer. General who replaced General Abercrombie.
Thomas Reynolds: United Irishman and treacherous traitor and informer.
Father John Murphy: The reluctant leader of the Wexford Rising .
General Hubert: French General. Victor at Castlebar, but too little, too late.
Lord Cornwallis: Appointed Viceroy and military commander in Ireland in June 1798.

The New Nation:

In 1782, the newly "almost" independent nation of Ireland showed signs of optimism, sovereignty and growth. Dublin, the capital, boasted several new buildings, including a custom house, a post office, the Four Courts, and the Bank of Ireland. Irish pride and nationalism was at an unsurpassed level. Poynings Law was gone, and the Penal Laws had been modified.

Theobald Wolfe Tone:

The inequity of the Irish political system, and the refusal of the ascendancy to allow Irish Catholics full participation in politics, caught the attention of another ascendancy barrister, Theobald Wolfe Tone. He was educated at Trinity College, and inspired by the American Revolution. He had taken an interest in what was going on in his country. Like Henry Grattan, he believed in religious tolerance, but did not share Grattan's view on the joint monarchy Ireland was compelled to share with Great Britain. He recognized independence as an absolute quality; that either you have, or you have not. He concluded that Ireland had not.(1)

The French Revolution:

The French Revolution began on July 14, 1789. The revolutionary battle cry, "Liberty, Equality, Fraternity, " caught the attention of the Irish people. They had not known liberty since the Norman conquest, and any thought of Protestant and Catholic equality vanished with the Tudor dynasty, as did the thought of brotherhood between the two groups. The concepts of liberty, equality and fraternity stirred the Irish imagination.

Tone vs. Grattan:

In 1790 Britain was on the brink of war with Spain over territorial disputes in western North America. In the Dublin Parliament, Wolfe Tone took strong exception to Gratten's assertion that the common interest of Britain and Ireland were inseparable. He then published several pamphlets refuting Grattan's point of view. He even favored closer ties with Spain. In 1791 he published a widely read pamphlet, titled, *An Argument on Behalf of Catholics in Ireland,* in which he espoused Catholic emancipation. In it he stated that Dissenters and Catholics had, *"but one common enemy:"* and ... *"it is necessary to forget all former feuds.... and to form for the future, but one people."* (2)

The Society of United Irishmen:

This caught the attention of Belfast liberals, who were primarily composed of Presbyterian dissenters. He was invited to meet with them in Belfast. These men listened attentively to what Tone had to say. One man, Samuel Neilson, a wealthy woolen merchant, had formulated the idea of a political party called the *United Irishmen.* This fit perfectly with Tone's philosophy. The group engaged Tone's services to draft a constitution for such a society. His draft was accepted, and the meeting of the *Belfast Society of United Irishmen,* occurred on October 18, 1791. Tone's next move was to contact Napper Tandy, an experienced and capable Dublin politician, and political organizer. With Tandy's able assistance, Tone was able to found the *Dublin Society of United Irishmen* in November of that same year. (3)

At first the United Irishmen attempted to secure the needed reforms merely by persuasion through their many published papers, and the pressure of public opinion. Volunteer corps also passed resolutions urging reforms, but to no avail. Ulster radicals held a repetitive convention in Dungannon urging the doing away with the tithes, reduced government spending, lowering taxes, and educational reforms. Parliament was not moved.

"Some are more equal than others…" (Orwell)

There was very good reason why Parliament was so unmoved by public opinion. Parliament, itself, was the one institution in Ireland that was most in need of reform. All of its members were, by law, Protestant, most of these Anglican, while 75% of the entire population was Catholic. But that was not the whole of it. Of the 300 members of Parliament, only 64 were elected by voters in the counties. The remaining 236 seats were occupied by men representing what has come to be called "rotten boroughs." These boroughs were owned by individual peers and wealthy men. Many of these boroughs had up to six voters. Some only had one voter. Whom, then, did Parliament represent?

The Catholic Committee:

In 1760, a group of Catholic members of the upper, and middle classes, mostly deprived land owners, merchants and professional men, formed a *Catholic Committee,* humbly seeking redress from the crown for their financial losses resulting from unjust treatment by the Protestant Parliament. They were ineffective and considered harmless, gaining a few small royal favors, and a degree of support from Presbyterian dissenters. But they persisted over the years, because the committee was the only hope they had.

In 1792, Great Britain was now on the brink of war with France. The Catholic Committee requested the parishes to choose delegates from all over Ireland to attend a convention in Dublin. The convention petitioned the government, asking for repeal of the remaining Penal Laws.

They even chose a delegation to go to London to appeal to the throne. They gained an audience with King George III, who did send a message to the Irish Parliament, asking them to repeal some of the Catholic constraints. The all-Protestant Parliament, ignored the King's request.

Westminster's Plan to Split the Committee:

The conservatives presented strong arguments against any concession, and any Catholic emancipation. They argued that such measures would "threaten the empire." Accordingly, a devious plan was developed to break the union between Catholics and Presbyterian dissenters in the Catholic Committee.

Facing a war with Napoleon, Parliament planned to court the Catholics to gain their good will. This was expected to play on the insecurity of the dissenters, causing them to feel threatened. Other measures would follow, to drive a wedge between the two parties. It was felt that failure to break this union could be an even greater threat to the empire. (4)

France Declares War:

On January 21, 1793, King Louis XVI, of France was deprived of his crown from the neck up. The new ruler, Napoleon Bonaparte then declared war on the Netherlands and their ally, Great Britain on February 1st. Westminster put pressure on the Dublin Parliament to accept the Catholic demands, resulting in the Catholic Relief Act on April 9, 1793. They reasoned that if they conceded the Catholics part of their demands it might cause the Presbyterian dissenters insecurity, and cause a split between the two groups. Thus the Catholics were given the right to vote, along with a few other minor concessions, but still denied the right to sit in the Irish Parliament, or to hold high office. (5)

The Convention and Insurrection Acts:

Conversely, on that same date, Dublin was pressured to disband the various volunteer corps and establish a militia of roughly 15,000. This was allegedly for home defense, strictly under government control. This was followed by the Convention Act on April 16th, which abolished the right of citizens to assemble, or hold public meetings. An Insurrection Act was also passed, giving the authorities a free hand to search homes for weapons, and to arrest and detain anyone suspected of favoring the union of all Irishmen. People were beaten and their property destroyed, and no-one was held accountable. (6)

United Irish Meet Covertly :

Under the terms of the Convention Act the United Irishmen were forbidden to assemble. Consequently they were forced to meet covertly, conspiring in secret militant societies, which were oath-bound to gain freedom from Britain and fight for reforms in the Dublin Parliament. Through a system of elected representatives, provincial committees were formed, leading ultimately to a national committee.

Rev. William Jackson, Spy :

In early 1794, William Jackson, an English clergyman who had been exiled to France for supporting King James, had become a French agent. He was sent to Ireland on a secret mission by the French Directory. While passing through London he was betrayed to the British authorities by an old friend. He was not arrested, but was watched carefully to see whom he would contact.

Jackson sought out the United Irishmen in Dublin. Through a barrister, Leonard McNally, he met with Tone, and several of the leaders of the Dublin group. McNally was affiliated with the United Irishmen, but he was in reality a spy for Dublin Castle. Tone and the others were implicated when Jackson was arrested before he could leave Ireland. He had on his person some papers indicating that a French invasion of Ireland would receive support from the nationalist element. Jackson was brought before the court to be tried for treason on April 30, 1795, but before he was convicted he took poison and died in the courtroom. So much for French Espionage! **(7)**

More Militia:

Following the Jackson incident, Britain was well aware of the threat of a possible invasion by the French, using Ireland as a platform. Unable to spare troops to control the Irish situation, Westminster put the pressure on Dublin to increase the strength of the militia to nearly 22, 000 men.

Tone Travels to France:

Tone was implicated and suspected of treason, but there was insufficient evidence for a conviction. His position was precarious, but he was permitted to emigrate to America. Tone, subsequently, traveled from America to France in early 1796, where he was warmly received as a representative of the Irish people. He immediately began pressing the French Directory, to make war on Britain by invading through Ireland. As it turned out, the French had actually been considering that very thing for the previous three years. **(8)**

"Battle of the Diamond":

The secret societies in Ulster had been battling for years, since the late 1740s. The Protestant "Peep o' Day Boys, " now called the "Protestant Boys" continued their holy war against any and all Irish Catholics and their principle antagonists, the "Catholic Defenders." The situation came to a boil at Loughgall in County Armagh on September 21, 1795. In what came to be called the "Battle of the Diamond, " the Protestant Boys killed thirty of the Catholic Defenders.

The Orange Society Established in Ulster:

That evening the Protestant Boys held a meeting at the home of a member, and established the first chapter of the Orange Society. In a solemn oath they each pledged to support the King, and to further swear to, "exterminate all of the Catholics of the Kingdom of Ireland. There was later denial about the "extermination" clause, but the subsequent action of the Orangemen spoke for itself. In just a few months there were over forty new chapters of Orangemen. **(9)**

Orange Terrorism:

The Orange Society went on a campaign of terror, posting Catholic homes with warnings to leave, or die, destroying home furnishings, burning homes and chapels. Over 7,000 Catholics, in five Ulster counties were driven out, homeless and destitute. The county magistrates took no action to protect the lives and property of the Catholic victims, nor was there any legal action taken. Not infrequently, the magistrates were actually the leaders of the terrorists.

The French at Bantry Bay:

In February 1796, Tone realized success in his mission to France. Forty-three French ships with 15,000 men at arms, sailed against England. They headed for Bantry Bay under the command of French General Hoche intending to rendezvous with the United Irishmen and overthrow the Irish government. Several of the fleet, including Hoche's ship, became separated from the others by fog, and then scattered by a winter storm. Hoche's second in command, General Grouchy, sailed about in Bantry Bay for a week, waiting for the other ships, which never arrived. The landing was not possible without the full fleet, so Grouchy returned to Brest, the invasion a failure. So much for French seamanship! **(11)**

More Orange Terror:

The Orangemen had many forms of torture they inflicted on Irish Catholics to intimidate them. I describe a few of them to explain the extreme hatred that they caused, and the terrible vengeance that was visited upon the Yeomanry and Militia during the subsequent uprising. One of the favorite methods of torture by the Orangemen was called, "Skull-capping." In this, a linen skullcap is filled with hot pitch, and jammed onto the victim's head. The pain was intense, and occasionally the hot pitch would flow down into the victim's eyes, rendering him blind, in addition to the pain. They then allowed the pitch time to cool. Thus assuring that there would be no way on earth to remove the cap, without removing a major part of the scalp. The blind, helpless victim would then be turned loose in the night. An alternative method, sometimes employed for their amusement, was to set fire to the cap, before turning the victim loose in the night. On other occasions they might moisten some gunpowder, paste it into the subject's hair in the shape of a cross, and light it off. The result would be a permanent scarring, or branding. A less imaginative method, sometimes inflicted, was to mutilate their captive by simply slicing off his nose, or his ears. **(12)**

Let's make It Legal:

On March 24, 1796 the Dublin Parliament passed the "Insurrection and Indemnity Acts, " which provided restrictive curfews for the Irish, and established the death penalty for unlawful oath taking. On November 9th, in order to further enhance the legality of the Orange actions, Parliament established a Corps of Yeomen to supplement the Militia. Members of the Orange Society flocked to the ranks of the new Yeomanry, eventually increasing to a strength of some 65,000, thus providing a semblance of legality to their outrages. This is called, "covering one's backside." **(13)**

United Irishmen Gear Up:

As a direct result of the actions of the Orange persecutions, and atrocities, Irish Catholics and Presbyterian dissidents joined the ranks of the United Irishmen in great numbers. By the end of 1796 that number would rise to roughly half a million members. The leadership of the United Irishmen now realized that the deck was stacked against them, and that persuasion and negotiation were fruitless. They had now begun to organize along military lines. A very popular, and experienced military leader, Lord Edward Fitzgerald, who joined the United Irishmen, was acclaimed as the commander-in-chief. It was estimated nearly 100,000 men were now drilling secretly, to support a French invasion, when the time came. **(14)**

Military Law Proclaimed in Ulster:

In 1797, military law was proclaimed in parts of Ulster and on March 13th Lord Lieutenant Camden sent General Gerald Lake, to search out Catholic and dissenter insurgents, and illegal weapons. He was instructed to use stern measures and "Not to be too squeamish, " about it. Irishmen were arrested without evidence or cause, on the flimsiest suspicion, and then tortured to make them "confess." Some were tortured until they lost consciousness, revived and tortured again, and again. The Militia and Yeomen burned homes, slaughtered old men, women, and children, and raped the younger women. No-one was safe. **(15)**

Sir Ralph Abercrombie:

Sir Ralph Abercrombie, commander of the British army in Ireland, resigned his command in protest to the atrocities of the Yeomanry and Militia, which he was powerless to control. General Lake, who was not offended by cruelty and torture, was appointed to replace Abercrombie. Under Lake's command, the illegal repressions and arrests were spread to the rest of Ireland.

The Informers:

Unfortunately, among the many who joined the ranks of United Irishmen, were those who had treachery in their hearts. They were Irishmen who valued the coin of the kingdom, higher than friendship and loyalty. They could live with, drink with, and laugh with their fellow countrymen, and then betray them to their doom. One informer even had himself arrested several times, just to direct suspicion away from himself.

The government was able to infiltrate them into the United Irishmen, from all classes. One such man, Thomas Reynolds, from Kildare, was a sworn United Irishman, a member of the Leinster Directory, and a friend of Lord Fitzgerald. Through him, Prime Minister Pitt knew what the United Irishmen were planning, almost before they knew it themselves. **(16)**

Leinster Directory Arrested:

On March 12, 1798, the leaders of the Leinster Directory of the United Irishmen were meeting at the home of one of their number in Dublin. The British new all of their names and their plans for an upcoming rising. All but three were arrested. Two members escaped to the continent, and Sir Edward Fitzgerald went into hiding. He refused to leave Ireland, feeling that as commander-in-chief, his duty lay there. The Directory was filled 0by new leaders, and Lord Edward continued to oversee the preparations for the rising from his hiding place in Dublin. On May 19th his location was discovered, and he was arrested. He was mortally wounded while resisting arrest, and died in prison fifteen days later. Without their leaders, the United Irishmen proceeded with the rising on May 23rd as planned. **(17)**

Risings in Dublin and Naas:

On May 23rd martial law was declared in Dublin, for the government was well aware of the time table. The rising was readily put down for the Militia and the Orange Yeomanry were forewarned and well prepared. The slaughter far exceeded the need. The Yeomen and the Dragoons outdid each other with unnecessary cruelty. An attack at Tara, County Meath, on the same day met with bitter defeat. On May 24th the insurgents attacked Naas, in County Kildare, but were easily subdued by the government troops. Combatants and bystanders were indiscriminately shot or hanged by the Militia. The government forces lost two officers, and thirty men killed.

Savage Revenge at Prosperous:

At Prosperous, Co. Wexford, the rebels trapped a company of Yeomen in their barracks building. The insurgents burned the building with most of the yeomen still inside. Those who leaped out of the windows were piked. None survived. In another engagement nearby, an entire troop of Dragoons was all but wiped out. This was revenge and payback, pure and simple.

Honor Dishonored:

Another group of insurgents under the command of a man named Perkins, was encamped on the Hill of Allan. General Douglas, of the Militia had them surrounded and offered them honorable surrender. Perkins accepted the offer, and the army of 2,000 surrendered, to lay down their arms. Major General Duff, to whom they delivered their arms, did not follow orders and honor Douglas's offer. After the insurgents were disarmed, he ordered his troops to fire into them. Then a Yeoman cavalry unit road them down with their swords. Many of the 2,000 were slaughtered in cold blood.**(18)**

Orangemen Warfare on Civilians:

On May 26th the North Cork Militia and Yeomanry paraded into Wexford.wearing their Orange Society sashes. They shot people without provocation, arrested men randomly and applied pitch caps and other forms of torture. For them it was a war with religious overtones. The population was frantic.

Boulavouge:

On Whit Sunday, May 27th, in the village of Boulavouge, Wexford County, a Catholic priest, Father John Murphy, had been trying to quell the rebellion and stop the atrocities being committed on both sides. The Yeomanry proceeded to burn several homes, including Father Murphy's, and totally destroyed the chapel in flames. This was, without doubt, a religious war for the Orange Yeomen.

Die With a Pike in Your Hand:

Several people of the parish had died in their burning homes. Others took to the woods, as did Father Murphy. The village people came to him asking him to comfort and help them. At that point Father Murphy's heart turned. He then rallied the men and told them to fight for their homes and families, rather than be passively murdered. "It's better to die with a pike in your hands, " he told them. In that moment he became the leader of the rebellion. He was soon joined by other priests: Father Michael Murphy, Father Philip Roche, and Father Doyle. To all intents, this was now a religious war on both sides. **(19)**

A young Irish poet, John Keegan Casey, composed the following verse, telling of the pike-men in this rising. It was sung as music, to the tune of "The Wearin' of the Green."

The Rising of the Moon

Oh then tell me, Sean O'Farrell, tell me why you hurry so,
Hush me bucall, hush and listen, and his cheeks were all aglow,
I bear orders from the captain, get you ready quick and soon,
For the pikes must be together by the risin' of the moon.

Chorus: By the rising of the moon, By the rising of the moon,
For the pikes must be together at the rising of the moon.

Oh then tell me, Sean O'Farrell, where the gatherin' is to be.
In the old spot by the river, right well known to you and me
One more word for signal taken, whistle up the marchin' tune
With your pike upon your shoulder, by the risin' of the moon.
Chorus:
There beside the singin' river, that dark mass of men were seen,
For above their shining weapons, hung their own beloved green
Death to every foe and traitor, forward strike the marchin' tune,
And hurrah, my boys for freedom, 'tis the risin' of the moon.
Chorus:
Well they fought for poor old Ireland and full bitter was their fate,
Oh what glorious pride and sorrow fill the name of ninety-eight
Yet thank God, while hearts are beating in manhood burning noon,
We shall follow in their footsteps at the risin' of the moon.

Armed with pikes and pitch forks, but with practically no firearms, the farmers, led by the clergymen, attacked the yeoman cavalry. A pike, when properly braced in the ground, spells disaster to an enemy on horseback. The Yeomen were, in this manner, forced to fight in close quarters, on foot, where their light cavalry swords are less effective. Farmers, with pitch forks quickly overwhelmed the Yeomen, and in the process gained possession of a number of firearms. The insurgents rapidly moved on to Camolin, Ferns, and Enniscorthy, where they encountered heavier resistance, but did prevail. The insurgents took no prisoners. From Enniscorthy they moved to nearby Vinegar Hill, where they set up camp.

By now the insurgents were pretty well armed with captured weaponry, and controlled most of Counties Waterford and Wexford. At Wexford they freed many citizens who had been arrested, and tortured by the Yeoman Garrison, which had fled before them anticipating the revenge the rebels would take. Some of the released prisoners joined the rebel movement.

More Revenge:

Some of the released prisoners, who had been tortured by the Yeomen, went to a site where a large number of Yeoman prisoners were being held in a barn. They overpowered the guards and were anxious to give the Yeomen a taste of what the Yeomen had given them. They burned the barn with the Yeomen inside and shot any who tried to escape. About one hundred Yeomen died in the flames, and 37 died of gunshot. Terrible atrocities on both sides, but with whom does the greatest burden of guilt reside?

Father Murphy's army of farmers, high on their success, moved on toward New Ross and Arklow. They captured New Ross, after fierce fighting, with heavy losses, to both sides. They were, however, unable to hold it against reinforced militia.

The Death of Father Michael Murphy:

On June 5th the rebels were also defeated at Arklow, after two hours of bitter fighting. Father Michael Murphy was killed at the head of the column, while leading a charge against the Ancient Britians Regiment. His death seemed to mark the turning point of the battle. Father Murphy's body was mutilated and roasted on a rack by his enemies. His saddened followers managed to withdraw to their camp on Vinegar Hill, near Enniscorthy. The insurgents were cut off, and forced to surrender after running out of powder. The survivors were cruelly executed.

Vinegar Hill is the high ground for many miles around. It is a natural fort, and commands a view of the Wicklow Mountains to the north, the coastal plains to the east, the Irish sea to the south, and Enniscorthy to the west. It was here the insurgents made their stand on June 21st. General Lake stormed the position with 13, 000 men and artillery.

The Death of Father John Murphy:

There was a gap in the government lines, and through this gap a small group of insurgents, led by Father John Murphy, was able to evade capture. They made their way to Kilkenny to try to raise more men, but were defeated in a small skirmish and dispersed. Some made their way home. Father Murphy was captured near Carlow and promptly executed, by hanging, like a common criminal. Thus ended the Wexford Rising. The rising is proudly recounted to this day, in the ballad "Boulavouge, " composed by an unknown bard.

Boulavouge

At Boulavouge as the sun was setting,
on the bright May meadows of Shelmaliar,
A rebel hand set the heather blazing,
And brought the neighbors from far and near.
Then Father Murphy from old Kilcormack,
Spurred up the rock with a warning cry,
"Arm, arm, " he cried, "For I've come to lead you,
For Ireland's freedom we'll fight or die."

He led us on 'gainst the coming soldiers,
The cowardly yeomen we put to flight,
'Twas at the Haara the boys of Wexford,
Showed Bookie's reg'ment how men could fight.
Lookout for hirelings, King George of England,
Search ev'ry kingdom that breathes a slave,
For Father Murphy from county Wexford,
Sweeps o'er the land like a mighty wave.

At Vinegar Hill o'er the pleasant Slane,
Our heros vainly stood back to back,
And the Yoes at Tullow took Father Murphy,
And burned his body upon the rack.
God grant you glory brave Father Murphy,
And open heaven to all your men;
For the cause that called you may call tomorrow,
In another fight for the green again.

Orange Justice:

A postscript to the rising occurred on the Wexford bridge. This had been the site where a Catholic priest had deterred a revenge seeking crowd, and saved the lives of many captured Yeomen. A courts martial was set up on June 10th. Father Roche and one of the rebel leaders, a Mr. Keogh were the first to be tried, in spite of a promise of amnesty, for being leaders in the insurrection. They were, of course found guilty, by a court of officers, who had not been sworn, and were executed by hanging from the bridge. It seems the court had developed a new standard: to wit, anyone who had saved an Orangemen, or Royalist from being killed, or his property saved, was to be considered as having influence among the rebels, and thus was proven to be a commander in the rebel army. Father John Redmond, and several others who had influenced the mob to mercy, were thus found guilty. Their reward, for their Christian acts, was instant execution. **(22)**

Reprisal:

On June 21st there occurred an incident in Scullabouge, Co. Wexford, in which a considerable number of Protestants were massacred by their Catholic neighbors. This was on a smaller scale than the Orange justice, but was equally regrettable and equally cruel and unjustified.

Here Come the French, Again:

The French again demonstrated their talent for arriving too late, and with too little to do any good. On August 22nd General Humbert arrived with a small force of 1,000 men, and landed in Killala, County Mayo. They also captured Ballina. They were joined by local Irishmen, and moved on to Castlebar, where they defeated a small British force of Yeomanry and Militia. Lord Cornwallis, the viceroy and commander of His Majesty's Forces in Ireland, arrived with a superior force of 20,000 and forced General Humbert to surrender at the Battle of Ballinamuck on September 8th. **(23)**

The Capture of Tone:

A few days later, on September 12th, a small French squadron, commanded by Admiral Bompart arrived in Lough Swilly in the north, off the coast of Donegal. These were all captured by the British Navy. Theobald Wolfe Tone was aboard one of the ships, in the uniform of a French naval officer. In appearance and language he was French, but he was recognized by an English officer, who was an old classmate from Trinity. He managed to get away, but was recaptured again at Buncrana, on November 3rd. He was tried and found guilty of treason, in spite of his French uniform. His sentence was not to be shot, but rather to be hung like a criminal. Tone had a pen knife on his person, and used it to cut his own throat, to avoid the disgrace of hanging.

Unfortunately, he botched the job and he passed a week of agony before finally dying on November 9th.

This is Not the End:

The failure of the risings, and death of Theobald Wolfe Tone marks the end of an attempt, but not the end of the Irish problem. That goes way back to the very beginning. It involved the Viking conquest, the Norman conquest, the Tudors, the Cromwellian conquest; the list is long. But the common thread is conquest. Brian Boru wanted national identity for Ireland, as did every Irish leader since. Tone was absolutely right. The Irish problem was foreign control, and influence. Ireland's problem was Great Britain. Future Irish leaders will all recognize that problem. Ireland needs to be Ireland, pure and simple. The struggle would continue. Some will try to solve it by political means, others by military means, or both. But the struggle would continue.

Chapter Twelve
Act of Union
1798-1821

A Man of Principle, The Orange Society, The United Irishmen, Pitt Makes His Case to the Populace, Parliament Opposes Union, The Irish Parliament, Union Proposed in Parliament, Pitt's Political Strategy, Dublin Passes Union, Westminster Passes Union, George III Reneges, The Bad Old Days All Over Again, More Stalling, Effects of Union in Ireland, Robert Emmett, The Best Laid Plans…, From Bad to Worse, Emmett's Last Words, The End of the Rising, After Union , O'Connell From Kerry, The Family Business, Daniel the Man, The Veto Question, A Young Lawyer's Debut, The Catholic Relief Bill, The People's Champion, The Trial of John Magee, The Orange Dublin Corporation, D'Esterre"s Threat, O'Connell's Response, The Field of Honor, Peace Brings More Suppression, Famine and Fever, King George III Dies, George IV and the Duke of Blarney,

They Made History:

William Pitt: Prime Minister of Great Britain (1783-1801), (1804-1806).

Henry Grattan: (1746-1820) Of the Ascendancy. Statesman, Strongly opposed Union, but supported monarchy.

Lord Cornwallis: Viceroy in Ireland since June 1798.

Robert Emmett: Young ascendancy Irish, educated at Trinity. Self-appointed general, Fermented the ill-fated rising.

Napoleon Bonaparte: Emperor of France after the French Revolution.

Michael Dwyer: Last rebel leader of the Rising of '98 who finally surrendered in December 1803.

Leonard McNally: Dublin barrister and treacherous informer. Defended Emmett in treason trial..

Daniel O'Connell: Young Irish-Catholic barrister from County Kerry. Founded the Catholic Association.

John Magee: Publisher of the Evening Post

King George IV: Succeeded to the throne in 1820, died 1830.

A Man of Principle:

British Prime Minister, William Pitt believed that the solution to the Irish problem, was Union with Great Britain. In spite of the horrific events of 1798, he still could not understand the force of Irish Nationalism. He simply could not imagine why a small, agrarian country would want to be separate from Great Britain. He was a sincere man, and honestly believed that what he proposed was best for Ireland. It might be necessary to make some concessions to make the Irish content. He had been one of the best friends the American revolutionaries had in English Parliament, not that he approved of the revolution. It is just surprising that he was unable to recognize the same force for national independence in Ireland, that he had witnessed in America in 1776-1783. **(1)**

He was very aware, as was Lord Lieutenant of Ireland, Cornwallis, that a hostile Ireland left Great Britain vulnerable to invasion by foreign powers. More than once, in the past, England's enemies had attempted to invade Britain through Ireland. This was an especially major concern at the moment, as Britain was again at war with Napoleon. Pitt and Cornwallis were certain that a successful union with Ireland would be a strength to England's security, not a weakness. They also believed that union was necessary to the survival of the Empire. It was obvious, however, that there were several different conflicting interests to appease, in order to bring union about. (2)

The Orange Society:

The Orange Society in Ulster also opposed Union with Britain. They had strong interests in the present Parliament, and were definitely opposed to any form of Catholic emancipation. Probably the largest obstacle Pitt had to overcome was the Protestant fear of being a minority surrounded by an empowered Catholic majority. The Catholics were unable to hold public office and the Protestants wanted to keep it that way, fearing what may happen if Catholics gained political power. Protestants owned most of the land, and all of the manufacturing and business interests in Ireland so there was also concern over Catholics gaining economic power. These concerns were heightened by the fact that there had been no love lost between the Irish Catholics and the Orangemen, following the atrocities committed by both sides during the recent rising. (3)

The United Irishmen: .

Since the recent rising the United Irishmen were outlawed and forbidden to meet, but there were still a couple hundred thousand of them out there. There was never any question that they were opposed to the Union. More than anything else, the Prime Minister and the Lord Lieutenant knew they would have to put the brakes on Irish nationalism.

Pitt Makes His Case to the Populace:

Pitt knew he would have to convert the Ascendancy in general and the Orange Society in particular. The first thing to accomplish would be to create a different perspective for the Protestant minority. His argument was that in Ireland the Catholics were the overwhelming majority, while in much larger Britain, the Protestants had the greater numbers. Consequently, if Ireland and Britain were joined in Union, the English and Irish Protestants would be the overwhelming majority, and the Catholics would be the minority.

His argument to the business community was that as a full member of the British Empire, Ireland would enjoy unimpeded trade and commerce with not only England, but with the former colonies in America. He further added that British investors would be much more willing to invest in Ireland, without the trade restrictions, and that everyone, including the working man would prosper. **(4)**

To the Catholic tenant farmers, or the "Old Irish Nation, " he offered the advantage of full British citizenship, and the ensuing rise in their standard of living. One might read into this that the land question would be resolved, which was the main sore spot with all Catholic tenant farmers. In reality, the land issue was not even to be considered. To the Irish Catholics, Pitt offered full emancipation and employment opportunities. Catholics would still be denied the right to sit in Parliament, but many government jobs, and commissions in the military would be open to them.

Parliament Opposed Union:

Then there was the Dublin Parliament itself. The Anglo-Irish, of the Ascendancy did not wish to give up the privileged position they held. They were the tail that wagged the Irish dog. The all-Protestant legislature was in a position to do favors for the manufacturers and merchants of the country; a service that has been amply rewarded.

They were, of course, strongly opposed to any idea of Catholic emancipation. Things were pretty cozy as they were, without messing them up with a lot of Paddy voters. Even the Irish Bar Association opposed Union, favoring a separate judicial system.

A young eloquent barrister from County Kerry named Daniel O'Connell made his initial public appearance, favoring an Irish national identity, stating that he would rather see the reinstatement of the Penal Laws, than a Union with Great Britain.**(5)** The House of Commons was led by Henry Grattan, a strong nationalist. He was very persuasive, and could influence others to favor Irish independence.

He did, on the other hand, favor the two countries sharing the same monarch, which would give Ireland a dominion status, and still be a part of the British Commonwealth. The House of

Lords also enjoyed a privileged position they wished to retain, so quite naturally they preferred the status quo.

The Irish Parliament:

The Irish Parliament was a peculiar sort of creature, as goes the general conception of legislative bodies. It was still an all-Protestant Parliament, as the newly liberated Catholics were still not allowed to sit in Parliament, but at least they were given an opportunity to vote But that was not the whole story. Parliament was comprised of two hundred ninety members. Of that number, fifty-eight were what you would call "place holders." That is to say, they were appointed, not elected.

Strangely enough, these "legislators, " were appointed by the "executive, " of the government, the Lord Lieutenant of Ireland. Strange? Yes! But there is more. These individuals were government employees. They held administrative jobs for the government, and serving in Parliament was part of the job. Yes, very strange!

But there is more. These individuals were not even Irish. They were British. Most of them, prior to taking the job, knew little or nothing about Ireland, nor did they even care.

There was another group of one hundred-sixty Members of Parliament, who were "elected, " in the various boroughs in Ireland, of which there were eighty. A borough was a town, or a city which was literally owned by an English nobleman, who may, or may not live in Ireland.

A rotten borough was one which had no actual population, but the land owner had his own representation in Parliament. These MP s were generally elected by as many as six voters, or as few as one, but it was always unanimous. The remaining seventy-two Members of Parliament were elected by voters of the five hundred thousand Irish-Protestant population, which was just about one-seventh of the total population of three million, five hundred-thousand. **(6)**

Union Proposed in Parliament:

On January 15, 1799 the Irish Parliament began what would be its last session. The proposal to join the Parliaments of Westminster and Dublin was proposed by the Lord Lieutenant Cornwallis. There was immediate opposition from Henry Grattan and several members. A motion against Union was made by Sir Laurence Parsons and debated. The debate went on day after day,

Grattan, and others, speaking out persuasively for Parsons's motion against Union.

Grattan left a sickbed and spoke persuasively to Parliament for two hours, from a sitting position When the vote was taken the count was 109 votes against the motion, to 104 votes in favor. Grattan had succeeded and Union was defeated for the time being. But Pitt and Cornwallis were determined to propose it over, and over, until it passed. (7)

Pitt's Political Strategy:

Pitt was aware of the best ways to influence the various members of Irish Parliament. At Pitt's direction, Cornwallis, as Lord Lieutenant, simply dismissed several of the MPs whom he had appointed, when they refused to be persuaded to his views. Others were persuaded by promise of advancement. Lord Castlereagh, Chief Secretary of parliament, did not refrain from bribery to move the greedy, and intimidation to persuade recalcitrant members where their best interest lay. The members representing the "pocket boroughs" were easily bought by offering the borough owner appropriate and generous compensation for his losses. The House of Lords offered little resistance, but the creation of twenty- eight new peerages in that house didn't hurt the chances of an overwhelming majority vote for Union. **(8)**

Dublin Passes Union:

On February 5, 1799 the House of Commons finally came up with a majority vote in favor of the preliminary proposals for Union. On February 6th the House of Lords also did what was expected of it, and passed an identical bill. It is interesting to note that during the following two months, the Orange lodges all passed resolutions against Union. The old members of the United Irishmen were, of course, strongly opposed to the Union, but there was not much anyone could do about it, or even say about it publicly. **(9)**

Westminster Passes Union:

On July 2, 1799, Westminster passed it's version of the Act of Union. It had taken considerable persuasion, and not just a little bribery. Parliament had, as the old saying goes, "Some of the best law makers that money could buy."

On August 1st Ireland's Parliament, such as it was, voted itself into oblivion by passing the Irish version of the Act of

Union. The Union became official on the first day of the year 1801. Ireland became a reluctant part of the British Empire. A new national ensign flew over London Tower, Dublin Castle and the Castle of Edinburgh, the design of which incorporated the crosses St. George, St. Patrick, and St Andrew. It was, and is, commonly called the Union Jack. **(10)**

Ireland was now a part of the United Kingdom of Great Britain and Ireland. The Union, however, had little, or no effect on the common people, the tenant farmers, or the working class. The laws were simply made in Westminster instead of Dublin. To the five-hundred and fifty-eight Members of Commons, would be added one hundred new Members from Ireland. Twenty-eight new peers, and four bishops were created, to sit in the House of Lords. The benefits of Union that everyone had been promised by William Pitt were never to materialize.

George III Reneges:

Pitt and Cornwallis were far from pleased with the way the Union was being carried out. The Catholics had been promised emancipation, and Pitt had every intention that it should be part of the deal. The fly in the ointment came when the King protested that, as the protector of the Church of England, he could not give his royal assent to modifying the oath of office for Parliament, by removing the test clause, to which no Catholic could subscribe. He believed that to do so would be a betrayal of his coronation oath.

Pitt was prevailed upon by the ministers not to oppose the King, for fear that to do so would push him past the edge of sanity. That was a narrow line that George III was prone to cross, from time to time. Consequently, emancipation was one of the first casualties of Union. No Catholic could take a seat in Parliament. Pitt would not oppose the King, but he felt he had been betrayed, and unable to keep his promise to the Irish Catholic people. He resigned his office in protest, but remained a member of Parliament. **(11)**

The Bad Old Days All Over Again:

Protestant controlled Parliament increased its grip on Ireland. Unjust laws were enacted, people were arrested without real cause and imprisoned or transported to the penal colony in Van Diemen's Land. (Australia). Lord Cornwallis now had 126,000 British troops at his disposal, with which to maintain order in Ireland, and order would be maintained. All constitutional guarantees were annulled. Martial law was proclaimed and habeas corpus suspended. Rural secret societies, such as the Whiteboys, Shanavests, Caravats, Ribbonmen, and Threshers, declared war on landowners and each other. Everything was as it was before the rebellion, or worse.

More Stalling:

The House of Lords presented an immoveable obstacle to Parliament with regard to the three biggest questions at hand. They simply exercised their veto power over legislation concerning the land, which was of greatest concern to the Irish tenant farmers, who were restricted in land ownership. The church hierarchy, most concerned with the established church and tithing, was also stonewalled by the veto, as were the nationalists, or former United Irishmen, who focused on the restoration of Irish government.

Effects of Union in Ireland:

The population of Ireland had now reached five million, the increase being mostly among the Irish Catholics. With Union, the emigration of Irish young people to the industrial cities of England increased dramatically. Industrial growth was also occurring in the areas of Dublin, Limerick and Cork, chiefly in the iron and textile industries.

A minor population shift occurred among the ascendancy land owners, as more of them took up residence in London. Their Irish properties were left in the hands of managers, whose success, and survival depended upon their ability to collect higher rents, and profits from the absentee's holdings. This had the effect of imposing an additional hardship on the tenant farmers, as eviction became a desirable option for the landlords, who could then convert the land to more extensive production, with crops of wheat and other grains.

On March 27, 1802 peace broke out between Napoleon and King George III, and a treaty was signed at Amiens, France. Robert Emmett, the son of a prominent Irish physician was traveling in France at the time of this peaceful interval. Young Robert had attended Trinity College in Dublin, but had resigned in protest in 1798 for having been disciplined for his membership in the United Irishmen. He had even insisted on having his name removed from their rolls. Being from a prominent ascendancy family, and member of a subversive Irish movement, Emmett had been able to arrange an interview with Napoleon. He became convinced that the Emperor was planning to invade England in August the next year. Robert had missed the rising in 1798, having been out of the country. Being an impetuous young man, he now started planning his own rising, to coincide with Napoleon's invasion of England. **(12)**

Robert Emmett:

On May 18, 1803 things got back to normal, with the resumption of hostilities between Britain and France. Robert Emmett had planned his rising carefully, with the assurance of French support. He had contacted the leaders of the, now low profile, United Irishmen in Wicklow, Kildare and Wexford, and coordinated his plans with them. He obtained their approval and support. He spent his own inheritance money, of 1, 200 pounds, to buy and manufacture weapons, and stored them in several secret depots in Dublin. **(13)**

The conspirators were all aware of the efficiency of the British spy network, and their use of informers, during the recent rising. They were determined not to make the same mistakes again. Unfortunately, they were so overly careful, that his communication system became complicated and inefficient. This flaw was to cause problems, and their contacts did not always get the information they needed in a timely manner.

The Best Laid Plans…:

On July 16th an explosion occurred at one of the Dublin arms depots. Emmett felt that his plans were now compromised, and in danger of discovery. He had also just been informed that Napoleon, in the French tradition, had changed his mind, calling off the invasion. Under the circumstances, there was danger in further delay. He made the decision to advance the day of the rising from the August date, to July 23rd. They would attack without the French troops, Emmett and the Dublin men attacking Dublin Castle, supported by Michael Dwyer and his boys from Wicklow. The men from Kildare would attack two other Dublin strong points. It was expected that when the rising began the Irish population would rise up and join them in support.

From Bad, to Worse:

Unfortunately, due to the last minute change of plans, things started to go wrong. More men turned out from Kildare than had been expected. There were not enough weapons for all of them. The attack had to be delayed. Many of the men became nervous, and upset. Many of them, got the word that the attack had been called off, and returned to their homes. Due to a foul up in communications, the men from Wicklow did not get word of the change of date, and failed to arrive at all. Emmett had expected to attack with a force of 2,000 men. By the time the attack was launched, at nine o'clock that evening, he had only about 74 men from Dublin and Kildare. **(14)**

The rising amounted to little more than a minor riot, and was easily put down. They stopped a coach carrying the Chief Justice and his nephew. Emmett lost control of the situation, and the undisciplined rebels murdered the pair. Realizing that they had failed, Emmett dispersed his troops. He himself was captured several days later in the Wicklow mountains, trying to find Michael Dwyer and his men. **(15)**

Emmett was charged with high treason and stood trial on September 19th. Defended by the Dublin barrister, Leonard McNally, whom you may remember as the informer who betrayed Theobald Wolfe Tone in 1798, Emmett's conviction was assured.

Emmett's Last Words:

On September 20th Robert Emmett was executed, in a Dublin street, by hanging before being drawn and quartered, and finally beheaded. His rising has been given little attention in the history books. He is remembered chiefly for his final statement, prior to his execution. When asked what his epitaph should be, he answered, **"Let no man write my epitaph…When Ireland takes her place among the nations of the earth, then, and not till then, let my epitaph be written."** These words forever earned him his place in the hearts of the Irish people, and sustained their desire for Irish nationhood. This unlikely general had succeeded to inspire future generations to struggle for its future achievement.**(16)**

The End of the Rising:

On December 14, 1803, Michael Dwyer, the last of the leaders of the 1798 Rising, was forced to surrender the small remnant of his troops, to the government forces of Lord Lieutenant Cornwallis. The surrender took place in the Wicklow Mountains.

Robert Emmett- Patriot

After Union:

In 1804 William Pitt was prevailed upon by King George III to resume his office as the Prime Minister of the Kingdom of Great Britain and Ireland. Pitt had to promise the King never to mention Catholic emancipation again, and was, regretfully, good to his word. Pitt died within two years, having failed to achieve his promise to the Irish Catholics. Relatively speaking, things were somewhat peaceful, with an occasional interruption of violence by some secret agrarian society. Government suppression continued in the form of the Convention Act, the Insurrection Act, along with the suspension of trial by jury and habeas corpus. Ireland was governed under martial law, and her jails and the transport ship to Botany Bay were kept busy.

Grattan entered Parliament in 1805. He entered a petition to both the Commons and the House of Lords, pleading the case for Catholic emancipation. They listened to him, but nothing much happened. Martial law was lifted in 1806, and there was some relaxation of the penal laws. This involved, mainly, the minor restrictions that were unenforceable anyway. Grattan would continue to campaign for emancipation, until his death in 1820.

O'Connell From Kerry:

Daniel O'Connell was born on August 6, 1775, in the remote back country of the Iveragh Peninsula, in County Kerry. He grew up speaking Irish, and received his early education in the "hedge school, " taught by a fugitive schoolmaster, and a fugitive priest. His father, a Catholic, was able to retain most of his own land by placing it in the legal custody of a trusted Protestant friend. Daniel was one of ten children, and in the custom of the Gael, he and his siblings were fostered to various aunts, uncles, and neighbors. **(17)**

The Family Business:

His family was able to acquire a reasonably good income, as they were in the import/export business, as were most of the families in the area. In the lonely bays of Iveragh they were able to carry on a brisk trade with their small boats, or smacks. They imported assorted wines and brandies and exported homespun flannels, butter, hides and wool. They were able to do this without bothering the poor overworked customs agents in Glengariff, Bantry, or Tralee. The Iveragh wives often shopped in Spanish markets.

Daniel, The Man:

When he was older, Daniel received some schooling in Cork, followed by some university studies in St Omer, in Flanders and Douay, in France. His studies were cut short by the French revolution. Dan completed his studies of law in London, in 1794. Daniel, having seen the bloodshed of revolution, became firmly resolved against violence as a means of bringing about reform. For the remainder of his life he was a devout advocate of democratic ways, working within the system to bring about change, and by making the system work for him. He became a master at it. **(18)**

The Veto Question:

In the spring of 1808 a bill was introduced in Commons by members Fox, and Greville, offering to remove a few small Catholic disabilities. This was to give it appeal to the minority population. The joker in the deck was, it empowered the government to exercise veto power over the appointment of Catholic bishops in Ireland. The ten Catholic bishops at Maynooth College had already, secretly consented to that provision.

A Young Lawyer's Debut:

It was at this point that our young Catholic barrister from County Kerry approached the Catholic Board in protest of the proposed arrangement. He spoke eloquently, and forcefully of the consequences of a temporal and predominantly Protestant authority having control over any organization aspect of the Catholic Church. The nominal leader of the Board, John Keogh favored "dignified silence" regarding the matter. O'Connell would have none of that. He raised such a fury, and apparently in the right places, that on September 1st twenty-six bishops joined him in repudiating the proposal. **(19)**

The Catholic Relief Bill:

On April 13, 1811, Henry Grattan introduced a Catholic Relief bill in the House of Commons. Principally it would remove the Catholic political disabilities that kept them out of Parliament and out of any high government office. Unfortunately, it also contained a clause regarding the infamous veto. It had the concurrence of the Catholic Vice Prefect Quarantoti, who was acting on behalf of Pope Pius VII, who at the time, was a prisoner of Napoleon.

The People's Champion:

O'Connell, and the Catholic Board, naturally opposed the bill. It was fortunate the majority of the House of Commons also disapproved of it. They, however, disapproved of the Catholic enabling portion, and defeated the bill 251 to 247. Daniel's dissenting speeches had been reported in all the papers, and he became known, not only in Dublin, but throughout Ireland, as a champion of the Irish Catholic. Under O'Connell's influence the Catholic Board had now become so outspoken, that the government proclaimed it as illegal, under the Suppression Act.

The Trial of John Magee:

In 1813 the publisher of the Evening Post, John Magee, a Presbyterian Irishman had published a scathing article about the recent Viceroy, the Duke of Richmond and his administration, including Lord Cornwallis. The government considered it libelous and would not stand for that type of criticism and exposure. Magee engaged the legal services of O'Connell. There was no doubt as to what Magee had published. Whether it was true, or not, would be a defense. The jury was composed of bigoted men, of Orange persuasion, and Lord Chief Justice Downes, and three other judges were blatantly proadministration. O'Connell knew going in that he had no chance for an acquittal, but determined to use the act of defense to make a political statement.

O'Connell berated the system, the jury and the judges. He told the jury of his respect for their Protestant faith, but cast serious doubt on their ability to honor their oath, to render a fair, impartial verdict. He accused them of being hypocrites, and unfaithful to their own religion by their very bigotry. His eloquence cast its spell as he berated the Lord Chief Justice as a man without principle, or fairness, and unloaded his contempt on the prosecuting attorney, branding him a libeler and a liar. So brilliant and compelling was his oratory, that his accusations went unchallenged, as his adversaries cowered before his outrage. He had confronted the British lion in its own den, and come out unscathed.

John Magee was sentenced to two years imprisonment, and the *Post* ran a partial summary of the trial. The *Post* also published a resolution approved by the Irishmen of Kilkenny, condemning the judges and the jury for their part in the trial. For publishing the resolution, John Magee subsequently had another six months added to the sentence. The government lackeys went so far as trying to have O'Connell disbarred, but they were way out of their class. O'Connell was now, in the hearts of the Irish people, a deliverer, a liberator, and just short of sainthood. In their eyes, he was now, without question, the greatest man in Ireland. **(20)**

The Orange Dublin Corporation:

O'Connell's stature was further enhanced a couple years later by the D'Esterre matter. D'Esterre was a wealthy Dublin pork merchant, and a member in good standing of the Orange Dublin Corporation. O'Connell, in one of his speeches for the Catholic Association, made some disparaging remarks, referring to the Orange Corporation, as the "beggarly Corporation." The newspapers quoted O'Connell's remarks, and the Orange group found it offensive, especially Mr. D'Esterre. As he was running for the Office of High Sheriff, he apparently thought it would gain him some points to publicly defend the corporation in question.

D'Esterre's Threat:

He wrote a rather nasty letter to O'Connell, demanding to know if he had acually made the remark, as reported in the paper. O'Connell's reply gave all of Dublin another laugh at the expense of the offended Corporation. He said, in effect, that no remark attributed to him could match his contempt for that group. D'Esterre was furious and announced that he was going to publicly chastise the offender. Now he was wise enough to know that he was no match for Dan in a verbal exchange, so his method of choice was the horse-whip.

D'Esterre, and his cronies, with horsewhip in hand, awaited on Grafton Street, to confront Dan on his way home from the Four Courts. A great crowd, including prominent members of the Orange Corporation and members of the city administration was gathering, to see the upstart receive his just deserts.

O'Connell's Response:

When O'Connell was informed of what awaited him on Grafton Street he grabbed his trusty blackthorn walking stick in his fist, donned his hat at a cocky tilt, and set out to meet his punisher. He and a couple of his sturdy friends, joked lightly as they strode defiantly down the thoroughfare. They smiled and waved to friends in the growing, cheering crowd that followed in their wake. When D'Esterre saw O'Connell and his multitude of followers coming his way, he was intimidated. Preferring discretion to further humiliation, he coiled up his whip and retired to a quiet place to think things over. O'Connell and friends passed on, waving and smiling to supporters and detractors alike. The multitude was ecstatic.

The "Field of Honor:"

D'Esterre was not finished. He still must avenge this humiliation, and save his honor. He had chosen his weapon poorly. He now challenged O'Connell to meet him on the field of honor. He felt that O'Connell would not dare to face him with pistols. D'Esterre was famous for his skill with that weapon. He demanded an apology, but Dan merely laughed. The Challenge was accepted, and the duel was to take place at four in the aftenoon on the appointed day.

The place was to be in nearby Kildare, outside the limits of Dublin. The word of the duel flew like the wind. As Dan and seconds made their way by coach to Kildare, all of Dublin seemed to follow with all types of carriage and cart, and men on horseback. The folks of Kildare all turned out, as well as a throng from nearby Naas.

D'Esterre kept Dan waiting at the field of honor, arriving at four thirty. The preparations were made and the principles took their places. The crowd was hushed with the tension. A handkerchief was dropped as the signal to begin. Both men stood, facing each other with pistols pointing at the ground. They stared at each other for about half a minute. D'Esterre took a step to one side as a distraction. Both weapons came up at the same time, but O'Connell got off the first shot. His challenger fell to the ground, mortally wounded.

A cheer went up from the watching crowd, and it continued for the next twenty-four hours as the news traveled throughout the island. O'Connell, the people's defender, had stood up, not just for his own honor, but for all of his down-trodden countrymen. He had faced down the Orange challenge. He had been forced to play by their rules, and he had prevailed. He was truly the people's champion, their defender of the faith, and the idol of the Irish. **(21)**

Peace Brings More Suppression:

The war with France came to an end on June 18, 1815 with the defeat of Napoleon at Waterloo. Post war Great Britain and Ireland had an economic downturn due to the decline in the price of wheat and corn. The high prices enjoyed by the farmer and their landlords were gone, and the increased demand for consumer goods brought inflation. Landlords were now charging their tenants as much as one third more than the value of their farms. The farmer could not afford the higher rents. Catholics were still being dunned for the tithe of 10% of their crops, which was ear marked to support the clergy of the Anglican Church of Ireland in relatively exorbitant luxury.The Catholic emancipation, that had been promised in 1800, had still not occurred, and the Convention Act, and the Insurrection Act were still being enforced.

Famine and Fever:

New laws, passed in 1816 made it even easier for land-lords to evict tenants delinquent with their rent, and turn the land to more profitable, extensive use. To make an intolerable situation even worse, in the autumn of 1816 the potato crop failed. Thousands faced eviction and starvation. The famine was compounded by an outbreak of Typhus that became a widespread epidemic that lasted until December of the following year. Over 50,000 people perished.

King George III Dies:

In 1820, that intermittently demented old tyrant, King George III, finally gave up his throne to the grim reaper, after a long run of sixty years. He was quickly replaced by King George IV, another anti-papist.

George IV and The Duke of Blarney:

The very next year the newly crowned King paid a royal visit to Ireland. He was greeted by an enigmatic Dan O'Connell, who for all his distain for British oppression, vowed undying fealty to his Majesty. While this may well cause some to question Dan's sincerity, knowing his silver tongued mastery of the art of Blarney, we must also take in to account the characteristic veneration with which the typical Celt viewed royalty.

It is even more remarkable when one considers that, in 1812 the Catholic Board, under Dan's leadership ridiculed the then, Prince of Wales for his anti-Catholic activities. The Board passed a widely circulated resolution, to the effect that it was probably the immoral influence of the young Prince's bigoted anti-Catholic mistress, that accounted for his attitude. It is safe to assume, that as King, his Majesty harbored no fond thoughts for Daniel O'Connell.

The strangest part of the whole business, however, was that O'Connell seemed to be pleased to pour praise and homage upon his Monarch. The king seemed equally pleased to receive it; and the more O'Connell poured it on, the more his Majesty lapped it up. The Irish people followed Dan's eloquent example, greeting the King with wild enthusiasm and devotion. The King was deeply moved by this spontaneous display of loyalty, by "his people." On the occasion of his departure, he addressed the cheering crowd from the deck of his ship and, with a lump in his throat, said, "Farewell, my beloved Irish subjects! May God Almighty bless you all until we meet again."(22)

In that same year the House of Commons passed still another Catholic Relief Bill. It made Catholics eligible for Parliament and for other high government offices. It also required them to take an oath of office, repudiating their Catholic faith; an oath no Catholic could take. It was of no consequence however, as the House of Lords could not bear to give the Catholics even that much. They refused to pass it. **(23)**

Chapter Thirteen
The Great Liberator
1822-1847

More Violence, The Catholic Rent, Catholic Clergy and the Peers Agree, The Association Flexes Its Muscle, Catholic Association Suppressed, The Clare Election of July 1828, O'Connell the Candidate, The Wearin' of the Green, King George Signs Under Protest, O'Connell in the House of Commons, O'Connell Refuses the Oath, O'Connell Returned Unopposed from Clare, The Anti-Union Association etc., The King is Dead-Long Live the King, The National School System, The Tithe War, The King is Dead- Long Live the Queen, A British "Solution to an Old Problem, O'Connell Focuses on Repeal, Population Explosion, Davis, Dillon and Duffy Support O'Connell, Rallies, Rallies, Rallies, The Rally at Tara, "A Nation Once Again, " O'Connell's Misconception, Clontarf Rally Cancelled, Young Ireland Party Formed, O'Connell Charged, O'Connell Vindicated, Potato Blight Noted, The Death of Daniel O'Connell.

They Made History:

Daniel O'Connell: First Catholic elected to Parliament, Opposed the Act of Union. Founded Repeal Associations
King George IV: King of England (1830-1830)
The Duke of York: Brother of George III. Strongly anti-papist.
Villars Stuart: Protestant MP, Pro-Emancipation, Supported O'Connell.
King William IV: King of England (1830-1837)
Vessy Fitzgerald: Protestant landowner & MP. Lost Clare Election to O'Connell.
Robert Peel: British Prime Minister under George IV, Supported emancipation.
Lord Wellington: Minister of the House of Lords. Supported emancipation
Duke of Brunswick: Another anti-papist brother of George IV.
Queen Victoria: Queen of England (1837-1901)
Thomas Davis: Protestant, Trinity grad. . Founded *The Nation* and Young Ireland
John B. Dillon: Catholic, barrister, Partner of Davis on *The Nation.*, Young Irelander
Charles G. Duffy: Young Irelander. A Belfast Catholic, journalist/ editor of *The Nation*

More Violence:

1822 brought another crop failure and more famine. Prices became even more inflated, and the profiteering landlords and government officials caused more hardship and suffering. In retaliation, landlords, or their agents were anonymously threatened and terrorized by the secret society of Ribbon-men. Some were even shot. Upper class families barricaded their homes, and lived in a constant state of fear, never opening their doors at night. **(1)**

The Catholic Rent:

Daniel O'Connell strongly opposed strong armed tactics, and bloodshed. He said, that even in the cause of Irish liberty, it was not worth the spilling of one drop of blood. On May 12, 1823, he and another barrister, Richard Lalor Shiel, founded the Catholic Association in Dublin. O'Connell's purpose was to use democratic methods to bring about political changes. The goal was to get repealed the remaining Penal Laws and to protect the tenant farmers from high rents and evictions. The Association was supported and run by the parishes under the leadership of the local priests. The first Sunday of each month, each farmer paid one penny at the chapel door. This was an amount that was affordable, but when paid regularly by 250,000 individuals, it added up, giving the Association a steady income of over one thousand pounds per week. The farmers referred to this as the "Catholic rent." **(2)**

Catholic Clergy and the Peers Agree:

In 1825, the House of Commons passed an Emancipation Bill which would permit Catholics to sit in Parliament and to hold other high government offices. It added another enticement, intended to make the bill even more acceptable to Catholics, by providing that the government would, henceforth, pay the salaries of the Catholic clergy, to include bishops, parish priests and curates. It was also designed to assure the loyalty, and hence the obedience of the Catholic clergy.

O'Connell found the compromise acceptable, because it would take the big step of securing emancipation. He was less concerned about the salary issue, because his next objective would be to secure repeal of the Act of Union. When that was achieved the salaries would no longer exist.

For once, however, the clergy, and the Catholic people, did not agree with Dan. The clergy did not want to be in the government's pocket and neither did the Catholic population.(3). The bill probably would have passed the House of Lords, had it not been for the Duke of York, the King's brother. He spoke to the Lords of the realm, threatened fire and brimstone, cajoled, pleaded, stormed and wept, accusing them of "subsidizing iniquity." The Lords voted it down and a new day of anti-popery dawned in Great Britain. Parliament dissolved and in the general election that followed, a new and bitterly anti-Catholic government ruled the Empire.

Daniel O'Connell – The Great Liberator

The Association Flexes Its Muscle:

The general election of 1826 went very well for the anti-papists in England, but it was a different story in Ireland. The Catholic Association decided it was time to see what they could do politically with a grassroots organization led by the parish priests and financed by the Catholic rent. In the Parliament race in County Waterford the Association backed Villiers Stuart, a Protestant who favored emancipation. Stuart was running against George Beresford, a land owner whose family had been members of the Dublin Parliament for over fifty years and the Westminster Parliament since the Act of Union in 1800. The Association, through the parish priests, mustered the needed votes, even among the Beresford estate tenants, and Villers Stuart was a shoo-in. The Association also backed successful candidates in Louth, Monaghan, and West Meath. O'Connell had flexed the political muscle of the Irish Catholics and they found they were empowered. (4)

Catholic Association Suppressed:

The new government wasted no time in proclaiming the Catholic Association and suppressing it. Nor did O'Connell waste any time in founding the New Catholic Association, having the purpose of "public and private charity." He was able to resume his campaign for emancipation without missing a beat.

The Clare Election of July 1828:

Vessey Fitzgerald a Member of Parliament, was appointed to a post in the British Cabinet. The law required that MPs appointed to a ministerial office stand for reelection in their home constituency. Fitzgerald had been County Clare's MP for the previous ten years and was a resident landlord, who had treated his tenants fairly. He was open minded regarding emancipation, but his appointment was to an office opposed to Catholic claims, and to the Catholic Association.

The Catholic Association felt they should oppose his candidacy, and a search began for a strong Protestant candidate who was sympathetic to emancipation. Not finding one readily, the suggestion was made that Dan O'Connell run for Parliament himself. The law only said that a Catholic could not be seated in Parliament. It didn't say that a Catholic couldn't run for the office. O'Connell liked the idea using a technicality in Britain's own law to serve the cause of emancipation, and the more he thought about it the better he liked it. Finally, he smiled a bit, and declared, " I'll do it!" Daniel speculated on what the government might do with an elected Catholic, not-seated, Member of Parliament.

O'Connell the Candidate:

Now the Association had to get busy and organize their campaign. Word went out to all the parishes in County Clare. The Priests knew the drill. They had been through it just two years previously, and got Fitzgerald elected. Now with the O'Connell, himself, as the candidate, they would have no trouble getting Fitzgerald un-elected.

The election would be held in Ennis. O'Connell and Fitzgerald were both nominated on Monday. On Tuesday the contest began. A crucial question was, which way would forty-shilling freeholders vote? These men were given votes, that in reality were intended as an endowment to their landlords. It was always assumed that these votes would go for the landlord's candidate, and invariably, they did. Although, in the 1826 election there were obvious indications that this assumption was no longer valid. This was confirmed on election day, as many of them came into Ennis in groups, cheering for Daniel O'Connell.

The parish priests played a key role, as their Sunday homilies urged the parishioners to vote their hearts, and cast their ballots for their faith, and O'Connell. The voters, carrying green boughs, were led to the poles by their priest, amidst shouting and cheering. The bands played a stirring Irish tune that recalled the struggles of Wolfe Tone, Napper Tandy, and the United Irishmen in the 1780s and '90s;

"The Wearing of the Green."

Oh! Paddy dear and did you hear the news that's going' round?
The shamrock is forbid by law, to grow on Irish ground.
Saint Patrick's Day no more we'll keep, his color can't be seen,
For there's a cruel law agin' the wearing of the green.

I met with Napper Tandy, and he took me by the hand,
And he said how's poor ould Ireland, and just how does she stand?
She's the most distressful country that ever you have seen;
They're hanging men and women there for wearin' of the green

Then if the color we must wear is England's cruel red,
Sure Ireland's sons shall ne'er forget the blood that they have shed.
You may take the shamrock from your hat and cast it on the sod;
But 'twill take root and flourish there, though under foot 'tis trod.

When the laws can stop the blades of grass from growin' as they grow,
And when the leaves in summertime, their verdure dare not show,
Then I will change the color that I wear in my caubeen,
But till that day, please God, I'll stick to wearin' of the green

All day Tuesday, O'Connell slowly pulled ahead. His lead increased on Wednesday, and continued the same on Thursday and Friday. By the time the poles closed on Saturday night, O'Connell had won by a landslide of 2,057 to 982. (5)

Prime Minister Robert Peel had gone on record as opposed to seating Catholics in Parliament. After the Clare election he had to rethink his position. He was sorely aware that England, at peace for the last thirteen years, currently occupied Ireland with over eighty percent of its infantry forces., just to maintain law and order. Lord Wellington conceded that the only alternative to emancipation was most likely to be civil war.

Even the King had asked Commons to be aware of the unrest in Ireland, and act prudently. Both houses of Parliament passed a bill removing the provisions in the oath that restricted Catholics from being seated in Parliament, or holding other high offices. The bill provided that the 40 shilling freeholders were disenfranchised, thus depriving O'Connell of eighty percent of his supporters. (6) The Catholic Association was also dissolved. It is interesting to note that the Archbishop of Canterbury and every Protestant Bishop in England, and Ireland, except one, voted against giving Catholics the full rights of citizenship in their native land.

King George Signs Under Protest:

King George IV was well aware of the public unrest, but was persuaded by his brother, the Duke of Brunswick, to oppose emancipation and not to sign the bill. Prime Minister Peel and Lord Wellington pleaded with the King for over five hours to change his mind. He stubbornly refused. Finally, they both handed in their resignations. Ultimately, the King had to reconsider his position, and finally agreed to sign the bill, under protest. On April 13, 1829, Catholic Emancipation became law. O'Connell had finally prevailed, and it had come about without bloodshed. (7)

O'Connell in the House of Commons:

On May 15th, O'Connell presented himself at Parliament presumably to take his seat. First, however, he was asked to take the oath of allegiance, in which he was asked to swear that the sacrifice of the Mass, and the invocation of the Blessed Virgin Mary, and other saints were impious and idolatrous, and to deny the dispensing power of the Pope, which never existed, except in the imagination of its framers. It seems that, even though the King had signed the Emancipation Act, it had not yet become effective.

O'Connell Refuses the Oath:

O'Connell, in a most composed and courteous manner, stated in a resonating voice that carried to every corner, "I decline, Mr. Clerk, to take this oath: Part of it, I know to be false; another part I believe not to be true." He then quietly marched out of the room. (8)

O'Connell Returned Unopposed from Clare:

Having declined the oath, after being elected to Parliament, and not been seated, O'Connell was required to stand again for election. On July 30th, 1829 he was again returned to

Parliament unopposed. At the next session he again entered Parliament, took a different oath, and on February 30th was seated as the first Catholic in the House of Commons. Emancipation being won, O'Connell, as a Member of Parliament, retired from his law practice to focus on repeal of the Union, and other matters concerning the people's cause. A national tribute had been organized, as an honorarium to compensate him for his public efforts to the tune of about 13,000 pounds per year. He now became a full time advocate for the Irish people, and was able to spend the honorarium in this cause.

The Anti-Union Association, etc. etc. etc.:

O'Connell founded what he called the *Anti-Union Association*. This did not find favor among the Ascendancy, or the northern Protestants.They feared that in an independent Ireland they would loose their privileged status over the Catholic majority, and bloody riots could ensue. The *Anti-Union Association* was immediately proclaimed by the government. O'Connell just as quickly reorganized under a new name, and of course, it, in turn, was proclaimed. Each week he would rename his association. He tried the *Repeal Breakfast Association,* and said if it were proclaimed he would have *Repeal Lunches*. After they were proclaimed, he formed, *Repeal Dinners,* which was succeeded by, *Repeal Suppers*. Next he started the General Association for Ireland.

He even proposed to make himself the Repeal Association, saying they could not disperse an individual by proclamation. He called his association, The *Irish Society for Legal and Legislative Relief.* Next he became an *Association of Irish Volunteers for Repeal of the Union,* and then an *Association of Subscribers to the Parliamentary Intelligence Office.* These assorted associations were organized in the same manner as had been the *Catholic Association* and resulted in greater financial support from the people than the "Catholic rent" had provided.

Finally they arrested him and charged him for violation of The Act for Suppression of Illegal Societies. O'Connell knew well, that this was a temporary act, so he pled guilty to a technical offense against a temporary act. In as much as he was a Member of Parliament, he arranged to have his sentence postponed until after the expiration of Parliament. The Chief Justice was undoubtedly surprised to learn that the Act for Suppression of

Illegal Societies had also expired at that time. Ultimately, the government recognized a stalemate, and O'Connell's anti-Union campaign continued. (9)

The King is Dead, Long Live the King:

On June 2, 1830, King George IV passed on to his royal reward, and was succeeded by his son, who was crowned as King William IV.

The National School System:

The Irish had always had great reverence for education, from the seanchaihies (storytellers) of pre-Christian Ireland, the early abbey schools in the Christian era, the bards of pre-Norman days, and to the hedge schools. In 1831 the National School System was established in Ireland, making elementary education widely available. This was a further effort by the government to Anglicize the Irish, as the medium used was the English language. Children were sometimes punished for speaking Irish, but Ireland has come to count the imposition of English a blessing, which was not, at first, recognized.(10)

The Tithe War:

On March 3, 1831 discontent, caused by the mandatory tithe of 10% of the value of their crop, or their income, that Catholics and Presbyterians were compelled to pay the Church of Ireland, resulted in violence. This had long been a sore point and was becoming a crisis. One hundred and twenty police were called upon in Graigurnamanagh, Co. Kilkenny, to seize cattle in payment of tithe. Farmers had branded all cows likely to be seized with a **T**, rendering them virtually un-sellable. People who paid the tithe would be ostracized. The police left empty handed. The government tried collecting the tithe using soldiers. Following several battles, riots, and assorted blood shed, they succeeded in collecting 12, 000 pounds, at a cost of 15, 000 pounds.

On December 14th, Carrickshock, Co. Kilkenny, police were routed by the mob, and twelve policemen were killed serving processes, while in Fermoy, Co. Cork, an incident, called the Massacre of Rathcormac, occurred when an Archdeacon, with the aid of soldiers, tried to collect 4 pounds, sixteen shillings from the Widow Ryan. In the ensuing riot, nine people died, including Widow Ryan's son. The soldiers seized four stacks of corn, in payment of the tithe.(11)

The King is Dead, Long Live the Queen:

King William IV, an obstinate, old man, died on June 20, 1837. His young, attracive niece, Victoria came as a distinct improvement to the British throne. Her reign over a period of change and industrial revolution would last for more than sixty-six years, and be known as the Victorian age.

A British "Solution" to an Old Problem:

The problem of the mandatory tithe was still a sore issue with Irish Catholics and Presbyterians. Daniel O'Connell did all that he could do to alleviate the situation, but the tithe proved to be beyond what anyone could do. In 1838 Parliament came up with a typical British solution to an Irish problem. They reduced the tithe by 25% and required that, in the future, the tithe be paid by the landlord. The landlords, in turn, merely applied the cost of the tithe to the tenant's rent, which was already too high. How typically bureaucratic of them!**(12)**

On July 31, 1838, Parliament passed the Poor Relief Act, extending the poor law system to Ireland. Under this system, care was provided for dispossessed farm families. Relief was extended to the able bodied poor, in the form of money or goods. Relief for children, or for the sick, or aged, was provided in work houses. By the year 1844 there would be ninety-eight work houses in Ireland, each one housing up to a thousand miserable souls, under the worst imaginable living conditions. **(13)**

O'Connell Focuses on Repeal:

In the early 1840s, having failed to achieve any satisfactory resolution to the tithe problem, O'Connell now focused his whole attention on trying to bring about the repeal of the Act of Union. Working peacefully, through constitutional means was a basic tenet of O'Connell's philosophy, but he was through lobbying at Westminster. He had tried that method with the tithe question, to little avail. His strength had always been with the people of Ireland, and to them he would turn again. This would require organization, so naturally, true to the O'Connell style, on April 15, 1841, he founded the *National Repeal Association*. In a relatively short time, the government proclaimed the new association.

It was just about this time that O'Connell was joined by a brilliant young, Protestant barrister, from Cork. Thomas Davis, had recently graduated from Trinity College, where he was a formidable debater, a noted essayist, and a talented composer. Catholic classmate, John Blake Dillon, was a close friend, and also a leading debater at Trinity. They were both drawn to O'Connell, and the repeal movement. One year after joining the National Repeal Association, they founded a weekly newspaper in Dublin with a strongly nationalist editorial policy. They recruited a noted Catholic journalist who was, at the time, the editor of a Belfast newspaper. Charles Gavan Duffy came on board as the editor of the *"The Nation."*

On July 16th, in standard O'Connell fashion, he renamed the Repeal Association, as the "Loyal National Repeal Association, " in deference to Queen Victoria. In August, to ease Irish unrest, the Parliament did pass the Municipal Reform Act, giving the major towns and cities a uniform constitution, providing for a popular electorate, and making municipal office available to Catholics. O'Connell's popularity was such, that he was elected as the first Catholic Lord Mayor of Dublin, for the period of one year.

Population Explosion:

The Act of Union in 1800, and the suppressive political and economic policies of Westminster, combined with the doctrines of Mother Church, had left the Catholic population in such a state of poverty, economically and culturally, that procreation had become the primary form of recreational pleasure that was left to them.. The population of Ireland increased from five million to eight million, a dramatic increase of three million people, within four decades, most of it occurring among the Catholic community.

Daniel O'Connell now thought to use this larger population in his fight to bring pressure to bear upon Sir Robert Peel, the current British Prime Minister. It had worked before, to bring about Catholic emancipation. O'Connell could not conceive that Peel and the Parliament could resist the public pressure of such a large mass of people. O'Connell toured Ireland, attending meetings, and speaking to the people.

Davis, Dillon, and Duffy Support O'Connell:

Meanwhile, Davis, Dillon, and Duffy strongly supported O'Connell, in *The Nation,* publishing stories of an historical political nature, and of current issues, especially repeal. They printed his speeches, and stories covering his travels and public projects. *The Nation* was circulated throughout Ireland, as poor farmers would pool their pennies to pay for a subscription. It was common practice for weekly readings to be held in the public house, or wherever men could gather to hear the priest, the school master, or a young student read them the latest news and editorials from Dublin. After profound discussions, the farmers would then retire to their own turf fires to share conclusions with their families. In this manner a national consciousness, and an awareness of national identity grew in Ireland.

Rallies, Rallies, Rallies:

On March 9, 1843, the Association, under O'Connell's direction, made the decision to hold even larger repeal meetings, at various sites of historical and cultural importance about the country. The word went out that Daniel summoned them, and they came by the thousands. These were well planned events and they were to be orderly, and lawful. Drinking and rowdiness were not to occur. That was the way it was, and that is the way it happened in over forty such rallies. Bear in mind that these were the days when the fastest means of travel was horseback. Nor was Ireland known for its fine roadways. They were but few, and what roads there were, were not much. The most common mode of travel was on foot, although many people did have buggies, and Irish jaunting cars. Many of those attending Daniels meetings would have to travel one, or two days, sleeping along the way, and carrying their food with them.

One of the earlier of these large rallies was held at Trim, on the River Boyne. Over 120,000 people showed up, to hear Daniel condemn the Act of Union, yet still espouse loyalty to the Queen. Another 120,000 people came to Limerick, where Patrick Sarsfield had surrendered to William of Orange. At the rally at Kells, the historic religious capital of Ireland, over 150, 000 attended. By this time these rallies were being called "Monster meetings." At the Rock of Cashel, ancient seat of the Kings of Munster, where King Brian Boru first conceived of an Irish Nation, the number attending swelled to 300,000. **(15)**

The Rally at Tara:

The high point of these rallies, and one that was, in truth, a "Monster" rally, was held on the Hill of Tara, the seat of the Ancient High Kings of Ireland. Five roads led to Tara, from each of the five provinces. People traveled for days, bands marched to Tara from forty different towns, followed by marchers in military fashion, four abreast. Beasts and buggies passed the walkers, as the vast procession continued. Buggies and carts were abandoned, in orderly fashion, at least three miles from the Hill as the numbers of people on foot made the road impassible. Bands surrounded the hill with music, as flags and banners everywhere proclaimed solidarity. People living within a half day's walk, continued to arrive until mid-day. The entire affair proceeded in a dignified, and orderly manner. An amazing feat in itself, which attests to the seriousness of purpose with which the people responded to the subject of repeal.

Estimates, at the time, placed the number attending at over one million people. There was, however, no place where one could actually view the entire crowd. Later historians have placed the numbers between 500,000 to 750,000. In any event, it was, and remains the largest single assembly of people ever to be mustered in Ireland. **(16)**

"A Nation Once Again:"

Thomas Davis had composed a stirring song titled, "A Nation Once Again" This composition was circulated through the crowd. It was played at the high point of the rally by the bands, and sung by the crowd with gusto. It was so stirring that it later was chosen as the Irish National Anthem.

"A NATION ONCE AGAIN"

When boyhood's fire was in my blood, I read of ancient free men,
For Greece and Rome, who bravely stood, Three hundred men and three
men,
And then I prayed I yet might see our fetters rent in twain,
And Ireland long a province be, a nation once again.

Chorus: *A nation once again, A nation once again,*
And Ireland long a province be, A nation once again.

And from that time through wildest woe, That hope has shone a far light
Nor could love's brightest summer glow, Outshine that solemn starlight;
It seemed to watch above my head, In forum, field and fane;
Its angel voice sang round my bed, "A nation once again."
Chorus:

O'Connell's Misconception:

O'Connell firmly believed, that with eighty percent of Ireland's population so demonstrably supporting the idea of repeal, Westminster would, naturally, just have to give in to the will of the people. This was the way it had happened in 1829, with the Clare election, and the winning of Catholic emancipation. He could not conceive of it being otherwise. What he failed to consider was that in 1829 a majority of the House of Commons and a considerable number of peers in the House of Lords, already leaned strongly in favor of emancipation. Such was not the case in 1843. In Commons both liberals and conservatives were united to save the Empire, fearing that repeal would be its downfall. Opposition was unanimous among the peers. (17)

Clontarf Rally Cancelled:

The last of the "Monster" rallies was scheduled to occur at Clontarf, on October 8, 1843, the site of Brian Boru's great victory against the Danes, and also where he, himself was slain. The crowd was expected to be even larger than at the Tara rally, as the location had strong emotional appeal with the population, and considering its proximity to Dublin. The government at Dublin Castle feared that a strong public reaction could result in violence. Mere hours before the rally, the government banned it. O'Connell, never condoning violence, and always espousing peaceful, and lawful means, called off the meeting.

The anti-repeal movement continued, but after the Clontarf episode things were not the same. The peasant support for rent repeal continued, pretty much as before. Meetings continued, but on a much smaller scale. O'Connell's basic assumptions, regarding peaceful persuasion, had been found to be ineffective.

He was not sure of what his alternatives might be. Slowly, the repeal movement, O'Connell style, lost momentum. **(18)**

"Young Ireland" Party Formed:

O'Connell had also lost the political support of Davis, Dillon, and Duffy, who considered the cancellation of the Clontarf meeting a big mistake. Other members of the Repeal Association, who wrote articles for *The Nation,* agreed with them: William Smith O'Brien, a studious young Protestant "country gentleman, " and prominent landlord from County Clare; John Mitchell, a young barrister from Banbridge, the son of a Unitarian minister; James Stephens, a civil engineer, who helped build the Limerick-Waterford railway; as well as Thomas Meagher, and Devin Reilly.

By November 1843, these men could no longer accept the peaceful, law abiding constitutional approach to winning repeal. Their writings became more and more militant. They interpreted O'Connell's policies as well intentioned, but ineffective. He could hypnotize the crowd with eloquence, raise them to a fevered pitch of patriotism, only to do nothing. They wanted to make the movement less Catholic, and involve more of the Protestant element. They wanted him to be amenable to the possible use of force. **(19)**

O'Connell took strong exception to this position and asserted that it had no place in the Repeal Association. At a two day meeting of the group, known as the peace resolutions debate, Thomas Meagher, another young barrister, and writer for *The Nation,* addressed the group. His words have since been called, his famous sword speech. In it, he repudiated the non-violence policy of O'Connell, and justified the sword as an instrument of policy, that had well served free men throughout history.

O'Connell was not present at the meeting, as he was occupied with trying to stay out of jail. His son, John, was then representing his father at Association meetings, and in O'Connell fashion, interrupted Meagher, and took strong exception to this kind of talk. He ended by threatening to walk out of the meeting. Meagher said that it would be inappropriate for him to leave the meeting of the Association founded by his father. He insisted that he, himself, be the one to walk out of the meeting, and he did. He was followed by Duffy, Mitchel, O'Brien, Stephens, Reilly, Father Meehan, and several others. They walked out of the meeting, and out of the Association.

The dissenting group, along with Davis and Dillon, had long been referred to, by O'Connell, in good humor, as "Young Ireland." They would now call themselves by that name, and they wanted more than mere repeal of the Act of Union. The Confederation wanted nothing less than complete independence from Great Britain. They were willing to fight for that independence, as had another Crown property across the Western Sea. Clearly, the "Great Liberator, " as he had affectionately been called by all, had failed to liberate. **(20)**

O'Connell Charged:

On October 14, Daniel O'Connell was charged by the government of attempting to alter the constitution by forcible means. The trial was held in January and February in 1844. Daniel defended himself and several others, against a partisan court, and an all Protestant jury. Naturally, all the defendants were found guilty. At the end of May 1845, O'Connell was sentenced to one year imprisonment. He was, however, given bail for three months. He made good use of this time by literally "barnstorming" England, holding meetings in major cities, including London itself. When his bail period was up at the end of August, he was imprisoned.

O'Connell Vindicated:

His imprisonment, however would be short lived. Apparently, someone was listening to him, during his three months of barnstorming. He had just begun serving his sentence in September, when the House of Lords, yielding to the pressure of public opinion, reversed the sentence. O'Connell was set free and returned to Dublin to be greeted by huge crowds, celebrations, and parades in his honor. **(21)**

Potato Blight Noted:

It was at harvest time in early September 1845, when farmers first noticed that some of their potato crop had turned to black, stinking mush. The arrival of another potato blight was first published in the Dublin papers. It drew minor notice, as had an earlier blight, no-one yet imagining the depth of the tragedy that was just around the corner. It was also at this time that *"The Nation"* announced the passing of their founder. Thomas Davis, the voice of Nationalism, and the leader of Young Ireland, had died of scarlet fever on September 16, 1845. O'Connell wept, as did Ireland, when he learned of Davis's passing. John Mitchell, a stronge militant, was soon to succeed Davis as publisher of *The Nation.***(22)**

The Death of Daniel O'Connell:

The Famine hit Ireland hard. Millions died and more were dying. People were more concerned with survival than they were with repeal. Daniel O'Connell, a tired old man of seventy, himself in failing health decided to visit Rome, in the spring of 1847. He almost made it, but was stricken while in Genoa. He died there on May 15th. In a sense, he did complete his pilgrimage, for his heart was sent on to Rome, where it is interred in the Church of St. Agatha. His body was returned to Dublin, where he was buried in Glasnevin Cemetery, following the largest funeral that Dublin had ever seen, before or since. There, rest the remains of The Great Liberator. **(23)**

Chapter Fourteen
Famine and Starvation
1840-1848

Not the first Famine, Set up For Disaster, The Coming of the Potato, Ireland Prospered for Awhile, Birthrate Soars, The Potato Blight, Phythphoa Infestans, Trevelyan's Economics, Peel Takes An Unpopular Stand, Public Works Systems, Full Famine- Peel's Government Falls, Trevelyan's and Russell's Priorities, Skibbereen, Britain's Everlasting Shame, The Conservatives' Approach, Some People Cared, When is a Famine Not a Famine? The Emigration Option, The "Coffin Ships," The Fields of Athenry, Loss of Irish Language, Social Structure, Primogeniture, Emigration as a Fact of Life.

They Made History:

Sir Robert Peel: Liberal Prime Minister of England. 1841-46
Charles Trevelyan: Permanent Assistant Secretary of the Treasury1840-59
Lord John Russell: Conservative Prime Minister of England, elected in 1846

Not the First Famine:

The potato blight, and the great famine of the 1840's were natural disasters. No blame should be assigned to any individual or, group of individuals. Nobody planned or directly caused the famine. As a matter of fact it was not the first famine that Ireland had experienced. There was a famine in the southern part of the island in 1727. Again in 1739, there was considerable crop failure due to an early frost, and the resulting famine. During the economic crisis that followed many tenant farm families were evicted from their homes. It has been estimated that 400,000 tenant farmers died of starvation, and related disease, but the economic crisis of 1740 had little affect on the majority of the population. No, this was not the first famine Ireland had seen, but it would prove to be the most severe. **(1)**

Set up for Disaster:

Ireland was set up for this type of disaster by a series of circumstances, some natural, some man created. First, Ireland did not have the mineral resources that other European countries possessed. Specifically, she did not have iron and coal in any great quantity. Consequently, following the middle ages, Ireland did not experience the industrial revolution that occurred elsewhere, so she was destined to remain an agrarian society, primarily limited to subsistence farming. The best lands were confiscated from the native population, and given to adventurers from England and Scotland, who established extensive pastoral plantations in the central, and eastern portions where the rich soils were conducive to pastoral agriculture. These large fields that were pasture lands, provide a sharp contrast today to the small plots allocated to the tenant farmers in the west. These were divided into small plots of less than five acres, and marked by an intricate patchwork of stone walls. On the positive side, Ireland's marine-west coast climate provided a more than adequate rainfall. **(2)**

The Coming of the Potato:

Secondly, during the Tudor period, and later following the Cromwell conquest, a major part of the native population had been forcibly confined to the rocky and mountainous parts of the island west of the Shannon. These lands were poorly suited to agriculture. Cattle could be grazed on the poorer land, but it was good for little else. Fortunately, the potato had come to Ireland in 1586, reputedly introduced by Sir Walter Raleigh, from America. The same Raleigh who confiscated land for Queen Elizabeth, and acquired a 40,000 acre plantation in Kerry. **(3)**

Potatoes grew well in the rocky, infertile soil, and produced a high yield per acre. Roughly, two thirds of the population became dependent upon the potato for survival. The potato actually turned out to be the perfect food for the impoverished farm population. A small plot of land could support a fairly large family for an entire year. With a supplement of milk it provided a diet of complete nutrients. By the end of the seventeenth century it replaced grain as the Irish staple. Many families lived solely on potatoes and milk. **(4)** The fact that such a large portion of the population depended upon a single crop for survival, rendered them totally vulnerable to the disaster that was to come.

Ireland Prospered, for Awhile:

Thirdly, there were a couple additional factors that exacerbated the scope of the famine; the effect of prosperity, and the effect of Church doctrine. Since the Treaty of Limerick, and the ending of the war between the Jacobites and the Williamites, Ireland had enjoyed nearly a century of relative peace. England had become engaged in a prolonged war with France, consequently the price of wheat increased considerably. In spite of the Penal Laws, and the theft of land from the Anglo-Catholic land-owners, Ireland enjoyed a period of relative prosperity. This afforded the small farmer the opportunity of producing a small cash crop. Ireland ports prospered and grew with the increased trade.

Birthrate Soars:

Prosperity resulted in a marked growth in the birth rate and population growth took a dramatic upswing during the first forty years of the nineteenth century. This was enhanced in a large part to Catholic Church doctrine regarding birth control and the duty of Catholic wives. It was common for many women to spend most of their married life in a state of pregnancy. The Irish tended to marry young and raise large families. As a result, Ireland's population increased by roughly 60% during this period, rising from five million in 1800, to eight million by 1845. **(5)**

The Potato Blight:

The potato blight was first noticed in September 1845. July had been extra rainy, even for Ireland. In August there was news of the potato crop in parts of south England being blighted. Then in September it hit the southern Irish counties of Waterford and Wexford. The blight spread quickly and soon half the potatoes in Ireland were affected. The affect was to turn the potato into a soft, black piece of stinking mush, that was totally inedible.

Phytophthera Infestans:

Britain's Tory Prime Minister, Sir Robert Peel, appointed a commission to study the problem. The commission botched the job and failed to diagnose the problem correctly. The blight was actually caused by a windborne fungus, *phytohththera infestans*. It had been seen in North America in 1844. The commission did not make that connection and determined that it was actually a disease of the potato itself. Their prescribed treatments of the disease were ineffective. **(6)**

Trevelyan's Economics

Peel's administrator for the famine program was the permanent assistant secretary to the Treasury, Charles Trevelyan, who did not believe in government relief measures. Like most British conservatives of the period, he subscribed to the Manchester school of economic theory, which stated that it was a mistake for government to interfere in economic matters, and that to do so, was a waste of time and effort. Left alone, the force of the market place would correct itself. This is sometimes referred to by the French term, *"Laissez-faire, "* meaning, "Let it happen, " or in other words, "Do not interfere with events." (Trevelyan must have viewed the corn laws, which were then protecting prices for English farmers, to be an exception to the Manchester theory).

Peel Takes An Unpopular Stand:

Regardless of the opposition, Peel did succeed in getting the "corn laws, " repealed. These laws had protected British farmers by keeping the price of imported grains high. This action was intended to keep the price of grain, and therefore the cost of bread, low. You can image how this was viewed by the farming interests and large land owners in England.

Public Works Systems:

The government work houses were full of impoverished farmers before the potato famine, so there was little help from that quarter. Peel's government then organized public works projects to enable people to earn money with which to buy food. A relief commission was established and local committees organized. Government grants subsidized local contributions at a cost of at least 365,000 pounds. At one point over 140,000 men, women, and children were employed by public works to improve harbors and roads. Peel's programs were successful, in-as- much, that no-one died of starvation during the winter of 1845-46. But we must take into account that in 1845-46 only half of the potato crop was blighted. **(8)**

Full Famine-- Peel's Government Falls:

In 1846 the famine hit all of Ireland in full force. The entire potato crop turned to black.stinking, inedible mush. It was also Ireland's misfortune that Peel's government fell to the Conservative Party, under Lord John Russell as Prime Minister **(9)**

Trevelyan's and Russell's Priorities:

Charles Trevelyan's job was made much easier for he and Prime Minister Russell were of one mind. Under Russell's government, Trevelyan decided not to buy any more food, and the government did not give free relief. Earlier it was stated that the famine was a natural disaster, and that no-one should be blamed for a natural occurrence. That much is true. But one must distinguish between a natural occurrence and a natural disaster.

Charles Trevelyan-Materialism Before Humanity

They are not the same, and should not be thought of in the same way. The Conservatives failed to make that distinction, and so did Charles Trevelyan. During this period tons of grain were exported from Ireland to Great Britain.

Their decision to sell this grain, corn and wheat, on the British market, for a higher price than the Irish market, exacerbated a natural occurrence, turning it into a natural disaster. Their further decision to hold landlords responsible, to pay taxes for their delinquent tenancies, compounded the problem. Consequently, landlords were anxious to evict non-paying tenants, in order to avoid paying the tax. No tenants, no tax! The result was an ever increasing number of people with no means, food, or shelter.

Skibbereen:

There's an old traditional ballad, by an unknown composer, which has been sung in Irish pubs since the famine days. It relates how one evicted farmer chose rebellion, and immigration to starvation. It illustrates the way traditional music and poetry become vehicles by which a memory of injustice may be passed through succeeding generations.

Skibbereen

Oh, father dear, I oft times hear you talk of Erin's Isle,
Her lofty scene and valley green, her mountains rude and wild,
They say it is a pretty place wherein a prince might dwell,
Then why did you abandon it? The reason do me tell;

My son, I loved our native land with energy and pride,
Until a blight came on the land and sheep and cattle died,
The rent and taxes were to pay, I could not them redeem,
And that's the cruel reason Why I left old Skibbereen.

It's well I do remember that bleak December day,
The landlord and the sheriff came to drive us all away;
They set the roof on fire with their demon yelllow spleen,
And that's another reason that I left old Skibbereen.

It's well I do remember the year of forty-eight,
When I arose with Erin's boys to fight against the fate,
I was hunted through the mountains for a traitor to the queen,
And that's another reason why I left old Skibbereen.

Oh father dear, the day will come when vengeance loud will call,
And we will rise with Erin's boys and rally one and all,
I'll be the man to lead the van beneath our flag of green,
And loud and high we'll raise the cry: "Revenge for Skibbereen."

Britain's Everlasting Shame:

It is to the everlasting shame of the British Empire, that at this time the ruling party in its Parliament considered it adequate to look upon this human tragedy as divine intervention to solve a social problem of over-population, by an undesirable and sub-human race of people. Parliament decided to do nothing to help. The attitude was, "Its a pity, but if they die, they die." **(10)**

The Conservatives Approach:

The Conservative government dismantled Peel's relief programs. Lord John Russell was more interested in work programs than he was in public feeding of starving people. All of the work programs were lumped together under an agency called the "Board of Works., " wherein 112,000 well fed bureaucrats were tasked with finding work for 750,000 starving, evicted peasants. They were less than successful. Work houses were established, where in return for backbreaking work, thousands of starving farm families were sheltered in squalor and paid a starvation wage. The winter of 1846-47 was cold and bitter, and surpassed all others in terms of death and human suffering. Tens of thousands died of starvation and exposure. **(11)**

Some People Cared:

Prime Minister Russell did not believe it was the responsibility of the government to feed the population, but that it should be up to private enterprise to meet the need. Many land owners did what they could to help their tenants by providing private work, rather than evicting their tenants. Private organizations, such as the Society of Friends, a Quaker charity, set up soup kitchens to feed the starving. In early 1847, the government reluctantly followed suit in setting up some soup kitchens. By mid-year over 3,000,000 people, half the population of Ireland, were being fed at these sites. **(12)**

When is a Famine Not a Famine?

It has been estimated that from 1846 to 1851 over one and a half million people died from hunger, exposure or disease. Another million people emigrated to the United States, Canada, and Great Britain. During the famine, the population was reduced to six million. You can't call it a **famine** when there is adequate food in the country, but it is being sold elsewhere for a better price. That is a **starvation**! In this case, when the government perceives the disaster as "God's way of adjusting over-population, " it might also be called **genocide. (13)**

The Emigration Option:

Liverpool, for the Irish, had long been the primary choice from which to emigrate. A short trip across the Irish Sea to Liverpool was a standard source of employment, and Liverpool had a resident Irish population, among its 250,000 people. There was very little additional emigration in 1845, as the blight struck in September, after the normal spring and summer emigration periods. In 1846 it was a different story, when the crop failure was total, Ireland developed a continuous emigration, even throughout the winter months. Since there were few, if any, ships sailing directly to the United States from Irish ports, by June of 1847, an additional 300, 000 desperate Irish had arrived in Liverpool, most seeking passage to Canada, or the United States. **(14)**

Passage to Boston or New York was six pounds, but passage to Montreal was only four pounds. Most emigrants chose the cheaper route if it was available. So great was the demand, that direct sailings from Cobh, (pronounced *"cove"*) were established. Cobh was Ireland's primary seaport for passenger vessels.

A statue in Cobh Harbor, memorializing
the 1840s famine emigrants

The "Coffin Ships:"

Ship owners in other Irish ports were quickly attracted to this new trade. Old ships that had previously carried only cargo were quickly redesignated. Lacking accommodation for passengers, the emigrants were crowded into the cargo holds. Conditions were wretched, sanitation inadequate, feeding marginal. Some vessels were not only unsuitable for passengers, but were totally un-seaworthy. A number of these wrecks foundered in the Atlantic storms and simply disappeared with all hands. Barring that misfortune, many of the emigrant passengers were already sick, or in a weakened condition, and succumbed to disease during the ten week journey. These were the infamous "coffin ships." There is no exact way of counting the thousands of passengers that died during, or as a result of, the conditions of the trip. **(15)**

A very moving song, composed by a twentieth century composer, Pete St. John, has taken its place among the traditional ballads of Ireland. It tells of the plight of a young Irish couple facing the famine years. Young Michael, for a very minor crime is sentenced to transportation to the penal colony in Australia, leaving his wife and child alone and facing starvation.

The Fields of Athenry

By the lonely prison wall I heard a young girl calling,
Michael, they are taking you away,
For you stole Trevelyan's corn, So the young could see the morn,
Now a prison ship lies waiting in the bay.

Chorus: Low lie the fields of Athenry,
Where once we watched the small free birds fly,
Our love was on the wing,
We had dreams and songs to sing,
It's so lonely 'round the fields of Athenry.

By a lonely prison wall, I heard a young man calling.
Nothing matters Mary when you're free,
Against the Famine and the Crown, I rebelled, they ran me down,
Now you must raise our child with dignity

Chorus:

By a lonely harbor wall, She watched the last star falling,
And that prison ship sailed out against the sky,
Sure she'll wait and hope and pray,
For her love on Botany Bay,
It's so lonely 'round the fields of Athenry

Loss of Irish Language:

A major change, in Ireland, as a result of the famine was the loss of the Irish language. The famine had the greatest impact on the counties in western Ireland. It was eastern, southern and northern Ireland that had been the most Anglicized. In fact the Education Act of 1831 established the National School System, with English as its official language. The Catholic farmers had been banned to "hell, or Connaught" (west of the Shannon) by Oliver Cromwell. Consequently, most of the old Irish speakers had been killed off by the starvation, and the Gaelic tongue survived only in a few isolated places in the west. The Irish in most other places associated Gaelic with poverty, and disgrace, and wanted their children to speak English. It became the language of commerce and prosperity, and was associated with success and respectability. **(16)**

This is what became of what the
emigrants left behind

Social Structure:

The social structure of Ireland, as well as the Irish culture itself, was devastated. Before the famine Ireland was a country of young families. The Irish married young and raised large families. After the famine this was not the case. Post famine, men usually waited until their late thirties or early forties before taking a wife. Women too married later in life, most past the age of thirty. Obviously, this resulted in smaller families, as wives had shorter period of child bearing age.

Primogeniture:

Another social change brought about by the famine was that the practice of primogeniture became the norm. The oldest son became the inheritor of the farm intact. No longer was it divided equally among all the sons. This left but a few options available to the young people. Younger brothers could perhaps learn a trade, enter the priesthood, or join the military. The oldest daughter, if she had a dowry, had a good chance of marriage. The dowry was generally passed on to her oldest daughter. The same dowry could be passed down generation after generation. Without a dowry, a girl's choice was pretty much limited to entering a convent. Of course emigration was an option for both sons and daughters.

Emigration as a Fact of Life:

Without a doubt, the most long lasting effect of the famine was the establishment of emigration as a fixed pattern of Irish life for the remainder of the century. By 1900 over 4,000,000 people had emigrated to the United States. There were at that time about as many Irish living in America as there were in Ireland. These Irish-Americans would play a significant part in Ireland's future struggle for independence. That pattern of emigration has continued although somewhat diminished, through the twentieth century. Today, there are over 43,000,000 Americans who proudly claim Irish heritage. **(17)**

Chapter Fifteen
Young Ireland and The Fenians
1847-1867

Mitchel Succeeds Davis on The Nation, The Nation Advocates Land Reform, Going His Own Way, The United Irishmen, Mitchel, O'Brien, and Meagher Charged, Mitchel Convicted of Treason Felony, The Government Strikes First, The "Rising" of 1848, Until They Are Dead, Van Dieman Alumni, Thomas Meagher, James Stephens, Stephens Founds the Fenian Brotherhood, American Fenians, Other Young Irelanders, Young Ireland's Legacy, Duffy Forms the Land League, The Protestant Minority, The Fenians, The Legendary Ancient Fenians, The Funeral of Terrence Bellew McManus, The Irish People Founded, Rising Promised for 1865, The Escape, The Fenians Invade Canada, A New Fenian Chief, The Rebellion of 1867, The Mancheser Martyrs, God Save Ireland, A Horrible Mistake, Glory Oh! To The Bold Fenian Men, Down by the Glenside

They Made History:

John Mitchel: Succeeded Davis as publisher of *The Nation*, Extremely militant.
John B. Dillon: Catholic, barrister, friend and partner of Davis on *The Nation*.
Charles Gavan Duffy: Noted Belfast Catholic journalist, and editor of *The Nation*.
James Fintan Lawlor: Writer for *The Nation ;* Proposed land ownership reform.
William Smith O'Brien: Country gentleman, nationalist, former Member of Parliament.
James Stephens: Civil Engineer. Founder of Irish Revolutionary Brotherhood.
Devin Rielly: Militant nationalist. Co-founder of IRB with Stephens
John O'Mahoney: Co-Founder of the Fenians, forced to flee to the U.S. in 1848
Thomas Meagher: Strongly militant and outspoken. The "Sword speech."
John Martin: Mitchel's brother-in-law. Replaced him and Founded *The Felon*.
Terence Bellew McManus: One of the Ballingary rebels of 1848

Mitchel Succeeds Davis on *The Nation:*

Following the untimely demise of Thomas Davis, John Mitchel succeeded him as publisher of *The Nation,* thus becoming the de facto leader of the Confederacy, or Young Ireland as they were now called. Mitchel was fanatically militant, far beyond most of the general membership. Ireland was facing a devastating famine, and the others were well aware that Ireland was in no way, capable of any kind of rising or rebellion. The Irish were struggling to stay alive. They had no equipment, nor were they trained to use it if they had it. It was not a popular idea. The people were concerned mainly with survival, not political movements. **(1)**

"The Nation" Advocates Land Reform:

In 1847 *The Nation* published a series of letters written by a James Fintan Lawlor, who was the son of a member of Parliament, from Queen's County, and a land owner. Lawlor advocated the radical idea that the tenancy arrangement of land ownership in Ireland was a major causative factor of the famine. Mitchel turned this into a campaign for tenure security for the tenant farmers. Lawlor's ideas found little acceptance at that time, but would prove to be a major issue in future land reform legislation. (2)

Going His Own Way:

Mitchel became more and more dictatorial, and dangerously militant. This did not sit well with Dillon and Duffy, and several others. They did not fear risking their lives to gain Ireland's freedom. They, correctly, believed that Ireland, in its present post famine condition, was far from ready for any sort of rebellion, and they had no intention of throwing their lives away, for no purpose. Their intent was to gain all they could by lawful means, while making preparation, and awaiting an advantageous opportunity. Mitchel was hard headed and did not see things their way. Consequently, he parted company with both *The Confederation,* and *The Nation.*

"The United Irishmen:"

In the early part of 1848, Mitchel, accompanied by Devin Reilly, and James Fintan Lawlor founded another paper he called, *The United Irishmen,* in order to proclaim his revolutionary principles. The paper was an instant success, and soon had a larger circulation than *The Nation.* He advocated armed rebellion, which was approvingly received by a population who had recently survived the "Starvation." With Irish public opinion leaning toward rebellion, a rebellion of which they were presently incapable, Dillon and Duffy, at *The Nation,* had no choice, but to follow suit. (3)

Mitchel, O'Brien and Meagher Charged:

Ireland had lost one quarter of its population during the past three years to emigration and starvation. In 1848, things were improving, the famine was abating, and the people were outraged, and bitter at their oppressors, for the mismanaging of the recent catastrophe. Mitchel called for a holy war, "to sweep Ireland clear of the English....." The time appeared to be ripe for revolution, but the Government took action first. The British Government was equally aware of the unrest, but had no intention of waiting for the Irish to be prepared for a rising. The offices of *The United Irishmen* were raided and O'Brien, Meagher and Mitchel were arrested and charged with the crime of sedition, or advocating rebellion. O'Brien and Meagher were tried first, separately from Mitchell. By some quirk of fate, and contrary to usual British procedure, two men, with open minds were accidentally seated on the jury. Consequently, it was not possible for the Government to obtain a guilty verdict. O'Brien and Meagher were set free. Lawlor was also arrested, but was soon released for ill-health reasons. He died within a year.(4)

Mitchel Convicted of Treason Felony;

Before trying Mitchel, the Government took the time to invent a new offense, they called "treason-felony." This act specified that it was a felony for any Irishman, to even utter a suggestion of revolution. They also took care to see that no Catholic, or open minded Protestant, got to sit in the jury box. Mitchel was, of course, convicted as charged, and sentenced to fourteen years transportation, in the Bermuda penal colony.(5)

John Martin, a Protestant gentleman farmer, married to John Mitchel's sister, stepped in to take Mitchel's place. *The United Irishmen* had been suppressed by the Government, so he founded a paper he called *The Felon,* and with the assistance of Kevin Reilly, took up the call for revolution. Still another Young Irelander, Kevin O'Doherty founded a third newspaper called *The Tribune,* and made the same appeal.

The Government Strikes First:

Again, the Government did not wait to give the revolutionists the luxury of picking the time. Within a few weeks the police made a simultaneous raid on all three papers, and arrested the editors. Duffy was sentenced to prison, but shortly released because of poor health. Martin, and O'Doherty, were convicted and sentenced to ten years transportation to Van Diemen's Land (Tasmania).

Warrants were sworn for O'Brien and Meagher, who had not been convicted the previous time, and again were being sought. McManus, Doheny, O'Gorman, Reilly, and Dillon were also on the run. They were out of options. The time had come for a rising, whatever the outcome. O'Brien was recognized as the leader, so the others spread out over the southern counties of Munster, to wait for him to strike the first blow. (6)

The "Rising" of 1848:

The general population was emotionally ready for a rising, but they were emaciated and without weapons, or a unified plan. They were in no shape to face the well trained, well fed, and well equipped British army. Never-the-less O'Brien, Meagher, and McManus were near Ballingary, in County Tipperary, addressing a group of local half-starved farmers, trying to rouse them to revolt. The meeting was interrupted by the arrival of forty-six members of the Irish Constabulary. The rising was on. The rising was over. It didn't take long, and amounted to little more than a brawl in a cabbage patch.(7)

Until They Are Dead:

O'Brien, Meagher and McManus, were arrested along with another follower named O'Donoghue. They were tried by the usual packed jury, convicted, of course, and sentenced *"to be hung by the neck until you are dead; and that afterwards your head shall be severed from your body, and your body divided into quarters, to be disposed of as Her Majesty shall think fit."* Then as an afterthought, *"May the Lord have mercy on your soul"*

Queen Victoria, the epitome of young womanhood, is said to have expressed regret that the rising did not actually materialize, so that British guns could have mowed down the Irish rebels, "….to teach the Irish a lesson." This sounds pretty vicious, coming from the young Queen, but to her credit, we must acknowledge that the sentence was soon commuted to life transportation to Van Diemen's Land. This could only have happened with her approval, if not her initiative. The reprieved rebels were soon joined by John Mitchel, who had been transferred from the penal colony in Bermuda. **(8)**

The Van Dieman Alumni:

James Stephens and John O'Mahoney fled to France together in 1848. Stephens remained in France for a period, and O'Mahoney continued on to New York City. Security in the penal colony was either very lax, or sympathizers facilitated escape for some Young Irelander's, as if through a revolving door.

Thomas Meagher:

In 1852, Thomas Meagher escaped from the penal colony in Tasmania, made his way to the United States, where he was able to establish a successful law practice in New York City.

During the American Civil War, Meagher was commissioned as a Brigadier General in the Union Army, He raised, and commanded the Irish Brigade, which was part of the 69th Regiment of infantry, from New York, later to be known as "the Fighting 69th." It was Meagher's intention, after the war, to take this battle hardened brigade to Ireland to fight for Irish independence. Even though he refused to join Stephens, in conspiring with the Fenians, he was still willing to fight for Ireland on the battlefield. Unfortunately, his Brigade sustained such heavy losses at Antietam and Fredericksburg, that it ceased to exist as a unit. After the war, Meagher stayed with the army, and was later appointed as temporary governor of Montana. During a flood of the Missouri River, he was accidentally swept away and drown. **(9)**

James Stephens:

While Stephens was in France, after fleeing in 1848, he heard of a Franco-Italian secret society of revolutionaries, known as the Carbonari. He learned that they were organized into different cells, with members unaware, with exception of the cell leader, of who belonged to any of the other cells. This rendered the Carbonari almost informer-proof. This made a very strong impression on Stephens. He recalled that every attempt of Irish revolt over the centuries had been betrayed by informers.

When he was finally able to return to Ireland in 1856, he spent the next two years traveling all over Ireland, talking to people, listening to their views, and contacting potential candidates. He developed a plan for organizing the Irish Revolutionary Brotherhood along similar lines as was the Carbonari. The name of the group was soon changed to the Irish Republican Brotherhood (IRB).

Stephens Founds The Fenian Brotherhood:

On March 17, 1858, St. Patrick's Day, Stephens and Thomas Clarke Luby took turns administering the Fenian oath to each other, thus officially founding the Irish Republican Brotherhood. They were soon joined by Charles Kickham and John O'Leary. Shortly after that, in Skibbereen, Stephens swore in Jerimiah O'Donovan Rossa, who was the leader of the *Phoenix National Literary Society*. This Society had branches in other parts of Ireland, which soon became the first cells of the Brotherhood.**(10)**

Later that year, Stephens traveled to New York to raise money for the Irish Republican Brotherhood. He called on John Mitchel and Thomas Meagher seeking their support for the Brotherhood. They had both had enough of revolutionary politics, and declined all but financial support. Terence Bellew McManus was another forty-eighter, and a Van Dieman alumnus, who lived out his life in San Francisco, although he remained an active supporter of the American Fenian Brotherhood.

American Fenians:

Stephens next called on his old comrade, John O'Mahoney, who enthusiastically came aboard. Together they founded the Irish-American version of the Brotherhood, with O'Mahoney as the leader of the American branch. O'Mahoney, being somewhat of a Gaelic scholar, named it the Fenian Brotherhood, after Finn MacCool's legendary ancient warrior band. The name caught on, and The Fenians also became the popular name for the Brotherhood in Ireland.

Other Young Irelanders:

John Mitchel escaped from Tasmania a year after Meagher, likewise went to New York, and made his home there. William Smith O'Brien was released from the penal colony in 1854, and returned to Ireland, where he retired from politics and lived a quiet life as the country gentleman he was. Doheny, Reilly, Dillon and O'Gorman evaded capture and escaped the country. They eventually returned to Ireland, but they all felt that they had had enough of Irish revolutionary politics.

Young Ireland's Legacy:

Many people would consider the Young Ireland movement to have been a failure; certainly the rising of 1848 was. But the movement, itself, was anything but a failure. It was a success in the many essays, poetry, and ballads they gave Ireland, such as the moving composition by Thomas Davis, *A Nation Once Again,* which for a time became Ireland's National Anthem.

James Fintan Lawlor, ahead of his time, recognized land ownership as a major problem in the Irish economy. The last half of the nineteenth century, saw it become one of the great national issues. Lawlor inspired Gavan Duffy to form the Irish Tenant League, in the 1850s, and Isaac Butt's home rule movement, of the 1870s. Thanks to Young Ireland, these issues would be addressed by constitutional, and parliamentary means. It was from them that Charles Stewart Parnell, and Michael Davitt, drew their inspiration.

The second great issue of the period, and in the early twentieth century, was the war for national independence. This was included among the objectives of societies, such as Irish Republican Brotherhood, and the Fenians. These dedicated men sought Irish Independence by rebellion, as a final resort. Without such men, the rising of 1916 may never have occurred. It was Young Ireland that motivated the following generations to aspire to independent nationhood.

Duffy Forms the Land League:

In 1850, Charles Gavan Duffy formed the Irish Tenant League, which was an organization of tenant farmers campaigning for better agreement with their landlords. Their platform was based upon what they called the Three Fs; fair rent, fixity of tenure, freedom for the tenants to sell their tenancy. They established an independent Irish party, and in the election of 1852, seated 50 tenant league supporters, out of 103 Irish Members of Parliament. The party failed, as several of its leaders sought personal political advancement, at the expense of their constituencies.The party just fell apart. Land tenancy continued to be a major concern in Irish politics well into the twentieth century. **(11)**

The Protestant Minority:

This, however, was not the case everywhere in Ireland. A substantial minority favored maintaining the Union with Great Britain. In the first half of the nineteenth century the northern counties had experienced the industrial revolution, and Catholics and Protestants alike had prospered, though not to the same degree. Catholics were still second class citizens, but they faired better than had Catholics in the southern counties. The tenant farmers had a greater degree of security in their land, and factory workers had a better standard of living than workers in the south, although it was still the Protestants who got the better jobs.

Belfast had become a great shipbuilding center, as well as the chief manufacturer of Irish linen goods. Consequently, maintaining the Union was not only vital to the northern counties, but also to Great Britain itself. The Union was also strongly supported by the land owning Protestant aristocracy throughout Ireland.

The Fenians:

In 1858 the Fenians Brotherhood in Ireland was not a majority in the nationalist movement. In fact, it was a rather small minority. It differed from other political organizations in several ways. First of all, it did not try to gain public support by virtue of the prominence of its members. Its membership was secret, and virtually unknown to the public. Secondly, it had but one objective, to achieve national independence, by armed rebellion. Finally, it was not organized and led by prominent men, professional men, or the land owning gentry. It was an organization made up almost entirely by farmers, and working men; clerks and tradesmen. For these reasons they were branded as communists, and lost the support of the Catholic Church. The fact is that they had no common political philosophy at all. Their only goal was Irish sovereignty.

In 1861 the Fenian Brotherhood was severely criticized and condemned by Dublin's Archbishop Cullen. He warned Catholics of the evils of secret societies, apparently forgetting that Christianity, itself, started out as secret societies, and pronounced anyone joining one to be excommunicated from the Church. He also ignored the fact that in 1859 Stephens, at the urging of O'Mahoney, had renounced secrecy, and removed it from the Fenian oath.

Believing as they did, that national independence would never be granted them by Great Britain, they were dedicated to the premise that they could only gain freedom by wresting it from Britain by force. To this end, they were prepared to wait until the time was right; hopefully at a time when The Queen's army would be under pressure from some other part of the empire. Meanwhile, Stephens had promised the American Fenians that there would be a rising by 1865. In preparation for that day, they needed to gain public support, and increase the membership of the brotherhood. **(12)**

The Legendary Ancient Fenians?

The Fenian Legendary Cycle tells us of Finn MacCool, an Irish High King of the third century, and his Fenian guards. The legend has much in common with the legend of King Arthur and the Knights of the Round Table. Their duty was to help maintain the peace among the lesser kings. To become a Fenian was not easy. A Fenian must first be a champion warrior and know the rules of poetry. Then he must swear to four pledges: To choose a wife for her virtue, not her wealth; To never be violent towards a woman; To always help those in need of help; and To never flee from less than ten champions. They, no doubt, represented actual people, but their story was passed down orally for centuries before being written down. Part of it may be factual, but much of it is pure fantasy, created in the minds of the story tellers. It does, however, reflect the codes and the ideals of the Fenian age. **(13)**

The Funeral of Terence Bellew McManus:

In 1861 Terence Bellew McManus died peacefully in San Francisco. As one of the veterans of the 1848 rising and an alumnus of Van Dieman's penal colony, he was a man revered by the American Fenian Society. It was the determination of that group, that this Irish hero should be honored and interred in his native soil. Arrangements were made for his body to be transported to Ireland, and laid to rest in Dublin's Glasnevin Cemetery, along with Daniel O'Connell.

As the remains traveled across North America, Irish Americans turned out by the hundreds, and by the thousands, at every whistle stop station, and prayed for McManus. In New York City thousands more waked the dead Fenian, while Archbishop Hughes bestowed his blessings. In Ireland over one hundred thousand more honored McManus in the city of Cork, and all along the road to Dublin. In that fair city, hundreds of thousands of mourners lined the streets and lanes, as fifty thousand men followed the hearse, swearing to live, and work, and if need be to die for Irish freedom. The great cortege may have surpassed even that of The *"Great Liberator, "* in 1847.

The honors paid to McManus brought the Fenian cause to the limelight and favorably modified the public image that had been created by the disapproval of the Catholic clergy. There was a dramatic increase in men taking the Fenian oath to join the Brotherhood. To O'Mahoney, Stephens claimed an Irish membership of 85,000 men, with another 15,000 sleepers in the British army. So bad was the situation, that many British regiments were considered by their officers to be unreliable. **(14)**

The Irish People Founded:

In 1863, the Fenians established a weekly newspaper, *The Irish People*, with Thomas Clark Luby as the publisher, Jerimiah O'Donovan Rossa as manager, and John O'Leary as the editor. Also on staff was Charles Kickham, who proved to have a talent for turning a phrase. The combined writings of Kickham and Luby proved to be a valuable asset to the Fenian cause. The circulation reached every corner of Ireland, but did not surpass that of its *Young Ireland* predecessor, *The Nation.*

Rising Promised for 1865:

In 1864 Stephens renewed his promise to the American Fenians that there would be a rising in Ireland in 1865 and he was busily making preparations for the occasion. The American Fenians planned shipment of arms for the rising. Unfortunately, due to differing opinions, the arms did not arrive as planned, and the rising was postponed.

The old problem that had plagued Irish conspirators for generations, reared its head again in 1865. Stephens and five others were betrayed by an informer who had infiltrated the staff of the, *The Irish People.* On November 11th, Stephens, John O'Leary, Thomas Luby, Joseph Kickham, Jeremiah O'Donovan Rossa, and John Devoy were all arrested and confined to the Richmond Jail in Dublin. **(15)**

The Escape:

While they were waiting for trial, an inexplicable occurrence took place. The jailors in Richmond had double locked them securely in their cells for the night. Everyone was accounted for. The next morning, however, one of the cells was mysteriously empty. James Stephens had simply departed, with both of the double locks undisturbed. The jailors were dumbfounded. How could this be? James Stephens, the Chief Fenian, had simply disappeared. The jail was in an uproar. England was in an uproar. A manhunt was immediately underway in Ireland, England, and Scotland. Every train, every coach, every ship and boat, was searched. He was nowhere to be found.

The remaining five were tried in December for high treason. The trial was, of course, loaded for the prosecution, as usual, the jury being hand picked. To absolutely no one's surprise, they were found guilty. Because this was his second conviction,

O'Donovan Rossa received a life sentence. Luby and Devoy were both sentenced to twenty years transportation. Both Kickham and O'Leary were released because of poor health.

Several weeks later, in Dublin, a prosperous appearing gentleman boarded a richly appointed coach, drawn by four magnificent white horses, a liveried driver up front and two footmen behind. The coach traveled through Dublin and up the coast to Balbriggan. There the gentleman left the coach, and boarded a small boat, which rowed him to a waiting lugger, in the harbor. Two days later James Stephens stepped ashore safely in France. From there he made his way to America.

The answer to the mystery is obvious today, but apparently not so obvious to the authorities at the time. Stephens had not fled Dublin, as the authorities assumed. He had simply "gone to ground" until things cooled off. It would seem that not only was the army full of Fenians, but the police force, and prison staff, was similarly infiltrated. Even the coach driver and the two footmen were armed Fenians, guarding their Chief. It seems strange that the British authorities, who were so successful at infiltrating informers into the Fenian ranks, never considered the possibility that their opponents were clever enough to do the same thing. But then again, the British actually did not consider that mere Irishmen, especially Catholics, had the mental capacity for successful covert actions.

Ireland was electrified by the news of Stephen's escape. The British were embarrassed. The European community was astounded. The Irish-American community was overjoyed. Stephens became an international hero, and the whole world became aware of the Fenian cause. Meanwhile, the Richmond Jail Superintendent, J.Breslin, and a night watchman, Joseph Byrne, both dedicated Fenians, quietly resumed their duties to the Crown. (16)

The Fenians Invade Canada:

Back in December, the American Fenians, were extremely upset that the rising did not take place, as planned, and held, their own leadership responsible for the postponement. An election was held and O'Mahoney was replaced by a Civil War veteran, a Colonel Roberts. Roberts was a man of action and had a plan for action. Roberts planned to distress the British by invading Canada, a dominion of the British Empire. For this purpose he had the tacit support of some element of the United States Government. The army had sold the Fenians a large supply of ammunition and supplies. Apparently even the customs service was in on the plot. In the summer of 1866, a large Fenian army, led by a former General, John O'Neill, was permitted to cross into Canada, near Buffalo, New York, without incident. The Fenians captured and occupied the British Fort Erie, and on the second, day met and routed a superior British force. They continued to occupy the Fort. About this time, another group of Fenians entered Canada from Vermont, but were easily captured. At this point, someone in the U.S. State Department, or the Army became aware of this unimaginable breech of international relations, and called a halt to it. Both forces were disowned, and forced to withdraw back to U.S. soil, where they were placed under, "technical" arrest.

One must wonder what were the expectations of the American Fenian leadership, from this ill-fated undertaking. Obviously they hoped to put pressure on the British Government; but to what end? In their wildest dreams, they could not have realistically expected the United States Government to have officially supported their actions. They may have hoped to trigger hostilities between the U.S. and Great Britain, but the United States had just fought the Civil War, and was still a nation divided, and weakened. Even with Ulysses S. Grant in the White House, the U.S. could have done little more than apologize to Great Britain. In the end, this could never have been any more than a grand gesture. **(17)**

A New Fenian Chief:

On August 17, 1866, Colonel Thomas Kelly, a veteran of the recent Civil War in America, had been chosen at the IRB convention, in New York, to replace Stephens as Fenian Chief in Ireland, and to lead a nation-wide rebellion, which was scheduled for February 11, 1867. The American Fenians outfitted a ship, the *Erin's Hope,* in Boston and a few dozen Irish-American officers, (Civil War veterans) sailed to Cork, for the purpose of leading the Fenians army in rebellion. Unfortunately, the British had been warned in advance of the plan, and all the officers were arrested in Cork. Their supplies, and arms were confiscated.

Due to this setback, the rising was postponed. Some of the Fenians, in Kerry, did not get word of the postponement, and launched their attack on Chester Castle, as scheduled. The fighting was sporadic, in isolated skirmishes, and failed to achieve its objective.

The Rebellion of 1867:

The rebellion was re-scheduled for March 5th, and the Fenians were prepared in Counties Clare, Tipperary, and Kerry, as well as in the cities of Dublin, Limerick, and Cork. As had happened in the past, the plans were betrayed by an informer, and the British were prepared for the events that were to follow. That in itself was enough to cause failure, but this time even the weather turned against the rebels. A freak snowstorm descended upon the combatants on March 6th. This was the mother of all blizzards, and totally atypical for Ireland. Neither side was prepared for this. It lasted for twelve days, and the country was paralyzed. The fighting ceased. The rebels went home, and the rebellion of 1867 was a bloodless failure. **(18)**

After the weathered-out rebellion, Kelly and his aid, Captain Tim Deasy evaded capture, and with the assistance of the Fenians, made their way to England. The intention was to covertly book passage to the U.S. They remained at large until September 11th, at which time they were betrayed by an informer and arrested near Manchester, England.

While they were being transported to court for trial, the van was stopped by a group of armed Fenians. Having difficulty with the lock, the rescuers decided to shoot the lock off. A policeman, inside the van, was accidentally struck by the shot and died. The rescuers and the prisoners made good their escape. A large manhunt resulted in the arrest of many suspects, non-Fenians, as well as a few Fenians.

The Manchester Martyrs:

The authorities decided that Philip Allen, Michael Larkin and Michael O'Brien looked guilty. They were tried, in the usual way, and, of course found guilty. They were sentenced to death, and hanged in Manchester on November 23rd. They have been long remembered in Irish history as "The Manchester Martyrs." They were three innocent men. **(19)**

An unknown Irish poet composed a lyric that was sung to the tune of a song from the American Civil War, *"Tramp, Tramp, Tramp the Boys Are Marching."*

A Horrible Mistake:

A few weeks after the Manchester incident, another attempt to rescue Fenians from an English prison became a disaster. The plan was to blow a hole in the prison wall to free the prisoners. Unfortunately, the rescuers over estimated the size of the charge needed to do the job. The explosion not only blew a hole in the wall, it totally destroyed it. Twelve people were killed outright, and eighteen others were fatally injured. Parliament was furious, the public was outraged, and the Fenians were branded as murderers and terrorists. This is an image that has persisted in many quarters.

Glory-Oh! To the Bold Fenian Men:

The Fenian Brotherhood declined after these incidents, but it did not disappear. It not only remained, but it evolved. It failed in that it did not achieve Irish independence by force of arms, but it succeeded in that it instilled that same flaming desire in those who came along a little later. Many Irishmen remember it as the Army of the Irish Republic, and recognize it as the model for the Irish Republican Army (IRA). Heroic warriors, struggling against overwhelming odds, but still struggling on. In January 1871, thirty-one Fenian prisoners were released from Van Dieman's Land including John Devoy, Jerimiah O'Donovan Rossa, John O'Leary, and Thomas Luby. Noted Irish poet and composer, Peadar Kearney, wrote of the Fenians in an inspiring work, the *"Soldiers Song, "* which has been Ireland's national anthem since 1926. He also praised them in the following ballad:

"Down by the Glenside, " **(20)**

Down by the glenside, I saw an old woman,
Plucking Young nettles, she ne'er saw me coming,
I listened awhile to the song she was singing,
Glory-Oh, Glory-Oh! To the bold Fenian men.

Some died by the glenside, some died 'midst the stranger,
And wise men have told us their cause was a failure;
But they loved dear old Ireland and never feared danger,
Glory-Oh, Glory-Oh! To the bold Fenian men.

I went on my way, God be praised that I met her,
Be my life long or short, I shall never forget her,
We may have good men, but we'll never have better,
Glory-Oh, Glory-Oh! To the bold Fenian men.

Chapter Sixteen
Home Rule and the Land League
1868-1885

Isaac Butt and the Fenians, William Gladstone, Glastone Challenges the Tithe Problem, The Disestablishment Act, Two Main Issues Remain, The Ulster Custom and the Land, Ireland and Home Rule, Gladstone's First Land Act, The Secret Ballot Act, The Home Rule League, The Election of 1874, Charles Stewart Parnell, Parnell vs. Butt. Michael Davitt, Two Giants Meet, The Land War Begins, Monster meeting in Mayo, The Death of Isaac Butt, More Trouble in Mayo, "A Firm Grip on Your Homesteads, " The Irish National Land League, Davitt Arrested, Parnell Campaigns in America, Trouble in South Ccnnemara, "Katie Bar the Door" The Bold Tenant Farmer, It's Gladstone Again, Still More Trouble in Mayo, The Boycott, The landwar Continues, Feet of Clay, Davitt Imprisoned Again, Trouble in County Sligo Gladstone's Second Land Act, Land Act Inadequate, Parnell Arrested, , The No-Rent Manifesto, The Kilmainham Negotiations, The Phoenix Park Murders, Irish Nationalism, Phoenix Park Incident Solved, Nationalism Gets a Boost, The Franchise Act.

They Made History:

Isaac Butt: Member of Parliament, Irish Party leader, defender of Fenian prisoners.
Charles Stewart Parnell: MP, Attorney, Leader of Irish Nationalism, , "The Chief"
Michael Davitt: MP, Attorney, Follower of Parnell, Founded Land League
William Gladstone: British Prime Minister-(1868-1874) (1880-1894 , Liberal, Friend of
      Irish cause.
Benjamin Disraeli: British Prime Minister-(1874-1880) Conservative.
Douglas Hyde: Advocate of Gaelic culture, Founded Gaelic League.
Catherine O'Shea: Parnell's mistress, and the cause of his downfall.
William O'Shea: Member of Parliament and cuckold husband of Catherine.
John Devoy: Leader of Clan-na-Gael in America
Charles Boycott : Land agent in Mayo and Target of the first incident called a boycott.
Anna Parnell: Sister of Parnell, who boldly headed the Ladies Committee.
Lord Frederick Cavendish: Chief Secretary of Ireland, murdered in Phoenix Park.
Lord Randolph Churchill: Agitator- "Ulster will Fight, and Ulster Will be Right."

Isaac Butt and the Fenians:

In the four or five years following the failed Fenian rising of 1867, it was open season on Fenians. Massive arrests of suspected insurrectionists were routine. Isaac Butt was a seventy-one year old, Anglican, Member of Parliament, leader of the Irish Party, and one of the ablest attorneys available at the time. While not a Fenian himself, he felt compelled to take up the defense of his countrymen. Conviction for high treason was a virtual certainty for the arrested Fenians in a British court. Never-the-less, Butt gave them an eloquent defense, though to little avail. Imprisonment for long terms, followed each trial, most being transported to Van Dieman's land.

Isaac Butt- Leader of the Irish Party in Parliament,
And an admired defender of Fenain insurgents.

Hundreds of Irish soldiers, who supported the Fenians were tried by courts martial for sedition. Butt also defended many of them, with the same pre-determined results. Their convictions also led to long imprisonment, but not until they were first flogged, to unconsciousness, in the military tradition of the times. It has been reported that the barracks yards ran red with their blood from their lashings, but that most still remained defiant of their oppressors.

Through his long effort on behalf of the Fenian prisoners, both civilian and military, Isaac Butt gained a tremendous respect and admiration for his clients. He was impressed by their courage, and devotion to their cause, and their stoicism in the face of their terrible punishments. He found none of them wanting. From that point on, he became an advocate for Irish nationalism, and home rule, for the rest of his life. (1)

William Gladstone:

In 1868, William Gladstone, a recognized leader in the House of Commons, was strongly impressed by the scholarly writings of the English philosopher, John Stuart Mill. Other political writers of the period, wrote much about England's *"Irish Problem."* Mill was the first to put the horse properly "before the cart, " and wrote daringly about Ireland's *"English Problem."* Gladstone, a liberal, was among the first of the English politicians, to recognize the logic of that approach. He soon became the best friend that Ireland ever had, among the English in Parliament. (2)

Gladstone Challenges The Tithe Problem:

In the House of Commons, that year, Gladstone, himself an Anglican, pointed out that the congregation of the Church of Ireland, comprised only one eighth of the total Irish population. With the exception of a very small minority of Scot Presbyterians, the vast majority of the population was Catholic. His point was, that in spite of her claim to being the Church of Ancient Ireland, she was no longer the Church of anything more than a small minority of upper class Anglicans. He challenged its right to establishment as the national church, and to be supported by the tithing of other Christian faiths. (3)

Back in 1831, when the government made it mandatory that all should pay ten percent of their crop, or their income, the result was agrarian riots. In the process, the government spent more collecting the tithe, than they were able to collect. The ensuing riot, at Rathcormac, County Kilkenny, cost nine lives, over a sum of 4 pounds, 16 shillings. Even Daniel O'Connell, himself, had been unable to resolve the issue. In 1838 Parliament made an inept attempt by reducing the tithe twenty-five percent, and charging it to the landlord, who in turn, simply passed it on to the tenant by raising his rent, which was already outrageous.

The Disestablishment Act:

Thirty years later, the problem still persisted. Parliament, however, was moved by Gladstone's eloquence, and the logic of his argument. There was some opposition from the anti-disestablishmentarians in Anglican England, so the issue forced a general election. In 1869, the Church Disestablishment Act was passed, and William Gladstone became Britain's Prime Minister. The Church of Ireland was placed on an equal footing with the other Irish churches, and there was no longer a state religion in Ireland. (4)

Two Main Issues Remain:

Now that the tithe problem was settled, there were two main issues that would dominate Irish politics the next half century. The primary problem was the land issue. The second issue in Ireland was the question of home rule, which would prove to be the more persistent of the two.

The Ulster Custom and the Land:

To all intents, the Irish lived under a feudal system, where the authority of the landlords was all but absolute, and the Irish farmers were merely vassals on land that was stolen from them. Following the "Flight of the Earls" in 1670, Ireland was left without its Gaelic leaders. King James I, who was also King James VI, of Scotland, had a plan for Anglicizing Ulster. Consequently, in 1622 the estates of departed Earls were confiscated, and heavily plantationed by some importing of 13,000 Scots, and Anglican English. These lands became the Counties Armaugh, Cavan, Londonderry, Donegal, Fermanaugh and Tyrone.

These imported tenants, as part of the bargain, were given an interest in their holdings. They had the right to protest eviction, as long as they paid the rent and, if they chose, they had the right to sell their interest in the farm. This arrangement came to be called, "The Ulster Custom, " and soon spread to the southern counties in the provinces of Leinster, Munster, and Connaught. However, it was only a custom, and had no legal standing. As far as the landlords were concerned, the land was theirs, to do with as they pleased. (5)

Ireland and Home Rule:

Even in the early days of the Norman invasion, when Edward I was king, there was a Parliament in Ireland, such as it was. In 1870, Ireland was ruled by an English Parliament, with a small minority of Irish members. Even at the county level, decisions were made by the foreigners. The Irish not only wanted to manage their own domestic affairs, but there was a growing number who wanted nothing less than complete independence. This would become the main thrust of the Fenians and the Irish Republican Brotherhood (IRB).

Gladstone's First Land Act:

Gladstone recognized the land question as an issue that had to be addressed, in the name of justice. As his first attempt to correct this centuries-old injustice, he introduced the Land Act of 1870. This act easily passed through Parliament, and made the Ulster Custom into law. It was intended to protect the tenant from unfair eviction. It had small effect, however, because the rights of the landlord were left unchanged. **(6)**

The Secret Ballot Act:

In 1872, the Irish peasants were empowered by the Passage of the Secret Ballot Act. The landlords had pretty much owned the peasant vote up to this time. The ballot had been public knowledge, and the landlords had the power to coerce their tenants to vote as directed. Once the ballot became secret, the peasants were free to vote their own choice. The result was that Irish conservatives were swept from office, and replaced with liberals who would represent peasant interests. **(7)**

The Home Rule League:

In 1873, Isaac Butt, at seventy-seven, took up the cause of home rule by forming the Home Rule Association, which very shortly was renamed the Home Rule League, with Isaac Butt as its president. The membership was made up of a cross section of the Irish political scene, including Tories, moderates, liberals, landlords, and a few nationalists. They passed a resolution to the effect that the answer to Ireland's problems would be found by the establishment of an Irish Parliament, which would exercise complete control over Irish domestic affairs. There was no assertion for the Repeal of the Union, nor was it their objective to separate from the Empire. **(8)**

The Election of 1874:

In the general election of 1874, the first use of the secret ballot, the Home Rule League became the Home Rule Party, and captured 59 of a total 103 Irish seats in Parliament, including the party leader Isaac Butt. Unfortunately for Ireland, the Liberals did not fair so well, and Gladstone was forced to resign from the office of Prime Minister. He was replaced by the Conservative (Tory) Party leader, Benjamin Disreali.**(9)**

Charles Stewart Parnell:

In 1875, the young, twenty-nine year old, Squire of Avondale, County Wicklow, Charles Stewart Parnell, was elected to Parliament for County Meath. His father was a Protestant landowner. His mother was an American of Irish descent, with a strong will, and a dislike of the English. Her father was Commodore Charles Stewart, of the United States Navy, who fought against the English in the War of 1812, which probably accounted for her anti-English sentiment.

Parnell was educated in English schools, and attended Cambridge University. Parnell was a quiet, and reserved young man, handsome and proud, possessing a passionate love for Ireland. He was a mediocre speaker, but exuded an energy, and self-confidence that inspired other men to follow him. Some historians have compared him with Red Hugh O'Donnell and Owen Roe O'Neill, regarding his ability to command respect and loyalty from his followers. To the poor Catholic tenant and his family, he was akin to old Gaelic tuath chieftains, and with affection, they came to call him, "The Chief." **(10)**

In Parliament, Parnell was greatly impressed by the Party leader, Isaac Butt, and his calm lawyer-like demeanor. Another member, Joe Biggar, an impressive genius of the Land League, was notable for his obstructionist tactics, in the House of Commons. Parnell took a page from Biggar's book and brought the art of filibuster to new heights. He developed a technique of delaying a bill he was opposed to by tying an amendment to it. He would then discuss his amendment at great length, in the greatest detail. Although he could not actually be accused of deliberate filibuster, he was extremely successful, in any event.

Charles Stewart Parnell, a charismatic and inspiring leader,
was idolized by the people, but had feet of clay.

In this manner he was actually able to put an end to the practice of disciplinary flogging in the British army and navy. On another occasion, when Parliament was considering a bill to annex the Transval, in South Africa, Parnell, and six other Irish members, held up action on the bill by continuous speeches for over twenty-six hours. Parnell had little confidence in the Parliament of itself. He placed his confidence in public opinion, and openly advised the Irish electorate to keep a close watch on the doings of their representatives.

Parnell vs. Butt:

Parnell had a great respect for Isaac Butt, but neither did he hesitate to take the opposite side of an issue, if their opinions differed. Parnell, by his manner had gained the respect of most of the Members, but by his tactics he gained the ire of many. As party leader, Butt was once called upon to rebuke Parnell for his obstruction of proceedings. Parnell effectively dismissed Butt with a single, curt reply. These two, strong willed men, were obviously not going to see eye to eye. Butt's approach to Parliament was one of conciliation. Parnell felt that England would never give Ireland anything willingly, but only that which Ireland could compel, "by treading on her toes." **(11)**

Michael Davitt:

Probably Parnell's most devoted follower was Michael Davitt. He was born in County Mayo, in 1846, at the height of the famine, the son of an impoverished tenant farmer. His family, like so many others, was evicted when Michael was only five years old. The family survived the famine, and somehow wound up in Lancashire, England, where his father gained a job as an insurance salesman. At age twelve, Michael had to help support the family by going to work in a cotton mill. He was assigned the job of operating a machine, for which he was too young, untrained, and inexperienced. His right arm became caught in the machinery, and was so badly mangled, it had to be amputated. This resulted in four years of schooling, followed by a job with the local postmaster.

Michael was a very intelligent boy, and made good use of the schooling he was given. He learned to read and write, read widely, and with self study, and a sharp mind, honed his writing skills. He joined the Irish Republican Brotherhood when eighteen years old, and later played a small part in the ill-fated attack on

Chester castle in 1867. By a quirk of fate, this fact was discovered, three years later. He was convicted and sentenced to fifteen years imprisonment at Dartmoor prison, but was released, with a "ticket of leave, " after serving just seven years. (12)

Michael Davitt- From a humble beginning, he became a national leader who made things happen.

In 1878 Davitt went to America to visit his mother, who had emmigrated while he was in prison. It was there that he met John Devoy, the leader of the American Fenians, the *"Clan na Gael"*. He discussed what had come to be called, in Ireland "the new departure, " the concept of uniting the Home Rule movement with the land ownership issue. Devoy agreed with Davitt, but several other leaders did not. However, Devoy and Davitt were free to pursue the matter.

Two Giants Meet:

Davitt and Devoy returned to Ireland where they met with Parnell. Parnell did not agree with them, but he did not disagree either. He did believe the two issues would be stronger together, and he also agreed that Irish farmers should own their own farms.

He did not, however, want to be identified with the new departure at that time. He preferred to just see what he could wring out of Parliament. **(13)**

The Land War Begins:

In 1879 times were bad. There was a poor harvest and the fear of famine stalked the land. The rents had not been reduced by the landlords, and thousands of tenant farmers had been evicted, some because they couldn't pay the landlord his rent, and others for no reason except the landlord wanted the land for another purpose. Agrarian acts of violence had occurred, and the possibility of a land war seemed very real. Two years earlier a notorious, rack-renting landlord, was shot to death in Donegal for sexually molesting a farmers wife and daughter. Another landlord in County Mayo had just recently been executed by a Protestant clergyman, for doubling the rent and imposing other fines on his tenants. More evictions were followed by still more evictions. Tenant cottages were razed, and more land was turned to pasture.

Monster Meeting in Mayo:

Connaught was becoming a tinder box. On April 20, a large public meeting was held in Irishtown, County Mayo, to hear a speaker from Dublin, and several others. It was here that Michael Davitt chose to open his land campaign. It was also from Irishtown that Davitt's family had been evicted back in 1851.

This was a meeting, the likes of which had not been seen, since Daniel O'Connell's monster meetings in 1843. Seven thousand people attended, and special protection was provided for the speakers. Their theme was peasant proprietorship, a distinctly different goal than merely the three Fs. The landlords got the message, and some of them left town. Parliament also got the message and immediately reduced the rents by 25%. **(14)**

The Death of Isaac Butt:

Amid the prospect of all this trouble, Ireland was about to loose one of her great statesmen. Isaac Butt had been in failing health, and had reluctantly retired from politics a few months earlier. He had been a long time defender of the Fenians and advocate of home rule. He loved Ireland, but its been said, he loved the House of Commons, and the Empire, more. He quietly passed away on May 3, 1879, at the age of eighty-five. He died a disappointed old man.

More Trouble in Mayo:

Parnell took a great interest in what was going on in Mayo. He saw this as a great social revolution, and he had always believed that public opinion was stronger than parliamentary procedure. In spite of Butt's warning to him concerning the dangers of large movements, Parnell decided to take a chance, fully realizing that he might be blamed for whatever events may follow his participation. He agreed to speak at a meeting to be held in Westport on June 8, 1879.(15)

"A Firm Grip on Your Homesteads:"

At that meeting he told them that a fair rent must be determine by the times, good, or bad, and that such rents must be insisted upon by the tenants. He told them that they must fight eviction, and forbid the parceling of the land. The phrase that stuck with them was that they must show the landlords their intention, and, *"to hold a firm grip of your homesteads and lands"*... The Land League of Mayo was organized on August 16, 1879 and" Hold a firm grip on your homesteads, " became its slogan. (16)

The Irish National Land League:

On October 21st, Davitt, in concert with Parnell, founded the Irish National Land League, in Dublin. They conceived that it would be a great advantage for the Irish cause, if the three advocating groups could work in unison. Parnell, who was now committed, since the Westport speech, was easily persuaded to accept the league presidency. This had the effect of uniting the land issue with home rule. The third element of the triumvirate, was to be John Devoy. Under his leadership, the American *Clan na Gael,* would provide financial backing for the movement. (17)

Parnell refused to endorse the Irish Republican Brotherhood, but neither did he condemn their methods. He was still hopeful of achieving land ownership, and home rule through the Parliament. As it was, the League had the needed support of the hierarchy of the Catholic Church, and the local priests. That would have been lost to them, had they endorsed the IRB.

Davitt Arrested:

On November 2, 1879, Davitt attended a large meeting in Country Sligo. John Dillon was there, as were a Mr. Daly from Castlebar, and a Mr. Killeen, a lawyer from Belfast. Also present was a Government observer. Davitt, Daly and Killeen all spoke at the meeting, advocating methods of resistance and coercion. Immediately after the meeting Davitt, Daly and Killeen were arrested. They were arraigned in Sligo on charges of sedition and coercion. Trial was set to be held at Carrick-on-Shannon.

The three defendants arrived at Carrick-on-Shannon the day before the trial and held a public meeting. At that meeting, they were good enough to say again, everything for which they had been indicted. This, of course, called for another change of venue, and the trial was rescheduled for Dublin. In Dublin, the case was dropped, and the League had won a small victory.

Parnell Campaigns in America:

Right after Christmas, following the trial fiasco, Parnell and Dillon, departed from Cobh, for the United States. Their mission was to raise support for the Land League, and Irish independence from England. They toured many of the major cities, lecturing, and stressing the importance of land ownership for the Irish farmers, and the "cutting of the last link." In February, through the influence of members of the *Clan na Gael,* Parnell was invited to address the U.S. House of Representatives, in Washington, D.C., espousing the Irish cause. The tour, and the addressing of Congress, were extremely successful, and resulted in the formation of the Irish National Land League of the United States. **(18)**

Trouble in South Connemara:

While Parnell was in the United States the land war continued in Ireland, as landlords increased evictions. Process servers always attracted a crowd, and frequently resulted in an incident. Relief money from America was provided by the Land League. Any farm that was seized, became banned, and no-one dared to replace the evicted tenants. In Southern Connemara, the farms were located on numerous small islands, which were so nearly connected, that one might not realize he was actually on an island.

Here, the landlords imposed unjust fines on several tenants, and raised rents for little reason. These injustices, on top of other problems, and a poor crop, led the farmers to revolt. Process servers accompanied by an armed force, were attacked by farm women and children. In the fray, several of the women were

injured. At this point the men, who had been spectators, joined in,
the police were routed, and several were beaten.

"Katie, Bar the door:"

The farmers were aware that the police would be back, so
they made preparations. Two days later the process server came
again, this time with a force of about two hundred and fifty
policemen. Suddenly the police found themselves surrounded by
two thousand angry, Irish farmers. The trap had been sprung.

Had the police forced the issue, and attempted to serve the
process, the bridge that they would have needed to cross in retreat,
would have been destroyed. Then it would have been a case of
"Katie, bar the door, " and some serious lessons would have been
learned, with heavy losses on both sides. It was fortunate that
discretion prevailed, and the police withdrew. Some lessons were
learned, anyway. **(19)**

An unknown balladeer, inspired by the tenant success,
came up with the following:

The Bold Tenant Farmer

One evening of late out of Bandon I strayed,
And bound for Clankilty I was making my way,
At Balin-a scathy some time I delayed,
For to wet me ould whistle with porter.

Chorus: Hey! Tiddlle le oh to, tiddle le oh to, tiddle le oh to toe tum
Tiddle le oh to, tiddle le oh to tiddle le oh to to tum
Tiddle le oh tah den, tiddle le oh to, tiddle le oh to tum,
Tiddlle le oh dahden doodle le do.

I scarcely had traveled a mile of the road,
When I heard a dispute in a farmer abode;
The son of the landlord, an ill looking toad,
And the wife of the bold tenant farmer.
Chorus:
"A robber, " the bold tenants wife, she replied,
You 're as bad as your daddy on the other side.
But the National Land League will put down your pride,
For they 're able to bear any storm.
Chorus:
Well, I spit in me fist and I picked up me stick.
And up to the coach road like a deer I did rip:
I cared not for bailiffs, landlords, or old nick!
And I sang like a lark in the morning.

It's Gladstone Again:

In March and April of 1880, general elections were held, and Disraeli's Conservative party was swept out, the Liberals again controlled Parliament, and Gladstone was once again the Prime Minister. Thirty Members of the Irish party were returned, and on May 27th they chose to elect Parnell as their party leader. **(20)**

Still More Trouble in County Mayo:

In September, in Lough Mask, County Mayo, things were coming to a boil. Captain Charles Boycott, the agent for Lord Erne, an absentee landlord, had a dispute with his laborers over wages. As a consequence, he fired them all, intending to easily replace them. His first surprise came when he found that no other laborers were available to take their places. Boycott became furious. He decided that if that was the way they were going to play, he would withdraw the rent reductions, to which he had agreed. Those who could not pay would be evicted. The next thing he discovered was that he could find no-one to serve the processes. Neither could he get the blacksmith to shoe his horse, and there was no-one to deliver his mail. His crops were rotting in the fields. He and his family were banned. No-one would even speak to them.

The Boycott:

Boycott appealed to other landowners in Ulster, and was relieved to have fifty volunteer, Orangemen workers sent to him. They were guarded by two thousand members of the Royal Irish Constabulary, (RIC). Upon their arrival in nearby Claremorris, it was discovered that there was not a single car, in running condition, to transport them the fifteen miles to Lough Mask. They had to walk the whole long way, in the rain.

At Lough Mask they encamped on the Captain's lawn, and since there were no provisions for them, ate the Capitan's live stock. They did manage to get the crop in alright, but at a cost to the government, above and beyond the personal losses of Boycott, of roughly ten pounds sterling, for every pound's worth of crops harvested. The agent inadvertently had lent his name to a new form of socio-economic coercion. **(21)**

The Catholic Church, in Rome was quick to condemn the process of "Boycotting, and coercion. It is interesting to note, that the Catholic bishops in Ireland, for once, disagreed with Rome.

Parliament on the other hand, was quick to agree with Rome, by passing a new Conspiracy Act. By the terms of this new act, the entire nation was declared an unlawful assembly.

The Land War Continues:

In other cases, where legal means were sought, and the facts were made public, the landlords generally came out the losers. The Land League established a system of courts which exercised more control than the courts of the government itself. In hundreds of cases, when tenants were evicted, the Land League was able to assure that the land remained without new tenants, and without profit. Huts were constructed to house evictees, and the needed food and supplies were provided by money from America.

Feet of Clay:

In Parliament, Parnell had become acquainted with Captain William O'Shea, of the Irish Party, and a Member of Parliament from County Clare. O'Shea became one of Parnell's followers, and a close associate. In 1880, in the course of this relationship, Parnell was introduced to O'Shea's lovely wife, Catherine, and he was quite taken with her. Over a period of time, as they became further acquainted, it turned out Catherine was somewhat taken with Parnell. Ultimately, and unfortunately, nature took its course, they fell in love, and began an adulterous affair.

It wasn't long before Captain O'Shea became aware of what was going on. Being a prudent, and resourceful man, O'Shea said nothing, and pretended that all was well. He was also an ambitious man, and it occurred to him that the affair might be useful to his political advancement. Another factor was that Catharine had an aunt, who was both wealthy, and in poor health. Her passing was expected to bring considerable inheritance to O'Shea. The cuckold husband continued to play the fool. **(22)**

Davitt Imprisoned Again:

In February of 1881, following the Boycotts, and violence, several leaders of the of the Land League were arrested, including Davitt. This possibility had been foreseen by Davitt, and he had made provision for it by establishing the Ladies Committee of the Land League, headed by Parnell's sister, Anna. The trial lasted for about a month. The crown had a weak case, and was out maneuvered by the defense. Davitt, as a "previous felon, " had been at liberty by means of a ticket of leave. This was immediately cancelled and he was returned to prison. Parnell, and his followers in Parliament, were suspended from the House of Commons, and forcibly ejected.(23)

Trouble in County Sligo:

Under the oversight of the Committee, which was now the Ladies Land League, land courts continued to be held, and Boycotting continued, supported by funds from the American Land League. Landlords continued with increased tenant evictions. This led to more violence. "Grabbers, who attempted to replace evicted tenants, were shot. In a confrontation, in County Sligo, police, protecting a process server, fired into an angry crowd. Two civilians were killed, as was the police sergeant, who gave the order to fire. The rest of the police officers barely escaped with their lives. Finally, Parliament realized that their tactics were doomed to failure. A new approach to the land issue was needed. (24)

Gladstone's Second Land Act:

Gladstone, for the second time, addressed the land issue, in The Land Act of 1881. This was easily passed, and assured the tenants the protection of what was referred to as, "The Three Fs:"
1. Fair rents, (reduced by 20%, with another reduction in 15 years)
2. Fixity of tenure, and
3. Free sale.

This time a special land court was established to assure that the provisions of the Act were, in fact, adhered to. Parnell favored acceptance of the Land Act, with certain amendments. Many of the Land League leaders agreed with him, but not all. (25)

Land Act Inadequate:

Others were not quite satisfied with the "Three Fs." They felt that provisions should be made to enable the tenant farmers to actually become the owners of the land. In practice, the Land Act proved to be riff with compromises favoring the landlords, at the expense of their tenants. Evictions continued in spite of the Three Fs. In the end, Parnell refused to endorse Gladstone's act, and agrarian violence continued unabated. It seemed certain that Parnell would now be arrested. A friend asked him, that if he were arrested, who would take his place?

Parnell quietly replied, "Captain Moonlight!" **(26)**

Parnell Arrested:

On October 13th, Parnell was arrested, under the Coercion Act, and charged with the land war violence. Even though he was not personally involved with the violence, Parnell was sent to Kilmainham gaol without a trial. Over night, he became more than just "The Chief." He became a national hero.

The "No-Rent" Manifesto:

On October 18, 1881, the Land League issued a No-Rent Manifesto, which had been signed by Parnell, Davitt, Dillon, Brennan, and Sexton. It specified that absolutely no rent was to be paid by tenants, until such time as the government abandoned terrorism, and restored the people's rights. The government replied by proclaiming the Land League an illegal organization, and banning it, by force, if need be. **(27)**

The "Kilmainham Negotiations:"

Anarchy ruled the land, as the land war intensified. Finally, after seven months Gladstone took a bold step. The British Prime Minister personally traveled to Kilmainham gaol to negotiate with Parnell. Under the circumstances, the negotiations were informal, and the agreement was unwritten. But the two men had a mutual respect for one another, and agreement was sealed by a handshake.

Parnell agreed to support the Land Act, and to use his influence to end the land war, and Gladstone agreed that the imprisoned Land League leaders would be released, and that the tenant's rent arears would be waived. Parnell, and the others were released from Kilmainham on May 2, and Davitt from Portland a few days later. **(28)**

The Phoenix Park Murders:

Four days after Parnell and the others were released from prison, a horrible crime was committed and public opinion was horrified. The newly appointed Chief Secretary of Ireland, Lord Frederick Cavendish, and the Under Secretary, Mr. T. H. Burke, while walking in Phoenix Park for a breath of air, were set upon, and murdered in a gruesome and bloody manner by several members of a small break-away group of the Irish Republican Brotherhood, IRB, calling themselves the *"Invincibles."* The assailants used surgical knives for the murder weapons, the bloody scene paralyzed the public perception.

Parnell wrote to Gladstone immediately, and offered his complete resignation from the political scene, as a gesture of his rejection and his abhorrence of such a monstrous act. Gladstone, of course, refused the offer. **(29)**

Irish Nationalism:

In October 1882, the Irish National League was founded in Dublin, as a successor to the proclaimed Land League. This was soon followed by the founding of the Irish National Leagues of America, as a successor to the American Land League. Irish nationalism was further reinforced by the 1883 founding of The Gaelic League, promoting Irish national pride through the revival of the Irish language, wherever it was still spoken. and campaigning for it as the national language of the country.

A year later, The Gaelic Athletic League was founded in Thurles, for the avowed purpose of replacing English sports with Irish sports. This would prove to be fertile ground for recruiting members to the Irish Republican Brotherhood, as English soldiers and policemen had banned from membership, by the governmant0.

Phoenix Park Incident Solved:

In January 1883, the police arrested twenty-seven known members of the brotherhood, as suspects for the act. One of the suspects turned Queen's evidence and implicated six others who had participated in the murder. Four of these men were executed, and two were transported to a penal colony for life. The Queen's informer was smuggled out of the country and released, only to be executed by a gunman from the *Invincibles,* who, in turn, was apprehended and hanged in Newgate prison in December. **(30)**

Nationalism Gets a Boost:

Two things occurred in late 1884 that had a major impact on future Irish politics. In November the Gaelic Athletic Association was founded in Thurles, and in December Parliament passed the Franchise Act. The lasting effect would be an indelible sense of Irish nationhood.

The Gaelic Athletic Association was founded by a school teacher named Michael Cusak, and an associate, Maurice Davin, who became its first president. Its purpose was to replace the English game of Cricket, with the traditional Gaelic games of hurling and Gaelic football. The Irish loved sports, and this de-Anglicization had a profound effect in revitalizing Irish pride. This also provided a fertile recruiting source for the Irish Republican Brotherhood, especially since the government had banned English soldiers and policemen from participation. **(31)**

The Franchise Act:

Parliament's passing a new Franchise Act for Ireland, extended the vote from the towns and cities to the rural areas. This enfranchised over 500,000 new Irish voters, bringing the total number to roughly 700,000. This would cause a significant difference in the outcome of the general election to be held the following year, and provide a revitalization for home rule.

Chapter Seventeen
The Gaelic Resurgence and the Orange Thorne
1885-1914

Ulster Will Fight, The Landlord's Dilemma, A New Beginning, The "Mud Cabin" Vote, Gladstone and Parnell Fight for Home Rule, Gladstone's First Home Rule Bill, Parnell Libeled, Parnell Cleared of All Charges, Trouble Brings More Trouble, The Downfall and Death of Parnell, Ireland After Parnell, Land Question Settled, The Balfour Act, Unrest in Ulster, The Gaelic League, Gladstone's Second Home Rule Bill, Gladstone Retires, The Election of 1895, Arthur Griffith and the United Irishmen, The National Literary Theatre Society, The Countess Cathleen, Cathleen ni Houlihan, Four Green Fields, Irish National Dramatic Society, The Abbey Theatre, Home Rule Not Viable, The Wyndham Act, Peasant Proprietors, Life for the Urban Poor, A Parallel Situation, The Ulster Unionist Council, Sinn Fein Founded, The Election of 1906, The Irish Party Holds the Balance of Power, The Parliament Act, Home Rule vs. Rome Rule, Carson Leads Unionist Party, Carson Threatens Secession, Churchill Responds, The Orange Covenant, Home Rule- Strike One! Home Rule- Strike Two! Connolly Forms Citizen's Army, MacNeill Forms the Irish Volunteer Force, The Curragh Mutiny, Gun Running in Ulster, Home Rule-Strike Three!

They Made History:

Herbert Henry Asquith: British Prime Minister 1908-1916
Arthur Balfour: British Prime Minister 1902 to 1906
Sir Edward Carson: Led Unionist Party, 1910-21, Opposed partition/ home rule,
Winston Churchill: First Lord of the Admiralty, Tried to assert law during the Ulster rebellion.
Lord Randoph Churchill: British Tory party leader and agitator.
James Connelly: Labor organizer, formed The Citizen Army,
Michael Cusak: Founder of the Gaelic Athletic Association.
William Gladstone: Liberal Prime Minister of Britain, , off and on, 1868 to 1898.
Lady Gregory: Writer, and Supporter of the Gaelic League
Arthur Griffith: Publisher of "United Irishmen" Founded Sinn Fein, Advocated complete separation of Britain and Ireland
Douglas Hyde: Co-founder of the Gaelic League. President of Sinn Fein, Became President of Ireland in 1938
James Joyce: Revered Irish poet and author.
Pedar Kearny: Composer of "The Soldier's Song" (National Anthem after 1926)
James Larkin: Founder of the Irish Transport and General Workers Union.
Eoin Mac Neill Member of Parliament, , Co-Founder of the Gaelic League,
Sean O'Casey: Controversial Irish playwrite, defended by W.B.Yeats
John Redmond: Successor to Parnell as leader of the Irish liberal party.
William Butler Yeats: Irish Poet and Play-write Author of "Cathline ni Houlihan"

"Ulster Will Fight"…:

In February 1885, Tory Leader, Lord Randolph Churchill, speaking to a crowd of Protestants in Belfast, "Played the Orange card, " by stirring them to resist home rule, in a famous speech in which he used the phrase, "Ulster will fight, and Ulster will be right." He pitted Protestants against Catholics, attributing the plan for home rule to the Catholics. He ignored the fact that many of the Irish leaders advocating home rule, Tone, Emmet, Davis, Butt, and Parnell, were, themselves, all Protestants. (1)

He was, however, very successful in his purpose. His Ulster audience took his words to heart and went right out and fought. They fought the first Catholics they could find. Many people were killed on both sides, but it was the minority group who suffered the most. The police were unable to control the situation. Ultimately, the military had to be called in to restore an uneasy peace. Gladstone feared a split in the Liberal party would adversely affect his plan to introduce a home rule bill.. (2)

The Landlords' Dilemma:

In 1885 the landlords felt that they were loosing too much interest in their holdings. In a three year period, following the Land Act, the fair rents the government had imposed had cost them a loss of 20%. The landlords despaired, feeling that the government was not backing them up. They appealed to Parliament for relief. They had begun to favor land purchase by the government, believing that it would be better to sell, with favorable terms, than to contend with dual ownership with the peasants, and a gradual chipping away of their assets, only to loose it all in the end anyway.

A New Beginning:

One good effect of the Ulster rioting turned out to be the willingness of Parliament to pass the Ashborne Act, which provided government assistance to the tenant farmers in purchasing their farms. The government hoped to divert some pressure from the home rule issue, by giving something to the newly enfranchised farmers. While this Act fell far short of those expectations, it did enable some farmers to ultimately purchase their land. It also fell short of what the landlords had hoped for, but it was better than nothing. It might even be considered the beginning of the end, of the land war. (3)

The "Mud Cabin" Vote:

The first general election, following the Franchise Act of 1884, was held in November and December of 1885. The Liberals won a victory in Britain, but the newly enfranchised "mud cabin" vote was an overwhelming turning point for Parnell's Irish Party. The Liberal Whigs got 335 seats and the Conservative Tories 249. Parnell's Irish Party captured 86 seats, giving them the deciding minority. Parnell delivered the votes needed by the Liberals, and Gladstone, once again, became Prime Minister, forming his third administration in January of 1886. (4)

Gladstone and Parnell fight for Home Rule:

Gladstone, at the age of seventy-six, now began the fight of his political career; the fight to give the Irish home rule. Parnell, who fought alongside Gladstone, was realistic enough to stop short of demanding independence. He knew that the British fear of eroding of the Empire could not allow independence. Parnell became an advocate for a subordinate Irish Parliament, feeling certain that Independence would be the eventual outcome.

Gladstone's First Home Rule Bill:

Meanwhile, in the midst of all this, Gladstone had introduced a home rule bill in the House of Commons in April of 1886. This provided more fuel for the violent rioting in Belfast, by the Protestants, who feared being controlled by a Dublin Parliament. As he and Parnell had concurred, it provided an Irish Parliament, subject to the control of Westminster and the Crown. In spite of their best efforts, Gladstone's worst fears were realized. Ninety-three Liberals, fearing a dismemberment of the Empire, went over to the other side, in June, and voted against it. It was defeated 342 to 311. In a general election in July, Gladstone was defeated, and Salisbury's Conservatives again took over control. This provided a shot in the arm for the Northern Irish Protestants, and the Orange order revitalized. The rioting in the North resumed and continued through the summer and fall. (5)

Parnell Libeled:

At this particular time, *The London Times* published a series of articles accusing Parnell of direct complicity in several agrarian murders, particularly the responsibility for the Phoenix Park murders, and general advocacy of physical insurrection. Parnell demanded a select committee from Parliament to investigate the allegations. The government went one better, and appointed a special commission of three judges for the job. The investigation continued, and finally, in February of the next year, Richard Piggott, a down and out journalist, who was always looking for a way to make a few quid, offered his services to the government as a witness, for the paltry sum of 1,500 pounds.

Piggott had produced the incriminating letters which had been published in *The Times.*

Parnell Cleared of All Charges:

These letters appeared to be less than credible to the defense, who then proceeded to break the witness down, and proved the letters to be forgeries. After three years under a cloud, The High Court Commission finally cleared Parnell of all charges. In the eyes of the public, the "Chief" was practically sanctified. The entire House of Commons cheered for him, even his enemies. Piggott, disgraced below even his standards, fled to Spain, and in a room, in a cheap Madrid hotel, took his own life. **(6)**

Trouble Brings More Trouble:

In the years between 1882 and 1884, Catherine O'Shea had borne three children, attributed to Parnell. Captain O'Shea had kept his own counsel and maintained the public illusion, that he was the father. In 1885, he had resigned his seat in Parliament, and he no longer anticipated a bequest from Catherine's aunt, as she had died without making any such arrangement. Now in the spring of 1889 he had had enough of being the cuckold, and filed for divorce, charging her with adultery. In November he named Parnell as correspondent. **(7)**

The Downfall and the Death of Parnell:

Parnell's indiscretion proved to be his downfall. In Catholic Ireland, such a betrayal could not be taken lightly. At first, Parnell's Irish party supported him, but soon a split occurred. Most of his own party, the non-conforming liberals, the conservatives and the Catholic Church denounced him as unfit for public office. Parnell refused to resign. In failing health he made a gallant effort to regain support, but public opinion had turned against him.

In May 1891, Parnell married Catherine, in a civil ceremony. Five months later, on October 6th, he died quietly in Brighton, England, at the age of forty-five years. Mourned by friends and adversaries alike, over 200,000 Dubliners lined the route to Glasnevin Cemetery to say goodbye to "The Chief." Two-thousand members of the Gaelic Athletic Association followed his coffin, carrying hurling sticks on their shoulders, draped with black ribbon. What might have been for Ireland, we can only imagine. **(8)**

Ireland After Parnell:

One might well assume that the loss of Parnell had a terrible impact upon the dream for an Irish nation. The spirit of nationalism was weakened considerably by the loss of his leadership, and the disillusionment of the young Irishmen, who had placed him on a pedestal, caused many to turn away from party politics entirely. They needed to find some other dreams to sustain them. Some turned to religion, some to poetry and some turned to Celtic mythology. Others expressed their heritage through literature, Celtic sports, and traditional music and dance. A few sought their dream in a bottle.

Land Question Settled:

The decade of the 1890s was a comparatively good time for the Irish farmer, following the Ashborne Act of 1885, which enabled, at least some, farmers to purchase their farms. Life, for the farmers, still wasn't easy, but it was certainly better, and there was, at last, some hope for the future. Life was also good for the Irish ascendancy. There was no agrarian agitation, and no violence. Irish nationalism, and thoughts of home rule were, temporarily eclipsed. There seemed to be a general acceptance of the fact, that Ireland was part of the British Empire. **(9)**

The Balfour Act:

John Redmond succeeded Parnell as the leader of the Irish liberal party. He was instrumental in securing the passage of the Balfour Act, thereby creating issues of land stock, backed by the British Treasury, to be issued to the selling landlords. This Act further enhanced the Ashborne Act and provided the needed incentive to persuade the landlords to sell their holdings. **(10)**

Unrest in Ulster

In mid-June 1892, with a general election coming up, the orange unionists held a convention in Belfast. Twelve thousand delegates, from the nine counties of Ulster, voted enthusiastically to reject any form of a home rule parliament. As they feared, in the July election the Liberals gained a majority, and Gladstone began his fourth term as Prime Minister. Home rule would, most surely, be on his agenda.

The Gaelic League:

The Gaelic Athletic Association, founded in 1885, gave rise to the founding of the Gaelic League in 1893, advocating the revival of the Irish language and Irish literature. Douglas Hyde, a Protestant linguistic scholar and Eoin MacNeill, a Member of Parliament, founded the League with avowed purpose of promotion of Irish national pride, through the survival of the Irish language, customs and dress. The ultimate goal was a resurrection of Irish, as the national language of the country. **(11)**

The League was supported by Lord Ashborne, who was the league president, and Lady Gregory, the widow of Sir William Gregory, who had been a distinguished government administrator. In the short span of one year, the league's membership soared to over fifty-thousand, (50,000) members, with five hundred and ninety-three (593) chapters. One could also reasonably assume that a member of the Irish Republican Brotherhood was, as a matter of course, a member of the Gaelic League. **(12)**

The inspiration of Parnell's leadership was not lost, in spite of his fall from grace. Irish nationalism did not die, but merely slept. The dream for home rule still survived, and even prosperity and proprietorship could not put it under. In time, it would reawaken as an unquenchable passion for total Irish independence.

Gladstone's Second Home Rule Bill:

In February of 1893, in the midst of this Gaelic revival, Gladstone introduced a second home rule bill in the House of Commons. This, of course, led to more bloody rioting in Belfast in April. With a liberal majority it was easily passed in Commons by a vote of 301 to 267, in early September, only to meet an insurmountable roadblock a week later in the House of Lords, with a vote of 419 to 41 against it.

Gladstone Retires:

Prime Minister Gladstone, affectionately known to the Irish as "The Grand old Man, " was now eighty-four years old. He had fought the good fight, but was now worn out. He realized that home rule would never be approved by the House of Lords. In March, he finally called it "quits' and retired in 1894, a disappointed old man. He had been the best English Prime

Minister that Ireland had ever known. Lord Rosebery became the new Prime Minister. **(13)**

The Election of 1895

In the general election in June, the liberal Whig party split into several segments, thereby giving the conservative Tories a sweeping victory. Lord Salisbury took over from Lord Rosebery, as Prime Minister, and the new lineup in Commons became Conservatives 340, Liberals 177, Liberal Unionists 71, and Irish Nationalists 82. **(14)**

Arthur Griffith and the *United Irishmen:*

In March 1899, Arthur Griffith published the first issue of *The United Irishmen.* It featured a collection of articles advocating deAnglicization of Irish politics and culture. He advocated a complete political and economic separation from Britain. His basic premise, simply stated, was that the Act of Union of 1800 was an illegal act and should therefore be nullified. **(15)**

The National Literary Theatre Society:

In May 1902, the National Literary Theatre Society, inspired by the Gaelic League, was founded by William Butler Yeats, and Lady Gregory. Yeats was a young Irish poet and writer, first published in the Dublin University Review in 1885. He met Lady Gregory in 1896, through a mutual friend. They were both enthralled by the tales of the mystical age and established an instant rapport. They established a working relationship, exchanged ideas, and even collaborated on some stories of ancient Celtic Ireland, involving Oisin, and Cuchulain. This marked the beginning of an Anglo-Irish Literary revival, a non-political movement that would have lasting influence on Irish politics.

The Countess Cathleen:

One of the first plays they produced in the Literary Theatre was Yeats' *The Countess Cathleen.* The play's suggestion, that an Irish person might even consider making a deal with the devil, so offended Irish morality, politics and religion, that performances required police protection to prevent riots.

Cathleen ni Houlihan:

Yeats' most politically significant work, *Cathleen ni Houlihan,* was presented in 1902, with Maud Gonne in the title role. It is the story of an old woman, calling upon her children to help her recover what strangers have taken from her. It is a parable, wherein the old woman is the personification of Ireland. She had four green fields, one of which had been stolen from her. The fields are the provinces of Ulster, Leinster, Munster and Connaught. When news arrived of the French forces landing at Killala, the old woman suddenly became a young girl, with "the walk of a queen."

Cathleen ni Houlihan was a powerful work which had a profound effect upon the audience. It was nearly sacramental to young Irishmen, who rushed to join the Volunteers, the IRA, or Sinn Fein. The story is timeless and partition has currently been denounced, in a song composed by Tommy Makem, with the title:

Four Green Fields **(16)**

What did I have? said the fine old woman,
What did I have? This proud old woman did say,
I had four green fields, each one of them a jewel,
'Til strangers came and tried to take them from me,
I had strong fine sons, who fought to save my jewels,
They fought and died, and that was my grief, said she.

Long, time ago, said the fine old woman,
Long time ago, this fine old woman did say,
There was war, and death, and plundering and killing,
My children died, on mountain, valley and sea,
And their wailing cries, they shook the very heavens,
My four green fields ran red, with their blood, said she

What have I now? said the fine old woman,
What have I now? This proud old woman did say,
I have four green fields, one of them's in bondage,
In strangers hands, that tried to take it from me,
But my sons had sons, as brave as were their fathers,
My fourth green field will bloom again, said she.

Irish National Dramatic Society:

In December 1902 the Irish National Dramatic Society, with Yeats as president, replaced the Literary Theater. Both Yeats and Lady Gregory became directors of the theatre, producing dramas that reflected the Irish culture, and inspired a national Irish identity.

The Abbey Theatre:

The most successful collaboration, of Yeats and Lady Gregory was the founding of the Abbey Theatre in 1904. In the Abbey, the works such writers as James Joyce, Oscar Wilde, John Millington Synge, Brandan Behan, Sean O'Casey, George Farquar, and Oliver Goldsmith, were performed. The Abbey also boasted some of the world's finest actors, such as Sara Allgood, F.J. McCormick, Arthur Sinclair, Arthur Shields, Barry Fitzgerald, and Maud Gonne. As of 1924, the Abbey has been subsidized by the Irish government, and even though the old Abbey was destroyed by fire in 1951, the new, present day Abbey, still entertains, and educates the public in an old, ongoing tradition. **(17)**

Home Rule Not Viable:

On June11, 1902, the Independent Orange Order formed in Belfast. In the July 12, 1902 Lord Salisbury's liberal party was defeated, by the conservatives and Arthur James Balfour became the new Prime Minister. At this point, the concept of Nationalism was popular in Ireland, but was at low ebb politically. Home rule was dead in the water.

The Wyndham Act:

In 1903, the Secretary of Ireland, Mr. George Wyndham was the moving force for an Act which provided bonuses for landlords willing to sell, and also made possible easy terms for 250,000 tenants to purchase the land, making interest free payments over a period of sixty-eight years. The interest was charged to the Imperial Exchequer, and overseen by an Irish Land Commission Court. It proved effective, as entire estates changed hands. **(18)**

Peasant Proprietors:

At last the farmers would be able to realized the benefits of their labor. They would no longer be plagued by unfair rents, and threats of eviction. They could, at last, make improvements to their farms, without being penalized for their effort. They could benefit from having a good crop, without their rent being raised. The land war was finally over. Ireland would become a land of peasant proprietors.

Life for the Urban Poor:

Home rule was not high on the priority list of the general population. Of course the people in the rural areas were doing better now, and most farm families had enough to eat, but survival was still their main concern. They had potatoes, and milk, so at least they were well nourished. Some even had eggs, and butter, and an occasional piece of mutton, or beef for protein. They were comparatively well nourished. In the larger urban areas, such as Dublin, Limerick, and Cork the situation was not as bright. Dublin for example, undoubtedly had the worst fed, worst housed, and most underpaid population in Europe. There were over 2,100 families surviving in one room, tenement apartments. Their main diet would consist of black tea and dry dark bread. Wages were low and unemployment was high. What little money, some of them may have come by, frequently did not get past the pub. These Irish were not concerned with politics, culture, literary revival or the Abbey Theatre.

A Parallel Situation:

In 1904, Arthur Griffith published *The Resurrection of Hungary,* in *The United Irishmen* relating how Hungary won its independence from the Austrian Empire. The situation was remarkably similar to Ireland's own relationship with the British Empire. **(19)**

The Ulster Unionist Council:

The Orange Protestants were getting restless in Belfast. In March, 1905, they established The Ulster Unionist Council, to oppose Home Rule. This resulted in parades and minor skirmishes. Catholic neighborhoods were targeted.

Sinn Fein Founded:

On November 28, 1905, Arthur Griffith combined his *Clan na Gaeldheal* with the *Dungannon Club*, forming a new organization, with a new doctrine, Sinn Fein, (Ourselves Alone). The basic advocacy of the organization was, that Ireland must stand by its own institutions, and boycott all foreign institutions. Griffith proposed that the Members of Parliament, elected by the Irish population, should withdraw from Parliament, and form its own governing body in Dublin, ruling with the consent, and the cooperation of the governed. Griffith's paper, *The United Irishmen* would be renamed, *Sinn Fein.* **(20).**

The Election of 1906:

In 1905 Balfour resigned as Prime Minister and was succeeded by Sir Henry Campbell-Bannerman. In the general election of 1906 the liberals, under, Campbell-Bannerman's leadership, won a landslide victory of a 106 majority over all other parties. Unfortunately for the Irish party, the liberals had a distinct majority without Irish support, consequently they had no reason to take the risky road of supporting home rule, and no chance of it getting past the House of Lords veto, if they did. Home rule was, politically, a dead issue. Redmond was astute enough to remain an ally of the liberals, in spite of their abandonment of home rule. **(20)**

Irish Party Holds Balance of Power:

In 1908, Herbert Henry Asquith became Prime Minister, and introduced a number of social reform legislations, which involved significant tax increases, especially among the more affluent. The "Peoples Budget, " as it was called, passed the House of Commons, but was vetoed by the House of Lords.

The Parliament Act:

In 1911 Asquith introduced the Parliament Act, a bill that would limit the veto of the House of Lords to two years. The House of Lords, of course, opposed the bill and threatened to veto it, but the liberals had a trump card to play. It seems that only the House of Commons had the power to create new peerages, and they threatened to create many new ones, unless the Lords agreed to the veto bill. New peerages would dilute their power, and most certainly dilute their wealth, so in August, the Parliament Act passed the House of Lords. By its terms, any future act passed by the House of Commons, three successive times, and vetoed by the House of Lords, three successive times, would automatically become law. **(22)**

"Home Rule vs. Rome Rule:"

The northern Protestants were seriously alarmed. They realized that home rule would be introduced again, and the position of the House of Lords had been weakened by opposition to the "Peoples Budget." They began holding rallies to oppose it, using the slogan, " Home rule means Rome rule."

Carson Leads Unionist Party:

They found a champion in the newly elected Tory leader of the Unionist party. Sir Edward Carson, a Dublin lawyer, not only opposed home rule, but strongly opposed the separation of Ulster. He wanted things to remain just as they were, with all of Ireland intact, as a part of Great Britain. Embittered by past political reversals, he became increasingly reckless, making it plain, that there was no length, to which he would not go, including civil war, to maintain the status quo. (23) In December 1910, Asquith called for a general election on the issue. The liberals won the election, but with a reduced majority. The budget bill passed, only with the support of Redmond's Irish party. The Irish, once again, held the balance of power. Asquith agreed to introduce home rule, but first, some changes would be required in the House of Lords.

Carson Threatens Secession:

In spite of his opposition to partition, Carson ran a bluff, threatening the separation of all nine counties of Ulster if Home Rule were passed. He was aware that he had only a slight Protestant majority in six counties, and most likely Donegal, Fermanagh and Cavan Counties would not go along. However, he felt certain that John Redmond would not accept partition, and would give up the idea of home rule. One can well imagine how this news was received in Ulster, with more riots and demonstrations. In January 1912, actions were taken in preparation of organizing a military force, to be called the Ulster Volunteer Force (UVF).(24) Remembering Carson's threat of secession of the nine counties, John Redmond, and the First Lord of the Admiralty, Sir Winston Churchill went to Belfast in February to address a large crowd in Celtic Park. The were met with hostility, shouted down, threatened with mob violence, and burned in effigy.

Churchill Responds:

Churchill did not take this treatment lightly, and he was determined that Ulster would obey the law. On March 11, he order the Royal Navy's Third Battle Squadron to hold naval exercises within sixty miles of the Ulster coast as a subtle hint of possible blockade. He also prompted the Military Commander-in-Chief in Ireland, Sir Arthur Paget, to make preparations to enforce the law in Ulster. Paget protested, but was counseled to comply. He did so reluctantly. In a speech on the fourteenth, Churchill spoke of Carson in terms of a "treasonable conspiracy," and accused Carson of pursuing a sinister and revolutionary purpose. **(25)**

Political matters in Belfast were temporarily eclipsed in April by the tragic sinking of the *Titanic,* on her maiden voyage, with the loss of 14,000 lives. The *Titanic* had been built in Belfast, for the White Star Line, by the Harland and Wolff shipyards. This loss hit pretty close to home for Belfast.

The Orange Covenant:

In September, the Orange Protestants of Belfast drafted a "Solemn League and Covenant, " whereby subscribers would vow to resist by any means necessary, to defeat the home rule conspiracy. This covenant was quickly signed by over 200, 000 men, who pledged that they would refuse to recognize the authority of any Irish home rule Parliament established in Dublin. Carson even went so far as to set up a provisional government of Ulster, to commence the day home rule became effective. This actually amounted to an act of treason, in as much as they were loyal to the crown, only as long as they got things their way. **(26)**

Home Rule- Strike One!:

In January of 1913, Asquith kept his word, and introduced a home rule bill in Parliament. It easily passed Commons but, of course, was vetoed by the House of Lords on January 30th. Strike one! The Unionists, in Ulster, reacted strongly to this development The very next day, senior retired British Officers completed the formal organization of the Ulster Volunteer Force (UVF), and by the end of March it numbered 100, 000 men. Carson reiterated that home rule would not be recognized in Ulster,

Home Rule- Strike Two!:

The home rule bill was introduced again in July, was passed in Commons, and vetoed by the Lords. Strike two! The Unionists could read the writing on the wall. By September 24th preparations were completed to establish the Provisional Government of Ulster in the event that home rule became the law. This government was to be backed up by the Ulster Volunteer Force, and Civil war was seen as a distinct possibility. The British Government, however, did not perceive Carson's treasonous actions as a threat to the Empire. **(27)**

Connolly Forms The Citizen's Army:

A labor dispute for better wages, and conditions involving the Irish Transport General Worker's Unions, led by union leader James Larkin, grew into a conflict between management and the Tramway workers in late August and early September. There was a strike, which resulted in a prolonged lock-out. The lock-out meant no wages at all, resulting in many people going very hungry. Before it was over, there was a baton charge by the Dublin police, resulting in several injuries. This resulted in James Connolly, a union organizer in Belfast, being recalled to Dublin, along with an associate who was a former British Army officer. Connolly lost no time in forming a citizen's army consisting of 200 men, to protect member workers from future police aggression. They began drilling by mid November. **(28)**

MacNeill Forms the Irish Volunteer Force:

A week following the formation of the Citizen's Army, saw the formation of the Irish Volunteer Force, by Member of Parliament, Eoin MacNeill. At this point both Connolly and MacNeill viewed their military groups as peace keeping forces, for the protection of Ireland. The idea of an insurrection was not part of their agenda.

While the Citizen's Army was composed of working union members, the Volunteer Force became a matter of strong interest to former Fenian, Tom Clarke, and Sean MacDermott of the Sinn Fein. Clarke, recently returned from America, had become the moving force in revitalizing the Irish Republican Brotherhood (IRB). Joined by Patrick Pearse, Joe Plunkett, Thomas Mac Donaugh, and others, the Irish Volunteers would become increasingly under the influence, and control of the Brotherhood, which advocated Irish independence through the use of force.

The Curragh Mutiny:

In early 1914, Carson was aggressively threatening civil war if home rule were imposed on Ireland, and Asquith was taking the threat seriously. The British Cavalry Brigade at Curragh, in County Kildare, was alerted to be prepared to take action against Ulster in the event of rebellion. Much to the dismay of the Prime Minister, and to King George himself, fifty-eight officers of the brigade offered their resignations, rather than to take action against, or even to coerce Ulster. The matter was handled discretely, and the resignations were not accepted. **(29)**

Gun Running in Ulster:

The Ulster Volunteer Force had collected a defense fund of one million pounds, with which to buy arms. On April 24th and 25th they openly "smuggled" 35,000 German rifles and 5,000,000 rounds of ammunition into Derry at the port of Larne, County Antrim, as the police stood by and watched the operation as spectators. Asquith chose to ignore Carson's rebellious behavior. No government action was taken, then or later. Sir Winston Churchill, was the only government official to have the courage to condemn the illegal Unionist activities, referring to them as criminal and treasonous. **(30)**

Home Rule- Strike Three!:

On May 25, 1914, The Home Rule Bill passed the House of Commons for the third time. Strike three! According to the Parliament Act it would automatically become law, pending royal consent. Upon approval, the Act provided for somewhat of a dominion status, and for a subordinate Irish parliament in Dublin, having control over all matters pertaining to Ireland, except defense, foreign policy, and fiscal matters. The other dominions, Canada, Australia, and South Africa had had complete national freedom since 1907, but Ireland would still be on a short leash. Apparently, her proximity to Mother England would have made an independent Ireland a perceived threat to the Empire.

Chapter Eighteen
The Rising of 1916
1914-1916

Gun Running at Howth, The Great World War, A Decision is Made, Home Rule Deferred, Civil War Averted, The IRB Military Council, Redmond Seeks Volunteer Enlistments, Volunteers Repudiate Redmond's Leadership, The Plan Takes Shape, German Aid Promised, Arms Shipment Pending, The Aud Arrives in Tralee Bay, Sir Rodger Casement, Rising Orders Countermanded, What Though the Odds, Decision, Countermanding Orders Countermanded, Dublin Force Decimated, A Fine Day for a Rising, New Irish Republican Army Deployed, The Irish Republic is Proclaimed, Action at the Four Courts, Action at Stephen's Green, Action at Dublin Castle, Boland Mills and Mount Street Bridge, Other Actions, Reinforcements, Unconditional Surrender, The Mood in Dublin, British Justice Was Swift , The Martyrs, Public Opinion Changes, Perspective.

They Made History

***Eamonn Ceannt** Member of Military Council, IRB, Commandant of Fourth Battalion, Dublin Brigade.

Robert Erskine Childers: Irish patriot, Smuggled guns into Howthe, in 1916 , for the volunteers.

Sir Winston Churchill: First Lord of the Admiralty, Tried, in vain, to assert law during the Ulster rebellion.

***Con Colbert:** Patrick Pearse's bodyguard during the rising.

***James Connolly:** Labor organizer, formed The Citizen Army, Commandant-General of the Dublin Forces.

Edward Daly: Commandant First Battalion, Dublin Brigade.

John Devoy: An old Fenian, and the leader of the Clan na Gael in America.

Eamon deValera: Commander of Third Battalion in 1916 rising. Imprisoned. President of Sinn Fein, Durable leader of Ireland until 1973.

***John MacBride:** Husband of Maud Gonne. Second in command of Second Battalion.

Sean MacDiarmada: Sinn Feiner and National Organizer for the IRB. Member of Military Council.

***Thomas MacDonaugh:** Commandant of Second Battalion, Dublin Brigade. Member of Military Council.

General Sir John Maxwell: Senior British Commanding Officer during the rising. Ordered the execution of the rebel leaders.

Eoin MacNeill: Irish Member of Parliament and founder of the Irish Volunteer Force.

***Michael Mallin:** Commander of the rebel Volunteers at Stephen's Green.

Countess Constance Markiewicz: Feminist, Founded Fianna Eireann, and Cumman Na hBan, Third in command at Stephen's Green.

***Patrick Henry Pearse:** Poet, Teacher, Member Supreme Council of IRA, Commandant General of the Volunteers during 1916 Rising.

***William James Pearse:** Noted Sculptor. Brother to Patrick Pearse.

***Joseph Mary Plunkett:** Member of Military Council, IRB, Chief -of -Staff and Director of Military Operations during the 1916 rising.

John Redmond: Leader of the Irish Party in Parliament.

* Executed after the rising.

Gun Running at Howth:

Sir Roger Casement, a distinguished English diplomat, and sympathizer to the Irish cause, had raised 1,500 pounds with which to purchase arms for the Irish Volunteers. He had purchased 1,500 old German Mauser rifles, and 45,000 rounds of ammunition. Plans were made with his friend, Erskine Childers, an adventurous yachtsman and popular novelist, to smuggle the weapons into Dublin. **(1)**

On July 26, 1914, John Redmond gave his approval for a formation of 800 Irish Volunteers to parade through Dublin, as a drill. The volunteers formed at the labor union's Liberty Hall, and marched out through Clontarf to the suburb of Howth. There they were met by a private yacht, owned and piloted by Erskine Childers. Nine hundred antiquated German Mauser rifles, that had been purchased in Hamburg, were smuggled into Howth Harbor, on Childer's yacht. The Irish volunteers took possession of the old Mauser rifles and the formation started back toward Dublin. A number of the rifles were taken away by motorcar. Five days later a remaining 600 rifles were landed at Kilcoole, without incident.

What had been intended as a show of force parade through Dublin, was soon stopped by a small squad of Dublin Metropolitan Police, along with about two hundred of The King's Own Scottish Borderers. The police demanded that they surrender their weapons. The Volunteers refused, and the Police armed only with batons, deferred the matter to the King's soldiers. A small scuffle ensued, in which the soldiers captured nineteen of the rifles. Tom Clark and Sean MacDermott quickly ordered the rest of the volunteers to scatter into the countryside, and hide their rifles. **(2)**

The "King's Own" returned to Dublin without having achieved their purpose. As they proceeded along the quay, on a section known as "Bachelors Walk, " they were heckled by a crowd of Dubliners, showered with shouts, and taunts, and belted with garbage. One thing led to another, and as the situation deteriorated, the soldiers ultimately panicked and fired into the crowd, killing four people, and wounding thirty-eight. The authorities were, of course, censured, but the contrast between the Howth incident and the earlier gun running at Larne was totally shameful. **(3)**

The Great World War:

June 28, 1914, Arch Duke Franz Ferdinand, heir to the throne of Austria, was assassinated, by a Serbian anarchist student at Sarajevo. The Austrian government issued an ultimatum to

Serbia, and when the Serbians requested clarification, Austria took it as a refusal, declaring war on Serbia. This prompted Russia to make threatening moves against Austria, causing Germany to get into the act, taking Austria's side. France made an unacceptable reply to a German inquiry, causing Germany to invade Belgium, on her way to attack France. So naturally, on August 4th, England declared war on Germany, "in order to help free the small countries of Europe that had been invaded by their larger neighbors, " namely Germany and Austria-Hungary. Somehow, that seems ironic for England.

A Decision is Made:

At this point, in September, the Supreme Council of the Irish Republican Brotherhood, (IRB) under the leadership of Tom Clarke, supported by Sean MacDermott, Patrick Pearse, and Eamon Ceant came to a major decision, based upon the axiom that "England's difficulty is Ireland's opportunity" They decided that there must be a rising before the end of the war. Patrick Pearse, master of a private boys' academy on the outskirts of Dublin, and a leading member of the military council, was chosen by the council as commanding officer of the Irish Volunteer Force. A letter was sent to Clan na Gael leader, John Devoy, in New York, urgently requesting assistance for obtaining weapons. **(4)**

Home Rule Deferred:

On September 15th the Home Rule Act was accorded the Royal Assent by King George V. It appeared that after all the years of struggle, failure, and disappointment, Ireland would at least be a nation again. Well, …….not quite yet! Great Britain had declared war on Germany six weeks earlier. The King, The Prime Minister, and the Parliament, feared to make constitutional changes in wartime, and the real prospect of an Irish civil war. Home rule would have to be deferred until after the war. **(5)**

Civil War Averted:

In mid September, Carson and Redmond came to a mutual understanding. In-as-much as home rule had been put on the back burner for the duration of the war, they agreed to put aside their differences for the good of the Empire, and Mother England. A civil war had been averted by one less civil.

The IRB Military Council

In early 1915, the Irish Republican Brotherhood had formed a Military Council, headed by Tom Clarke. The other members were Patrick Pearse, Sean MacDermott, Eamonn Ceannt, Thomas MacDonaugh, and Joseph Mary Plunkett. Eoin MacNeill, an Irish Member of Parliament, was the founder, and Commandant of the Irish Volunteer Force. He was not, however, a member of the Irish Republican Brotherhood. He did not share their views regarding offensive action, and held the point of view that the volunteers were, and should remain, strickly a defense force. Consequently, he remained "out of the loop, " and was unaware of the military council's plans. (6)

Redmond Seeks Volunteer Enlistments:

On September 20, 1915, MP John Redmond spoke to a large gathering in Wicklow, urging Irish volunteers to sign up with the British Army, "to serve wherever the firing line extends, in defense of right, freedom, and religion, in the war against the Hun." Apparently, a large number of Irishmen took him up on it, with about 150,000 enlistments. Unlike volunteers in Ulster, who were kept in local Ulster regiments, the enlistees from the southern counties were dispersed to various units throughout the British Army.

Volunteers Repudiate Redmond's Leadership:

On September 24th, Eoin MacNeill, and the leaders of the Irish Volunteer Force repudiated Redmond's leadership, entirely. James Connolly and Arthur Griffith were similarly of the opinion that it was England's war, and that Ireland had no problem with Germany. (7)

The Plan Takes Shape:

The Irish Volunteer Force, with a total of 10,000 men, as a counter part to the Ulster Volunteer Force, was looked upon as a sort of militia, and thus enjoyed a measure of tolerance from the British Government, in southern Ireland, including the ability to move freely, and hold military maneuvers from time to time. James Connolly's Citizens Army enjoyed the same freedom of movement. The Military Council planned to capitalize on the situation in order to take the government forces by surprise during the rising, which had now been planned for Easter Sunday, April 23, 1916. Connolly, who was not a member of the Irish

Republican Brotherhood, was openly calling for rebellion, but he was unaware of the planned rising. The Council was concerned that he may start one on his own, with his Citizen's Army, thus compromising the nation-wide rising in April. Connolly was, therefore, practically recruited into the Brotherhood by force, and made aware of the plan. It was thought best, on the other hand, that Commandant Eoin MacNeill, still remained unaware of the plan, and was led to believe Easter Sunday would merely be more maneuvers. **(8)**

German Aid Promised:

At the request of the IRB Military Council, Sir Roger Casement traveled to New York to meet with John Devoy. The two of them met with the German Ambassador to United States, urging German assistance for the rebellion. Germany was in no position to render any active assistance, but Casement, with Devoy's approval, traveled on to Germany and did obtain a promise of an arms shipment prior to the rising. **(9)**

Arms Shipment Pending:

Word was received by courier that 20,000 rifles and ammunition would arrive at Tralee Bay, in the German freighter, *The Aud,* on the night of Thursday April 20th. IRB Council received this information with alarm. That would be four days before the rising on Sunday, April 23rd. They feared that the Royal Navy may intercept the freighter and compromise the rising. That would give the British time to bring in reinforcements from England. They felt it essential that the arms be delivered April 24th, after the rising had begun. Because the Council was unable to contact Germany directly, they dispatched a courier to Devoy, with instructions to pass the word to the Germans.

***The Aud* Arrives in Tralee Bay:**

Apparently, the Germans did not get the word in time to delay the shipment. *The Aud* arrived at Tralee Bay on Thursday night, April 20th, four days early, after slipping past the British blockade disguised as a Norwegian vessel. The German freighter steamed up and down Tralee Bay, flashing the agreed upon signal to the shore. There was no return signal of green lights. Fate had intervened. The men assigned to send the signal took a wrong turn in the road, drove their car off a pier near Killorglin and plunged into the sea. All three men were drowned. *The Aud* flashed her signal over and over, the whole long night. There was no response from Banna Strand. (beach).

The next day *The Aud* was discovered and forced to surrender to the Royal Navy and escorted into Cobh Harbor (pronounced *Cove)*. The German captain, rather than have his cargo confiscated by the enemy, scuttled his ship, sending 20,000 rifles, ten machine guns and one million rounds of ammunition to the bottom of the harbor, along with the last hope of success for the rebel forces. **(10)**

Sir Roger Casement:

That night, Sir Roger Casement, and two other men, came ashore from a German submarine. The reason for his returning to Ireland was to warn the insurgents that the artillery, which was critical to the success of the rising, was not included in the shipment, as planned, and that the rising would surely fail. The three men were captured in Kerry, shortly after they landed. **(11)**

Rising Orders Countermanded:

Meanwhile, Blumer Hobson, the Volunteer's secretary for Eoin MacNeill, discovered that the outlying Volunteer units were preparing for a rising on Easter Sunday. He immediately informed MacNeill, who was outraged at the news. They immediately drove to Pearse's home to confront him, and the turf hit the fan.

After a heated discussion, MacNeil issued orders, which countermanded the nation-wide "Easter Maneuvers" and sent Blumer Hobson on an urgent three day tour of Ireland to all of the remote units, to pass the word. He even placed prominent announcements in all the newspapers.

When the Volunteers in the outlying areas received MacNeill's countermanding orders, most of them stood down and went home. Unknown to the Voluteers, British Military Intelligence had cracked the German code, and was already aware of the impending rising. They had already been more than somewhat suspicious of the proposed nation-wide maneuvers. But with the interdiction of the *Aud,* and MacNeill's countermanding announcements in the newspapers, their concerns were put to rest.

What Though the Odds!

Michael Collins, the Volunteers intelligence officer, had received word from his spies in Dublin Castle, that there were plans to arrest the leaders, and disarm Volunteers. The Military

Council, held a crisis discussion. They finally concluded that if they did not proceed as planned, they would never have another opportunity. They were fully aware that without the *Aud's* rifles and machine guns, and especially without the artillery, the situation was hopeless. They also knew that the obsolete, single shot, Mauser rifles they had received at Howth, were no match against the modern British Enfield rifles, in the hands of thousands of British Tommies. Defeat would be certain, for themselves, and for the Volunteers, most of whom were still under the impression that they were merely holding maneuvers.

Decision:

They entertained the hope that once the rising had begun, the general population would join them in support. Realistically speaking, however, this was false hope. They stood no chance at all, and they knew it. The decision was determined by a majority of one vote. This kind of sacrifice was required, to rouse the nation to fight for its independence, and nationhood; if not now, then the next time. **(12)**

Countermanding Orders Countermanded:

They decided to set the date back one day, to Easter Monday, hoping more of the Volunteers would get the word. Women of the Cumann na mBan were sent out as couriers to the volunteer units in the outlying towns of Belfast, Limerick, Wexford, Galway, Enniscourthy, Tipperary, and Cork with orders that countermanded MacNeill's countermanding order. Unfortunately, most of these men had gone home after receiving MacNeill's order. Of the 10,000 Volunteers, only about 2,000 participated in the rising. **(13)**

Dublin Force Decimated:

Even in Dublin, from a force of 2,000 men, at least 800 of them believed what they read in the newspapers, and stayed home. With reduced ranks, a battalion strength would number only about 200 to 300 men. These would be augmented by a few dozen women of Cumann na mBan, who served as nurses and prepared meals for the men.

A Fine Day for a Rising:

Easter Monday, April 24th was a bright cloudless day. It was a bank holiday, and the streets were full of Dubliners, out enjoying the sunny weather. At Liberty Hall, the union headquarters, two hundred and fifty uniformed members of Connolly's Citizen Army formed in two columns, while a little over nine hundred partly uniformed members of the Irish Volunteer Force, formed ranks in four battalions, led by Patrick Henry Pearse as Commander-in-Chief., James Connolly as Commandant-General, and Joseph Mary Plunkett, as Chief of Staff and military strategist.

Patrick Pearse-
Poet, Schoolmaster, Citizen Soldier, Martyr.

James Connolly- Labor leader, Citizen Soldier, Martyr

It was Connolly who gave the marching orders to the officers.The following strong points were to be taken, and occupied:

The Dublin General Post Office was to be occupied by the Headquarters Battalion of about 150 mixed Citizen's Army and Irish Volunteers, and serve as the central command post.

The First Battalion, commanded by Edward Daly, was to take and occupy the Four Courts Building.

The Second Battalion, under Sean MacDonaugh, was to occupy and hold Jacob's Biscuit Factory.

The Third Battalion, commanded by Eamon deValera, was assigned to occupy Boland's Mills, on the Kingstown Road and interdict any reinforcements coming from Kingstown.

A Company of Citizen's Army troops, under Michael Mallin was to Occupy Stephen's Green.

Sean Connolly, with a company of fifty men, was to capture Dublin Castle.

Sean Heuston's squad was to occupy the Mendicity Center.

Three remaining squads were assigned to occupy the three railroad terminals in Dublin. **(14)**

New Irish Republican Army Deployed:

Orders having been given, the various elements moved out to their assigned positions. The command post element of one hundred fifty men formed up for the parade down Lower Abbey Street, to Sacksville Street, (present day O'Connell Street) up to the General Post Office. Pearse, as Commander-in-Chief, led the column, flanked by Commandant General, James Connolly, one step behind on his right, and Chief-of-Staff Joe Plunkett in a similar position on his left. Tom Clark marched alongside the column and Sean MacDermott limped along with him.

The citizens of Dublin took little notice, as the volunteers were a familiar sight, on their training line marches, to various locations around the city. Pedestrians often walked in the street because of the narrow sidewalks, but they did give the volunteers curb room as they marched by. Traffic stopped as they entered the Boulevard and proceeded north toward Nelson's Pillar. When they reached the Post Office, the Column halted smartly to command, and did a left-face.

On Command the first and fourth squads wheeled left and right, into protective positions. Each man knew what his assignment was. On commands from James Connolly, "Squads two and three, the Post Office, **Charge!"** Troops charged into the post office, weapons at the ready. Others took up positions, forming a defensive perimeter.

Inside the post office, there was surprise and confusion. Several British officers and a policeman were present in the lobby. They were arrested, taken prisoner and advised that they would be treated with respect. The civilians present on personal business were told to leave quietly. The post office staff was also told to leave. One squad was sent to the second floor to seize the telegraph office. On the stairway they encountered a small group of armed soldiers. One of them was shot. The others dropped their rifles. The lone female operator in the telegraph office also surrendered without resistance.

Once the building was secured, a detail was sent out front to bring in the extra weapons and ammunition. Those inside were busy breaking windows, and barricading them with whatever was available. Sniper posts were established in the surrounding buildings. **(15)**

The Irish Republic is Proclaimed:

Once positions were established, Patrick Pearse, accompanied by James Connolly went outside to raise the tricolor flag and address the crowd of curious onlookers, who had gathered in front of the Post Office. The crowd consisted mostly of the poor of Dublin, who lived in the tenements in the surrounding area. They found the situation to be entertaining, and they enjoyed heckling the soldiers. Their mood was generally bored, or hostile. They were little impressed with the historic significance of what was happening.

The British Union Jack was hauled down and the Irish Tricolor was run up the flag pole. A second flag, the old Irish green flag, with a harp, and emblazoned the words, IRISH REPUBLIIC, "was flown beneath the Tricolor.

Commandant General Pearse read the formal declaration from the steps of the Post Office.(See text at end of chapter.)

Action at the Four Courts:

The First Battalion under Edward Daly, was assigned to occupy the Four Courts Building. Because of the bank holiday there were few people in the building, except for custodial employees. They told them to leave and proceeded to fortify the building by barricading the doors and windows. Sean Heuston, with a small squad, was occupying the Mendicity Institute on the opposite side of the Liffey. His job was to hold the position for four hours, to provide covering fire, while Daly's men fortified the Four Courts. They held it for fifty hours.

Action at Stephen's Green:

Michael Mallin, with a company of less than one hundred was assigned to occupy Stephens Green and establish a command post there. He was then to capture the Shelbourne Hotel and other buildings around the Green, to control adjoining streets, and interdict British troops from nearby Portobello Barracks. He was soon joined by Countess Markiewicz, who served as his second in command.

Unfortunately, British troops siezed the Shelbourne Hotel first and were able to rake the Green with machine gun fire, the trees and shrubbery offering no cover. Mallin quickly withdrew his exposed troops to the opposite facing College of Surgeons Building, where they made a gallant stand, but accomplished nothing. They had no place to go. (16)

Action at Dublin Castle:

Sean Connolly, with a force of only fifty men was assigned to take and hold Dublin Castle, the seat of British government in Ireland. It being a bank holiday, they expected only a skeleton staff to be on duty. They encountered a single policeman at the gate. When he tried to stop them, he was shot. In the guardroom, they encountered six soldiers, but took them by surprise, and tied them up. As they entered the upper yard they were fired upon by someone in an upper window. Mistaking this lone defender to be overwhelming fire from a superior force, Connolly forthwith withdrew from the Castle, locking the gate behind him, and succeeded in storming the deserted City Hall. He then set up sniper positions in the City Hall and surrounding buildings to "cover" the Castle. (17)

Boland Mills and Mount Street Bridge:

The Third Battalion, commanded by Eamon deValera occupied Boland Mills, on the Kingstown Road, with orders to interdict the expected reinforcements. Maxwell was able to bypass

Boland Mills, but at the Mount Street Bridge his forces encounterd seventeen of deValera's men who had set up defensive positions in three corner buildings, which commanded the bridge. Their fire was so effective that the British thought they were fighting two hundred men. They suffered terrible casualties and were held off for hours. Four British officers were killed, and fourteen were wounded. One hundred and thirty-two enlisted men were killed, and three hundred and ninety-seven were wounded, before the insurgents were overrun. Eleven of the defenders were killed, five were wounded, and one possibly escaped. In the Dublin area, the total republican losses were sixty-four men killed. British losses were two hundred sixty-eight killed. Approximately three hundred non-combatants were killed. **(18)**

Other Actions:

In County Meath the insurgents captured the Royal Irish Constabulary (R.I.C.). Enniscorthy and much of northern Wexford County was under republican control. At Ashborne the R.I.C. inflicted heavy losses on a small force of republicans. A large group of insurgents attacked in Galway, with little effect, and the volunteers were easily dispersed at Athenry. Country wide the total casualties were over 3,000 and most of these were non-combatants.

Reinforcements:

When word of the rising reached Kingstown, seven miles south of Dublin, a Royal Navy vessel in the harbor notified its headquarters in Britain. Within hours reinforcements, under the Command of General John Maxwell, were on the way to Ireland. Maxwell had plenary orders to deal severely with the insurgents.

Unconditional Surrender:

The rebels were dramatically over-matched, and were easily defeated by over-whelming force. By May 1st the Rising was over; crushed by the British Army. Pearse knew they must surrender, and asked for honorable terms from the British Commander, General Maxwell. The only terms Maxwell offered were that they must surrender unconditionally. Pearse was forced to accept these harsh terms.

The last night before the surrender, Pearse called the survivors of his company to assemble, for the last time, to tell them of the terms. There in the dark night, in the basement of the demolished post office building, someone began singing a familiar marching song of the volunteers. Slowly, they all joined the singing. It had been composed by a gifted young man, Pedar Kearney, and recently introduced in the Abbey Theatre. Fourteen years later it would be adopted as Ireland's National Anthem. It was titled simply as:

The Soldier'sSong. (19)

Verse: We'll sing a song, a soldier's song,
With cheering, rousing chorus,
As round our blazing fires we throng,
The starry heavens o'er us:
Tonight we man the bear-na baoghal,
In Erin's cause, come woe or weal,
Mid cannon's roar and rifle's peal,
We'll chant a soldier's song.

Refrain: Soldiers are we, whose lives are pledged to Ireland
Some have come from a land beyond the wave.
Sworn to be free, No more our ancient sire land
Shall shelter the despot or the slave.
Impatient for the coming fight,
And as we wait the morning light,
Here in the silence of the night,
We'll sing a soldier's song.

The Mood in Dublin:

The next morning they surrendered in disgrace, and were abused by their captors. Even the citizens of Dublin were angry with the insurgent republicans and taunted them, as they were marched through the streets on their way to jail. The people blamed them for the enormous amount of destruction, disorder, and looting, along with the heavy civilian casualties, caused by the British response. The rising was viewed as a criminal act, by a bunch of fanatics. The minds of the people had been conditioned by the censored, pro-British press. All republican papers had been proclaimed and suppressed. Most of the Dublin public was in poverty, and more concerned with day to day survival, than they were with dreams of a republic.

British Justice Was Swift:

General Maxwell had been given plenipotentiary powers for Courts Marshall, and the death sentence, in order to make examples of the disloyal, Irish rebels. Immediate and secret military tribunals were convened, and quickly reached predetermined verdicts. One hundred and twenty-one rebels were tried, one of them a woman. Countess Constance Markievivz and thirty men were found guilty and sentenced to life imprisonment. Ninety men were found guilty and sentenced to death. The use of firing squads would be the only miliary courtesy afforded the rebel leaders. **(20)**

The Martyrs:

On Tuesday, May 3rd, Patrick Henry Pearse, as the leader, would be the first to die. He was soon followed by Thomas Clarke and Thomas MacDonaugh.

The next day, May 4th, Joseph Mary Plunkett was to be executed. He had been allowed to be married to Grace Gifford, as four guards with fixed bayonets witnessed. Permitted exactly ten minutes to spend with his bride, he was then taken out and promptly shot. He was followed by Edward Daly, Michael O'Hanrahan, and Willie Pearse. Willie had not taken part in the rising. His only offense was being the brother of Patrick Pearse.

On May 5th, John MacBride, the husband of the famed actress, Maud Gonne, noted for her role as *Kathleen ni Houlihan*, died alone, being the only Republican shot on that day.

On Sunday, May 8th, Eamonn Ceannt, Michael Mallin, Sean Heuston, and Con Colbert joined the ranks of the martyrs.

On Thursday, May 12th, Sean Mac Dermott, and James Connelly paid the supreme price. Connolly had been shot in the ankle during the hostilities, and was unable to stand. His British executioners thoughtfully tied him in a chair, facing the firing squad, to meet his God.

Sir Roger Casement was the last to die. He was not accorded the honor of a firing squad, as he was tried and convicted of treason. He was considered to be a British subject, had been knighted by the King, and as such was found guilty of consorting with the German enemy. He was hanged as a traitor, on August 3rd, in England.

Eamon de Valera was not executed because of his American birth, and dual citizenship. The British wanted the support of the United States, which had not yet entered the War, and the British did not want to antagonize the American public.

The Irish press strongly condemned the rising, and the public itself viewed the rebels as foolish, misguided fanatics. The women were particularly harsh, especially some of the Dublin poor, who were receiving subsistence checks for their husbands in the British army. They viciously derided the rebel prisoners, who were marched through the streets of Dublin on their way to prison.

Public Opinion Changes:

But as the week wore on, came word of new executions. The public attitude underwent a remarkable change. Word leaked out that Pearse, Clark and McDonaugh had been buried in quicklime. The circumstances of Joseph Mary Plunkett's execution aroused the public ire. The British public, as well as the Irish public were outraged and aroused by the manner of the executions, of honorable Irish soldiers, that went on day after day.

John Redmond, who had supported the British during the rising, was also alarmed, even though some of his volunteers were actually killed trying to suppress the rebellion. Even Prime Minister Asquith was alarmed by the public outcry, and wired General Maxwell of his concerns. Still the executions went on.

After the execution of the first fifteen martyrs, General Maxwell reconsidered his position, reduced the sentences of the remaining seventy-five to life imprisonment in England.

Perspective:

The rising was a major mistake, and was doomed from the very beginning. The decision to proceed, even after the loss of the weapons, and the confusing Countermanding of orders was foolhardy. It was a futile, but noble, gesture which resulted in the loss of leaders who could not be replaced. Had they lived, Irish history would have been totally different, and a bloody civil war might never have divided the country.

The rebels, due to various poor judgments, did not capture Dublin Castle, which would quite likely have been a better objective than the Post Office, and it would have been easier for them to defend. They also failed to capture the telephone exchange, thus leaving the British the means to send for reinforcements from Curaugh and Belfast, including artillery.

Stephen's Green was a poor choice on which to locate a command post. The Sherbourne Hotel would have served them better. The decision to proceed without artillery and machine guns was the biggest mistake. The Volunteers could have buried their weapons, and the leaders could have gone into hiding, or exile. Pearse had expected widespread public support, which had never existed.

The rising did, however, shake the public out of the political lethargy, and the acceptance of tyranny that had taken the country. Public condemnation of the republican rebels had been reversed by their martyrdom. They had lost the war, but had won the hearts, and the veneration of the Irish people. Their dream of an Irish Republic had captured the public imagination, and the spirit of revolt would grow in the land. The rebellion had just begun.

POBLACHT NA EIRIANN
THE PROVISIONAL GOVERNMENT
OF THE
IRISH REPUBLIC
TO THE PEOPLE OF IRELAND

IRISHMEN AND IRISHWOMEN:

In the name of God and the dead generations from which she receives her tradition of nationhood, Ireland through us summons her children to her flag and strikes for her freedom. Having organized and trained her manhood through her secret revolutionary organizations the Irish Republican Brotherhood, and through her open military organizations, the Irish Volunteers and the Irish Citizen's Army, having patiently perfected her discipline, having resolutely waited for the right moment to reveal itself, she now seizes the moment and supported by her exiled children in America and by gallant allies in Europe, but relying in the first on her own strength, she strikes, in full confidence of victory.

We declare the right of the people of Ireland to the ownership of Ireland and to The unfettered control of Irish destinies to be sovereign and unfeasible The Long Usurpation of that right by a foreign people and government has not extinguished the right, nor can it ever be extinguished except by the destruction of the Irish people. In every generation the Irish people have asserted their right to national freedom and Sovereignty; six times during the past three hundred years they have asserted it in arms. Standing on the fundamental right, and again asserting in arms in the face of the world, we hereby proclaim the Irish Republic as a Sovereign independent State, and we pledge our lives and the lives of our comrades-in-arms to the cause of its freedom, of its welfare, and of its exaltation among the nations.

The Irish Republic is entitled to, and hereby claims, the allegiance of every Irishman and Irishwoman. The Republic guarantees religious and civil liberty, equal rights and equal opportunities to all its citizens, and declares its resolve to pursue the happiness and prosperity of the whole nation and all its parts, cherishing all the children of the nation equally, and oblivious of the differences carefully fostered by an alien government, which have divided a minority from the majority in the past. Until our arms have brought the opportune moment for establishment of a Permanent National Government, representative of the whole people of Ireland and Elected by the suffrages of all her men and women, the Provisional Government hereby constituted, will administer the civil and military affairs of the Republic in trust for the people

We place the cause of the Irish Republic under the protection of the Most High God, Whose blessing we invoke upon our arms, and we pray that no one who serves that cause will dishonor it by cowardice, inhumanity, or rapine. In this supreme hour The Irish nation must, by its valour and discipline and by the readiness of its children to sacrifice themselves for the common good, prove itself worthy of the august destiny to which it is called.

Signed on behalf of the Provisional Government

THOMAS J. CLARKE
SEAN Mac DIARMADA THOMAS Mac DONAOGH
P.H. PEARSE EAMON CEANNT
JAMES CONNOLLY   JOSEPH PLUNKETT

Chapter Nineteen
The War for Independence
1917-1920

Partition, Prime Minister Lloyd George, Frongoch "University of Insurrection, " Rebels Released, The Rise of Sinn Fein, Sinn Fein and the Volunteers, Michael Collins-Man of Action, "The Chief, " Conscription, General Election, First Dail Erieann, The General Elections, Republic Proclaimed Again, First Shot Fired, Sensational Escape, President deValera, American Sojourn, Official Army of the Republic, Undeclared War, Flying Columns, , R.I.C. Supply Service, Black and Tans and Auxiliary "Cadets, " Against All Odds, Top Offical Murdered, Counter Intelligence Ops, "IRC Supply Service, " Disturbance in Derry, Rule of Law in the Republic, Lord Mayor of Cork Arrested, Incident in Balbriggan, Kevin Barry, Ambush in Clare, Man Murdered by Mistake, Another Mistake, Shootout on Talbot Street, Double Tragedy Stirs Public Opinion, "BLOODY SUNDAY, " Retaliation from the Castle, Retaliation, Retaliation, Retaliation, Government of Ireland Act-1920, Stalemate.

They Made History:

Michael Collins: Survivor of the 1916 Rising, Organized IRA intelligence net, Directed covert ops.

Arthur Griffith: Editor of *United Irishmen*, Publisher of *Sinn Fein* , President of Dail Erieann, founder of Sinn Fein.

Countess Markievicz: Founded Na Fianna Erieann. An officer in the Citizens' Army *Fought in 1916 Rising.*

David Lloyd George: *British Prime Minister 1916 to 1922. Shrewd negotiator. Imposed partition in 1920*

Eamon deValera: *Survivor of 1916 Rising, Crafty poltician, President of Dail Erieann, Free State President*

Tomas MacCurtain: *IRA Commandant, Southern Division, Lord Mayor of Cork, Murdered by RIC*

Terence MacSwiney: *Lord Mayor of Cork, Arrested, died on a hunger strike.*

Tom Barry: *Leader of Flying column in Cork Brigade IRA. at Kilmichael Ambush.*

Sean Treacy: *Noted IRA gunman and assasin.*

Dan Breen: *Noted IRA gunman and assasin.*

Kevin Barry: *Young IRA soldier, unjustly hanged* in Mountjoy Prison. His death impacted public opinion.

Sir Edward Carson: *Prime Minister Northern Ireland.* Resignd in 1920, succeeded by Sir James Craig.

Liam Lynch: *Member Supreme Council IRA., Southern Division Commandant General.*

Partition:

Concerned over the rapid shift in Irish public opinion after the 1916 executions, Prime Minister Asquith decided to implement Home Rule as agreed in 1914, instead of waiting until the end of the war. This caused trouble with the unionists in the northern counties. Lloyd George, who was responsible for the negotiations, persuaded Carson to go along with Home Rule, provided the six counties were permanently partitioned. He separately assured Redmond the partitioning would be merely temporary. On July 22, 1916, Redmond was informed that the partition would be permanent. He was outraged, and refuted the agreement, but the damage had been done. (1)

Prime Minister Lloyd George:

Shortly thereafter, Lloyd George replaced Asquith as Prime Minister. He was concerned with the possible loss of Irish support for the war with Germany. He had 90,000 southern Irishmen, serving in the British army whose loyalty he wanted to retain. He also wanted to regain the good graces of the Americans, who reportedly, were displeased with Britain, and still maintained their neutrality.

Frongoch "University of Insurrection"

The majority of the rebel prisoners were confined to Frongoch Camp, in England, which soon became an "insurrectionist university." Michael Collins had become the moving spirit and organized classes in military skills and Irish history. He surrounded himself with a group of hard cases, who were as dedicated to the republic as himself. With them, he took command of the Army of the Irish Republic that Pearse had proclaimed from the Post office steps, and reorganized James Stephen's Irish Republican Brotherhood. With information from other prisoners, he made notes on where arms and ammunition had been cached and compiled lists of contacts who had been helpful during the rising. In an effort to court the Irish nationalists, and influence the talks between Carson and Redmond, six hundred prisoners, including Collins, were released from Frongoch in December. (2)

Rebels Released:

In June of 1917, the remaining rebel prisoners were released from Frongoch, including the senior surviving member of the rising, Eamon deValera, who had been sparred from execution because he had been born in the United States. Lloyd George later held discussion with Redman and deValera concerning home rule and the issue of partition. These talks did not include Sinn Fein directly, and therefore had little meaning.(3)

The Rise of Sinn Fein:

The Sinn Fein Party won bi-elections in the spring of 1917, in the counties of Roscommon and Longford, occupying seats formerly held by members of John Redman's party, thus making Sinn Fein the main political force of the republican movement. In July, de Valera was elected to Parliament as MP for East Clare.

As a member of Sinn Fein, he worked closely with Arthur Griffith restructuring the organization to make it more unified and bipartisan. They developed a more inclusive set of policies, that were acceptable to both Republicans, and Griffith's Home Rulers. These were presented at the *Ard Fleis*, (conference) in October. The acceptance of these policies established Sinn Fein as the political wing of the republican movement, with the stated purpose of achieving international recognition for Ireland as an independent republic. That having been accomplished, they could then determine what form of government they would choose.

Sinn Fein, and the Volunteers:

On April 1, 1917 deValera was elected as President of Sinn Fein, replacing Arthur Griffith, who founded the organization. Griffith was chosen as the vice-president. In November, Michael Collins organized a convention of the Irish Volunteers, at which time de Valera was elected president of that organization. **(4)**

Michael Collins, Man of Action:

De Valera appointed Collins Dail Minister of Home Affairs and a short time later reappointed him as Minister for Finance. In March of 1918 Collins was appointed as Director of Organization. In that capacity, Collins directed the organization of the General Headquarters Staff, he, himself, becoming Adjutant General. This job title was, possibly, intentionally deceptive. In reality he would function more in a capacity of *"Director of Military Intelligence, and Covert Operations, "* a job for which he was innately suited. Collins was, first and foremost, a soldier.

"The Chief:"

Collins was an enigma. He was a big man, who stood out in a crowd, yet he had the chameleon-like ability to alter his appearance and blend-in. He would even appear shorter, merely by bending his knees slightly and slouching. He had a long time habit of avoiding cameras, and there were no existing photographs of him. Most of his adversaries did not know what he looked like. He coul avoid arrest by simply going unnoticed. **(5)**

Michael Collins, a soldier, a patriot, the Chief.

Nearly all of the General Staff were also members of the Dail, and hence, were more inclined to be politicians. As such, they would be somewhat disinclined to use military force against British soldiers, or the police. Collins, on the other hand, would feel no such constraint. Consequently, military operations were initially executed by local Volunteer units, "on their own initiative, " and without "official" authorization.

Conscription:

By 1918, the British had sustained heavy losses on the Western Front. The 90,000 young Irishmen who had volunteered for service, at the urging of John Redmond, or for the pay and pension to support their families, were still not enough. Having a need for additional cannon fodder, they attempted to introduce conscription in Ireland. Needless to say, this idea was not well received. As a result, Sinn Fein called for a general, nation-wide strike, on April 21st, protesting conscription in neutral Ireland. Redmond's Home Rule Party MPs walked out of Parliament in support of the strike.

The British government responded by sending a new Lord Lieutenant to Ireland, in the person of Field-Marshall Lord French, an old war-horse, empowered to enforce conscription. Within a week, he had arrested the leaders of Sinn Fein, and the Volunteers, including Griffith and deValera . They even arrested the leaders of the Gaelic League, and any other suspected nationalists they could find. Strangely enough, they had somehow overlooked Michael Collins, and Cathal Brugha. The World War came to an end on November 11th, with the defeat of Germany. Conscription in Ireland became a non-issue. **(6)**

The General Election:

On November 21st, Parliament passed an act empowering women, for the first time, to hold a seat in Parliament. In the general election in December, Sinn Fein won 73 of 105 available Irish seats. The Unionists Party captured 26, Redman's Irish party returned only 6 members. Instead of taking their seat in Parliament, the newly elected Sinn Fein MPs met in secret at the Mansion House in Dublin, on the 21st of January, 1919 with Cathal Brugha serving as Provisional President. They had sent invitations to the Unionist and Nationalist MPs, to join them, but both groups declined. Twenty-seven Sinn Fein MPs formed the first Dail Eireann. One of these seats in the Dail was occupied by Countess Markiewicz, the first Irish woman, and the first woman in Europe, to ever hold an elected political position. Thirty-four other members were absent, for the reason of being in jail, and there was one who had been deported. **(7)**

Republic Proclaimed Again:

In an effort to secure recognition for the republic, the Members of the Dail ratified the Republic which had been proclaimed by Patrick Pearse, in 1916, drafted a declaration of independence and a message to the free nations of the world. They approved a provisional constitution, recognizing a twenty-six county state, and developed the republic's socio-economic policy. **(8)**

First Shots Fired:

Coincidentally, on the same day that the Dail adopted the Constitution of the Irish Republic, an incident occurred, that would become all too familiar, in the coming months. Near the town of Soloheadbeg, County Tipperary, a small IRA force, led by Sean Treacy, and Dan Breen, acting "independently, " attacked a Royal Irish Constabulary convoy, that was transporting a quantity of gelignite explosive. Two constables were deliberately shot and killed. The incident is often referred to as the first shots of the Irish

War for Independence, which would begin in earnest some months later. The gelignite was buried to hide it, which, unfortunately, degraded it, rendering it useless. **(9)**

Sensational Escape:

On February 3, 1919, Collins arranged the escape of deValera from Britain's Lincoln jail. A key was smuggled into the jail, believe it or not, in a cake. Enabled by the absence of a couple bribed guards, whose "duties" took them elsewhere, deValera, and two other Fenians, simply walked out of jail in the dark. Quickly whisked away by waiting Volunteer operatives to a safe house in Manchester, he was later smuggled back into Ireland, and sequestered comfortably in the Gatehouse of the Bishop of Dublin. The escape of deValera made sensational news all over Europe. It was particularly foremost in the minds of the Irish public, as the British authorities carried on a massive manhunt throughout Britain and Ireland. The fugitive became an inter-national hero, as he continued to "elude" capture. **(10)**

Eamon deValera, politician extrodinaire,
patriot, President, American citizen

President de Valera:

It is not surprising, that, on April 1st, the Dail unanimously elected Eamon de Valera the President of the Dail Erieann, in absentia. His political power had reached a zenith. He was not only President of the Republic, but also of Sinn Fein and the Irish Volunteers. He rewarded Collins by appointing him Minister of Finance, with the task of raising a loan of a quarter of a million pounds, to be used to maintain Dail administration, and for propagandizing Irish independence to the American public. **(11)**

The winter of 1919 also brought a major outbreak of influenza in the British prisons, killing an un-named imprisoned member of the Dail Erieann.

In June, the British government belatedly decided it would be expedient to release the rest of the Sinn Fein prisoners, who survived the influenza outbreak, including the much sought after de Valera.

American Sojourn:

Now a freeman, President deValera decided that he could best serve the Republic by going to America to propagandize the Irish cause and raise public support. In June of 1919, leaving Arthur Griffith as acting president of both the Dail Erieann, and Sinn Fein, he had Michael Collins smuggle him out of the country, enroute to America. He would spend the next year and a half on tour, and would raise over five million ($5,000,000) for Ireland's struggle for freedom. Meanwhile, while he was absent, that struggle would become more and more violent. **(12)**

In July, in the wake of deValera's departure, leading Republicans elected Michael Collins as President of the Supreme Council of the Irish Republican Brotherhood, a secret, oath-bound society, which had great influence over the IRA . In this capacity, Collins would actually have more control over the IRA than either the Dail, or Sinn Fein. Many would consider *'the Chief"* to be the *"real president"* of the Republic.

Official Army of the Republic:

In spite of the propaganda value of distancing IRA activities from the Dail, most republican leaders came to realize the danger of having two separate organizations representing the Irish Republic. From the examples demonstrated by the American

Revolution, and of John Redmond's failure to gain British recognition of the Irish Republic by political negotiation, the prospect of military action became more acceptable to both groups as an instrument of policy.

On August 20th the Dail Erieann passed a resolution, that the IRA was the official Army of the Irish Republic, and would henceforth be officially referred to as the **Irish Republican Army.** A new army constitution was drafted and adopted, and a new oath of allegiance was subscribed to by members of both the Dail and the IRA, wherein all members of both bodies swore, "to defend the Irish Republic and its government, the Dail, against all enemies, foreign and domestic." The new constitution, with the Dail's approval, gave the Army approval authority for the Dail's appointment of the Minister of Defense. **(13)**

Undeclared War:

A major historic failure, that had always plagued Irish conspiracy and insurrection, had been the vulnerability to betrayal by informers. The British had a talent for either bribing, or coercing impoverished Irish conspirators. Collins had followed the model, copied from the Franco-Italian Carbonari, and introduced by James Stephens in 1848, using only small cells, or squads, whose members, and their activities were known only to their respective cell leaders.

By September, not only were operations more secure, but Collins turned the game around. He was able to actually infiltrate the Dublin Castle headquarters with his own informers. Collins would know of British intentions long before they were implemented.

"Flying Columns:"

At Collins' direction, IRA commanders organized "Flying Columns, " squads consisting of fourteen to thirty men, which operated throughout Ireland, against the Royal Irish Constabulary (RIC). The columns were particularly successful in the southern division, under the command of General Liam Lynch. The final months of 1919 also saw the covert deployment of Collins' personally selected Squad of twelve assassins. They were all young men and Collins was strict with them, insisting that only targets designated by his order be terminated. There was to be no random killing. **(14)**

"Black and Tans" and Auxiliary "Cadets:"

The British response, to the apparent ineffectiveness of the Constabulary, was to enroll demobilized army troops from the recent war. They apparently "scraped the bottom of the barrel, " for they came up with the dregs of British society; a drunken, indigent collection of under educated, and mostly unemployable misfits.

They were sent to Ireland in January 1920, by Prime Minister Lloyd George, ostensibly to "keep order, " but in reality they were, what the next generation would come to know as, "Storm troopers." They were hastily outfitted in a mixed uniform that was a combination of black constabulary trousers, and left over khaki army shirts, and paid 10 shillings a day to raise hell with the Irish population. Following a rampage in Limerick, the Irish derisively nicknamed them, "The Black and Tans."

The cruelty and disregard for human life, of the Black and Tans, would be surpassed only by another group of misfits, which was later mobilized in August. This corps was misleadingly called "Auxiliary Cadets." They were made up of ex-officers, a little older, generally more intelligent, and more capable than the first group. They were pretty much given a "free hand" to do as they pleased, and were paid one pound sterling per day to terrorize the public.

They practiced a strict and brutal form of law enforcement, involving random arrests of the innocent, and the use of torture to extort confessions. The IRA waged guerrilla warfare against the Black and Tans, and the Auxiliary, who in turn, imposed reprisals on the public, with random murder and destruction of property. (18)

Against All Odds:

The deployment of the Black and Tans, together with the Auxiliary Cadet force provided the British with about forty-three thousand well equipped troops, to supplement the Royal Irish Constabulary which originally numbered about ten thousand, before IRA inspired mass resignations, and defections. All that stood between these forces and an unarmed public was the poorly equipped Irish Republican Army, which on its best day, never numbered more than fifteen thousand.

Top Official Murdered:

On March 20, 1920 Tomas MacCurtain, Commandant of the First Cork Brigade, IRA, and Lord Mayor of the City of Cork, was murdered by disguised operatives of the RIC. District Inspector Swanzy, was found guilty by Coroner's court of participating in this atrocity. With blackened faces, they forced their way into his home, and shot the Lord Mayor in his bedroom, in front of his wife, and as he lay dying they rampaged through the house, smashing furniture, as they searched for incriminating evidence. **(15)**

Counter-Intelligence Ops:

In early April 1920, Michael Collins took further steps to penetrate Dublin Castle's intelligence system. With the aid of a defected Castle detective, he had himself smuggled into secret police headquarters in Brunswick Street. He spent the night studying their files to determine their intelligence gathering methods, and how the information was disseminated. He discovered that all routine information, of a political nature, recorded by the Dublin Police, was passed on to the G Division of the Royal Irish Constabulary in the Castle. He deduced that if these individuals were removed, the intelligence gathering system would break down.

On April 9th he ordered that designated "G men" would be warned anonymously, of the ultimate hazards to their health, if they continued in their occupational activities. This was clarified a short time later by the involuntary, and permanent removal, of one of their more prominent colleagues, by Collin's special squad. **(16)**

"The R.I.C. Supply Service:"

In the Counties of Wexford , Cork, Kerry, Limerick, and Tipperary, in the south, and County Clare in the west, RIC barracks proved to be a primary supply source, from which the IRA could acquire arms. These hit and run raids were so successful, that, one by one, the barracks were abandoned by the RIC.

After a few months the Constabulary existed only in the fortified towns. On a single night, in April 1920, IRA units attacked and burned to the ground three hundred fifteen (315) of the abandoned barracks. The *Irish Times* proclaimed, and not without a touch of partisan pride, that the British government no longer existed, "South of the Boyne and west of the Shannon." By mid year 1920, RIC casualties amounted to fifty-five killed, and seventy-four wounded. By July's end over twenty percent of the constables had seen fit to resign from the force. Some of them even switched sides and joined the IRA. This was highly risky, and they were closely watched. Suspected informers lived only long enough to have regrets. **(17)**

Disturbance in Derry :

Persecution of Irish Catholics in Ulster was fermented by Sir Edward Carson by appealing to the piously bigoted nature of 48,000 Specials comprising the Ulster Volunteer Force (UVF), recruited primarily from the Orange Order.

Riots and assaults continued through April, May and most of June. The Ulster Police did nothing to dissuade the rioters. On August 20, 1920, five thousand Catholic workers were driven out of the Belfast shipyards. Thousands of Belfast Catholics were driven from their homes, as hundreds of homes were burned to the ground.

This was, in effect, a pogrom, a "deliberate and organized" campaign, under the oversight of a Member of Parliament, Sir Edward Carson. Instigated by the Orange Society, disturbances broke out in Belfast from July 21st through the 24th, as workers expelled Catholics from the shipyards and engineering works. On August 22nd and 23rd there were more riots in Belfast. Thirty people were killed in the Catholic Bogside neighborhood, and the Ulster Constabulary actually responded by enforcing a curfew to restore order. **(19)**

Rule of Law in the Republic:

By July 1920, the Dail had established a system of courts, in twenty-eight counties to arbitrate civil matters and enforce the law, a function that the British could no longer perform effectively. This was soon followed by the establishment of land courts. Many land owners, loyal to the crown, were uncomfortable in the new Irish Republic and anxious to sell their property. The republican courts assured them of fair treatment, and a fair price for their land.

Lord Mayor of Cork Arrested:

Terrence MacSwiney, who had replaced the late Tomas MacCurtain, as the Lord Mayor of Cork, was arrested on April

13th and charged with possessing subversive documents. Fully aware of the nature of British justice in Ireland, and conditions in British prisons, he decided that his only recourse was to stage a hunger strike. He began his fast on day one, of his incarceration. Four days later he was tried in a military tribunal and summarily found guilty. He was immediately sent to Brixton Prison, in England, where he would languish for the last seventy days of his life.

Incident in Balbriggan:

On September 20th in a small pub in the Dublin County village of Balbriggan, a group of Black and Tans were rousting the locals in drunken sport. Suddenly a shot rang out and one of them fell dead, and another wounded. The other Black and Tans fled the scene, and made their way quickly back to their barracks in Gormanstown, just three miles away.

It was only minutes before one hundred fifty (150) Black and Tans descended upon Balbriggan in armored cars. With flaming torches, and loud ribald singing, they set fire to the pub, and swept through the town, looting and shooting at anything, or anyone that moved. Two civilians were killed, by bayonet, one a woman. Nearly fifty houses were burned down, as well as four pubs and a factory. No-one was ever held accountable for this outrage. **(20)**

Kevin Barry:

On September 20th, an IRA column attacked a lorry carrying several British soldiers, intent on capturing their rifles and ammunition. They met strong resistance and returned fire, killing two of the soldiers. One of the attackers was wounded, and a second one, Kevin Barry, an 18 year old medical student at Belvedere College was captured when his gun jammed. Barry was beaten, arrested, and interrogated. His captors threatened that unless he revealed the names of his accomplices, he would be hanged as a spy. Barry refused to betray his comrades. He was cruelly tortured, but still maintained his silence. **(21)**

Ambush in Clare:

On September 21, another IRA flying column ambushed five Black & Tans in west Clare, to capture their rifles and ammunition. They met with strong resistance, so it was necessary to kill all five of them. This led to reprisals on the nearby village of Ennistimon, where the Black and Tans randomly killed two men, and a twelve year old boy, and burned several houses. Moving on to the coast, they put the torch to Lahinch, incinerating the whole town. Then they drove through the county, randomly shooting at fleeing people, and wound up their spree ten miles to the south, several hours later in Milltown. **(22)**

Man Murdered by Mistake:

On September 22, an innocent man, John A. Lynch was shot to death in his Dublin hotel room, by members of the Royal Irish Constabulary. He was killed because he had the same last name as General Liam Lynch, Chief of Staff of the Southern division of the IRA. A simple case of mistaken identity. **(23)**

Another Mistake:

October 11th, British soldiers located IRA gunmen Dan Breen, and Sean Treacy in a Dublin "Safe-house." Ambushed in their beds, in the middle of the night, they were able to fight their way free, Breen sustaining a head wound in the escape. Strangers helped him to a nearby Catholic hospital, where the sisters treated his wound and hid him in the maternity ward to recover. Soldiers surrounded the hospital and discovered another wounded man in the trauma ward. Mistaking him for Breen, they dragged him out of the hospital, and so aggravated his wounds that the poor man died. The soldiers congratulated themselves, thinking they had killed "Notorious Dan Breen." **(24)**

Shoot-out on Talbot Street:

Three days later Dan Treacy was discovered on Talbot Street by a detective from the Castle's G-Division, and several Auxiliaries. In the subsequent exchange of gunfire, the detective shot Treacy, and at the same moment Treacy shot the detective. Both men were dead at the scene. **(25**

Double Tragedy Stirs Public Opinion:

On October 25 Terence MacSwiney, the Lord Mayor of Cork, expired in Brixton Prison on 74th day of his protest hunger strike. The Dail decreed a day of national mourning. One week later, Kevin Barry, an eighteen year old medical student, and IRA member, was hanged by the neck in Mountjoy Prison, because he would not reveal the names of his companions. A huge crowd had gathered outside the prison to protest the execution, and to pray for the young patriot. All to no avail. Both men died tragic deaths, and their martyrdom greatly stirred public opinion in both Ireland and America. A ballad mourning young Barry was soon composed, which has kept the tragic memory alive to this day. **(26)**

Kevin Barry

In Mountjoy jail, one Monday morning, High upon the gallows tree,
Kevin Barry gave his young life, For the cause of liberty.
But a lad of eighteen summers, Yet no one can deny,
As he walked to death that morning, He proudly held his head on high

Just before he faced the hangman, in his dreary prison cell,
British soldiers tortured Barry, just because he would not tell,
The names of his brave companions, and other things they wished to know,
"Turn informer, or we'll kill you, " Kevin Barry answered "No."

Calmly standing at attention, while he bade his last farewell,
To his broken-hearted mother, whose grief no-one can tell.
For the cause he proudly cherished, this sad parting had to be,
Then to death walked softly smiling, that old Ireland might be free.

Another martyr for old Ireland, another murder for the crown,
Whose brutal laws may kill the Irish, but can't keep their spirits down ,
Lads like Barry are no cowards, from the foe they will not fly,
Lads like Barry will free Ireland, for her sake they'll live and die.

"BLOODY SUNDAY:"

On Sunday, November 21st Collins ordered the execution of a number of G-Division secret agents. Collins' special squad, along with picked members of the Dublin Brigade efficiently performed the assignment. The subjects were shot in their homes, or hotel rooms, almost simultaneously, at 9:00 a.m. at locations throughout Dublin. The official government bulletin set the number of deaths at fourteen, but unofficial sources place that number at nineteen or twenty. This was the beginning of what would always be remembered as "Bloody Sunday." When the news was reported, hundreds of civil servants and military personnel, fearing they would be next, sought sanctuary in Dublin Castle. One secret agent, who had been overlooked, is reported to have broken under the strain, and dispatched himself. **(27)** Now that's what you might call, being a real good sport.

Retaliation From The Castle:

The official response was both infamous and swift, and it was inflicted upon the city of Cork, not Dublin. Cork was, undoubtedly, the most likely place in Ireland, where the British would find a large gathering of potential republicans. This was the day of the All-Ireland Gaelic Football Championship, between Tipperary and Dublin. The Irish take their football seriously, and over eight thousand (8,000) spectators had crowded into Croke Park for the grand event. At three o'clock the game had just barely begun, when Auxiliaries, and Black and Tans surrounded the Park. Without warning they began firing into the crowd, with rifle and machine gun. Fourteen people were killed outright, including a player, a woman, and a child. Fifty-seven spectators were seriously wounded by gunfire, and hundreds were trampled in the ensuing panic and stampede. **(28)**

The world would not witness such inhumanity, and wanton disregard for human life, until twenty-nine years later, in Nazi-Germany. The British attempted to pass the incident off as "merely return fire, ' directed at fugitive assassins in the crowd; One wonders how British imperial authority came to be personified by a characterization identified as John **"Bull."**

Retaliation, Retaliation, Retaliation:

A week later, a flying column, commanded by Tom Barry, ambushed a convoy of Auxiliaries at Kilmichael, County Cork, killing all eighteen of them. Three of Barry's men were also killed. Two weeks later, on December 10th, Lord-Lieutenant French declared martial law in counties Cork, Kerry, Tipperary, and Limerick. The next day, the city center of Cork was sacked and burned to the ground by the Black and Tans, destroying one entire major street, including the City Hall, and the Free Library. Shops and business establishments were looted and gutted. At least two firemen were shot, while fighting the fires. Morning revealed smoldering ruins. **(29)**

Sinn Fein politicians were getting nervous about the events that had developed. Three events occurred at this point that paved the way for a truce: A member of the Dail, Roger Sweetman, from County Wexford, published a statement suggesting a peace conference; The Sinn Fein, Galway County Council, passed a resolution, requesting that the Dail negotiate a truce; and Father Michael O'Flanagan, Acting President of Sinn

Fein, sent a telegram to Lloyd George, stating that Ireland (Sinn Fein) is willing to negotiate.

Government of Ireland Act- 1920:

Michael Collins, acting as head of the Dail, expressed concerns of the Dail being stampeded by false promises. Then, another event occurred that would influence the course of events. Eamon deValera decided that this was the time for him to return from America. So on Christmas Eve, he arrived in Dublin, full of ego and woefully out of touch with the current reality of the situation. As it happened, the day before deValera's return, *The Better Government for Ireland Act*, (1920) which had been kicking about in Parliament for the last three and a half years, had finally been passed and became effective on December 23rd.

The Act imposed a settlement on Ireland, without further negotiation. It provided for two parliaments, subordinate to Westminster, one in Belfast and one in Dublin. It partitioned Ireland, into six strongly Protestant counties, in the north, instead of the nine as laid out by Lloyd George in 1916. Donegal, Cavan, and Monaghan Counties, having large Catholic populations, would be part of the remaining twenty six counties comprising Southern Ireland

Stalemate:

This pretty much put the frosting on the cake. Lloyd George had established partition as a *fait accompli,* and would never accept any part of Ireland leaving the Empire. The Irish republicans, on the other hand, would not accept anything less than a thirty-two county Ireland, and complete independence. There seemed to be nothing left to negotiate

Chapter Twenty
Partition & The Irish Free State
1921-1923

Carson Retires, General election 1921, "Dev" is Back, Friction Between deLavera and Collins, Change in Tactics, The Custom House Attack, IRA ill-Equipped, Sir James Craig, PM, Lloyd George vs DeValera, The "Scapegoats," No Pre-Conditions Reneged, A Crack in the Dam, War Within Three Days, The Anglo-Irish Treaty, Will The Real Government Please Stand Up? Misappropriated By "Mother England" By Coersion A "Civil" Stand-off, A Ray of Hope, Army Convention Declared Illegal, Army Convention at Mansion House, Pogrom in Ulster, Trouble Continues in Ulster, Justice Delayed, Special Powers Act, British Turn Over Weapons, IRA Seizes Four Courts, IRA Retaliation in the North, Northern IRA Outlawed Royal Ulster Constabulary, Election of Dail Erieann and/or Parliament, Wilson Assassinated, The Civil War Begins, Death of the Giants, William T. Cosgrave, Emergency Powers Act, Republicans on the Run, The Death of Childers, Reprisal Counter-Reprisal, , More Reprisal, The Civil War Ends, Mass Hunger Strike.

They Made History:

Sir Edward Carson: Prime Minister Northern Ireland. Resigned in 1921, succeeded by Sir James Craig.

Winston Churchill: British Secretary for War.

Michael Collins: Director of Military Ops, Treaty Delegate Commander-in Chief of Irish Free State Forces.

Sir James Craig: Leader of Unionist Party. Succeeded Carson as Prime Minister

David Lloyd George: British Prime Minister 1916- 1922. Imposed partition with the Government of Ireland Act.

Arthur Griffith: Publisher of Sinn Fein Erieann, Founder of Sinn Fein Party. Treaty delegate, President of Dail .

Liam Lynch: Chief of Staff of Irish Republican Army after the Treaty

Richard Mulcahy: Dail Minister of Defense.

Rory O'Connor: Member of the IRB Anti-treaty IRA leader at Four Courts seizure.

Eamon deValera: Survivor of 1916 Rising, President of the Free State.

Field Marshall Sir Henry Wilson: Formed and armed the B specials &the R.I.C.

Carson Retires:

Following the *Better Government for Ireland Act (1920)*, Sir Edward Carson, the newly appointed Prime Minister of Northern Ireland, retired from politics, having achieved his goals of partition, and a separate Belfast Parliament. The six counties no longer had to fear being a secular, and economic minority, controlled by a Dublin Parliament. The Unionist Council quickly replaced him with Sir James Craig, as Prime Minister, on February 4, 1921.

General Election 1921:

In May there was a general election for both Parliaments. In Dublin Sinn Fein swept 124 seats, with only the four Trinity University seats going to Nationalists, unopposed. In the North, the Belfast Parliament seated 40 of the Unionist Party, as the Nationalists, and Sinn Fein split the 12 remaining seats, 6 to 6. The Sinn Feiners, of both parliaments, joined together to form the second Dail Erieann, claiming to represent all 32 counties, north and south.

"Dev" is Back:

Having recently returned to Ireland, following his extended tour of the United States, Eamon deValera, with five million dollars in his coffer, was chosen President of the Second Dail Erieann. DeValera had concerns that the guerilla type warfare, of ambush and assassination, was not looked upon favorably by U.S. public opinion. The Irish Republican Army was now officially acknowledged as the Army of the Republic, and had sworn allegiance to the Dail.

Friction Between deValera and Collins:

There can be little doubt that deValera resented Michael Collins and was envious of his achievements. This is clearly obvious from a statement he made to Tom Cullen and Bat O'Connor upon his return from America.. In response to deValera's inquiry as to the state of affairs, Cullen replied, "Great, the Big Fellow is leading us, and everything is going marvelous." (sic)

DeValera responded to this angrily, "Big Fellow, eh? We'll see who's the Big Fellow!" [1]

He followed this up a few weeks later by ordering Collins to go to America, under Bruga's direction. Fortunately, he was over-ruled by the outraged reaction from within the Irish Republican Brotherhood, and forced to countermand the order.

Change of Tactics:

President deValera was also insisting upon a change of tactics, contending that public opinion in America did not look favorably upon the guerilla tactics currently employed. He felt that the IRA should meet the British forces in open battle, at least once a month, with a force of about five hundred men. Michael Collins was bitterly opposed to such a plan. He pointed out that the British had superior numbers, were better equipped, better trained, and better armed. He further contended that Irish losses of men and weapons could not be replaced, nor be afforded. His protest was useless, and he ultimately had to give in to the pressure.

The Custom House Attack:

Collins was at least successful in reducing the size of the force to one-hundred twenty men, instead of five-hundred. The chosen objective was to be the impressive 18th Century Dublin Customs House, on the River Liffey. The building was to be taken by surprise, and set on fire, the afternoon of May 21st. The attack, was to be carried out by the Dublin Brigade. Each volunteer, going into battle, had no more than four, or five rounds of ammunition, but the surprise was complete, and the building was burned as planned. The fire burned all night, the great golden dome collapsing into the rubble. Morning light revealed only smoldering rubble, where once stood a splendid architectural wonder.

It was a huge propaganda success, making sensational, world-wide headlines. Militarily it was a disaster. The attackers were soon surrounded, greatly outnumbered, out gunned, and overrun. Six of the volunteers were killed, and twelve were wounded. Seventy-five of the Brigade's best men were taken prisoner, along with their weapons One, or two more victories such as this would put the IRA out of the insurrection business for good.

IRA ill-Equipped:

After the burning of the Custom House, the IRA was confronted with a growing problem of shortages. They had little mobile equipment to begin with, but weapons were becoming less available, and there was practically no ammunition to serve the few weapons they still had. It reached the point where Collins felt that he could only field about 3,000 effective troops. They were forced to resort to the burning of soft targets, such as unionist houses and other private property. The British had begun to flood likely target areas with troops, forcing the IRA to fight a more defensive war.

But the government forces were also getting worn down. The Prime Minister realized that he was still opposed by a dangerous, and determined enemy. He finally concluded that he had but two options. He must either totally defeat the IRA, which could take time and be costly in more ways than one, or he could negotiate. He chose to negotiate.

Sir James Craig, PM:

On June 7th, King George V. went to Belfast, to officially open the Parliament of Northern Ireland, and Sir James Craig appointed his cabinet ministers. In his address, the King appealed to all Irishmen for conciliation, and forbearance.

Lloyd George vs. DeValera:

Lloyd George took this as a face-saving opportunity to open the door to negotiations. Selecting deValera as the man to deal with, he wrote him a letter, urging a meeting with himself, and Sir James Craig, to discuss a possible peace agreement. After conferring with his own people, north and south, and the remnants of the IRA, deValera accepted. With a delegation of six, he went to London to negotiate with Lloyd George. Collins was not included, as a calculated snub.(2) One wonders why he bothered to take the other delegates, as deValera left them entirely out of the talks, while he alone negotiated with the Prime Minister. A truce was signed on July 11th, and the fighting stopped. Discussion went on for the rest of the summer, and into the fall. Finally, agreement was reached to hold a conference with no preconditions regarding Ireland's unity with, or independence from Great Britain. At this point Craig withdrew, as he had no concerns with remaining issues.

The "Scapegoats:"

Being the clever politician that he was, deValera also chose not to continue to personally meet with Lloyd George. There has been much speculation regarding his reason for this decision. It appears that he had already concluded that agreement on acceptable terms could not be reached. Having met with Lloyd George, he knew him to be a crafty negotiator. Anticipating his insistence on partition and the oath to the crown, he chose to distance himself from an unpopular decision. In his stead, he appointed Arthur Griffith and Michael Collins, and five others as plenipotentiaries. Robert Barton, a member of the delegation, later recalled a revealing remark made by deValera, at the time, "We must have scapegoats." (3)

On October 11th, the "scapegoats" traveled to London to meet with Lloyd George, and his cabinet. DeValera's instructions to them specifically specified that partition was not acceptable, nor should they agree to any form of loyalty oath to the crown. If things went according to his instructions, all would be well. Alternatively, he was insulated from responsibility, if they did not.

"No Preconditions" Reneged:

Things started to go wrong right at the beginning. Lloyd George, reneged on his "no pre-preconditions" agreement with deValera, and dictated that the proposed terms must be in accordance with the Better Government for Ireland Act.

1. The British government would acknowledge the independence of the twenty-six southern counties as the new Irish government, called

2. *The Irish Free State,* with dominion status as Canada.

3. The six northern counties would be regarded as a part of Britain, thus allowing Northern Ireland to remain outside of the new state.

4. The Free State would assume its share of the National debt, incurred by Great Britain.

5. The control of the Irish Sea, would be retained by Great Britain, as well as several strategic harbors in Ireland, and other needed facilities.

6. A final provision would require all Members of Parliament, all members of Dail Erieann, and all officials to sign an oath of allegiance to the Crown. (4)

A Crack in the Dam:

He further pointed out that, in-as-much as deValera, himself, had agreed to the conference to include the Northern Ireland Prime Minister, and Arthur Griffith had previously signed an agreement regarding establishing the boundary commission, partition had already been established.

In all fairness to Griffith, at the time he agreed to the boundary commission, he felt that it would result in such small segmentation of Ulster that it would surely prove unworkable. (5) However, he was a man of honor, and refused to disavow his previous commitment. Therefore, he agreed to sign the treaty.

"War Within Three Days"....:

Michael Collins, and the other plenipotentiaries were taken aback by Griffith's concession, but they still objected to the oath of allegiance to the crown, and refused to sign. Lloyd George insisted that it would be necessary for all the delegates to sign the treaty. He showed them two sealed letters that he had written to

Sir James Craig. The first letter announced that the treaty was agreed to, and would be implemented. The second letter stated that the treaty had not been agreed to, and consequently, he said, "It is war--- and war within three days! Which letter am I to send?" (6)

Michael Collins was aware of the inability of the IRA to sustain the war, and win. He signed for the Sinn Fein, and the others followed his lead. Collins later commented to a friend, "I have just signed my own death warrant.

The Anglo-Irish Treaty:

The *Anglo-Irish Treaty,* was signed by Ireland and Britain on December 6, 1921. The Irish Free State was established as a dominion of Great Britain. The Provisional government was established on the same day, for a period of one year. On January

7, 1922 the Dail Eireann gave approval to the treaty, by a small margin of 64 to 57.

Eamon deValera wept at the result of the vote. He resigned as President, and along with the fifty-seven members opposed to the treaty, walked out of the Dail. On January 14, the remaining sixty-four members met in the Mansion House and again approved the Treaty.

Michael Collins was elected Chairman of the Provisional Government. On the same day, the British forces began to withdraw throughout the country, some barracks, and mobile equipment were turned over to the Provisional Government, which began to set up its headquarters in Dublin Castle.

Will The Real Government Please Stand Up:

At this point, the situation becomes rather clouded. Arthur Griffith was chosen to succeed deValera, as President of the Dail. Richard Mulcahy, was chosen as the Dail's Minister of Defense, By the terms of the Treaty, the Provisional Government, was established on January 14th, with Michael Collins as its Chairman. By virtue of his position as President of the Irish Republican Brother-hood, (who considered themselves to be the "real government of the Republic) he was also the Commander of the Irish Republican Army, as well as Commander in Chief of the Free State Army. (who still considered themselves to be the IRA.)

By some quirk of Gaelic logic, the two governments co-existed, by and large, with overlapping membership. Arthur Griffith, who was President of the Irish Dail, became Michael Collin's deputy in the Provisional Government, which answered to only Westminster. Richard Mulcahy, as Dail Minister of Defense, tried to maintain control of the Army, by reminding them of the oath they took to the Dail when the IRA was voted to officially be the Army of the Republic, which he insisted, it still was.

Meanwhile, fifty-seven members of the Dail, who followed deValera, still claimed to be the Dail which represented the Irish Republic, and that the segment of the Army opposing the Treaty, was the official Army of the Republic. They claimed that the Dail which accepted the Treaty had, in effect, voted itself out of existence. Consequently, they refused to acknowledge the Provisional Government of Southern Ireland, or take the oath to the crown.

Misappropriated by "Mother England, " by coercion!

Thus, Sinn Fein was divided into two opposing camps; the anti-treaty group, under deValera, with former Dail members, and two segments of the Army, opposing the Treaty. One division was under command of Liam Lynch, in Cork, and another division led by Rory O'Connor, in Dublin. They all represented the Republic, and they all refused the oath to the crown. The opposing camp, the Provisional Government, was led by Michael Collins, and Arthur Griffith. Their forces, comprised of former IRA members, was operating out of Dublin Castle, and was now called the Free State Army. The Parliament, composed of former Dail members, was meeting at the Mansion House, in Merrion Square.

A "Civil" Stand-off:

On February 18th the Army's mid-Limerick Brigade, which was opposed to the Treaty, moved to occupy the barracks that were being evacuated by the British. However, the First Western Division, pro-treaty, had already been ordered to occupy the same barracks. A dangerous standoff developed. Civil war threatened. The mayor of Limerick attempted a reconciliation between the two forces, without success. Liam Lynch, commanding the Southern Division, and Oscar Traynor, commanding the Dublin Brigade, were called in by Collins and Mulcahy to work out a solution. Fortunately, they were successful, and the barracks were turned over to the First Western Division. A civil war was, for the moment, averted.

A Ray of Hope:

Sinn Fein held its Ard Feis (*High convention)* on February 28, 1922. The situation looked hopeful when agreement was reached between the two opposing camps; deValera and Austin Stack on the one side, and Arthur Griffith and Michael Collins, the Provisional Government, on the other. The decision was made that Dail Eireann, (sometimes called the Parliament) would continue as it had, before the Treaty issue, with one hundred-twenty members, the existing president and cabinet remaining in office. The prospect of a civil war seemed less likely.

In early March a meeting was called in Dublin by Defense Minister Richard Mulcahy. Attending were Chief of Staff O'Duffy, a number of officers from the various divisions, and several officers of General Headquarters (GHQ). The purpose was to find some means of reconciliation between the pro-treaty, and anti-treaty elements of the Army. The solution would be presented at the Army convention, which was to be held March 26th.

Army Convention Declared Illegal:

The meetings went on for several days. While they were deliberating, they received notice of a decision of the Dail Cabinet, that a resolution they planned to present at the convention, removing the Army from the Dail's control, would be illegal. Hence the convention itself would be illegal, and was therefore cancelled.

Noting that this decision came from the Dail, namely Griffith and Mulcahy, and not the provisional government, (Collins), Rory O'Connor, a leader of the anti-treaty faction, insisted that they hold the convention anyway. His argument prevailed.

By resolution, the convention would be postponed until March 26, to enable all of the Army's, elected delegates to attend. The resolution was signed by all of the fifty-two officers attending.(7)

Army Convention at Mansion House:

The convention was held, as scheduled, at the Mansion House with 211 delegates attending. They reaffirmed their allegiance to the Irish Republic, and resolved that the Army continue as the Army of the Irish Republic. They also repudiated the authority of the Dail's Minister of Defense, Richard Mulcahy, to exercise any control over the Army. They elected six officers as a temporary executive. On April 9th the convention reassembled and adopted a constitution. They also elected Liam Lynch as Army Executive.

Pogrom in Ulster:

Immediately after the Dail's acceptance of the Treaty, the Ulster Volunteer Force, and B Specials, unleashed a pogrom of terror and murder, in the six northern counties, during the early months of 1922. Two hundred and thirty two Catholics were randomly murdered including two Catholic Members of Parliament, and nearly one thousand people were wounded.(8) This resulted in continuing retaliatory raids, in the boundary counties, by the IRA.

Trouble Continues in Ulster:

On February 21st, retired General Sir Henry Wilson was the successful Unionist MP candidate for County Down. On March 14, Craig appointed him as military advisor for Northern Ireland, with unlimited authority. One of the first things he did was to disband the Royal Irish Constabulary, which he considered to have too many Catholics among its ranks.

April brought renewed violence in Belfast. Entire Catholic families were randomly beaten to death, or shot by the Constabulary, or Sir Henry's B Specials. Sometimes the children were spared, only to see their parents shot down in front of them. Five year old Johnny Devlin, a threat to no-one, was brutally shot and killed, while playing with his friends.(9)

Justice Delayed:

The violence was exacerbated by the IRA's execution of former RIC District Inspector Swanzy, who had been found guilty, in 1920, by a coroner's court, of the murder of the Mayor of Cork, Tomas MacCurtain. Swanzy had never faced punishment for his crime. The execution had been ordered by Michael Collins. (10)

Special Powers Act:

On April 7th the Parliament of Northern Ireland passed the Special Powers Act, which allowed the B Specials virtually unlimited powers to stop and search, arrest without a warrant, and to imprison without a trial. Mere possession of a firearm was punishable by death. Whipping and torture became part of the routine.(11)

British Turn Over Weapons:

On April 12th, the British Secretary for War, Winston Churchill announced that the British forces would turn over 4,000 rifles, 2,200 revolvers, six machine guns and a large quantity of ammunition to the Irish Free State Army. (12) The Army of the Irish Republic (IRA), of course, would not benefit from this, or future turnovers.

IRA Seizes Four Courts:

On April 13th, in the wee hours of the night, anti-treaty members of the First and Second Battalions of the IRA's Dublin Brigade, commanded by Rory O'Connor, seized and fortified the Four Courts building. Situated on the north side of the River Liffey with its immense, copper-clad dome, the building extended some five hundred yards along the river. This impressive edifice had long been a symbol of British authority, and would now, for a time, become the headquarters for the Irish Republican Army. Before the sun rose, a second IRA force had taken control of the infamous Kilmainham Jail.(13)

IRA Retaliation in the North:

The government of Northern Ireland remained totally indifferent to the ongoing attacks and murders of Catholics. In May, the IRA Northern divisions carried out widespread attacks on Royal Irish Constabulary (RIC) barracks in counties Tyrone and Kerry. This was followed by bombings, and arson attacks in counties Antrim and Down. Violence in Belfast increased, on one weekend resulting in fourteen deaths, and countless injuries. On May 22nd, Unionist Member of Parliament W. J. Twaddell was assassinated in a daylight raid.(14)

Northern IRA Outlawed:

On May 23rd, 1922, the Government declared the IRA an illegal organization, and quickly arrested and interned over two hundred IRA members, including most of its leadership. This was a most fatal blow to Northern IRA activities.

Royal Ulster Constabulary:

On May 31st, Sir Henry Wilson replaced the disestablished RIC, with the Royal Ulster Constabulary (RUC), the ranks of which were entirely Protestant, and recruited primarily from the Orange Order. The new force was heavily armed for its primary mission of counter-insurgency, and general suppression of Catholics.

Election for Dail Erieann and/or Parliament

On June 16th, Southern Ireland held a general election for the Dail, and/or the Free State Parliament. The results were, Pro-Treaty seats fifty-eight, Anti-Treaty seats thirty-six; a clear majority in favor of the treaty. The Dail would be replaced by the Free State Parliament on June 30th, but before the delegates would be able take their seats, the situation would change drastically.

Wilson Assassinated:

On June 22nd, 1922, RUC commander, Sir Henry Wilson was assassinated. He was shot, and killed in front of his London home by two IRA hit men, under orders from Michael Collins. The credit, or blame for the deed, was mistakenly assigned to Rory O'Connor and his IRA brigade occupying the Four Courts. At the insistence of Winston Churchill, the Provisional Irish Government was forthwith required to remove and arrest those IRA members.

The Civil War Begins:

On June 26th, 1922, the Free State Army, using British provided 18 pound field guns, began shelling the Four Courts, which by June 28th was rendered to rubble. After a two day siege Rory O'Connor and one hundred of his troops had surrendered. The fighting lasted for five more days in other parts of Dublin. Hundreds more surrendered and were imprisoned. Cathal Brugha fought to the end, refusing to surrender.

The Irish Civil War which had begun in Dublin, spread very quickly to the rest of the country. General Liam Lynch of Cork, the Southern Division Commander, became the leader of the Republican side of the IRA. Eamon deValera enlisted as a private in the Third Battalion of the Dublin IRA.

The Death of the Giants:

Arthur Griffith, Irish scholar, journalist, founder of Sinn Fein, President of Dail Erieann, and first President of the Irish

Free State, died suddenly, of a cerebral hemorrhage, on August 12th, at the age of fifty years. After attending Griffith's funeral, Michael Collins traveled south to county Cork, in an effort to contact Liam Lynch, and hopefully, negotiate an end to the war. On August 22nd, at Beal na mBlath, his party ran into an ambush. In the exchange of fire, Collins was struck in the head by a single bullet. He died instantly. He was thirty-one years old. With him died the hopes of an early end to the civil war. His death plunged the entire country into a state of shock. What a leader, with his abilities, may have achieved, had he lived, can now only be imagined.

William T. Cosgrave:

Griffith was succeeded, as President of the Dail, and the Irish Free State by William T. Cosgrave on September 9th. Cosgrave had been a founding member of Sinn Fein, and the Irish Volunteers, and was a member of the Dail Cabinet. The Constitution of the Irish Free State was approved by Parliament on October 25th. It was officially ratified on December 5th by the Parliament and the British Government. President Cosgrave officially declared that the second Dail had come to an end on June 30. The sovereign assembly of the Irish Free State was now the Parliament elected the previous June.

Emergency Powers Act:

Without the moderating influence of the late Michael Collins, who had been reluctant to act against his former comrades, President Cosgrave and the new cabinet wasted no time in having the new Parliament pass the most insidious Emergency Powers Act, which basically empowered the Government to execute members of the irregulars, as the Irish Republican Army was now referred to, for any act of war it may choose.

Republicans on the Run:

Eamon deValera had been urged by the IRA executive to reorganize the Republican Government. The second Dail had never officially been dissolved. It had merely ceased to function after the death of Arthur Griffith. DeValera called upon the anti-treaty members of the Dail to convene as a government for the Irish Republic, thus maintaining a political entity for the Republicans. As time went by, however, the futility of their cause became more and more obvious. After the Emergency Powers Act, deValera and the members of the Dail were forced to go into hiding.

The Death of Childers:

On November 17th, Erskine Childers, patriot gun-runner of 1916, had been captured by Free State soldiers, in possession of a small revolver. Cosgrave's cabinet decided to make an example of him, but Childers was too well known and admired for the cabinet to appear to be acting summarily. To prepare public opinion they felt they must first establish a precedent. To this end, four non-ranking members of the IRA, who had earlier been arrested under Emergency Powers, for possessing weapons, were randomly selected, and executed by firing squad.

Childers had been convicted by a Military Court, and then appealed to the Dublin High Court for an order of *habeas corpus.* On November 24th, without waiting for the High Court's judgment, he was taken out for execution. Childers, forgivingly, shook the hand of each man on the firing squad, then, refusing a blindfold, stood against the wall, and was shot to death, by the authority of the Provisional Government.

Reprisal, Counter Reprisal, More Reprisal:

On November 30th, 1922, Liam Lynch issued an order to the Republican Army (IRA), that all members of Parliament who had voted for the "Murder Bill, " as it was now called, were to be shot on sight.

On December 6th, the anniversary date of the Treaty, the British Government ratified the Free State Constitution as provided in the Treaty, and approved by the Free State Parliament. The next day two members of the Parliament were fired upon. MP Sean Hales, who had been a close friend of Collins, was killed. Another MP Padraig O'Maille was wounded. The Government retaliated by executing Rory O'Connor and three other leaders of the Four Court take over.

These nine executions were the first of seventy-seven such killings that would be ordered by the Free State Government in the course of the next five months. Reprisal fostered counter reprisal, and on, and on. The killing and burning continued. Eventually the Republican forces would have to lose to the superiority of the Free State Army in manpower, weapons, ammunition and equipment.

Liam Lynch was killed on April 10th, near Clonmel, Country Cork. On April 27th deValera and Frank Aiken, the IRA Chief-of-Staff, issued an order to cease fighting.

The Civil War Ends:

The fighting slowly petered out, the Civil War officially ended on May 2nd, 1923, without formalities. It has been estimated that during the eleven month war, there was a total of over 4,000 men lost. The imprisonment of IRA members continued for the rest of the year. The IRA, or what was left of it, went into hiding. Rather than surrender their weapons, they buried them, for future use. By July there were over 11,000 men and about 250 women in Free State prisons, many without the formality of a trial.

Mass Hunger Strike:

In protest, hundreds of the prisoners staged a mass hunger strike, in the course of which, several of them died. In response, the government decided to release them, a few at a time. Slowly, in the course of several months, they were all set free, but the bitter memory, on both sides, of acts committed, lives lost, and property destroyed, would impact Irish public life for decades to come.

Chapter Twenty-One
The Republic of Ireland
1923-1949

Cumann na nGaedheal, Garda Siochanna Established, The Hogan Act, Sinn Fein Heard From, A Propaganda Ploy, A Nation Among Nations, The Warriors of Destiny, DeValera Hits New York Again, O'Higgins Assassinated, DeValera Fakes the Oath, Irish Press Founded, The Statute of Westminster, Army Comrades Association, The General Election of 1932, The Economic War, DeValera Dismissed O'Duffy, Large Farmers Stop Annuities, Maintaining Law and Order, Violence Continues, DeValera Abolishes Senate, Exit O'Duffy, Constitutional Amendment Act, New Constitution for Erie, Economic War Settled, Controversy Over Remaining in the Commonwealth, Prevention of Violence Bill, Erie Declares Neutrality, Attacks in Dublin, The War Years, Churchill Declares Victory, DeValera Responds, There'll Be Some Changes Made, The Republic of Ireland Act., Britain Recognizes the Republic, AT LAST! A NATION ONCE AGAIN!

They Made History:

William T. Cosgrave: Member of Sinn Fein, 1916 Volunteer, Supported Treaty, President Executive Council of the Irish Free State.

Eamon deValera: Commander 3rd Batallion 1916, President of Irish Republic 1921, Anti-Treaty, founded Fianna Fail, , President of Free State 1932

Kevin O'Higgins: Deputy and Free State minister of Justice, Assassinated 7/27.

Desmond Fitzgerald: Free State Minister of Industry and Commerce.

Patrick McGilligan: Free State Attorney General

Frank Aiken: Minister for Co-ordination of Defensive Measures 1939-45,

Eoin O'Duffy: First Commissioner of Guarda Siochan Fired by deValera, Fascist leader of the Blueshirts, President of Fine Gael

Douglas Hyde: A scholar and noted writer, co-founder of the Gaelic League, Chosen as the First President of the Republic of Ireland

Cumann na nGaedheal:

In March 1923, shortly before the end of the war, President Cosgrave had founded the Cumann na nGaedheal as the government pro-treaty party. This would be the ruling party for the next decade. Meanwhile, Eamon deValera and his Sinn Fein followers were either on the run, or already in jail, under the Emergency Powers Act.

Garda Siochanna Established:

On August 8th, 1923, the Free State Government passed an act establishing the Garda Siochanna. President Cosgrave appointed Eoin O'Duffy as the Garda's first commissioner. Like O'Duffy, a major portion of the officers were former IRA officers, and the ranks were made up of former volunteers many of them friends of Michael Collins. Most were men, who like Collins and Griffith, supported the Treaty. The pay was low, and often late, and the hours were long. This was the beginning of Ireland's highly regarded unarmed police force.

The Hogan Act:

On August 9th, the government passed the Hogan Act, wherein they agreed to the payments of annuities to the British Government, of 5,000,000 pounds per year, to reimburse the British Government the cost of buying out the estates of the Anglo-Irish landlords, as per the previous land act. **(1)**

Sinn Fein is Heard From:

In order to secure a new mandate against deValera, and his followers, the government set up a special election for August 27th. The constituencies had now been amended to provide 153 seats in the Parliament instead of the 128 seats there had been in the Dail. There were 87 Sinn Fein candidates, including deValera, who decided to stand for election, in spite of their tenuous status as fugitives, or prisoners.

A Propaganda Ploy:

DeValera made a public announcement that he would speak at Ennis, in County Clare, at the election rally on August 15th. It is believed that his intention was to get himself arrested as publicly as possible, to gain a well publicized platform, from which to speak out against the treaty. Taking a page from "Michael Collins book, " he made it to the speakers platform without being recognized. At that point he was discovered, and accommodated, by the Free State soldiers who quickly arrested him. The authorities soon realized his purpose, and decided not to bring charges that would afford him a free platform. He was held for nearly a year.

What the government party found most distressing however were the results of the election. Cumann na nGaedheal Party lost their majority, winning only 62 seats, to Sinn Fein's 44 seats. The Farmers Party won 15 seats, the Labour Party 14, and the Independents 17. This meant that Sinn Fein would now become the most powerful opposition party, if it weren't for the fact that so many of the electees were in jail. Even in jail, deValera had become a political force, with which to be reckoned.

A Nation Among Nations:

On September 10th, 1923, The Free State of Erie (Ireland) was admitted to the League of Nations. This was still a far cry from the dream of a republic, composed of a thirty-two county independent nation, but it was a step in that direction. Ireland was now officially recognized by the other nations of the world as a member of the world community.

The "Warriors of Destiny:"

On May 26th, 1926 deValera founded a new republican party, which would soon be called the "Fianna Fail, " taking its name from the legendary Fenian warriors. The new party made a poor showing in the special election, taking only 35 of the 153 seats. The government, pro-treaty party, Cumann na nGaedheal, was not much impressed by the "Warriors of Destiny."

DeValera Hits New York Again:

After Fianna Fail had been firmly established as a political party, deValera scheduled a trip to the United States for a two month, nation-wide fund raising campaign.. On March 5th, 1927 deValera landed in New York, where he was received with open arms and open pocketbooks. The popularity he had gained in 1919 and 1920 had not waned a bit. People clamored to get into the meetings where he spoke. While in New York, he managed to gain control of the $3,000,000 dollars remaining in the New York Banks from his earlier trip, in spite of Cosgrave's attempt to obtain an injunction to prevent it. On May 1st, deValera, a man of means, left Boston to the cheers of thousands of Irish-Americans. (2)

The next year on June 9th, 1927 the general election was a different story. Fianna Fail captured 44 seats, only 3 less than the Cumann na nGaedheal's 47 seats. The remaining 66 seats were closely divided among three smaller parties. This weakened the Cumann na nGaedheal, and make Fianna Fail its largest opposition party. Except for one little detail: deValera and his followers still refused to take the oath, and were therefore denied their seats. (3)

O'Higgins Assassinated:

On July 10th, 1927, President Cosgrave's deputy, and Minister for Justice, Kevin O'Higgins, was assassinated on his way to mass, by three unidentified former IRA men, acting independently. This atrocity resulted in a crack down on the IRA, under the Public Safety Act .

DeValera Fakes the Oath:

A secondary result was that the Parliament ruled that Fianna Fail members, recently elected, would be required to either take the oath, or forfeit their seats. DeValera decide to take the oath and his seat, but before doing so he quietly placed the Bible aside, and then placed a blank sheet of paper to cover the oath, before signing below in the space provided. Thus he later claimed that he never really took the oath. **(4)**

That sounds somewhat like the old trick used by children, when making a false promise, or telling a lie, but at the same time crossing their fingers. They did not think it dishonorable, merely clever. Apparently, Mr. deValera was a very "clever" politician. In any event, Mr. deValera took his seat in Parliament, as did his Fianna Fail followers. One wonders if they were all as clever as deValera.

Irish Press Founded:

In September, 1931, Eamon deValera founded the *Irish Press*. This was to be the public voice of Fianna Fail, funded by bond issues, controlled by a board of seven directors. The chief director actually had absolute control, and as you probably have guessed, his name was Eamon deValera. The paper, with national circulation, would be a major factor in the general election that would be held in 1932.**(5)**

The Statute of Westminster:

Three cabinet members, Minister for Defense, Desmond Fitzgerald, Minister for Industry and Commerce, Patrick McGilligan, and Attorney General John A. Costello, worked closely with officials of the other dominions of the British Commonwealth, Canada, and Australia to reshape the dominions into a free association of self governing states. Due, in large part to their efforts, the British Parliament passed the Statute of Westminster on December 11, 1931. By its terms, laws enacted by Dominion Parliaments could no longer be voided or overridden by the Westminster Parliament, and the laws enacted by Westminster, without the concurrence of the Dominion shall have no affect. It further provided that any existing laws enacted by Westminster, pertaining to a given Dominion, may be repealed by the concerned Dominion. In effect, the Dominions were free to control their own destinies.**(6)**

The Army Comrades Association:

On February 9, 1932 the Army Comrades Association was founded. Much of its membership was drawn from the recently released IRA prisoners, who had been, and still were, supporters of the treaty.

The General Election of 1932:

Fianna Fail was the big winner in the 1932 general election capturing 72 of the 153 seats. Cumann na nGaedheal retained only 57 seats. 11 Seats went to the Independents, 7 to Labour, 4 to the Farmer's Party, and 2 to the Independent Labour Party. DeValera, of course, was subsequently elected President of the Irish Assembly and formed a new government, with the support of the Labour Party.(7)

The first order of business for the new government was keeping deValera's campaign promise, to remove the oath of allegiance to the Crown from the constitution. The second order of business, a major priority, was the release of the IRA prisoners. DeValera was of the opinion that former President Cosgrave was a little too enthusiastic in his enforcement of The Public Safety Act, as was his choice of Garda Commissioner O'Duffy. Some of these prisoners were against the treaty, but many more now favored the treaty. DeValera, to his credit, made no distinctions. All were released.

A third order of business was the termination of payment of annuities to the British Government. This seems reasonable, in as much as the purpose of annuities was to reimburse the British Government for property that they confiscated from Ireland, during and after, the Norman conquest.

The Economic War:

Mother England did not take kindly to this development. To compensate for the loss of 5,000,000 pounds of annual annuities, she retaliated by taxing the import of cattle from Ireland. The Irish Free State, in turn, began taxing British goods imported into Ireland (including coal). This, of course, greatly exacerbated the effect of the worldwide economic depression of the thirties, on Ireland, specially for the farmer. DeValera proposed settling the matter by international arbitration. Britain refused the offer, stating that the arbitration court should be within the British Empire. **(8)** *Like a fox to guard the hen house.*

DeValera Dismisses O'Duffy:

On February 22, 1933, deValera fired General Eoin O'Duffy as Chief Commisioner of the Garda Siochana. Not only had O'Duffy enjoyed, too much, the job of arresting members of the IRA, but there were credible rumors that he, along with two highly placed government officials, was planning a coup d'etat. There were also counter-rumors that deValera was planning to establish a dictatorship, and that he was a communist. On July 20th O'Duffy was offered the leadership of the recently formed Army Comrades Association (ACA). He accepted the offer. The ACA had adopted the Blueshirt as a uniform. O'Duffy, it seems, had developed some rather radical ideas of his own, regarding public morality, masculine virility, and law enforcement. (9) He changed the name of the ACA to the National Guard, and introduced the one arm salute that was so popular with the national-socialist party, now growing in Germany. Ireland now, had two independent armies operating within its borders: The IRA, and Blueshirts, as they were now called.

Large Farmers Stop Annuities:

A public issue arose as a result of the economic war. The large farm owners, who purchased grazing land from the Free State Government, stopped paying their annuities for the purchase. Violent acts were committed by individuals. Lines were drawn. In September 1933, Cumann na nGaedheal joined with the Centre Party and the ACA, to form the United Ireland Party, in Irish called "Fine Gael, " with General O'Duffy as its leader. Many of the large farmers were in Fine Gael. On the other side was the Fianna Fail, the Labour Party, and the IRA.

Maintaining Law and Order:

DeValera, and the Dail, as the Government, tried to maintain a public appearance of maintaining the law, revoked all fire arms certificates. He stated that the Government would not tolerate private armies. Still, incident, followed incident. DeValera was criticized by Fianna Fail for not taking a stronger republican position. In April 1935, Sean Russell, IRA Chief-of-Staff met with deValera in an effort to negotiate IRA and Fianna Fail cooperation. DeValera wanted the IRA to stand-down and forsake the use of violence. Russell wanted deValera to agree to declare the Republic within five years. DeValera was unable to agree to those terms.

Violence Continues:

Violence flared in Kerry, and spread to other parts of the country. O'Duffy went on a fascist rampage throughout Ireland, purportedly to "save the country from the communists." Ulitimately, deValera's main effort was turned against the Blueshirts, and the National Guard, both of which he proclaimed on August 22, 1933. Over the next year public opinion turned strongly against the Blueshirts, and Fine Gael Party. Eoin O'Duffy was under extreme pressure as president of the Fine Gael Party, and in September 1934, resigned from that position, and from the party.

DeValera Abolishes Senate:

The IRA had also come under fire by deValera for its unlawful use of violence as an instrument of policy, and its association with *Saor Erie, (Free Ireland)* and other communist organizations. The Dail had passed legislation condemning the IRA, the Blueshirts, and subversive organizations, but the Senate had been a road block. On May 29, 1936 deValera abolished the Senate because of its obstruction of his anti-Blueshirt and IRA legislation. This was followed up on June 18, by legislation declaring the IRA to be an illegal organization. I found it somewhat remarkable that the President of the Assembly had the authority to simply abolish the Senate but he did it anyway.

Exit O'Duffy:

In November, Eoin O'Duffy, and what was left of the Blueshirts, traveled to Spain to fight in the Civil War for the fascist forces of General Franco, as the Irish Brigade. O'Duffy would return to Ireland in 1937, and political obscurity. He would become a recluse, and die in 1944, …"a broken, aged man, only in his mid-fifties."(10)

Constitutional Amendment Act:

On December 11, 1936 the Dail passed an amendment to the Constitution of 1922, which removed all reference to the British Crown, and/or the King's governor General of Ireland. This was followed the very next day by the External Relations Act. By its terms, the effect was the same as if the King had abdicated as King of Ireland, and was thereafter recognized, and acknowledged as a neighboring monarch, with whom Ireland had various trade relations, and some areas of mutual interest.(10)

New Constitution for Erie:

On June 14, 1937 the Dail approved a whole new constitution for the Irish Free State, which replaced the Treaty of 1921, and all the terms thereof. There were several new changes. Sean Lemass, deValera's minister for industry and commerce was able to establish Aer Lingus, as Ireland's national air service. In addition to instating the President of the Dail, the new document also provided for a Prime Minister (Taoiseach) and restored the Senate (Seanad), which deValera had abolished the previous May. The powers of the Seanad, however, were limited, having only the ability to delay legislation.

In the late thirties, with the new constitution, came new efforts by Fianna Fail, for development of industrialization, and for the creation of infrastructure.The constiution re-established a national police force, the Garda Siochana, and replaced the judicial system. A civil service, fashioned after the British model was established. The tri-color flag, of green, white and orange was adopted as the national ensign.

The National School System was also created, establishing compulsory education for all Irish children, and requiring that Irish, as a language, be taught in all schools. It provided for the future development of the Shannon hydro-project, to provide power for the rural areas, and provide assistance in establishing an industrial base, similar to that which existed in the six northern counties. Major changes were also made to upgrade agriculture by opening more lands to grazing, as an alternative to subsistence farming. It provided help for farmers to diversify agriculture, and make improved use of the land.

Provision was made for religious freedom of all faiths. Article 44 provided for a special position for the Catholic Church, but at the same time freedom of religion was guaranteed for all people of all faiths. (Article 44 would be overwhelmingly repealed by referendum in 1972.) Today, all churches are treated equally. The document stated that these laws would apply to all of Ireland, but added that, pending the re-integration of the national territory, the laws would apply only to the twenty-six counties of Southern Ireland. (11)

A public referendum vote was held on July 1st, and the new constitution was approved by a substantial majority of the voters, and became effective on December 29th, 1937. Douglas Hyde, a co-founder of the Gaelic League, 1893, was elected as the First President of Erie.

Economic War Settled:

Agreement was reached between Great Britain and Erie on April 25th, 1938. Britain agreed to a final settlement on the annuities question and an end to the trade war, for a total amount of 10,000,000 pounds. Ireland conceded free access to the ports of Cobh, Berehaven, and Lough Swilly. Irish goods were to be admitted to the British market tariff free. The quantity of agricultural products would be regulated, of course, as were certain classes of British goods imported into Ireland controlled, to protect Irish industry. **(12)**

Controversy Over Remaining in the Commonwealth:

Following the removal of the oath of allegiance to the crown, the External Relations Act, the approval of the new constitution, and the economic settlement, there remained considerable question as to whether Ireland would remain in the British Commonwealth. The question was not decided at that time, but as it worked out, Ireland did not attend Commonwealth Conferences from 1937 until 1948.

In late December of 1938, the Irish Republican Army Council unlawfully presumed the authority to act for the legitimate government of Ireland. It issued an ultimatum for British forces to withdraw from Ireland. Quite naturally, with war looming in Europe, the British ignored the threat. Consequently, the IRA bombing campaign began in Britain on January 12, 1939. In the beginning only property was intended as targets, but before long, some the bombers changed the rules, placing their explosives in crowded public locations. Civilian casualties mounted. **(13)**

The Prevention of Violence Bill:

The terrorist attacks resulted in a response from the British Government. It came in the form of the Prevention of Violence Bill on July 24, 1939. It made it easier for the authorities to obtain search warrants, which resulted in the seizure of large quantities of explosive materials. It also provided the authority to expel Irish nationals from Great Britain, on suspicion, for little, or no cause.

Many Irish farmers had been forced to emigrate to England for work, as a result of the economic war. Returning them to Ireland worked great hardships on the hundreds of deportees, as well as the Irish Government, who was then faced with the problem of what to do with them.

On August 25, 1939, a psychopathic bomber rode his bicycle into a crowded market area. Realizing that the device on his bicycle was about to explode, he left it parked on a crowded street. Five people were killed outright and over 50 were severely injured. At that point there had been 127 bombing attacks by the IRA, 57 of them occurring in London. **(14)**

Erie Declares Neutrality:

On September 2, 1939, Eamon deValera, as Taoiseach, firmly declared Ireland's intention to remain neutral in the anticipated war between Great Britain and Germany. This would be a difficult position to maintain, by deValera, who perceived it as essential to Ireland's assertion of sovereignty. Frank Aiken very carefully explained it: *"It has always been one of the difficult problems in human relationship (sic). Instead of earning the respect and goodwill of both belligerents it is regarded by both with hatred and contempt. 'He who is not with me is against me.' In modern total warfare it is not a condition of peace with both belligerents, but rather a condition of limited warfare with both; a warfare whose limits, under the terrific and all prevailing force of modern total warfare, tend to expand to coincide with those of total warfare. In cold economic and military fact it is becoming more and more difficult to distinguish between the seriousness of the two emergencies called war and neutrality, "* **(15)**

Attacks in Dublin:

Not all of the IRA attacks of this period occurred in London. Seventy of them happened in Ireland. But on December 23, 1939 they went too far. They raided the Magazine Fort, in Dublin's Phoenix Park. Unfortunately, the magazine was poorly guarded, and a gate left unlocked. The raid was well planned, and no-one was injured. The raiders, however made off with the bulk of the ammunition of the Irish Army, over a million rounds. It required thirteen lorries to carry it off. It was such an easy heist, that there was much speculation to the effect that it was a set up by the government in order to provide them with an excuse to declare war on the IRA.

But declare war, they did! Ten days later Emergency legislation was passed by the Dail, authorizing detention without trial. The government went to war against the IRA, and set up a security force of over 13,000 men throughout Ireland. Within a few weeks all but one lorry of ammunition had been recovered. The increased number of arrests filled the prisons, resulting in prison riots and hunger strikes. Stephen Hayes, IRA Chief of Staff called off hunger strikes, but by March 1940, the bombing campaign was over.

On August 16, 1940, the Dail deleted the right of appeal from a military tribunal, convened under the Emergency Powers Act. The death sentence could be, and would be imposed. During the war years, or during "The Emergency, " as it was called, twenty-seven IRA men were either executed, or permitted to starve themselves to death. The IRA virtually disappeared. **(16)**

The War Years:

On September 3rd, Winston Churchill declared war between Great Britain and Nazi Germany. During the "Emergency" years as they were referred to in Ireland, deValera scrupulously maintained Ireland's neutrality. But not all the Irish remained neutral. Some 44, 000 of Ireland's sons enlisted in the British Army. Throughout the war Germany maintained diplomatic relations with Ireland, and to some extent an intelligence effort was made by German agents, through IRA contacts. This was of a limited nature, due in part to ineptitude, and partly because there just wasn't that much going on to report.

Both Northern Ireland and Southern Ireland suffered casualties from German air strikes. Dublin was bombed accidentally on May 30, 1940 when German pilots were confused by British radio frequency jamming and bombed the wrong target. Thirty four people were killed. The North was attacked twice, because it was part of the British Empire. The first attack on Belfast occurred on April 15, 1941, when one hundred eighty German planes dropped one hundred tons of explosives on a residential area. Seven hundred forty-five civilians were killed. The second attack was on May 1, 1941 with two-hundred four planes dropping 95,000 incendiary bombs on the Belfast shipyards, killing one hundred-fifty people. **(17)**

Churchill Declares Victory:

The war ended in 1945. Winston Churchill, in his victory speech on BBC spoke very derisively of the Irish Government, regarding its position of neutrality: *"However with a restraint and poise with which I say history will find few parallels His Majesty's Government never laid a violent hand upon them though at times it would have been quite easy and quite natural. And we left the deValera Government to frolic with the Germans and later with the Japanese Representatives to their hearts content."*

DeValera Responds:

Three days later Eamon de Valera replied to Mr. Churchill's rebuke: *"Mr. Churchill is proud of Britain's stand alone, after France had fallen and before America entered the war. Could he not find in his heart the generosity to acknowledge that there is a small nation that stood alone not for one year or two, but for several hundred years against aggression; that endured spoliations, was clubbed many times into insensibility, but that each time on returning consciousness took up the fight anew; a small nation that could never be got to accept defeat and has never surrendered her soul.* **(18)**

There'll Be Some Changes Made:

In the three years immediately following the war, change was in the air. The decline of the Cumann na nGaedheal Party gave rise to a new party called Fine Gael. This new party, working with the Labour Party, and another new party, called Clann na Poblachta, joined forces with Clann na Talmhan, and the Independents, to form a coalition. Together they were able to defeat the former majority party, Fanna Fail, headed by deValera. This inter-party government elected former attorney general John A. Costello, as Taoiseach, on February 18, 1948.

Republic of Ireland Act:

In September Costello announced the intention of the new government to repeal the External Relations Act of 1936. This was accomplished in December with the passing of the Republic of Ireland Act which finally proclaimed that Ireland was a Republic. This automatically repealed the External Relations Act.

Britain Recognizes the Republic:

On June 2, 1949, Westminster passed the Ireland Act, which declared that Ireland was not a part of British dominions, but was to be regarded as a foreign country. Great Britain recognized the free and independent Republic of Ireland. The Act also stated that Britain would retain control of Ulster until the Parliament of Northern Ireland agreed to join the Republic of Ireland. **AT LAST! A NATION ONCE AGAIN!**

REPUBLIC OF IRELAND
26 Counties
1949
DONEGAL
SLIGO
MAYO
LEITRIM
CAVAN
LOUTH
ROSCOMMON
LONGFORD
WEST MEATH
MEATH
GALWAY
OFFALY
DUBLIN
KILDARE
LEIX
WICKLOW
CLARE
CARLOW
KILKENNY
TIPPERARY
WEXFORD
KERRY
CORK
WATERFORD

Chapter Twenty-Two
The Post "Emergency" Years
1949-1971

IRA Hiatus, DeValera Looses Some Support, Partition Causes Divergence, Emigration Again an Option, Act of Oireachtas, Mother-Child Health Program Crisis, The Maura Lyons Case, The Troubles Begin, DeValera Taoiseach Again, Economic Growth Increased, President Kennedy Cites Irish Progress, DeValera Takes a Back Seat, The Modernization of Ireland, More Trouble from Paisley, Television Comes to Ireland, DeGualle Vetos Common Market Bid, Captain Terence O'Neill, Change of Focus on Partition, A Brief Period of Peace, The Lynch Commission, Changes in Northern Ireland, Some Things Don't Change, IRA in Decline, All It Takes is a Spark, The Ulster Volunteer Force, Paisley Again, Northern Ireland Civil Rights Association (NICRA), Trouble in Derry, More Trouble in Derry, Elections Changes in Britain and Northern Ireland, The Battle of Bogside, Rioting in Belfast, The Downing Street Declaration, Westminster to the Rescue, The Hunt Committee. The Provisional IRA, More Riots in Armagh, Belfast and Derry, B-Specials Disbanded, Political Crisis in the Republic, Conservatives Control Westminster, The Marching Season, Running the Blockade, The Social Democratic Labour Party (SDLP), A New Bombing Campaign, Sterner Measures Called For, Internment Without Trial, Every Action Has An Opposite Reaction, The Ulster Defense Association.

They Made History:

Neil Blaney: Cabinet member under Jack Lynch, Accused in arms plot.

Dr. Noel Brown: Noted for his efforts to control TB, and author of "Mother Child Health Scheme."

James Chichester Clark: Northern Ireland Prime Minister(1961-1971.)

John A Costello: Taioseach 1948-51, 1954-57.

Bernadette Devlin: Elected Stormount MP for Mid-Ulster 1969.

Gerry Fitts: A Belfast socialist and early leader in the N.I.C.R.A..

Charles Haughy: Cabinet member under Jack Lynch, Accused in arms plot.

John Hume: Derry school teacher, and civil rights leader. Elected to Parliament.

John Fitzgerald Kennedy: President of the United States, (1956-1962.)

Jack Lynch: Taoiseach following Lemass. (1966-1973).

Professor Patrick Lynch: Head of the Commission on Education in 1960.

Maura Lyons: Fifteen year-old Catholic girl, abducted and converted by Paisley.

Sean Lemass: Minister for Industry & Commerce, Taioseach (1959-66).

Sean MacBride: Chief of Staff of the IRA, and founder of Clann na Polachta.

Eddie McAteer: Nationalist Member of Parliament and civil rights leader.

Eamon McCann: Northern socialist civil rights leader.

Sean T. O'Kelly: President of the Irish Republic (1945-59).

Capt. Terence O'Neil: Prime Minister of Northern Ireland(1963-69).

Rev. Ian Paisley: A Presbyterian minister, anti-papists, and eloquent speaker, extreme ethnic bias.

T.K Whitaker: Secretary of the Department of Finance in the Republic:

IRA Hiatus:

The IRA was somewhat in-active in "post-emergency" Ireland, its public image having been damaged by its connection to the German intelligence service during the war. But it was far from dead. The leadership had begun to redefine its purpose, and to reinvent itself, in order to achieve the goal of a thirty-two county republic. They would focus their attention on trying to entice Northern Ireland into union with the South. There was still much inequality in the North, between Irish-Protestants, and Irish-Catholics, so the IRA concentrated on campaigning for civil rights and equal treatment of all citizens.

DeValera Looses Some Support:

The harsh treatment meted out to the IRA during the "emergency years, " and in the post war years, under the Offenses Against the State Act, had cost deValera some republican support. They concluded that he was more concerned with obtaining power, than he was for achieving the unity of a thirty-two county republic. The IRA believed that the proclaiming of Ireland as a republic amounted to nothing more than a name change for the Irish Free State.(1) The leadership of the IRA was, more or less, of the collective opinion that the separation of the republic from Great Britain would facilitate ending partition, and reuniting the thirty-two counties. Prime Minister Clement Atlee's government did all they could to disabuse them of that notion, and make it perfectly clear that such a course would be of no avail. The Ireland Act clearly specified that, Northern Ireland could only cease to be part of the British Empire with the specific consent of the Northern Ireland Parliament.(2)

Partition Causes Divergence:

The general feeling in Ireland was that by taking the Republic out of the British Commonwealth, the partitioning of the Island had become more and more permanent. Indeed, northern and southern Ireland had, in fact, become increasingly isolated from one another.

Emigration Again an Option:

As a result of remaining neutral during the war, southern Ireland had become somewhat isolated from the other nations of the world. Still primarily an agrarian country, lacking industrial development and infrastructure, Ireland found herself in the grip of unemployment and stagnation. Emigration again became an option for many, rivaling the depression of the 1880s. Ulster, on the other hand, being part of the British welfare state, with its National Health Service, was highly motivated to maintain the *status quo*.

The Social Security Act of 1947 initiated a program in Ulster, the likes of which, did not even exist in the South. The frosting on the cake, however, was Westminster's Northern Ireland Education Act, which enabled everyone, including impoverished, Catholic students, to attain higher education. (3) The gap widened.

Act of Oireachtas:

In 1950, however, the two Irelands came a step closer together, when an agreement was reached on June 13th, to cooperate on a drainage, and power development plan, by an Act of Oireachtas, (a joint session of the Dail and the Senate) in the republic, and later approved by the Belfast Parliament on June 27th. Another important agreement between Dublin and Belfast was reached in January of the following year for a joint operation of the Great Northern Railway.

The Mother-Child Health Program Crisis:

Inner-party conflict, was precipitated by objections concerning the "mother-and-child" health program, which was advocated by the highly respected Dr. Noel Brown. Two major institutions of Irish society had concerns.

The medical profession felt that absence of financial means, should be a criteria for eligibility. Doctors were concerned that it was, as written, providing socialized medical care for all mothers, whose children were under the age of sixteen.

The Catholic Church opposed the program because it included an educational program for the mothers, which went beyond instruction in child care. Prevention of insemination was implied, or at least suspected. This was deemed immoral by "Mother Church" due to the possibility of artificial birth control advocacy, or even abortion. In spite of Dr. Brown's reputation and public esteem, once the Catholic Church voiced its disapproval of the matter, it was a dead issue. (4)

The Fall of Clann na Poblachta:

Advocacy of the program, led by the leader of the Clann na Poblachta, Sean McBride, weakened Costello's government. McBride called for Dr. Brown to resign, and one month later Costello was swept from office, in the general election of 1951, and Clann na Poblachta ceased to exist. John Costello was succeeded by Eamon deValera as Taoiseach, and Dr. Noel Brown was, himself, re-elected as minister of health. Three years later, 1954, the revolving door of the Dail went around again, and deValera was out and Costello was back in. In that same year, Sean T. O'Kelly was elected for his second term as President of Ireland, and the republic was admitted to membership in the United Nations Organization. Erskine Childers, Costello's minister for posts and telegraphs, was appointed to the Commission Radio Ireland, *Comhairle Radio Erieann*, with authority to establish a national broadcasting system.

The Maura Lyons Incident:

In October 1956, a fifteen year-old Catholic girl, Maura Lyons, disappeared from her home in Belfast. Her family and friends searched frantically for her. A police effort turned up nothing. She reappeared, however, seven and a half months later in the home of Reverend Ian Paisley, a Presbyterian minister. She was now a member of Paisley's Protestant sect, the "Free Presbyterian Church of Ulster, " which had been founded by Paisley five years earlier. The court quickly removed the teenager from Paisley's home, and placed her in a remand center. She was ruled a ward of the court by Lord Dermot, lord chief justice. Paisley was not held accountable. (5)

The Troubles Begin:

In the early nineteen fifties a splinter group of the IRA, called Saor Uladh, opposed to partition, launched a series of successful attacks on police barracks in Counties Fermanagh and Armagh, for the purpose of acquiring weapons. This was but a preview of the violence to follow in the coming years. The IRA opened its campaign in Northern Ireland in November, 1956 with attacks on border customs posts. Guerrilla columns continued these attacks in an effort to protect vulnerable Irish-Catholics in Ulster. They were met with stiff resistance from a well organized military, and police force, which kept them fighting a defensive war for the next five years.

DeValera Taioseach Again:

Meanwhile, the revolving door of politics went around again in 1957, taking Costello out, and bringing deValera in again as taioseach. With Sean Lemass, as minister for industry and commerce, the republicans passed an act establishing the Agricultural Research Institute in Feb 1958. In April of that year,

Lemass was successful in initiating an air service, Aer Lingus, to North America.

Economic Growth Increased:

In 1958, the secretary of the department of finance, T.K. Whitaker published the results of a survey, titled *Economic Development,* proposing that the government should increase its capital investment, accompanied with appropriate economic planning. Whitaker advocated a policy of free trade, rather than the then current protectionist program which had led to stagnation. Foreign investment was encouraged, and sought. Light industry such as communications, and electronics was developed. Farming was modernized, and hydro-development was expanded.

President Kennedy Cites Irish Progress:

U.S. President, John F. Kennedy, visiting Ireland in 1963, showed his Irish-American pride when he addressed the Oireachtas. He said to the joint session, "You have modernized your economy, harnessed your rivers, diversified your industry, liberalized your trade, electrified your farms, accelerated your rate of growth, and improved the living standards of your people."(6)

The government subsequently published its first *Programme for Economic Expansion (sic).* This is credited for doubling the annual economic growth rate to four per cent for the next several years, and reduced emigration.(7)

DeValera Takes a Back Seat

In 1959 deValera retired from active politics, and was elected to replace the retiring Sean T. O'Kelly, as President of the Republic. This was primarily a symbolic position, but for the next fourteen years it would be occupied by Mr. deValera, who would continue to exert a strong indirect influence in both the national and the international arenas.

The Modernization of Ireland:

Sean Lemass, was elected to replace deValera as Taoiseach. Previously, as minister for industry and commerce, Lemass had been instrumental in establishing innovative programs in industrial development, and creating public enterprise to fill needs which were not being provided by private investment. As taioseach, he would continue these polices, providing the leadership which would bring Ireland into the modern world.

More Trouble from Paisley:

Ian Paisley, who had been ordained six years earlier as a Presbyterian minister, was dissatisfied with the status quo. He hated Catholics, and apparently, couldn't even get along with other Presbyterians. He demonstrated that in August, when he disrupted a meeting in Ballymena, conducted by the Reverend Donald Soper. Paisley heckled him so badly, that Reverend Soper was unable to continue with his speech. This time Paisley, and others were each fined 30 pounds for unlawful assembly. Paisley refused to cease the disturbance, or to pay the fine. Consequently, they were all remanded, without trial, and held from July 26, to October 19, 1959. **(8) #26**

It is surprising to find a minister of the Christian faith, so vehement, and vituperative in his hatred, and condemnation of other Christians. It is also surprising to find a Protestant court, in Northern Ireland, willing to incarcerate a Protestant clergyman, but let the punishment fit the crime. In the following year, the Reverend Paisley became politically active as a Protestant-extremist, and a persecutor of "Roman papists."

Television Comes to Ireland:

An Act of Oireachtas, on April 12, 1960, established a board of nine directors, for Radio Erieann, which had been established in 1954. The board was charged with the responsibility for conducting, and overseeing national radio and television services in Ireland. Television, inaugurated in 1961, would soon become a national sounding board for public opinion and debate on controversial social and economic issues.

DeGaulle Vetoes Common Market Bid:

In 1963 Great Britain and Ireland each applied for entry into the European common market. Great Britain and Prime Minister Margaret Thatcher were viewed with skepticism in much of Europe, at that time, and when Britain's application was vetoed by France's Charles deGualle, Ireland was tarred with the same French brush. **(9)**

Captain Terence O'Neill:

In 1963 Captain Terence O'Neill was elected Prime Minister of Northern Ireland. A new Catholic leadership was evolving as a result of the national higher educational system, a beneficiary of the British welfare program which had been established in Northern Ireland. O'Neill, himself, was a product of that program, which had benefited many Catholic young men and women. As Prime Minister, O'Neill set about trying to bridge the gap between the two ethnic groups. **(10)**

Change of Focus on Partition:

Rather than condemning partition, Lemass directed his focus on establishing better relationships between the two Irelands, both politically and economically. In 1963-64, Lemass introduced the *Second Programme for Economic Expansion*. resulting in a minor balance-of-payments crisis, requiring the overly ambitious program to be cut back to a more conservative level.

A Brief Period of Peace:

In January 1965, Taioseach Sean Lemass drove to Belfast to confer with Prime Minister Terrence O'Neal, in an attempt to improve North/South relations. The situation was slightly exacerbated by the appearance of the Reverend Ian Paisley, and his followers, at the gate of Stormount, to pummel Lemass's car with snowballs, in protest. **(11)**

How incredibly childish of Paisley! What could he possibly have hoped to achieve? O'Neill and Lemass had their talk anyway, and apparently got on well together. In February, O'Neill reciprocated, by visiting Lemass in Dublin, to continue their discourse. The result was a period of peace, which lasted for over a year.

The Lynch Commission:

In 1960, Lemass had appointed Professor Patrick Lynch, to head a commission on education in Ireland, to report to the government on all aspects of the educational system. Their report, published in 1966, would result in sweeping changes, particularly in higher education.

Changes in Northern Ireland:

Northern Ireland, in 1966, was undergoing a period of major economic and social change. The unemployment rate was high due to the decline in its primary industries, ship building, linen manufacturing, and agriculture. This was offset by the new industry developing around man-made fibers. Northern Ireland was becoming one of the leading manufactures of fibers in

Europe. The infrastructure, new highways, utilities and housing showed an annual growth rate of 4%, equal to that of the Republic, and higher than elsewhere in the United Kingdom.

Some Things Don't Change:

The ethnic barriers in Northern Ireland remained in place, being firmly fixed by social custom. Mixed marriage between a Catholic and a Protestant was severely frowned upon by both groups. Education was separate, which was, more or less, assured by housing segregation. Social interaction between the two groups was discouraged, and people were wary of strangers. Gerrymandering of electoral boundaries assured the perpetuation of Protestant rule, job discrimination against Catholics, housing segregation and unequal law enforcement.

IRA in Decline:

Political military activity of the IRA, in the six counties, was in decline at this time. The leadership was focusing its attention more on the social and economic disparities. Life was relatively peaceful .....for the moment.

All It Takes is a Spark:

In the wee hours of the morning of March 8, 1966, some unknown, and overly zealous republicans blew up the statue of Great Britain's greatest hero, Admiral Horatio Nelson, of the Battle of Trafalgar fame. The statue and one-third of its three story pillar was reduced to rubble, on Dublin's O'Connell Street. No-one was injured due to the hour of the incident. The bombers had taken adequate precautions to avoid such an outcome. Never-the-less, it was perceived in Ulster as an IRA challenge to the empire, and thus it was a threat to Ulster. It provided the spark in a highly volatile atmosphere.

The Ulster Volunteer Force- UVF:

In April 1966, as a direct result of the Dublin bombing, the Ulster Volunteer Force (UVF), a Protestant paramilitary organization was founded. On June 26, an eighteen-year old Catholic bartender was murdered by gunfire in Belfast. Several members of the UVF were arrested and convicted of his murder. Consequently, on June 28, the Northern Ireland Government declared the Ulster Volunteer Force to be an illegal organization. Apparently, the order was never enforced.

Paisley Again:

In Belfast on June 6, 1966 the Reverend Paisley, and several others, were arrested, and convicted, following a civil disturbance, protesting the Presbyterian General Assembly for disclaiming the "Rome-ward Trend" of the Presbyterian Church. Paisely, and his followers were fined 5 pounds each for breach of the peace.

Northern Ireland Civil Rights Association: (NICRA)

In January 1967 the Northern Ireland Civil Rights Association (NICRA) was founded under the leadership of young Catholic men of Ulster, who had been educated as per the provisions of the United Kingdom's education act. The police, and right wing Protestants labeled them as subversive, but the organization was not out to abolish partition or to undermine the Stormount government. Its only aim was merely to redress civil rights abuses against Catholics, which that government supported.

Trouble in Derry:

On October 5, 1968, NICRA's leaders, socialist activist Eamon McCann, nationalist Member of Parliament Eddie McAteer, Belfast Socialist Gerry Fitt, and Derry school-teacher John Hume, organized a march from Coalisland to Dungannon, as a protest of housing discrimination. William Craig, minister for home affairs, unintentionally called additional public attention to the situation by officially banning the march.

As the marchers approached the town center, they were confronted by an opposing group of right-wing orange unionists, called the *Apprentice Boys*. The two groups clashed violently. People were injured on both sides. The police entered the fray with a baton charge, in support of the *Apprentice Boys*. More people were injured. This was followed up with water cannon, to disperse the crowd.

This could have been a peaceful demonstration of protest of little significance, were it not for one little thing. The whole world got to see it through the presence of the television media. The police brutality was captured electronically, and vividly, and the rest of the world was aware of a small corner of it, called Northern Ireland. John Hume, spokesman for the marchers, suddenly became a prominent figure in Irish politics. **(12)**

This was followed in early November by a massive march into Derry, with over 15,000 people participating. This resulted in Prime Minister O'Neill announcing a five point program, agreeing to NICRA's demands, with the exception of the "one man, one vote, " reform. Other major reforms were to be made in the Derry administration. In the Stormount government, early December saw the dismissal of William Craig as Northern Ireland's minister for home affairs. **(13)**

More Trouble in Derry:

On New Years Day 1969, students from Queen's University, referring to themselves as *the People's Democracy,* led a long range civil rights march from Belfast to Derry. It was a peaceful demonstration, but when they reached a town called Burntoller, Co. Derry on January 4th, they were ambushed by a mob of Protestant militants. There were many injuries on both sides, as the Royal Ulster Constabulary (RUC) stood by as spectators. Some members of the mob were identified as off-duty police B-Specials, members of a select strong-arm squad. As the riot went on into the night barriers were erected, and the police, who finally attempted to force their way into Bogside, were denied entry. The morning revealed a sign that had been painted on the side of a house.

"YOU ARE NOW ENTERING FREE DERRY." (14)

Election Changes in Britain and Northern Ireland:

In the British election of February 1969, newcomer John Hume replaced Eddie McAteer in Westminster Parliament. It was also a good year in the Stormount Parliament as fiery Bernadette Devlin became MP for mid-Ulster. Unfortunately, in the next month Terence O'Neill resigned as Prime Minister, and was replaced by James Chichester Clark.

The Battle of Bogside:

The next major eruption occurred in Derry, on August 12, 1969, when the annual march of the Apprentice Boys through Derry provoked a riot in the Catholic section. It soon escalated into a full-scale battle, and the Royal Ulster Constabulary rushed in to support the Apprentice Boys. The Catholic youths from Bogside were well prepared, considering that they were unarmed defenders, but with a good supply of stones and fire bombs, they gave a good account for themselves.

Barriers were erected, and the Royal Ulster Constabulary (RUC), which was ineffectively attempting to restore order, was denied entry into the neighborhood. The Bogside was under siege by the Apprentice Boys, and the Royal Ulster Constabulary.(15)

Rioting in Belfast:

Two days later, on the night of August 14th, rioting spread to Belfast in the section between the Shankill, and the Falls, when an armed Protestant mob, supported by a civilian part-time militia, also known as the B-Specials, (an all-Protestant organization), stormed into the area, shooting at Catholics and setting their homes on fire. One Protestant man was shot to death. The RUC moved in with heavily armored cars and heavy-caliber machine-guns, ostensibly to restore order. Machine-gun fire was irresponsibly directed into flats, which were occupied by Catholic families. A nine year-old Catholic boy was shot and killed in his own bed. The rioting spread and more Catholic homes were set on fire. Bombay Street, in the Clonard section, was burned, and a teenager was murdered in broad daylight.

Finally, British troops were brought in and order was restored. The troops were welcomed by the Catholics as protectors, as indeed they were. Catholics in Northern Ireland, particularly those in Derry and Belfast, were hopeful, but not quite willing to believe that all would be well. Eight people had been killed and 1,500 Catholic families had been made homeless.(16) In Dublin, the Dail reacted by voting 100,000 pounds for the relief of distress in Northern Ireland, most of which would be misappropriated for the purchase of arms.

The young nationalist survivors of these outrages became the nucleus of a new branch, of the Irish Republican Army. Unhappy with the impotency of the 'official' IRA to protect nationalists in Northern Ireland, they formed the Provisional IRA. They took an oath that, "Never again would Catholic areas be left unprotected." Their slogan became: "From the ashes of Bombay Street rose the Provisionals."

The Downing Street Declaration:

On August 19th, British Prime Minister Harold Wilson, signed the Downing Street Declaration, a seven point, joint agreement between the United Kingdom and Northern Ireland, reaffirming the same equal right for every citizen, throughout the United Kingdom.

Westminster to the Rescue:

In August, Westminster took action and passed several provisions to remedy the Northern Ireland problem, and granted nearly all of the demands of the Civil Rights Association. New electoral boundaries were drawn to provide more equitable representation, housing managed by a non-partisan administration, and measures were taken to assure against discrimination in public employment. The reforms were strongly resented by the Protestant right wing, the Orange Society and the Reverend Ian Paisley.(17)

The Hunt Committee:

On October 10th, the report of the Hunt Committee on Police Reform was submitted to Mr. Wilson. It was especially critical of the partisan conduct of the Royal Ulster Constabulary regarding riot control. The Prime Minister was especially pleased to order the disestablishment of the B-Specials. (17)

What follows portrays the most violent period that Ireland has known in modern times. The 'Troubles' which had exploded in Derry and Belfast in the late 1960s, would continue through the 1970s, and claim over two thousand lives; mostly in the North, but also in the Republic. The Provisional IRA, or Provos, as they were called, would arise from the West Belfast rioting, and be responsible for over half of those losses.

The Provisional IRA:

Created initially for the protection of Catholic areas from mob, and/or police terrorism, the Provos soon developed a broader agenda; more specifically, getting rid of the Stormount government by rendering the six counties ungovernable, and to bring an end to partition. To these ends, they attacked both military and economic targets, using petrol bombs, high explosives, and firearms. By February 1970 the British army had decided to get tough with the Provos, and GOC Freeland, the General Officer Commanding issued orders that petrol bombers could be shot. The Ulster unionists were, obviously, calling the tune for the British army.

More Riots in Armagh, Belfast and Derry:

In early April, commemorations of the Easter Rising of 1916 were held in Armagh, Belfast and Derry. Naturally, such nationalist rallies were subject to contrary unionist demonstrations, and violence by the Apprentice Boys, the Orange Society, the

Royal Ulster Constabulary, (RUC) the B-Specials, and other Protestant mobs. This was quite a realistic expectation and did, in fact, lead to the customary rioting and head busting.

B-Specials Disbanded:

On April 30, 1970, the B-Specials, of the Ulster Defense Force, were disbanded, as ordered by Prime Minister Wilson back in October.(these things take time) Their *duties*, such as they were, were transferred to the Ulster Defense Regiment. The inference here was that this was a significant change. One wonders to what extent the character, of such an undisciplined group of bullies and murderers, would be affected by an order to disband. One must also wonder how much the Ulster Defense Regiment differed from its predecessor. Ironically, loyalist rioting, protesting, Mr. Wilson's action, would be the cause of the first fatal casualty of the Royal Ulster Constabulary (RUC).

Political Crisis in the Republic:

On May 6th, Taoiseach Jack Lynch announced the dismissal of two of his cabinet ministers. Mr. Neil Blaney, and Mr. Charles Haughey were dismissed following allegations that they were involved in the misappropriation of funds, which were voted by the Dail for relief of distress in Northern Ireland. It was alleged that these funds were used to obtain arms for the Provisional IRA. The two men were officially charged on May 28th with conspiracy to import arms into the Irish Republic. The court ruled that there was no case against Mr. Blaney. Mr. Haughey was found not guilty.(18)

Conservatives Control Westminster:

The general election in the United Kingdom in June brought the conservatives to power. Edward Heath replaced Harold Wilson as Prime Minister, and Ian Paisley won himself a unionist seat in the House of Commons. One of the first things Mr. Heath did was to remove the restraints that Wilson had placed upon Stormount and the British army in Northern Ireland. The army became a primary tool for the unionist administration. **(19)**

The Marching Season:

June 27, 1970, brought the annual Orange marching season to Northern Ireland. The local Orange Societies turned out, resplendent in their bowler hats and orange sashes, arrogantly marching to the beat of the big Lambeth drum. Of course, they would have to pass through the Catholic neighborhood, and that would, naturally, draw the desired response. In lieu of confetti, someone would inevitably bestow garbage upon the proud marchers, which was not received graciously. Suddenly, mayhem reigned and people on both sides were hurt.

When the rioting broke out in West Belfast, on July 23, more than cabbage flew through the air. The Provos were deployed to protect the Catholic neighborhood. Six people were killed in the ensuing riot. Three thousand British troops were turned loose, without restriction, to do a house-to-house search. The Provos responded, and when the smoke cleared, five more people lay dead. Curfews were imposed, and violated, but slowly, order was restored. (20)

The following Friday an (official) IRA arms cache was discovered in the Falls area in West Belfast. There was a confrontation, which developed into a riot, which soon developed into a full scale battle. Local citizens, who were not members of the IRA, took on the British army's Black Watch battalion with stones, home made petrol bombs, and nail bombs, against grenades and small arms fire. Three people were shot, and one was run over by an armored vehicle. One of the shooting victims was a British newspaper photographer from London.

Running the Blockade:

Another curfew was imposed by the Black Watch, "to teach the republicans a lesson." This was in a poor neighborhood of tenement flats, without proper plumbing, and without refrigerators. Food was not stored for long periods and the curfew worked a great hardship on the people. Food for the babies ran out. The soldiers of The Black Watch were young Scottish men, from pretty much the same ethnic stock as the people they were confronting. They soon found themselves faced by an army of middle aged women, who closely resembled their own mothers and sisters, pushing prams filled with baby food. This was a violation of the curfew, but the women were accompanied by a cortege of television cameramen and journalists. The soldiers had no choice, but to step aside. The blockade was broken. (21)

Two weeks following the riot, two officers of the Royal Ulster Constabulary were killed by parties unknown. Two weeks after that three off-duty British soldiers were wounded by unidentified gunfire.

The Social Democratic and Labour Party (SDLP):

On August 21.1970, The Social Democratic Labour Party (SDLP), the brain-child of John Hume was formed under the leadership of Gerry Fitt, of Belfast. The agenda of the new party was to stress reforms and seek compromise with the unionists. The ultimate goal was to reunite Ireland, by the consent of a majority of the northern population. The first aim was admirable, but would have required the restructuring of the Stormount government, which would be a prolonged process. The second one was unrealistic, as the primary purpose of the unionist party was to prevent unification of Ireland from ever happening.

A New Bombing Campaign:

On October 23rd, a rejuvenated IRA began a bombing campaign in Northern Ireland, and occasionally in Great Britain, which caused numerous civilian deaths. On rare occasions they would strike within the republic, with similar results. There were also Protestant paramilitary groups, who committed less frequent, but equally deadly attacks. (22)

Sterner Measures Called For:

The reaction of the British army to the lethal attacks by the IRA, and the organized stone throwing by Irish youths, resulted in turning the Catholic public against the soldiers, whom they had originally welcomed as protectors. Early in 1971 a soldier was killed by IRA gunfire, marking the first British fatality of the 'Troubles.' As the IRA offensive continued, with more bombing, month by month, the number of fatalities, both civilian and military increased. The unionists began to pressure the Stormount government for sterner measures. On March 10th, Chichester-Clark resigned as Northern Ireland Prime Minister, and was replaced by Brian Faulkner.

Internment Without Trial:

Internment without trial had been successful for the British three times in the past, so Falkner decided to try it again. The military made a wide sweep and rounded up some three hundred forty-two people suspected of being IRA terrorists. One might consider it strange that Protestant terrorists were not included in the round up, but apparently the British only wanted certain kinds of terrorists. That marked one of the few occasions that Protestants had experienced discrimination. It should also be pointed out that many of the Catholic internees were totally innocent of any political involvement of any kind. Perhaps some people just looked more guilty than others. In any event, one hundred-five internees had to be released within two days. This is an indication of the degree of cause needed for the arrest, by British standards. (23)

Every Action Has an Opposite Reaction:

As might be expected, the internment program produced a wide spread negative reaction on the part of republicans, both North and South. Demonstrations erupted everywhere which resulted in strong repressive measures in the North. The barriers went up around the Bogside and the Creggan again, but this time the people were protected by the Provos.

Elsewhere, riots occurred, and twenty-two people were killed within a three day period. The IRA responded in a way, that for some reason, Brian Faulker had not anticipated. Numerous economic targets in Belfast were struck on a massive scale with high explosives, not to mention the various security forces subjected to a small arms offensive, which killed forty-one of them. These actions also caused seventy-three fatal civilian casualties.

The Ulster Defense Association:

It appears that the IRA response to the unlawful internments caused another reaction. Late in August 1971, the Ulster Defense Association (UDA) emerged. This was a paramilitary group consisting of working class Protestants in Northern Ireland.

Chapter Twenty-Three
The Troubles
1970 to 1985

Paisley Forms His Own Party, NICRA Against Internment, Bloody Sunday, Remembrance, Official IRA Ceasefire, Direct Rule from Westminster, A Brief Period of Peace, Bloody Friday, Death Toll Climbs, Working Toward Power Sharing, Republic, Joins European Economic Community, Torture of Prisoner, More Bombs General Election in the Republic, Northern Ireland Assembly, Oiling the Skids, President Erskine Childers Died, The Sunningdale Conference, The Council and the Assembly Fall, Unionists and SDLP Seek a Compromise, Past-President Eamon deValera Died, Prisoners Lose Political Status, A New Atmosphere in Prisons , The Peace PeopleMovement, General Election in the Republic, Mountbatten Assassinated, Taoiseach Charles Haughey, Hunger Strike Over Prisoner Status, Thatcher and Haughey Meet in London, Huger Strike Reinstated, Sands For Parliament, General Election, Fitzgerald Taoiseach, Thatcher and Fitzgerald Meet in London, Republic National Debt, Rotating Taoisachs, Northern Ireland Assembly Meeting, The New Ireland Forum, The Anglo-Irish Agreement, Sinn Fein and the IRA, Violence Begets Violence Begets More Violence, Arms Shipment Seized, The Harrod Incident, SAS Strikes Back, Vengeance is Mine Sayeth the IRA, Legitimate Military Targets, Fair Employment Act. Peter Brooke Secretary for Northern Ireland,

They Made History:

Gerry Adams: Commanded the Belfast IRA, Later MP, President of Sinn Fein 1983 Present.

Liam Cosgrave: Taoiseach 1973-77. Son of William Cosgrave, Free State Prime Minister, Executive Jan 1922.

Eamon deValera: Taoiseach 1951-66, 57-59, President of Republic 59-6

Alan Duke: Fine Gael party leader who put Ireland ahead of personal gain

Brian Faulkner: Prime Minister Northern Ireland Dec.73-Mar. 74

Gerry Fitt: Leader SDLP party, Northern Ireland deputy executive.1/73

Garret Fitzgerald: Taoiseach 6-81 to 3/82, 12/82 to 3/87

Charles Haughey: Taoiseach 12/79 to 6/81 3/82 to 12/82..

Edward Heath: British Prime Miister, Succeeded by Wilson 1972-79

Jack Lynch: Taoiseach 11/66 to 3/73

Lord Earl Mountbatten: British hero, Assasinated Aug 27, 1979, Cousin to the Queen

Reverend Ian Paisley: Leading Protestant unionist agitator, Founded his own DUP party, member of Parliament.

James Prior: British secretary of state 1982.Mach 1971-December 1972

Margaret Thatcher: British Prime Minister, 1979 to 1990.

William Whitelaw: Secretary of state for Northern Ireland.

Harold Wilson: British Prime Minister 1964 to 1972.

Paisley Forms His Own Party:

The Reverend Ian Paisley, after being ordained, formed his own religious sect. Then, in October 1971, following his election to the House of Commons, he decided to form his own political party, the Democratic Unionist Party, (DUP). The man was an enigma of the first order. He was a man of God, yet he advocated hatred. He did not invent the "Troubles, " but certainly exacerbated them. He was a brilliant speaker and spellbinding orator. His demogogery could arouse his followers to perform terrible acts of violence. Under his influence, biogotry had become a general characteristic of the Orange movement. But, in all fairness, the Reverend Paisley was but a product of his environment.

The larger problem actually resided with a large segment of the Protestant population; economically privileged by chance of history, and insanely fearful of loosing their privileged status, should they ever unite politically with their southern neighbors. The economic separation was made further complicated by the fact that the two groups were separated along secular line, as well as temporal. The Protestants distrusted the Catholics, and the Catholics distrusted the Protestants. It would take time and genuine faith to break such a cycle.

NICRA Against Internment:

On January 22, 1972, the Northern Ireland Civil Rights Association planned a peaceful march in the Creggan, planning to proceed to Derry's Guildhall Square. The march was in protest of internment without trial that was happening to suspected rebublicans. The internment incidents had caused great indignation in the Republic, and concern in the United States as well. The march was, of course, immediately banned by Northern Ireland's Prime Minister, Brian Faulkner.

The local chief of the Ulster Constabulary argued against banning the march, but Faulkner was intransigent. In spite of the ban, roughly ten thousand people assembled in Creggan to join the march. The event was well covered by the media, as internment without trial had created world-wide attention.

Bloody Sunday:

The decision was made to contain the marchers to the confines of the Bogside area, and the British army's parachute regiment was called out to enforce the decision. Unexpectedly, a single shot range out, followed by many more shots. The British troops were firing into the crowd. Mayhem and confusion followed. The march ended in panic, as people were being cut down. As the smoke cleared, fourteen unarmed civilians lay dead, and countless more were seriously wounded.

The paratroopers claimed that they were fired upon first, and they were merely returning fire. However, no weapons could be found anywhere, and no soldiers were killed, or even wounded.

In fact, it was evident that they were never even shot at. This was the bloodiest and most lethal day of the "Troubles, " to date, and it was well covered by the press.

The British government insisted upon the version told by the army, and the matter was pretty well white-washed in the British press. This was not the case in the Irish Republic, or the rest of the world. The facts spoke for the truth.

In Dublin, Taoiseach Jack Lynch declared that February 2nd, would be a day of national mourning, to commemorate "Bloody Sunday." The day reached its climax at the British embassy in Dublin. It was burned to the ground. (1)

Remembrance:

On February 22nd, on the one month anniversary of Bloody Sunday, the official IRA bombed the officers mess at the base in Aldershot, England, which was the headquarters for the parachute regiment. Unfortunately, five civilians and a chaplain were killed by the blast.

Official IRA Ceasefire:

As a direct result of this attack, and because of the collateral casualties, the Official IRA announced a ceasefire, and turned to a course of political action, and renunciation of violence. (2)

Direct Rule from Westminster:

Westminster viewed the fallout from Faulkner's Northern Ireland policies with extreme displeasure. On March 4th, Faulker's government was rebuked by Westminster for refusal to accept a number of reforms of security measures proposed by Prime Minister Heath.

At this point, Westminster prorogued, or suspended the Northern Ireland Parliament, and imposed direct rule from London. William Whitelaw was appointed as secretary of state for Northern Ireland. March 28, 1972 marked the end of one-party rule for Northern Ireland. A power-sharing plan would now be sought, which might be acceptable to both unionist and nationalist parties.

A Brief Period of Peace:

During the months following Bloody Sunday, The Provisional IRA increased its bombing campaign, and the killing of RUC men, members of the Ulster Volunteer Association (UVA), and the Ulster Volunteer Force (UVF). The random murder of Catholics became more frequent, in retaliation.

The Official IRA's change of direction, and their suspension of northern operations in May, possibly influenced the Provisional IRA. On June 26th the Provos suddenly declared a truce with the British army. Unfortunately, that truce only lasted about three and a half weeks before it fell apart.

Bloody Friday:

Hostilities were resumed on July 21st, and Bloody Friday truly deserves the name that has been given it. The Provos outdid themselves with a series of explosions in Belfast, which killed nine people, and injured one-hundred and thirty others. During the turmoil following this irresponsible act, the army regained control of the Catholic areas in Belfast and Derry, and things quieted down after that. (3)

Death Toll Climbs:

The year 1972 set a new high for violent killing. More than twice as many people were killed in 1972 as had been killed in the two previous years combined. Four hundred and sixty-seven people had their lives taken from them in 1972, compared to two-hundred eleven since 1969. The three year total was six hundred seventy-eight lives taken. What a loss of potential, and a waste of human beings! (4)

Working Toward Power Sharing:

Meanwhile, secretary of state for Northern Ireland, William Whitelaw was trying earnestly to bring the unionists and the nationalists together on a power-sharing plan. The unionists were reassured by a guarantee from Westminster, that the North would remain part of the United Kingdom, for as long as the majority desired. The SDLP was mollified by the promise of a share in the executive power, and the establishment of all-Ireland institutions.

Gerry Adams, who had been arrested following Bloody Friday, was flown to London, as the most senior officer of the Belfast IRA. Martin McGuinness, the senior officer of the Derry IRA, was also present. They were there to meet with first northern secretary Whitelaw, as delegates for the IRA, to provide input regarding the proposed assembly, and power-sharing executive for Northern Ireland. (5)

Republic Joins European Economic Community

The Republic of Ireland was admitted to the European Economic Community, along with Great Britain and Denmark, on January 1, 1973, in spite of European misgivings regarding Great Britain. As part of the Common Market, Ireland benefited from substantial financial assistance from wealthier countries of Europe, by a "cohesion" process, which enabled smaller countries to catch up regarding infrastructure. It was also beneficial for the advancement of agricultural practices. Electrification, which had been started years earlier, was now extended to the rural areas.

Torture of Prisoners:

Stories had been circulating for some months, of new torture techniques, known as sensory deprivation, being used by the British army on selected political internees. This was recently reported, and photographs of prisoners beaten by soldiers were published. The British government was made to look very bad, indeed.

More Bombs:

Apparently, the Official IRA had second thoughts regarding its ceasefire of February, the previous year. On February 20, 1973, a car bomb explosion in Dublin killed one person, and injured seventeen others. This was followed three weeks later with two car bombs exploding in London. This time, also, only one person was killed, but there were one-hundred and eighty serious injuries. These incidents were both attributed to the Official IRA.

General Election in the Republic:

The results of the March election in the Republic came as a surprise. The Fianna Fail party received the most votes, but managed to lose six seats. This made it possible for Fine Gael and the Labour party to form a coalition, thus replacing Jack Lynch as Taoiseach with Liam Cosgrave. (The son of William Cosgrave.)

Northern Ireland Assembly:

William Whitelaw's efforts led to an election in Northern Ireland in June, for a new Assembly. Seventy-eight members were elected, for the first time, by proportional representation. Faulker's

Unionists and Gerry Fitt's SDLP, comprised the majority of the Assembly. Six more months of hard bargaining, between the two parties, finally brought agreement for a joint power-sharing administration, composed of ministers from both communities of Northern Ireland.

Oiling the Skids:

On October 16, 1973, six OPEC countries, in the Persian Gulf, increased the price of crude oil, from $3 to $8 per barrel. This meant that Ireland would not be spared the hardships of the oil crisis of 1973, and the international recession that would come with it.

President Erskine Childers Died:

The President of Ireland, Erskine Childers, died on November 17th. He was succeeded by Cearball O'Dalaigh, unopposed on December 3rd. Also in December, the OPEC countries raised the price of oil to $11.50 per barrel. World economic recession followed.

The Sunningdale Conference:

On December 6, 1973, a conference was held at Sunningdale, in Berkshire, between the British and the Irish governments, and the executive designate for Northern Ireland, to establish a Council of Ireland. The Council would be comprised of the power-sharing executive of Northern Ireland and representatives of the Republic of Ireland. It would provide a stage for cooperation between the two Irish governments, regarding matters of common interest, and concern, including measures to bring to justice the persons committing the February/March killings in Dublin and London.

Suspicion pointed strongly toward the Irish National Liberation Organization. But whoever the perpetrators had been, it was deemed an unmanly act, and a wasting of innocent lives, for no purpose; committed by cowards, afraid to do more than to seek soft targets.

On January 1, 1974, Gerry Faulkner took office as the power-sharing executive of Northern Ireland, with SDLP leader Gerry Fitt as his deputy. Faulkner was repudiated by the Unionist party and still faced opposition from Paisley's DUP, concerning the Council of Ireland. On May 14th Ulster Workers' Council called a general strike, in opposition to the Sunningdale

Conference. On the same day, a car bomb in Dublin killed twenty-five people.

The Council and the Assembly Fall:

On May 28th, Faulkner and the unionist members of the executive resigned, in the face of strong opposition, and a total lack of support. The Workers' Council was planning a general strike, protesting unionist intransigence. The next day Westminster abolished the Northern Ireland Assembly. The general strike was called off by the Workers' Council. The Council of Ireland became a dead issue. (6)

Unionists and SDLP Seek a Compromise:

Unionist negotiating team leader, William Craig and the SDLP leader Gerry Fitt discussed the possibility of a compromise on a voluntary coalition. The unionists would agree to power-sharing for an experimental period, if the SDLP would put off its demand for a Council of Ireland.

Unfortunately, at this particular time, the IRA chose to increase its activity. This caused the unionist convention, led by Ian Paisley, to repudiate the idea of a compromise. They refused any kind of power-sharing with the SDLP, even on a temporary basis. They insisted upon returning to majority rule, as it was before 1972, with no significant safeguards for the minority. (7)

The SDLP refused to even acknowledge the proposal, and Westminster subsequently rejected it. The Assembly was dissolved and direct rule from London was re-established for Northern Ireland.

Past-President Eamon deValera Died:

Former President Eamon deValera, veteran of the Rising of 1916, and former Taoiseach, died on August 29th. He was ninety-two years old. He had served in elected office in various capacities from 1923 until 1948.

Prisoners Lose Political Status:

On December 5, 1975, internment without trial was discontinued. This seemed to have reduced the level of violence, but a separate, and new issue, then arose to keep the pot boiling. Up until then, republicans arrested were treated as political prisoners, which of course they were. Under the new policy, in a new prison, they would loose their political status and be treated as common criminals.

The British apparently reasoned that what appeared to the world to be a colonial problem could be ameliorated with modern two-man cells. These would replace the barracks compounds, which they thought resembled a concentration camp, at the same time, reduce the number of guards required. The prisoners would be given brand-new prison garb, which they would be required to wear. They would also be required to do prison work, and be subject to the same rules as criminal prisoners. Failure to conform would result in a loss of privileges, such as receiving food parcels, and having visitors.

A New Atmosphere in Prisons:

Of course, the jailors should have known, that being Irish, the prisoners would resent being treated as common criminals, and that, most certainly, they would not conform. Instead, they refused to wear the prison cloths. They refused to leave their cells, and they refused to wash or shave. They wore their bed blankets, and became grizzly, and odiferous.

Of course, the prisoners should have known, that their jailors, being British, would keep a stiff upper lip and carry on. But then, off-duty guards began to disappear mysteriously. Other guards began resigning their posts, as the bodies of missing guards began to turn up. It was suspected that the Provisional IRA had something to do with it. A rather sticky wicket! Eh whot?

Ultimately the mysterious killings stopped. But nothing had changed and the passive protests continued.

The Peace People Movement:

Toward the end of 1976, a grass roots peace movement had developed, with people from both communities at mass meetings in Drogheda. This group called themselves the Peace People, and their message was merely that the people were tired of war. The movement gained wide support, and resulted in giant demonstrations. The message was clear, but the leaders of the Peace People were unable to articulate any kind of workable program. Ultimately, the group simply faded away. **(8)**

General Election in the Republic:

In July 1977, Fianna Fail received the largest majority ever, in an Irish general election. Liam Cosgrave took the heat for the economic recession, resulting from the oil crisis. He was replaced as Taoiseach by Jack Lynch. He was also replaced by Garret Fitzgerald as leader of the Fine Gael party.

In the late '70s, various British secretaries of state made repeated attempts to help the Unionists and the SDLP come to some kind of compromise on a devolved government. Both sides remained immoveable.

In 1978, Gerry Adams, who had been in and out of jail, was released again. He was re-seated as a member of the IRA army council and elected as the vice-president of Sinn Fein.

In the United Kingdom general election in May 1979, Prime Minister Callaghan was succeeded by Margaret Thatcher.

Mountbatten Assassinated:

On August 27, 1979 an IRA bomb attack killed Lord Earl Mountbatten, two family members, and a guest. The attack took place on his boat near Mullaghmore, Co. Sligo. This incident caused an uproar in Britain. Lord Mountbatten was extremely popular. He had commanded the British Mediterranean fleet during World War II. He became first lord of the admiralty, and was a cousin to Queen Elizabeth II.

In a separate attack, on the same day, eighteen British soldiers were killed. Sixteen of them were members of the parachute regiment involved in "Bloody Sunday" in Belfast. The attitude of the British government, especially that of Margaret Thatcher, was hardened by the event. **(9)**

Taoiseach Charles Haughey:

Jack Lynch lost party support through internal Fine Gael matters relating to the recession. He resigned as Taoiseach on December 5, 1979, to be succeeded by Charles Haughey, his former internal minister for health and welfare. Haughey had previously been dismissed by Lynch, for alleged involvement in illegal arms importation. He was the son-in-law of former Taoiseach, Sean Lemasse.

Hunger Strike Over Prisoner Status:

The prisoners in the so-called "H-Block, " in the new Maze prison, had been resisting the loss of political status since 1975, by refusing to conform to the change in rules. On October 27, 1980, seven prisoners decided to go on a hunger strike in protest. They were joined, thirty-five days later, by three women prisoners in Armaugh, and fourteen days later by twenty-three more prisoners at Maze. By December 19th an apparent agreement had been reached and the strike was ended.

Thatcher and Haughey Meet in London:

Meanwhile, on May 21st Taoiseach Haughey and Prime Minister Thatcher had a meeting to exchange views. They agreed to examine the possibility of forming an Anglo-Irish parliamentary council between Britain and the two parts of Ireland. (Though the plan was not later repudiated by Thatcher,) The plan would fall apart in 1982 when Ireland would refuse to support Britain in its dispute with Argentina over the Falkland Islands. **(10)**

Hunger Strike Re-instated:

Doubt soon arose among the prisoners as to whether the authorities had bargained in good faith. The consensus among the prisoners was, that they had been duped. The bargaining resumed, but by March 1, 1981 the prisoners decided that the authorities had deliberately misled them.

The strike would continue. Bobby Sands, the officer in command of the prisoners, decided that he would lead the strike himself. He stood down as OC, as he felt that his judgment could become questionable, as he weakened.

Sands for Parliament:

On March 6, 1981, Frank McQuire, MP for Femanaugh, South Tyrone, died of natural causes, leaving a vacant seat in Westminster. After much political discourse, Bobby Sands was nominated for that seat in Parliament, unopposed. After fifty days of fasting, political prisoner Bobby Sands became a member of the House of Commons.

It was generally believed in the Catholic community, that the British government would not permit a Member of Parliament to die. Unfortunately, they completely misjudged the mood of the British establishment, following the bombing attacks that killed Lord Mountbatten, and eighteen British soldiers.

After sixty-five days fasting, Bobby Sands died, and over ten thousands people attended his burial. During the next three months, nine of his comrades followed his example and fasted to death.

Rioting and arson spread through many of the northern towns and sixty-four people were killed by the authorities, in their efforts to subdue the riots. **(11)** The Strike finally ended on October 3rd.

The voluntary deaths of these brave young martyrs in Maze prison received world-wide attention and empathy from Catholics in North America. It was difficult for the British establishment to argue that nationalist prisoners were mere criminals. It is politically significant however, that in the election for Sands' vacant seat, Owen Carron, an Irish-Catholic, running on a Sinn Fein ticket, received a greater number of votes than even Sands himself. What had greater significance is that after that election, republicans were even more eager to take up the Ballot box as a weapon.

General Election, Fitzgerald Taoiseach:

Haughey's administration had been troubled by economic problems. The depression, following the oil crisis, did not go away. Haughey had hoped to avoid budgetary cutbacks by borrowing from abroad. The depression continued and the national debt increased. Severe budget cuts were necessary, and Haughey called for an election on June 11, 1981, hoping to gain support. Things went the other way and Haughey lost his office to Fine Gael's Garret Fitzgerald.

Thatcher and Fitzgerald Meet in London:

Prime Minister Margaret Thatcher was perceived by most nationalist to be intransigent and immovable. It's been suggested that the increased strength of Sinn Fein at the ballot box moved her to meet with Taoiseach Fitzgerald, to discuss matters of mutual interest regarding Northern Ireland.

In any event, their talks in November 1981 proved productive, and resulted in the signing of the Anglo-Irish Agreement, which for the first time, afforded the Republic a consultant role in matters concerning the North.

This was followed on January 19, 1982 by the first meeting of the Anglo-Irish Governmental Council, under the oversight of the new secretary-of-state. James Prior. The purpose of the Council was to come to agreement between the SDLP and the unionists, on a plan of "rolling devolution" and to schedule an election of the Northern Ireland Assembly in October. **(12)**

Republic National Debt:

The economic problems, Fitzgerald inherited from Charles Haughey, would plague his administration. By the beginning of 1982 the national debt had risen to 4.8 billion pounds. The only answer was to stop borrowing and make the much-needed budget cuts.

Fitzgerald's minister of finance, Ray MacSharry secured the sponsorship of Fine Gael leader Alan Dukes, who unselfishly helped Fitzgerald and secretary MacSharry to secure the needed votes for the cut. The act ultimately cost MacSharry his coalition. These personal sacrifices were for the good of the country, and made it possible for Ireland to regain financial stability. This, in turn, made it possible for Ireland to benefit from the unprecedented economic growth that was to follow in the near future.

Rotating Taoiseachs:

A general election in March 1982, resulted in Fitzgerald, who had lost his coalition, surrendering the job of Taoiseach back to Charles Haughey. In October, the Labour/Fine Gael coalition having been repaired, called for a vote of no confidence for Charles Haughey, who was forced to resign. In a general election in December, he was succeeded by Garret Fitzgerald again.

Northern Ireland Assembly Meeting:

Also in October, the first meeting of the new Northern Ireland Assembly ended in chaos. At first both the Unionist and SDLP members refused to take their seats. Secretary Prior refused to devolve power to a Unionist dominated assembly. Deadlock!

The SDLP called for a United Ireland by consent. The IRA called for a United Ireland by coercion. The Unionists made an equally ridiculous proposal. The very concept of compromise seems to have been totally foreign to both Irish and English mentality.No-one was satisfied with anything, and they all went home fuming. So much for the assembly plan!

The New Ireland Forum:

In May 1983, a debate was held among the main constitutional nationalist parties: Northern Ireland's SDLP, the Republic's Fianna Fail, Fine Gael, and the Labour parties. In the course of the debate they examined three different options for Northern Ireland:

(1) That it should become part of a unitary Irish state,
(2) or a part of a federal/confederate state,
(3) or be governed by a joint authority under Dublin and London, giving equal validity to each of the two traditions in Northern Ireland.
Apparently, the debate was a draw.

The Anglo-Irish Agreement:

In November 1983, Prime Minister Thatcher and Taoiseach Fitzgerald held a meeting of the first session of the Anglo-Irish Intergovernmental Council (AIIC) to discuss Anglo-Irish relations. They issued a report, stating that the identities of both communities in Northern Ireland should be recognized and respected in ways that are acceptable to both.

Both governments agreed to support the devolution of powers within Northern Ireland. It also reaffirmed the provision, that there would be no change of status for Northern Ireland without the consent of a majority of the population, and the majority at that time wished for no change of status. It also stated that, if at some future time a majority of the population of both countries did wish for a united Ireland, and formally consented to it, they may request such change through appropriate legislation by both the respective parliaments.

Both Thatcher and Fitzgerald signed the agreement on November 15, 1985.The Dail in Dublin approved the agreement on November 21st. The House of Commons in London approved the agreement on November 27th, For the first time, the Republic was given a consultive role in managing the affairs of Northern Ireland. It represents a beginning.

Generally speaking, political parties in Ireland believed, with the exception of the unionist, that a united Ireland might be desirable, but at the same time recognized that it would not be practical, or likely to be in the foreseeable future. During the election in the Republic in 1987, the electorate was poled regarding with which issues the politicians should be concerned. The wish for a united Ireland was never even mentioned. From this, we may conclude that for the man on the street, or the man in the field, unity of the Irelands held a low priority.

Sinn Fein and the IRA:

Gerry Adams and Martin McGuiness, the Sinn Fein president and vice-president, respectively were members of the

Irish Republican Army military council. Both men strongly believed that force alone could never drive the British out of Ireland, but at the time, it was the only way to get their attention.

They were aware that careless, or sloppy operations, resulting in civilian casualties would earn them the "terrorist" label. Their avowed purpose was not to cause casualties, nor military defeat of the British, but rather to demoralize them and to motivate negotiation. Adams and McGuiness advocated in the council, choosing targets for their tactical value, to obtain the maximum public effect, and to wear the British down.

On May 8, 1987, eight members of a highly experienced IRA assault team were ambushed by the British Special Air Service (SAS)during an attempt to destroy the Royal Ulster Constabulary (RUC) barracks at Loughgall, County Armaugh. All eight were mowed down by machine gun fire. An innocent civilian, who drove into the line of fire, was also killed. These losses were keenly felt by the IRA.

There were other cases of mistaken identity, or where authorities failed to take proper protective measures, such as clearing an area when a warning was called in. In any event, the public effect was very negative and detrimental to Sinn Fein, the political face of the IRA. **(14)**

Violence Begets Violence, Begets More Violence:

Sinn Fein lost considerable public support four months later, following the Enniskillen bombing in November. An IRA explosive device did not go off at the time for which it was intended. It exploded later, near a crowd, at a Protestant Remembrance Ceremony. It killed twelve innocent people. It had been set for an earlier time, when the police and soldiers would have been performing a security sweep of the area.**(15)**

Arms Shipment Seized:

In November 1987, the British seized a Libyan freighter off the French coast carrying a cargo of arms for the IRA. The British were dismayed to learn from the captain of the vessel that this was his fifth trip. He told them that since August of 1985, he had delivered one-hundred fifty tons of weaponry; consisting of AK-47 rifles, pistols, heavy machine guns, flame throwers, rocket launches, and surface to air missals. He also confessed delivering several tons of Semtex plastic, which was extremely explosive, easily disguisable, odorless and undetectable.

The Harrod Incident:

A week before Christmas, 1987 a thirty pound bomb had been set, irresponsibly, and inexcusably, outside of Harrod's Department Store, in London. Six people died in the explosion and nearly one hundred people were injured. This was not a sloppy operation. It was the careless and deliberate murder of innocent civilians. Such an operation should never have even been considered by the IRA.(16)

SAS Strikes Back:

On March 6, 1988, three IRA operatives were shot and killed in Gibraltar by the British Special Air Service. (SAS) They were, purportedly on a mission which had gone sour. At the time they were unarmed and carried no explosives.

A week later, in Belfast, thousands of people turned out for their funerals in the Miltown Cemetery. An Ulster Defense Association (UDA) gunman showed up and opened fire with a hand gun and grenade, at the gravesite. He was immediately pursued and attacked by hundreds of young, unarmed mourners.

The chase was prolonged, as they were repeatedly shot at and bombed with grenades. The gunman was eventually out of ammunition, and was apprehended. Three men had been killed, and sixty others injured.

Vengeance is Mine, Sayeth the IRA:

The next week, three more funerals! The funeral cortege of one man, who had been an IRA member, was interrupted by two men in a Volkswagon car, one of them firing an automatic pistol into the air. The two men were seized, badly beaten, and hauled to a nearby park, and strip searched. They were identified as two British corporals, in civilian clothing. They were then driven off to a nearby alley by two IRA gunmen, and shot to death.

Legitimate Military Targets:

On August 20, 1988, an IRA 30 pound roadside bomb killed eight British soldiers along Ballygawley-Omagh road. The victims were members of a light infantry regiment, traveling in an unmarked bus. Nineteen others were injured. Ten days later the Special Air Service (SAS) ambushed and killed three men believed to have been IRA bombers. Prime Minister, Margaret Thatcher was so lividly furious with the IRA that she banned any, and all, statements, or "propaganda" from Sinn Fein from being broadcast over British, or Northern Ireland airways. **(17)**

Adams and McGuiness now found it difficult, if not impossible, to publicly explain, or justify IRA actions, and likewise to persuade IRA military committees to amend their policies and practices to use force only sufficient to pressure the unionists and the British to negotiate. They firmly believed that the way to achieve their ultimate goals was through the political process. Regardless, the IRA was in public disfavor, and Sinn Fein was losing support

Fair Employment Act:

In Northern Ireland, the Fair Employment Act of 1989, (FEA) was designed to address the problem of discrimination against Catholics. It was, and had been, a major political issue that placed Catholics at a tremendous economic disadvantage, and a markedly lower standard of living than their Protestant Neighbors. Determined campaigners in the United States had built up the Catholic disadvantage as "laying at the root of Northern Ireland's political conflict." The discrimination in employment levels remained a basic source of tension between the two communities. **(18)**

Peter Brooke, Secretary for Northern Ireland:

Margaret Thatcher wrote a letter to Gerry Adams, stating that "Britain had no long term interest in Northern Ireland, " and that she would be agreeable to any settlement arrived at peaceably, and by consent. She further acknowledged that if the IRA declared a ceasefire, she would have no objection to discussing a settlement with Sinn Fein.

In August 1989, Peter Brooke was appointed as secretary of state for Northern Ireland. Speaking in November 1990, to members of Parliament, she said that, "Britain had no strategic or economic interest in Northern Ireland, "but to ensure democratic debate, and free democratic choice.

Chapter Twenty-Four
We're Almost There

1990-2007

Thatcher Out, Major In, Politics Make Strange Bedfellows, A Valentine for John Major, A Strategy for Peace and Justice, Election in the Republic and the UK, Sir Patrick Mayhew, Adams Looses His Seat in Parliament, Hume and Adams Meet Secretly, The Missing Element, UDA Banned, The Hume-Adams Document, London's Financial District Targeted, IRA Offers Ceasefire, Major and Reynolds Meet, Second Attack on Financial District, Amerians for a New Irish Agenda (ANIA), The Shankill Bomb, The Downing Street Declaration, Adams Granted a U.S. Visa, London's Heathrow Airport"Bombed, " One Last Bit of Business, The Bombing Stops, TUAS, Decommissioning, Loyalist Weapons in Northern Ireland, Shovels as Weapons? More Than one Private Army, Peace Forum Scheduled, The Forum, Taoiseach John Bruton, U.S. Senator George Mitchell, A New Framework, Major's Man Bruton, Gerry and Bill, The Brits Say Yes, Then They Say No, The David and Ian Show, They're Still Here, President Clinton Takes Belfast, The Mitchell Report, Assembly Proposed, Enough Stalling, The Voters Make Needed Changes, Ceasefire Restored, The Good Friday Agreement, More Violence by Radicals, The Patten Commission, Power Sharing at Last, The Unionist Way or No Way, Trimble Consents, Stalemate-Everyone Looses, Trimble Looses Seat in Commons, Knighted By the Queen, Adams moves Sinn Fein, DUP Playing Same Old Game, Hains Cites Bread and Butter Issues, Large Turnout for Assembly Elections, Party Leaders Meet, Executive Cabinet Named, Peter Hain Given Eviction Notice, Devolved Power-Sharing at Last, We're Almost There

They Made History:

Gerry Adams: President of Sinn Fein, Member IRA council, MP for W. Belfast.
Bertie Ahern: Taoiseach June 97 to present.
Tony Blair: British Prime Minister, May 97 to June 2007.
Peter Brooke: Secretary of State for Northern Ireland –Jul 89 to Apr 92
John Bruton: Taoiseach June 95- Jun 97
William Clinton: President of the United States 1993 to 2001.
John de Chastelain: Ex- Canadian general, Member of Mitchell Commission
Garret Fitzgerald: Taoiseach Jun 81 to Mar82, Dec82 to Feb 87
Charles Haughey: Taoiseach Dec79-Jun81, Mar82-Dec 82, Feb 87- Feb 92
Hari Holkari, Former PM of Finland, Member of Mitchell Commission
John Humes: Leader of SDLP party.
Ted Kennedy: Brother of the late President Kennedy
Sir Patrick Mayhew: Sec. of State for Northern Ireland in Apr 92 to May 97
John Major: British Prime Minister, Nov 90 to May 97
Martin McGuinness: Vice President Sinn Fein, member IRA council, MP.
George Mitchell: Advisor to President Clinton, Sec. of State on economic initiative in
    Ireland..
Ian Paisely: Unionist clergyman, Demgogue, Leader of Unionist Party,
Albert Reynolds: Taoiseach Feb 92- Jun 97
Nancy Soderberg: Appointed by President Clinton, as Staff director of the National
    Security Council.
Margaret Thatcher: British Prime Minister May 79 to Nov 90.
David Trimble: Leader of unionist party, First minister to the assembly of Northern Ireland

Thatcher Out, Major In:

In the November 1990 elections in Great Britain, John Major succeeded Margaret Thatcher as Prime Minister. Unlike his predecessor, Major had no anti-Irish baggage. In fact, he became Prime Minister with little, or no, pre-formed opinions regarding Ireland at all, as his previous government experience had not been related to Irish issues. (1) His dependence upon the unionists for support, however, was another matter.

Politics Make Strange Bedfellows:

The Tories had won a majority, but some of them were skeptical regarding relations with Europe, and were not inclined to support Major on these issues. Consequently, Major was deprived of a majority vote from his party. He entered into an informal understanding with unionist leader, James Molyneaux, for his continued support in certain matters regarding the European Union; matters in which his conservative Tory MPs' non-support could cost him a majority.

He came to depend upon the twelve votes of the Unionist party. In return, Major would grant the unionists major concessions, regarding issues with Sinn Fein. This in effect, made it possible for the Ulster unionists to covertly 'veto' any proposals made regarding Sinn Fein. This rendered it impossible for him to bargain in good faith with the nationalists. The unionists were unwilling to participate in peace talks, unless the Anglo-Irish Agreement was suspended, and Sinn Fein was excluded from the process. Thus, Major became even more intransigent than Margaret Thatcher, where the IRA was concerned. Sinn Fein was out of the loop.

A Valentine for John Major:

The IRA, as a gesture of good will, announced a Christmas ceasefire. This was the first such gesture since 1970. The good will ended after Christmas. The ceasefire ended on February 7, 1991, when the IRA launched a mortar attack on Number Ten Downing Street, to show their displeasure with its occupant. There was some minor damage, but nothing 'Major.' The closest shell landed fifteen meters short of the building (2)

A Strategy for Peace and Justice:

On October 6, 1991 John Hume, taking input from Gerry Adams, Peter Brooke, Charles Haughey, and other senior Irish officials put together a plan for peace and justice in Ireland. John Hume's plan called for a three stranded approach to peace talks.

Strand 1. Between Belfast and Dublin,
Strand 2. Between Belfast, Dublin and London,
Strand 3. Between the opposing parties in Northern Ireland, (Unionist, Alliance, SDLP)

In a fourth strand, Brookes secretly continued to talk with Sinn Fein through the "back channel." Martin McGuinness was a principle player, among several, for Sinn Fein's back channel exchanges.

Election in the Republic and the UK:

In February 1992, Charles Haughey resigned as taoiseach, and was succeeded by Albert Reynolds. The new taoiseach announced that his main focus would be on the northern situation. Hume reassured Reynolds regarding the Sinn Fein leadership, and Adams's ability to get things done. Reynolds had a good awareness of northern problems. He also had a previous friendship with new British Prime Minister, John Major.

Sir Patrick Mayhew:

Also in April, Sir Patrick Mayhew, an old political ally of John Major, succeeded Peter Brooke as secretary of state for Northern Ireland. Actually, it had been Sir Patrick, who gave John Major his first political appointment.(3) In a speech in Coleranine, Mayhew praised the Sinn Fein leadership and acknowledged their desire for a peaceful solution. The overall substance of his remarks was, *If republicans end the violence, the government will respond positively.* This became the basis of British policy for the mid 1990s, but further obstacles would develop. (4)

Adams Looses his Seat in Parliament:

In the April 1992 elections in the UK the SDLP made some gains in votes, but Sinn Fein lost ground, and Gerry Adam's seat for West Belfast went to the SDLP candidate. The Provisional IRA (a splinter group not connected to Sinn Fein) detonated two bombs in London's Hyde Park and Regent's Park, targeting The Queen's Mounted Royal Household Cavalry, and members of the Royal Band. Ten Soldiers were killed.

Humes and Adams Meet Secretly:

In June 1992, John Humes (SDLP) and Gerry Adams (Sinn Fein) met secretly, and found that they were in agreement on numerous matters. Together, they produced a document, which would later be referred to as the Humes-Adams Document. On September 25, 1992 they issued a statement announcing their meeting and a copy of the document was sent to Taoiseach Albert Reynolds, in Dublin. (5)

The Missing Element:

The years 1991-92 were essentially unproductive in the peace process. There was a change of leadership in the United Kingdom, and in the Republic. Talks took place among all concerned parties except Sinn Fein, which was excluded, supposedly because of IRA violence, but in reality because Ian Paisley and his DUP party controlled John Major. This was unfortunate, because Sinn Fein was the missing vital element for any progress. Consequently the violence continued, however, it was far from one-sided. The loyalists were not idle. By the end of 1992 the body-count was: Republicans-thirty-six, Loyalists-thirty-nine. (6)

UDA Banned:

The nature of the killings by the Ulster Defense Association (UDA) was such that the organization was banned by the Northern Ireland government. There were those who protested that Sinn Fein should also be outlawed, because of its ties to the IRA, the approach of the government toward Republicans at that time was more conciliatory than coersive. The government's policy had become to "speak softly to Sinn Fein." (7)

The Humes-Adams Document:

In early April 1993, Adams and Hume issued a joint statement. re: The Hume-Adams Document, released the previous September. The document stated that the Irish people, as a whole, have a right to national self-determination. It also proposed a time scale for future unification of Ireland, which was strongly opposed by the unionists. Whereas, the British government, (namely John Major) was dependent upon unionist support in Parliament, the time table could not be accepted by the British Government.(8)

The Hume-Adams document brought the underlying issues to the fore: Who made policy for Ireland, Mayhew, Hume,

Reynolds, or Major? An Irish toaiseach was proposing policy to satisfy a Tory British Prime Minister, who was dependent upon Unionist support on European issues. (9)

London's Financial District Targeted:

In April 1993, an IRA blast destroyed the Baltic Exchange in London. This immediately caused foreign investors to be skeptical about making investments in London. A loss of confidence among international financiers could seriously damage the British economy.(10)

IRA Offers Ceasefire:

In May, the IRA offered a ceasefire for a fortnight (two weeks). The British, ostensibly sought a settlement, but in reality, for some reason they failed to respond. This lack of response was not well received, and led the IRA leadership to wonder about the motives of the British government. John Major, speaking for the British Government, rejected Gerry Adams and declared that because of the IRA attacks, he would accept nothing that had Gerry Adams's fingerprints on it.

Major and Reynolds Meet:

In December 1993, the British and the Irish governments agreed that The Humes-Adams Document was not acceptable, and drew up their own watered down version of the document, eliminating the references to time scale unification. (11)

Second Attack on Financial District:

On April 24, 1993, a 2,000 pound bomb destroyed the National West Tower at Bishopgate, in London, following more than a dozen warning phone calls. There were many buildings destroyed, including the Hong Cong and Shanghai Bank. The damage to London's financial district, amounting to over three hundred million pounds, caused tremendous concern to the government. A trespassing photographer from *News of the World* was killed, when he slipped past security guards to get his picture of the threatened area.

Americans for a New Irish Agenda:

In September 1993, Americans for a New Irish Agenda (ANIA), the main contact for the Irish-American lobby, met with, Nancy Soderberg, who had recently been appointed by U.S

President Clinton, as staff director of the National Security Council. As a result of this meeting, a delegation of the ANIA visited Ireland. The IRA called a seven day ceasefire, and the delegates met separately with all the parties to the conflict, Unionist, and Nationalist leaders, and the Dublin and London representatives.

They carried a letter from President Clinton expressing criticism of anti-Catholic discriminatory employment polices in Northern Ireland, and support given to Loyalist paramilitary groups by the British security forces in Northern Ireland. Upon their return to the U.S. they recommended to Clinton that Gerry Adams be given a visa to visit the country to seek support for the peace process. This would also have the effect of mainstreaming Adams and the Sinn Fein as a legitimate party to the process. **(12)**

The Shankill Bomb:

On October 23, 1993, a bomb, intended for the Ulster Defense Association leadership, exploded prematurely in a crowded fish shop, on the Shankill road in Belfast. It killed the IRA bomber and nine unintended Protestants. The targets had previously departed. On October 30, two Ulster Freedom Fighters entered a bar in Derry, and randomly murdered seven Halloween costumed patrons. The worst period of fatalities occurred in December of 1993, just before the Downing Street Declaration. There were numerous attacks by the Ulster Defense Association (UDA) with automatic weapons, indiscriminately murdering large numbers of Catholics, and even a few Protestants who happened to get in the way. During the three year period of 1991 through 1993, the UDA and the Ulster Volunteer Force (UVF), killed more people than the IRA did. **(13)**

The Downing Street Declaration:

October 29, 1993- Taoiseach Albert Reynolds and Prime Minister Major issued a joint statement distancing themselves from Adams and Hume. They stated that Britain and the Republic will continue to work together to design a framework for peace, and they disavowed the possibility of any secret agreements between a government and an organization supporting violence. Clearly they were referring specifically to Sinn Fein. In December they met at the residence of the Prime Minister on Downing Street, London to formulate a joint statement clarifying their position. They declared that, "it is for the people of the island of Ireland alone, by agreement between the two parts respectively, to exercise their right of self-determination on the basis of consent freely, and concurrently given, North and South, to bring about a united Ireland, if that is their wish." The Downing Street Declaration also made it very clear "that the British government has no selfish, or strategic, or economic interest in Ireland.

Adams Granted a U.S. Visa:

U.S. Senator Ted Kennedy had intervened, and President Clinton agreed that granting the visa for Adams to enter the United States would help to mainstream Sinn Fein and convince the Republicans that political action would work where military action would not. Clinton personally signed the authorization admitting Adams to the U.S.(14) Despite British objection, Adams was given a forty-eight hour visa. Taoiseach Reynolds very much supported the move, and provided him with all the information and assistance at his disposal.

Adams arrived in New York at the end of January 1994. At the White House he met the President, the Security Council, the White House Staff, Ted Kennedy and many others. He was totally convinced that the Republican movement must abandon use of violence as an instrument of policy.

He was wined and dined everywhere he went. John Majors was furious, and even tried, unsuccessfully, to ban the satellite telecasts of Adams's speeches. Irish and American officials were unable to convince Majors that Adams's visit would have a positive effect upon the peace process.

London's Heathrow Airport "Bombed:"

On March 9, 1994 London's Heathrow airport became the object of an IRA attack, by means of five mortar rounds being dropped onto the runway. On March 11th, four more mortar rounds struck the airport administration building. On March 13th, the airport was struck with four more rounds, one of them landing on Terminal Four. There were no deaths, or injuries. There were no explosions. The mortar shells had been disarmed, so there were no explosives involved, nor were the "bombers" ever apprehended.

The British authorities were embarrassed, and just to rub it in, the IRA issued a public statement criticizing the 'negative attitude' of the British government, and stressing the positive attitude of the IRA toward the peace process. John Major was furious. The Irish government and President Clinton were exasperated, to say the least. The Public was somewhat amused.

One Last Bit of Business:

The IRA still had other scores to settle with the Ulster DefenseAssociation, (UDA) Ulster Volunteer Force, (UVF) and the Ulster Defense Force (UDF) for killings which took place over the previous three years. Through the summer months the IRA killed several senior members of the Ulster Defense Association, including its political chairman. Other loyalists suspected of murdering Catholics were also eliminated as late as mid-August.

The Bombing Stops:

Suddenly, on August 31, 1994, the IRA announced a complete cessation of all military operations. No time limit was set, no pre-condition set. If on the other hand, circumstances should occur that contravened any of their objectives, the cessation would end. The loyalists were stumped. What did it mean? What would the IRA do next? They were, figuratively, "waiting for the next shoe to fall." The waiting went on.

TUAS:

The reasons, known only to the senior members of the Republican movement as "TUAS;" *Totally Unarmed Strategy,* were to achieve the following objectives:

1. To gain the strongest possible consensus among Dublin Gov, Sinn Fein and SDLP.
2. Establish a common position for advancement toward their goal.
3. Present a common nationalist negotiating position.
4. International dimension of consensus with the United States and Europe.(15)

"Decommissioning:"

Unfortunately, John Major did not accept the ceasefire, and had one further issue to introduce into the process; decommissioning of weapons. What this appears to mean, is that the Unionists wanted to maintain the status quo. Decommissioning had never been raised, prior to the announcement of the cease fire. If it had been, the cease fire would never have happened. The Republicans had never given up their weapons, not even at the end of the Irish civil war.

One IRA leader, Frank Aiken, actually ordered the weapons to be dumped, but not surrendered. Many IRA members also considered the possibility that the Catholic population in Northern Ireland would be defenseless, if the RUC and Loyalist death squads should resume hostilities. There were 160,000 licensed weapons in Protestant hands at that time. Nothing was mentioned about confiscating those weapons.

Loyalist Weapons in Northern Ireland:

There had also been large caches of weapons that had been smuggled into the six counties by British intelligence, and placed into the hands of Loyalist organizations, with memberships of 32,000. Nothing was mentioned about decommissioning them.

Shovels as Weapons?

It should also be pointed out that the weapon which had caused the most destruction, the fertilizer bomb, was impossible to decommission. Two men, using shovels, and a schoolboy formula can construct such a 1,000 pound weapon in a cowshed, in about two hours. If discovery was threatened, the 'bomb' could easily, and harmlessly, be concealed by spreading over the near-by field. Yet nothing was ever mentioned about decommissioning shovels.

More Than One Private Army?

One cannot support an argument condoning the existence of private armies in a democracy. On the other hand, there was no serious contention that Northern Ireland is, or was, a democracy. It was either under the control of a foreign power, or a sectarian tyranny of a loyalist government that denied the basic human rights to over forty percent of its people. It is also an established fact that the IRA was not the only private army with which to be concerned. **(16)**

Peace Forum Scheduled:

As yet unaware of the new decommissioning constraint, on September 6th, Taoiseach Reynolds convened a meeting between himself, Gerry Adams and John Hume. They called for a Forum in Dublin Castle, to discuss Peace and Reconciliation. It was to include all political parties, and be convened on October 28th.

The ceasefire held through September and into October. The IRA cease fire had made it feasible for the direct negotiations between Sinn Fein, the British and the Northern Irish government's two loyalist parties. Not wishing to be left out of the proceedings, the Loyalist para-militarists who had been engaged in "reprisals" for IRA operations, declared a ceasefire of their own, on October 13[th.] This turned out to be a major truce, involving the Ulster Defense Association, The Ulster Freedom Fighters, The Ulster Volunteer Force, and the Red Hand Commandos also called a ceasefire. One must wonder why John Major said nothing about decommissioning the loyalist para-militarists.

The Forum:

When the Peace and Reconciliation Forum convened in Dublin Castle, on October 28th, it would have been the first public meeting between Sinn Fein and British government. Taoiseach Reynolds even removed the longstanding ban on broadcasting Sinn Fein statements. A real break through was imminent. Unfortunately, John Major and the Unionists parties did not choose to attend. **(17)**

Another major blow to the peace process happened on November 17, 1994, when Albert Reynolds was forced to resign as taoiseach. John Bruton introduced a no-confidence vote concerning a political appointment made by Reynolds, Attorney General Harry Whelehan, as President of the High Court. Whelehan was heavily criticized for failure to adequately prosecute a case involving a pedophilic Catholic priest. **(18)**

Taoiseach John Bruton:

The 1995 election in the Republic, produced a "Rainbow coalition, " of Fein Gael, Labour, and Democratic Labour, which elected John Bruton as taoiseach. As it turned out, Bruton was almost as negative about Republicanism as was John Major.

Bruton immediately met with Major, after which he stated that "substantive progress' on decommissioning would be required, exactly mirroring the British position. **(19)** An essential part of TUAS was Irish governmental support. (Whose side was Bruton on?) The peace talks would be stalled.

U.S. Senator George Mitchell:

On January 9, 1995, President Clinton's appointment of retired senator George Mitchell as special advisor to the President, and as Secretary of State on economic initiatives in Ireland, became effective.

A New Framework:

In February the British and Irish governments came up with *A New Framework for Agreement,* for proposing constitutional changes in both the North and South. This would be done without upsetting either group's traditions, yet provide plans for new structures, and a commitment in respect for human rights, and applying the principle of the Downing Street Declaration. All of this would be subject to referendum in both parts of Ireland.**(20)**

Major's Man Bruton:

In March, taoiseach John Bruton, speaking in Washington, made a series of speeches supporting the position of requiring decommissioning of weapons as a pre-condition for Sinn Fein participating in peace talks.

Gerry and Bill:

In March Gerry Adams was given an unlimited visa for visiting the United States. On March 15, he and President William Clinton shared a photo-op, shaking hands at the White House. Clinton agreed to permit Sinn Fein to openly collect political contributions in the U.S. He also invited Adams to attend a St. Patrick's Day reception at the White House. These occasions were directed at demonstrating to the IRA that political activity bore fruit. John Major was really enraged by both of these actions, to the extent that he refused to accept a phone call from Clinton. A later call was accepted and Clinton added insult to injury, when he told Major that if he continued his refusal to invite Sinn Fein to a dinner which he would host in Belfast the following December, to inaugurate an investment conference, there would be no dinner, or conference. He pointed out to Major that the object of the exercise was to end discrimination, not to extend it. **(21)**

The Brits Say Yes, Then they Say No:

On March 29th the British government announced that they were prepared to "hold an exploratory dialogue" with Sinn Fein. Prime Minister Major visited Washington in April, and was praised by President Clinton for his courage in opening talks with Sinn Fein. Unfortunately the Ulster nationalists still maintained the position that the IRA must decommission weapons before they would be willing to talk to them. After returning to London, John Major forgot about Clinton's remarks and announced that Sinn Fein would not be allowed to take part in all-party talks, until the

IRA had decommissioned its weapons. In June, Sinn Fein announced that they were no longer prepared to talk with British officials. **(22)**

The David and Ian Show:

On July 18 David Trimble made an arrangement with the RUC, whereby he and the Rev. Ian Paisley would lead the Orangemen's parade through the Catholic area down Garvaghy Road, but without the band and drums, and making no effort to provoke the inhabitants. They did this, marching proudly, hand in hand together. They held their joined hands high over their heads to the delight of the triumphant Protestant throng, and to the humiliation of the watching Catholic residents. This colluded demonstration of sectarian solidity, was the political making of David Trimble. He was subsequently elected leader of the Ulster Unionist Party. **(283)**

They're Still Here

On August 13th, Gerry Adams raised the ire of the unionists, while speaking at a unionist rally in Belfast. He reminded his audience, "They" (the IRA) "haven't gone away, you know!" He wrote a newspaper article in, *An Phoblacht Republican News,* offering a blunt warning as to continued insistence upon decommissioning. He said: "The British government and others (meaning Bruton and Trimble) may be miscalculating the IRA's position on decommissioning. ….If a surrender of weapons had been imposed, as a precondition, prior to cessation, there would have been no IRA ceasefire."**(24)**

President Clinton Takes Belfast:

On November 30th, President Clinton, speaking in Belfast to employees and guests at the Mackie Metal Plant, told them, "We are proud to support Northern Ireland. You have given America a very great deal. Irish Protestants and Irish Catholics together have added to America's strength. From our battle for independence to the present day, the Irish have not only fought in our wars, they have built our nation, and we owe you a very great debt."

"But, " he continued, "The greatest struggle you face is between those who, … are inclined to be peacemakers, and those who, …cannot embrace the cause of peace. …old habits die hard."

He assured his audience that the United States would stand with the peacemakers. **(25)**

The Mitchell Report:

On January 26, 1996, the Mitchell Report was published. It was arrived at through the efforts of Senator Mitchell, the former Prime Minister of Finland, Hari Holkari, and former general John de Chastelain of Canada. The Commission Recommended a formula for by-passing the decommissioning issue, so the parties could deal with more urgent matters. The report required six procedural commitments from all parties. It also recommended revising police issues, such as a protocol for use of plastic bullets, more Catholic recruitment in the Royal Ulster Constabulary(RUC), and remediation of the situation by which weapons had been legally licensed to Protestant citizens.

Assembly Proposed:

British Prime Minister Major chose to ignore most of the Mitchell Report, except for a paragraph that mentioned the idea of an elected body. He revived David Trimble's proposal for an assembly and announced elections to a forum. His announcement was greeted with delight in the unionists camp, but somewhat differently by the nationalists and republicans. **(26)**

Enough Stalling:

Frustrated by intolerable delays by the British, the unionists and the loyalist, the IRA ended its seventeen month ceasefire on February 9th by detonating a 1,000 pound bomb near the impressive Canary Warf skyscraper in the London Docklands. Two workmen were killed by the 7:00 p.m. explosion, which did 150 million pounds worth of damage to the financial service district. The IRA demanded "an inclusive negotiated settlement." **(27)** A statement released by the IRA claimed, …"the British government acted in bad faith, with Mr. Major and the Unionist leaders squandering this unprecedented opportunity to resolve the conflict." **(28)**

On June 15, 1996, the Arndale Center of Manchester was destroyed by a 3,000 pound bomb, which was detonated in a parked lorry. Numerous false bomb threats were also called in to the police, causing further disruptions. July 12th, of course, brought about another Orangeman parade, which forced its way down Garvahey Road, near Drumcree, with the aid of the Royal

Ulster Constabulary and the British army. There was the usual rioting, and head bashing, but nothing lethal. In October, IRA exploded two bombs inside British army barracks in Northern Ireland. **(29)**

The Voters Make Needed Changes:

In May 1997, British Labour party leader Tony Blair was acclaimed as Prime Minister of Great Britain by a landslide victory. John Major was gone and Unionist MPs no longer held the balance of power in Parliament. It is interesting to note that Tony Blair also had a family tie to Ireland, his mother being of Donegal origin. As a child Tony had spent many happy holidays in Ireland.The new PM sanctioned the opening of talks with Sinn Fein's Gerry Adams, and Martin McGuinness. Regrettably, the talks had to be temporarily suspended when the IRA shot and killed two RUC men, in Lurggan, County Armagh. **(30)**

In the same general election Sinn Fein became the largest political party in Northern Ireland. In the process Gerry Adams regained his seat in Parliament as MP for West Belfast. Sinn Fein vice-President Martin McGuinness was also elected MP for Mid-Ulster. The people turned out to vote for Sinn Fein because they wanted them to represent them in the peace talks **(31)**

On June 6th, the general election in the Republic gave Bertie Ahern the office of taoiseach. Things were looking up. First John Major was voted out, and now John Bruton had joined him in political oblivion. Now the Republic had a leader who would represent the Republic.

Twenty-one people were killed in sectarian attacks in 1997. The IRA was responsible for eight of those deaths. Loyalist Orangmen were responsible for thirteen of them, as the Orange parade on July 12th, forced its way through the Portatown-Garvaghy Road again, with the aid of police and the British army.

Ceasefire Restored:

In July former U.S. Senator George Mitchell led intense talks between the British, the Northern Protestants and Sinn Fein. As a result, it came as a surprise when the IRA announced resumption of the ceasefire on July 20th .

Consequently, Sinn Fein was admitted to peace talks on September 9th. British Prime Minister, Tony Blair on a visit to Belfast, enraged many unionists by shaking hands with Gerry Adams. Blair did it again at 10 Downing Street at a later date. **(32)**

The Good Friday Agreement:

In April 1998 the Good Friday Agreement was signed by all of the Northern Ireland parties participating in talks. Both the Irish and British governments also signed the agreement. Island-wide referenda, endorsed by all parties, north and south, set up a new assembly in Northern Ireland, a North-South Council, and a British Irish Council. Provision was made for new and better protection of civil rights, and equality of opportunity. Commitment was made to achieve weapons decommissioning within two years, and a special provision for the rapid release of prisoners was agreed upon.

More Violence by Radicals:

On July 12, three young Catholic boys were killed, in a predominantly Protestant neighborhood in the Ballamoney area, when Loyalists petrol-bombed their home. On August 16, a traditional Catholic holiday, twenty-eight people were outright killed, one died later, and hundreds were injured. A Republican splinter group, calling itself, The "Real" IRA" detonated a 500 pound car-bomb in a crowded shopping center in Omagh, County Tyrone. This was seen as one of the worst outrages of "The Troubles." The total number of people killed in Northern Ireland, in 1998 was fifty-five; mostly Catholic.**(33)**

In September, President Clinton, with his wife and daughter, joined Tony Blair and his wife, to visit a large group of the injured victims, and their families. They placed a plaque at the site in memoriam. On December 13, President Clinton addressed a crowd of eight-thousand people in Belfast, telling them, "I believe in the peace you are building, I believe there can be no turning back.

The Patten Commission:

Under the terms of the Good Friday Agreement, a commission was set up, under Chris Patten, to investigate the Royal Ulster Constabulary (RUC) and make recommendations for needed reforms. The commission did a thorough study, taking over a year, and made its report on September 9th. They concluded that the force needed to represent both traditions, which would require more Catholics in the ranks. They also recommended that the name of the force be changed to "the Northern Ireland Police Service." It also suggested that the organizational emblem, a

British crown over an Irish harp, be discontinued, along with the practice of flying the British Union Jack outside the police stations. They also recommended that the size of the force be reduced. Needless to say, these recommendations were viewed with anger by the Unionists, and joyfully accepted by the Nationalist.

Power Sharing At last:

There was much bickering, arguing and name calling over various issues. The Unionists objected to the Patten Commission report, and demanded the ousting of Sinn Fein from the Assembly because the IRA had not decommissioned its weapons. This was followed by resignations, and threats of resignation by key people, more objections from the Unionists, shouting, pouting, and scowling. Adams and Trimble made eloquent statements, and General de Chastelain announced that the decommissioning plan was proceeding and recommended devolution of powers. Resignations were withdrawn, and everybody calmed down again. Finally, after twenty-five years of direct rule, Northern Ireland regained a power-sharing executive on November 29, 1999, and a devolved government took office.

The Unionist Way, or No Way:

It looked as though a settlement had been achieved, but there was a fly in the ointment. The vote for power-sharing had passed with a comfortable majority, made possible through a deal with the Unionist Party. That majority had a price tag on it. The price was a check, in the form of a pre-signed letter of resignation from First Minister David Trimble, if the IRA decommissioning was not accomplished by the deadline of April 2000, as the two years agreed upon in the Good Friday Agreement. The Unionists cashed that check in February 2000, leaving the Assembly without an executive. It would seem that in the event a government, for whatever reason, should lose its chief executive (first minister), the position would automatically devolve to the first deputy minister, in this case Seamus Mallon, (SDLP). However, that was apparently not the way things worked in Northern Ireland. In any event, the Assembly ceased to exist, and direct rule was reinstated from London on February 11th.

Political and diplomatic pressure was applied from Dublin, Belfast, London and Washington, seeking a way to restore a power-sharing Assembly. General de Chastelain said he was certain the IRA could fulfill its mandate. Everyone was satisfied except the Unionists, who now added the provision that the decommissioning be accomplished in full view of the television cameras. That, of course, was unacceptable to the IRA, and the discourse continued.

On May 6, the IRA reiterated its commitment to "put arms beyond use completely and verifiably in the context of full implementation of the Good Friday Agreement. They would allow two, distinguished, third-party, international observers, to inspect their dumps to confirm that the weapons remain secured. Provision would also be made to re-inspect the dumps periodically. The IRA opened its dump to the inspectors on June 26.

Trimble Consents:

Meanwhile, David Trimble finally condescended to resume his position as first minister of the assembly, and on May 29, 2000 devolution had been restored to Northern Ireland. This was followed on June 26th by IRA announcing the opening of its arms dumps to the inspectors. This, in turn, was followed by the release of four hundred twenty-eight political prisoners from the Maze prison on July 28th, as provided in the Good Friday Agreement, two years before. (34)

On August 21, 2000 Loyalist feuding caused the return of British soldiers to the streets of Belfast. The violence continued. "The Real IRA, " with no political connection to anyone, mounted its own rocket attack on M16 headquarters in London

Stalemate! Everyone Looses:

On June 30, 2001, David Trimble again resigned as first minister of the assembly, because of the IRA failure to decommission, according to the Unionist latest standard. The IRA responded to Trimble, on August 6, offering to continue with previously agreed to plan to put weapons beyond use in co-operation with the decommissioning body. The next day, Trimble rejected the IRA plan out of hand. On August 14th the IRA withdrew its decommissioning offer, because of Trimble's response.

That was five years ago. At the time of this writing nothing has changed much; not Ian Paisley, not David Trimble, not the DUP. Your may, indeed, wonder what the D stands for, and well you might!

Rev. Ian Paisley, Member of Parliament, Leader of DUP.

The reason is clear. The Unionists did not want to share devolved power with the Republicans. Their goal was to maintain the status quo: Rule by Westminster.They wished to remain within the British Empire in order to maintan their class-structured society, in which Protestants comprise the privileged class. In anybody's book, that is not democracy. Look at this story from the pages of the *Wall Street Irish American,* August/September, 2006: (36)

N.I. Talks Show Slow Progress

Irish and British governments continue to push the November 24 deadline for power sharing in Northern Ireland, but there is little sign of actual progress on the ground. Unionist and nationalist parties have been unable to find a way to restore devolved government at the N.I. Assembly, but Dublin and London hold the majority Democratic Unionist Party (DUP) chiefly responsible for stalling the return to devolution under the terms of the Good Friday Agreement. The DUP and Sinn Fein represent the largest blocs of unionist and nationalist votes respectively, and progress depends on agreement between the two parties. Sinn Fein has already indicated it is prepared to share power with the DUP, but the offer has not been reciprocated. Governments in Dublin and London are satisfied that the IRA has met demands on decommissioning, but DUP leader Dr. Ian Paisley wants greater proof that republicans are committed to decommissioning of arms, ending criminality and supporting the PSNI legal system in Northern Ireland. Sinn Fein is unlikely to bow to any DUP demand for further concessions and unless agreement is reached before November 24, the N.I. Assembly will be wound up and direct rule from London restored. Dermot Ahern, Irish Minister for Foreign Affairs met with Northern Secretary Peter Hain, reporting that both governments were somewhat "under whelmed by the progress to date at the talks." He added that "Both governments are adamant about the November 24 deadline and we expect people to be up to the mark. Ultimately it's a matter for them, but November 24th is sacrosanct.

Trimble Looses Seat in Commons, Knighted by The Queen:

In the Westminster elections in 2006 David Trimble lost his seat in the House of Commons. Following Trimble's defeat, his Ulster Unionist Party(UUP) went over to Ian Paisley's Democratic Unionist Party, making it the dominant party in the North.(40) For past services rendered, Trimble was knighted by the Queen, and now sits in the House of Lords.

Adams Moves Sinn Fein:

On Sunday, January 28, 2007, Sinn Fein president Gerry Adams addressed the Sein Fein *Ard Feis* (party congress) in Dublin, and was able to counteract one of those added provisions of Rev. Ian Paisley, cited above, specifically Sinn Fein's lack of support for the Police System of Northern Ireland (PSNI), which was previously known as the Royal Ulster Constabulary (RUC).

The Sinn Fein membership had, for some time, been strongly opposed to supporting anything to do with the RUC because of collusion between the RUC special branch, and loyalist gangs of the Ulster Volunteer Force (UVF), resulting in the cold blooded murder of scores of Catholic men, women, and children from 1991 to 1993.

A recent report by Police Ombudsman Nuala O'Loan regarding this collusion had revived the memory and Adams used that memory as ammunition to make his point. He contended that this type of collusion must never be allowed to happen again, and that supporting the PSNI and participating in the policing board would be the best method of prevention.

Their support of PSNI would also remove the last barrier blocking the March 7th elections, for the Stormount Assembly. Following six hours of hard debate, the motion to support PSNI was passed by the convention by a 90% vote.

Adams stated, "This decision we have taken today is truly historic. This is one of the most important debates in the history of republicanism and of this country. Let's not be upset by how others respond to today's decision." Referring to previous DUP tactics, he added, "The higher they build their barriers the stronger we become." (37)

Peter Hain, Britain's Secretary of State for Northern Ireland, speaking to U.S policy makers in February, reiterated Adams remarks, saying that the power-sharing Executive must support policing and rule of law, as the twin pillars of the St. Andrew's Agreement, in order to meet the March 26th deadline.(43)

DUP Playing the Same Old Game:

True to form the Democratic Unionist Party threw up another road block by demanding a provision to throw Sinn Fein out of power, if the DUP deems that the IRA has been involved in any action.(39)

Hains Cites Bread and Butter Issues:

Secretary of State Peter Hains reaffirmed that if the power-sharing Executive is not set up by March 26th, he would be compelled to abolish the Good Friday Agreement of 1998. He continued, saying that people were now concerned with the "Bread and butter"issues, such as taxes, jobs, health, the economy and education." He continued, "When there used to be shipbuilding and a linen industry, there might have been some value in a connection with the Union. Now our argument is, If there is a Celtic Tiger, (in the republic) why should it stop at the border? Why can it not come to Belfast? Are people not going to accept jobs and economic dividends, if there were a thirty-two county Celtic Tiger?" (40)

Large Turnout for Assembly Election:

March 7th saw a large turnout of voters to determine how 108 assembly seats would be divided in the Stormount Assembly. The results were not surprising, with the DUP and Sinn Fein being the leading winners, respectively: DUP 36, Sinn Fein 28, UUP 18, SDLP 16, and the remaining ten seats divided among the four smaller parties.(41)

Party Leaders Meet:

Party Leaders Gerry Adams and Ian Paisley had a face-to-face meeting within 48 hours following a DUP Party meeting where the membership voted 90 % for a request of six weeks delay in establishing a power-sharing Executive. The meeting was reported as private, cordial, but not friendly. Paisley was reported to have said, "This is a 'work-in' not a 'love-in'." The two men did not shake hands. The requested delay was quickly approved by both the London and Dublin governments.

The new deadline for establishing devolved power-sharing was set at May 8, 2007. Had Paisley and Adams not met and agreed on the request, the secretary of State would have dissolved the assembly permanently. At that point, the contingency B-Plan would have been implemented, involving joint rule of Northern Ireland by London and Dublin.(42)

Following the "work-in, " Paisley was quoted, "We must not allow our justified loathing of the horrors and tragedies of the past to become a barrier to creating a better and more stable future. In looking to the future we must never forget those who have suffered during the dark period, from which we are, please God, emerging."

Adams was similarly quoted, "We have all come a very long way in the process of peace-making, and national reconciliation. Collectively we have increased the potential to build a new, harmonious and equitable relationship between nationalists, and republicans and unionists, as well as the rest of the people of the island of Ireland."(43)

Executive Cabinet Named:

Party Leaders Ian Paisley and Gerry Adams named their appointments to the power-sharing Executive Cabinet to be installed on May 8th:

First Minister Rev. Ian Paisley,
Deputy First Minister Martin McGuiness,
Minister of Finance and Personnel Peter Robinson,
Minister of Enterprise, Nigel Dodds
Minister of Environment Arlene Foster,
Minister of Culture and Leisure, Edwin Poots
Minister of Education, Caitriona Ruane,
Minister of Agricultrue, Michelle Gilernew,
Minister of Regional Development, Conor Murphy,
Ministerof Health /Social Services, Michael McGimpsey
Minister of Higher Education, Sir Reginald Empey. (44)

Peter Hain Given Eviction Notice:

The First Minister and the Deputy First Minister, in waiting, sent a joint letter to Secretary of State Peter Hain, requesting him to please relocate and vacate his offices at Stormount. Secretary Hain told the BBC that he will be delighted to do so.

Devolved Power Sharing, At Last:

On May 8, 2007, the bilateral government of Northern Ireland was smoothly established at Stormount, as Ian Paisley, and Martin McGuiness were sworn in as First Minister and Deputy First Minister respectively. Present at the ceremony were British prime minister Tony Blair, Taoiseach Bertie Ahern, and U.S. Senator Ted Kennedy.

Sinn Fein President Gerry Adams remarked, "I genuinely believe that we are all shaping a real process of national reconciliation, and building a new relationship between the people of this island, and between Ireland and Britain. (45)

We're Almost There!

Since the days of the first Irish Ard Ri, and the loose confederation of Kingdoms of Ireland, through the Viking invasion, the Norman invasion, and the resulting Anglo domination, Irishmen have dreamed of a free, and United Ireland. They have fought and died for that dream. Such men as Brian Boru, Patrick Sarsfield, Theobald Wolf Tone, Father John Murphy, Daniel O'Connell, Charles Parnell, Michael Collins, Patrick Pearse, have all shared that dream. The dream has been told to the generations, through the poetry, and music of the land. That dream of nationhood has been kept alive in Irish hearts. We are almost there!

Bibliography

(1) Adams, Gerry, *A Farther Shore,* Random House, New York, 2003

(2) Bhreathnach and Newman, *Tara,* Government of Ireland, Dublin, 1997

(3) Bright, David James, editor, *Let's Go Ireland 2003,* St. Martin's Press, New York

(4) Coogan, Tim Pat, *Ireland in the Twentieth Century,* Palgrave MacMillan, NewYork, 2003

(5) Cruise O'Brien, Marie & Conor, *Ireland, A Concise History,* Thames and Hudson, New York, 1972

(6) Curtis, Edmund, *A History of Ireland,* Routledge, London, 1936

(7) Cusack, Mary Francis, *History of Ireland 400 to 1800,* Senate Press Ltd., Middlesex, UK, 1868

(8) Duffy, Sean, *The Consise History of Ireland,* Gill & MacMillan, Dublin 12, Ireland, 2005

(9) Feeney, Brian, *Sinn Fein, A Hundred Turbulent Years,* University of Wisconsin Press, Madison, 2002

(10) Foster, R.F., *Modern Ireland 1600-1972,* The Penguin Press, London, 2000

(11) Garibhi, Marie NicDomhnaill, *A Traditional Music Journey 1600 to 2000,* Drumlin Publications, Leitrim, 2000

(12) Grogan, Robert, *130 Great Irish Ballads,* Music Land, Dublin, 1997

(13) Hayes, G.A. and McCoy, *Irish Battles- A Military History of Ireland,* Appletree Press, Belfast, 1969

(14) Kee, Robert, *Ireland A History,* Little, Brown and Co. Boston Toronto, 1992

(15) Kennedy, Conan, *Ancient Ireland- The User's Guide,* Morigna Media Co Teo, Killala, Co. Mayo, 1994

(16) Llyweylen, Morgan, *Lion of Ireland,* Playboy Paperbacks New York, 1979

(17) Ibid, *1916,* Tom Doherty Associates, New York, 1998

(18) Ibid. *1921,* Tom Doherty Associates, New York, 200

(19) Ibid. *1949,* Tom Doherty Associates, New York, 2003

(20) Ibid. *1972,* Tom Doherty Associates, New York, 2005

(21) MacAnnaidh, Seamas, *Irish History,* Parragon Publishing, Bath, UK, 1999

(22) MacGarry, Fearghal, *The Making of An Irish Fascist,* History IRELAND, Vol 13, No. 6, Bray, Co. Wicklow, 2005

(23) Manning, Conleth, *Rock of Cashel,* Duchas- TheHeritage Service, Dublin, No date given.

(24) Massie, Sonja, *Irish History and Culture,* Alpha Books, Indianapolis, 1999

(25) McAffrey, Carmel & L. Eaton, *In Search of Ancient Ireland,* New Amsterdam Books, Chicago, 2002

(26) McManus, Seumas, The *Story of the Irish Race,* Wings Books-Random House, New York 199

(27) Moody, T.W. & Martin, F.X., *The Course of Irish History,* Mercier Press, Cork, 1967(28)

(28) O'Crohan, Tomas, *The Islandman,* Oxford University Press, NewYork, 1951

(29) Purdon, Edward, *The Irish Famine,* Mercier Press, Dublin, 2000

(30) Ranelagh, John, *Ireland, An Illustrated History,* Oxford University Press, New York, 1981

(31) Ryan, Meda, *The Real Chief Liam Lynch,* Mercier Press, Cork, 1986

(32) Uris, Leon, *Trinity,* Doubleday & Company, *New York,* 1976

(33) Wallace, Martin, *A Short History of Ireland,* Apple Tree Press, Belfast, 1975

Endnotes

Chapter One

1. Mc Affrey, et. al., *In Search of Ancient Ireland.* p. 7
2. Moody & Martin, *The Course of Irish History,* p.15
3. Ranelaigh, *Ireland, An Illustrated History,* p.12
4. Ibid. p.13
5. Moody & Martin, *The Course of Irish History,* p.20
6. Ranelaigh, *Ireland, An Illustrated History,* p.16
7. McManus, *The Story of the Irish Race,* p.p.7, 8
8. Ibid.p.p.28-35
9. McAffrey, et. al., *In Search of Ancient Ireland. P. 54*
10. McManus, *The Story of the Irish Race,* p.2
11. McAffrey, et.al., *In Search of Ancient Ireland. P.31*
12. Ranelaigh, *Ireland, An Illustrated History,* p.30
13. Ibid. p.31
14. Ibid. p.232
15. Ibid.p.p.24-28

Chapter Two

1. McManus, *The Story of the Irish Race,* p.113
2. Ranelaigh, *Ireland, An Illustrated History,* p.43
3. McManus, *The Story of the Irish Race,* p.111
4. Ranelaigh, *Ireland, An Illustrated History,* p.42
5. McManus, *The Story of the Irish Race,* p.112
6. Ibid.p.p. 113-114
7. Ibid. p.115
8. MacAnnaidh, *Irish History,* p.30
9. Ibid.p.35
10. Ibid. p.p. 38-39
11. Ranelaigh, *Ireland, An Illustrated History,* p.47
12. McAffrey, et.al. p.122

Chapter Three

1. Moody & Martin, *The Course of Irish History,* p.p.67-68
2. Ibid.p.70
3. Ibid. p.p. 74-75
4. Curtis, *A History of Ireland,* p.20
5. Ibid. p.21
6. Ranelaigh, *Ireland, An Illustrated History,* p.58
7. McAffrey, *In Search of Ancient Ireland,* p.230
8. Curtis, *A History of Ireland,* p.22

9.   McAffrey, *In Search of Ancient Ireland, p.232*
10. Llywleylen, *Lion of Ireland,* p.22
11. Curtis, *A History of Ireland,* p.23
12. Llywleylen, *Lion of Ireland,* p434
13. Moody & Martin, *The Course of Irish History,* p.78
14. Llywleylen, *Lion of Ireland,* p.60
15. Ibid. p.p. 555-56

Chapter Four

1.   Moody & Martin, *The Course of Irish History,* p.87
2.   Cusak, *History of Ireland, 400 - 1800,* p.222
3.   Moody & Martin, *The Course of Irish History,* p.p. 95-96
4.   Curtis, *A History of Ireland,* p.32
5.   *History of Ireland, 400 - 1800,* p.226
6.   Ranelaigh, *Ireland, An Illustrated History,* p.63
7.   Moody & Martin, *The Course of Irish History,* p.97
8.   Ranelaigh, *Ireland, An Illustrated History,* p.64
9.   MacAnnaidh, *Irish History,* p.p. 54-59
10. McManus, *The Story of the Irish Race,* p.324
11. Moody & Martin, *The Course of Irish History,* p. 101
12. McManus, *The Story of the Irish Race,* p.325
13. Ranelaigh, *Ireland, An Illustrated History,* p.66
14. Moody & Martin, *The Course of Irish History,* p.p.103-04
15. Massie, *Irish History and Culture,* p.77
16. McAffrey *History of Ireland, 400 - 1800,* p.p. 292-93
17. Curtis, *A History of Ireland,* p.57
18. Cusak, *History of Ireland, 400 - 1800,* p.294
19. Massie, *Irish History and Culture,* p.30
20. Ranelaigh, *Ireland, An Illustrated History,* p.p. 68-74
21. Cusak, *History of Ireland, 400 - 1800,* p.80
22. Curtis, *A History of Ireland,* p.74

Chapter Five

1.   Ranelaigh, *Ireland, An Illustrated History,* p.p. 68-71
2.   Ibid.p. 71
3.   Ibid. p.71
4.   Ibid. p.71
5.   Massie, *Irish History and Culture,* p.81
6.   Curtis, *A History of Ireland,* p.p. 99-102
7.   Ibid. p.p.108-113
8.   Ranelaigh, *Ireland, An Illustrated History,* p.73
9.   Massie, *Irish History and Culture,* p.89
10. Ranelaigh, *Ireland, An Illustrated History,* p.75

Chapter Six

1. Ranelaigh, *Ireland, An Illustrated History*, p.p. 77-78
2. Duffy, *The Concise History of Ireland*, p.96
3. McManus, *The Story of the Irish Race*, p. 358
4. Moody & Martin, *The Course of Irish History*, p.p. 140-41
5. Ranelaigh, *Ireland, An Illustrated History*, p.p. 80-81
6. Duffy, *The Concise History of Ireland*, p.p. 100-01
7. MacAnnaidh, *Irish History*, p. 91
8. Massie, *Irish History and Culture*, p.95
9. McManus, *The Story of the Irish Race*, p.p. 170-71
10. Ranelaigh, *Ireland, An Illustrated History*, p.89

Chapter Seven

1. Cusak, *History of Ireland, 400 - 1800*, p.p. 441-42
2. Ibid. p.444
3. Duffy, *The Concise History of Ireland*, p.p. 100-01
4. Ranelaigh, *Ireland, An Illustrated History*, p.86
5. Ibid.p.89
6. Curtis, *A History of Ireland*, p.p. 176-77
7. Cusak, *History of Ireland, 400 - 1800*, p. 450
8. Ranelaigh, *Ireland, An Illustrated History*, p.90
9. Curtis, *A History of Ireland*, p. 179
10. Hays, *Irish Battles A Military History of Ireland*, *p.p. 125-27*
11. MacAbbaidh, *Irish History*, p.98
12. Cusak, *History of Ireland, 400 - 1800*, p. 457
13. Ibid. p.p. 457-58
14. Ranelaigh, *Ireland, An Illustrated History*, p.92

Chapter Eight

1. Cusak, *History of Ireland, 400 - 1800*, p.464
2. Curtis, *A History of Ireland*, p.191
3. Ranelaigh, *Ireland, An Illustrated History*, p. 93
4. Wallace, *A Short History of Ireland, p.30*
5. Duffy, *The Concise History of Ireland*, p. 111
6. Moody & Martin, *The Course of Irish History*, p.p. 154-55
7. Ibid. p.156
8. Ranelaigh, *Ireland, An Illustrated History*, p.p. 100-01
9. Curtis, *A History of Ireland*, p.p. 206-09
10. Moody & Martin, *The Course of Irish History*, p.p. 159-60
11. Ranelaigh, *Ireland, An Illustrated History*, p.104
12. Hayes, *Irish Battles- A Military History of Ireland, p.p. 179-97*
13. Curtis, *A History of Ireland*, p. 214
14. Ibid.p.215
15. MacAnnaidh, *Irish History*, p. 215

16. McManus, *The Story of the Irish Race*, p.425
17. Ibid. p. 426

Chapter Nine

1. Moody & Martin, *The Course of Irish History*, p.162
2. McManus, *The Story of the Irish Race*, p.p. 424-30
3. Curtis, *A History of Ireland*, p.p. 217-19
4. Duffy, *The Concise History of Ireland*, p.p. 117-18
5. Moody & Martin, *The Course of Irish History*, p.167
6. *History of Ireland, 400 - 1800*, p. 556
7. Curtis, *A History of Ireland*, p.231
8. Ranelaigh, *Ireland, An Illustrated History, p.108*
9. Moody & Martin, *The Course of Irish History*, p.170
10. McManus, *The Story of the Irish Race*, p.p. 439-40
11. Curtis, *A History of Ireland*, p.233
12. MacAnnaidh, Irish History, p.120
13. Cusak, *History of Ireland, 400 - 1800*, p.564
14. Ibid. p.566
15. McManus, *The Story of the Irish Race*, p.p. 444-47
16. Ibid. p.p. 448-52
17. Curtis, *A History of Ireland*, p.p. 234-35
18. McManus, *The Story of the Irish Race*, p453
19. Curtis, *A History of Ireland*, p.235

Chapter Ten

1. Massie, *Irish History and Culture*, p.108
2. Ibid.p.109
3. Moody & Martin, *The Course of Irish History*, p.177
4. Ranelaigh, *Ireland, An Illustrated History,*
5. McManus, *The Story of the Irish Race*, p.459
6. MacAnnaidh, *Irish History*, p. 125
7. Ranelaigh, *Ireland, An Illustrated History*, p.117
8. Ibid. p.117
9. MacAnnaidh, *Irish History, p.p. 126-27*
10. Ranelaigh, *Ireland, An Illustrated History*, p.132
11. MacAnnaidh, *Irish History*, p.p. 130-31
12. Ranelaigh, *Ireland, An Illustrated History*, p. 115
13. Muzzey, *Our American Republic*, p.p. 47
14. Moody & Martin, *The Course of Irish History*, p.190
15. Ibid. p.190
16. Ibid. p. 191-92
17. Ibid. p. 192-93

Chapter Eleven

1. Ranelaigh, *Ireland, An Illustrated History*, p.134
2. MacAnnaidh, *Irish History*, p.138
3. Moody & Martin, *The Course of Irish History*, p.196
4. McManus, *The Story of the Irish Race*, p.507
5. Curtis, *A History of Ireland*, p.p. 285-86
6. McManus, *The Story of the Irish Race*, p.507
7. Moody & Martin, *The Course of Irish History*, p.p.198-99
8. Ibid. p.199
9. Duffy, *The Concise History of Ireland, p.139*
10. McManus, *The Story of the Irish Race*, p.p.509-10
11. Moody & Martin, *The Course of Irish History*, p. 189
12. Cusak, *History of Ireland, 400 - 1800*, p.p. 622-23
13. Ibid. p.618
14. McManus, *The Story of the Irish Race*, p.511
15. Curtis, *A History of Ireland*, p. 290
16. Moody & Martin, *The Course of Irish History, p.210*
17. Curtis, *A History of Ireland*, p.293
18. Cusak, *History of Ireland, 400 - 1800*, p. 626
19. McManus, *The Story of the Irish Race*, p. 502
20. Cusak *History of Ireland, 400 - 1800*, p. 628
21. Curtis, *A History of Ireland*, p. 295
22. Cusak, *History of Ireland, 400 - 1800*, p.p. 628-29
23. Curtis, *A History of Ireland*, p.296
24. McManus, *The Story of the Irish Race, p.p. 523-25*

Chapter Twelve

1. Moody & Martin, *The Course of Irish History* , 202
2. Curtis, *A History of Ireland*, p.p.296-97
3. Ranelaigh, *Ireland, An Illustrated History, p.144*
4. Moody & Martin, *The Course of Irish History*, p.202
5. Curtis, *A History of Ireland*, p.p. 298-99
6. McManus, *The Story of the Irish Race*, p.530
7. Curtis, *A History of Ireland*, p.299
8. McManus, *The Story of the Irish Race* , p.p. 527-28
9. Moody & Martin, *The Course of Irish History*, p.411
10. Cusak, *History of Ireland, 400 - 1800*, p.639
11. Ibid. p.639
12. Ranelaigh, *Ireland, An Illustrated History*, p.p. 145-46
13. Moody & Martin, *The Course of Irish History*, p. 203
14. McManus, *The Story of the Irish Race*, p.536
15. MacAnnaidh, Irish History, p.p. 148-49
16. Ranelaigh, *Ireland, An Illustrated History*, p. 146
17. Ibid. p.148

18. Duffy, *The Concise History of Ireland, p.148*
19. McManus, *The Story of the Irish Race,* p. 542
20. Ibid. p.p. 545-47
21. Ibid. p.p. 548-50
22. Ibid. p. 551
23. Ibid. p.p. 551-53

Chapter Thirteen

1. McManus, *The Story of the Irish Race,* p.553
2. Moody & Martin, *The Course of Irish History,* p.206
3. McManus, *The Story of the Irish Race,* p. 554
4. MacAnnaidh, Seamus, *Irish History,* p.154
5. Moody & Martin, *The Course of Irish History,* p.p. 207-09
6. MacAnnaidh, Seamus, *Irish History,* p.155
7   Ranelaigh, *Ireland, An Illustrated History,* p. 149
8   Cusak, *History of Ireland, 400 - 1800,* p. 647
9   McManus, *The Story of the Irish Race,* p.568
10 MacAnnaidh, Seamus, *Irish History,* p.158
11. Ibid, p.p. 157-59
12. Ibid. p158
13. Ibid. p.p. 160-61
14. Ranelaigh, *Ireland, An Illustrated History,* p.p.151-52
15. MacAnnaidh, Seamus, *Irish History,* p.p. 163-64
16. Moody & Martin, *The Course of Irish History,* p.p. 211-12
17. Ibid. pp.213-14
18. Ibid. p.214
19. Ranelaigh, *Ireland, An Illustrated History,* p.p. 152-57
20. Moody & Martin, *The Course of Irish History, p.214*
21. Ranelaigh, *Ireland, An Illustrated History,* p.150
22. Ibid. p.150-51

Chapter Fourteen

1. Ranelaigh, *Ireland, An Illustrated History,* p. 159
2. Moody & Martin, *The Course of Irish History,* p.p. 218-26
3. Curtis, *A History of Ireland,* p. 173
4. O'Crohan, Thomas, *The Islandman, p.p. 22-23*
5. Uris, Leon, *Trinity,* p.55
6. Moody & Martin, *The Course of Irish History,* p.221
7. Uris, Leon, *Trinity,* p.73
8. Ranelaigh, *Ireland, An Illustrated History,* p.159
9. Ibid. p.160
10. Massie, *Irish History and Culture,* p.129
11. Moody & Martin, *The Course of Irish History,* p.p. 222-23
12. Massie, *Irish History and Culture,* p.130

13. Duffy, *The Concise History of Ireland*, p.160
14. Moody & Martin, *The Course of Irish History*, p225
15. Ibid. p.225
16. Ranelaigh, *Ireland, An Illustrated History*, p.p. 163-64
17. Ibid. p. 162

Chapter Fifteen

1. McManus, *The Story of the Irish Race*, p.595
2. Ranelaigh, *Ireland, An Illustrated History*, p. 154
3. McManus, *The Story of the Irish Race*, p. 595
4. Ibid. p.596
5. Ibid. p.p. 598-99
6. Ibid. p. 599
7. Ranelaigh, *Ireland, An Illustrated History*, p.157
8. McManus, *The Story of the Irish Race*, p.317
9. Ranelaigh, *Ireland, An Illustrated History*, p.p. 166-67
10. Ibid. p.p. 167-68
11. McManus, *The Story of the Irish Race*, p.320
12. Ranelaigh, *Ireland, An Illustrated History*, p.167
13. Massie, *Irish History and Culture*, p.43
14. Ranelaigh, *Ireland, An Illustrated History*, p.p. 614-16
15. Ibid. p.169
16. McManus, *The Story of the Irish Race*, 616-17
17. Ibid. p. 619
18. Ibid. p.619
19. Curtis, *A History of Ireland*, p.p. 320-21
20. Ranelaigh, *Ireland, An Illustrated History*, p.p. 170-71

Chapter Sixteen

1. McManus, *The Story of the Irish Race*, p.621
2. Ranelaigh, *Ireland, An Illustrated History*, p.176
3. Curtis, *A History of Ireland*, p. 321
4. MacAnnaidh, *Irish History*, p.184
5. Ranelaigh, *Ireland, An Illustrated History*, p.177
6. Duffy, *The Concise History of Ireland*, p.169
7. Ranelaigh, *Ireland, An Illustrated History*, p.178
8. Curtis, *A History of Ireland*, p. 323
9. Moody & Martin, *The Course of Irish History*, p. 234
10. Curtis, *A History of Ireland*, p.p. 324-25
11. McManus, *The Story of the Irish Race*, p.624
12. Moody & Martin, *The Course of Irish History*, p.p. 236-37
13. McManus, *The Story of the Irish Race*, p.627
14. Ibid. p.628
15. Moody & Martin, *The Course of Irish History*, p. 237

16. McManus, *The Story of the Irish Race*, p.629
17. Ranelaigh, *Ireland, An Illustrated History*, p.p. 179-80
18. McManus, *The Story of the Irish Race*, p. 631
19. Ibid. p.p. 631-32
20. Moody & Martin, *The Course of Irish History*, p. 416
21. McManus, *The Story of the Irish Race*, p.p. 637-38
22. Massie, *Irish History and Culture*, p. 147
23. McManus, *The Story of the Irish Race*, p. 638
24. Ibid. p.640
25. Ranelaigh, *Ireland, An Illustrated History*, p.181
26. McManus, *The Story of the Irish Race*, p.643
27. Ibid. p.644
28. Curtis, *A History of Ireland*, p. 326
29. Ranelaigh, *Ireland, An Illustrated History*, p.182
30. Ibid. p.182
31. MacAnnaidh, *Irish History*, p.p. 206-07
32. Curtis, *A History of Ireland*, p.328

Chapter Seventeen

1. Ranelaigh, *Ireland, An Illustrated History*, p.139
2. Coogan, *Ireland in the Twentieth Century*, p.1
3. Duffy, *The Concise History of Ireland*, p.p. 174--75
4. Curtis, *A History of Ireland*, p. 328
5. McManus, *The Story of the Irish Race*, p. 636
6. Ibid. p.p. 657-58
7. Massie, *Irish History and Culture*, p.147
8. McManus, *The Story of the Irish Race*, p.p. 661-64
9. Ibid. p.652
10. Curtis, *A History of Ireland*, p.334
11. Ranelaigh, *Ireland, An Illustrated History*, p.p. 194-95
12. Cruise O'Brien, *Ireland, A Concise History*, p.p. 128-29
13. Curtis, *A History of Ireland*, p. 332
14. Ibid. p.333
15. Moody & Martin, *The Course of Irish History*, p. 248
16. Cruise O'Brien, *Ireland, A Concise History*, p.129
17. Ranelaigh, *Ireland, An Illustrated History*, p.p. 196-97
18. Coogan, *Ireland in the Twentieth Century*, p. 14
19. Moody & Martin, *The Course of Irish History*, p. 248
20. McManus, *The Story of the Irish Race*, p. 686
21. Ranelaigh, *Ireland, An Illustrated History*, p.199

Chapter Eighteen

1. Ranelaigh, *Ireland, An Illustrated History*, p.209
2. Llywleylen, *1916*, pp.171-184

3. Ibid. p.p. 185-87
4. Coogan, *Ireland in the Twentieth Century*, p.41
5. Massie, *Irish History and Culture*, p.150
6. Coogan, *Ireland in the Twentieth Century*, p.p. 42-43
7. Ibid. p.p. 43-45
8. Ranelaigh, *Ireland, An Illustrated History*, p.p.211-14
9. Coogan, *Ireland in the Twentieth Century*, p.49
10. Massie, *Irish History and Culture*, p.p. 150-51
11. Coogan, *Ireland in the Twentieth Century*, p.p. 49-51
12. Ibid. p.p. 52-53
13. Ranelaigh, *Ireland, An Illustrated History*, p. 214
14. Ibid. p. 216
15. McManus, *The Story of the Irish Race*, p.p. 696-701
16. Llywleylen, *1916*, p.p. 425-27
17. Ibid. p.p. 423-24
18. Ranelaigh, *Ireland, An Illustrated History*, p.216
19. Llywleylen, *1916*, p.p. 477-81
20. MacAnnaidh, Irish History, p.p. 248-49
21. Ranelaigh, *Ireland, An Illustrated History*, p.p. 219-223

Chapter Nineteen

1. Ranelaigh, *Ireland, An Illustrated History*, p.p. 226-27
2. Ibid. p.p. 224-25
3. Ibid. p. 227
4. Duffy, *The Concise History of Ireland, p. 198*
5. Llywleylen, *1921*, p.p. 112-13, 121, 153-54
6. Cruise O'Brien, *Ireland, A Concise History*, 142-43
7. MacAnnaidh, *Irish History*, p.p.253-59
8. Ranelaigh, *Ireland, An Illustrated History*, p.230
9. Llywleylen, *1921*, p.196
10. Ranelaigh, *Ireland, An Illustrated History*, p.230
11. Massie, *Irish History and Culture*, p.158
12. Coogan, *Ireland in the Twentieth Century*, p.p. 75-77
13. Ranelaigh, *Ireland, An Illustrated History*, p. 231
14. Ibid. p. 232
15. Coogan, *Ireland in the Twentieth Century*, p.124
16. Ibid. p. 76
17. Ranelaigh, *Ireland, An Illustrated History*, p. 233
18. Coogan, *Ireland in the Twentieth Century*, p. 82
19. Ibid. p 123
20. Ibid. p.83
21. Llyweylen, *1921*, p.p. 244-45
22. Ibid. p. 254
23. Ibid. p.255
24. Ibid. p.257

25. Ranelaigh, *Ireland, An Illustrated History*, p.236
26. Llyweylen, *1921*, p.p.259-60
27. Coogan, *Ireland in the Twentieth Century*, p. 84
28. Ranelaigh, *Ireland, An Illustrated History*, p.237

Chapter Twenty

1.   Coogan, *Ireland in the Twentieth Century*, p. 91
2.   Ibid. p.p. 93-96
3.   Ibid. p.100
4.   McManus, *The Story of the Irish Race*, p.711
5.   Moody & Martin, *The Course of Irish History*, p. 275
6.   Coogan, *Ireland in the Twentieth Century*, p. 105
7.   Ibid. p.115
8.   Moody & Martin, *The Course of Irish History*, p.264
9.   Llywelyn, *1921*, p.383
10. Coogan, *Ireland in the Twentieth Century*, .124
11. Feeney, *Sinn Fein, A Hundred Turbulent Years*, p.155
12. Llyweylen, *1921*, p.378
13. Ibid. p.p. 378-79
14. Feeney, *Sinn Fein, A Hundred Turbulent Years*, p.151

Chapter Twenty-One

1.   Moody & Martin, *The Course of Irish History*, p.276
2.   Coogan, *Ireland in the Twentieth Century*, p.158-59
3.   Ibid. p.p. 159-60
4.   Ranelaigh, *Ireland, An Illustrated History*,   p.251
5.   Coogan, *Ireland in the Twentieth Century*, p.182
6.   Ibid. p. 177
7.   Ibid. p. 184
8.   McManus, *The Story of the Irish Race*, p.719
9.   MacGarry, Fearghal, *The Making of an Irish Fascist, p.p. 33-74*
10. Ibid. p.30
11. Foster, R.F., *Modern Ireland. 1600-1972* p. 719
12. Moody & Martin, *The Course of Irish History*, p.p. 276-78
13. Coogan, *Ireland in the Twentieth Century*, p.327
14. Ibid. p.p. 327-28
15. Foster, R.F., *Modern Ireland. 1600-1972*, p.p. 559-60
16. Coogan, *Ireland in the Twentieth Century*, p.p. 329-333
17. Foster, R.F., *Modern Ireland. 1600-1972*, p.p. 560-62
18. Kee, *Ireland, A History*, p. 220

Chapter Twenty-Two:

1.   Feeney, *Sinn Fein, A Hundred Turbulent Years*, p.p. 190-1
2.   Cruise O'Brien, *Ireland, A Concise History*, p.160

3. Duffy, *The Concise History of Ireland, p.p. 226-7*
4. Ibid.p. 215
5. Moody & Martin, *The Course of Irish History*, p.425
6. Duffy, *The Concise History of Ireland*, p.220
7. Moody & Martin, *The Course of Irish History*, p.p. 282-7
8. Ibid. p.p. 426-7
9. Duffy, *The Concise History of Ireland*, p. 220
10. Moody & Martin, *The Course of Irish History*, p.p. 288-9
11. Ibid, p.289
12. Duffy, *The Concise History of Ireland, p.p 228-9*
13. Moody & Martin, *The Course of Irish History*, p.428
14. Duffy, *The Concise History of Ireland*, p.229
15. Feeney, *Sinn Fein, A Hundred Turbulent Years*, p.p. 254-5
16. Duffy, *The concise History of Ireland, p. 229*
17. Ibid. p. 231

Chapter Twenty-three

1. O'Brien, *Ireland, A Concise History*, p.173
2. Feeney, *Sinn Fein, A Hundred Turbulent Years*, p. 265
3. Ibid. p. 265
4. Ibid. p, 266
5. Cruise O'Brien, *Ireland, A Concise History*, p. 173
6. Feeney, *Sinn Fein, A Hundred Turbulent Years*, p.p. 270-1
7. Duffy, *The Concise History of Ireland*, p.p.232-3
8. Feeney, *Sinn Fein, A Hundred Turbulent Years*, p. 272
9. Moody & Martin, *The Course of Irish History*, p.292
10. Ibid. p.430Ibid. p.292-3
11. Cruise O'Brien, *Ireland, A Concise History*, p.p.174-5
12. Moody & Martin, *The Course of Irish History*, p.295
13. Duffy, *The Concise History of Ireland*, p.p. 221-2
14. Moody & Martin, *The Course of Irish History*, p.295
15. Feeney, *Sinn Fein, A Hundred Turbulent Years*, p.286
16. Moody & Martin, p.305
17. Feeney, *Sinn Fein, A Hundred Turbulent Years*, p.p.287-91
18. Duffy, *The Concise History of Ireland*, p.236
19. Moody & Martin, The Course of Irish History, p.p. 306-7

Chapter Twenty-four

1. Feeney, *Sinn Fein, A Hundred Turbulaent Years*, p.p.337-9
2. Moody & Martin, *The Course of Irish History*, p.p. 306-8
3. Feeney, *Sinn Fein, A Hundred Turbulaent Years*, p. 339
4. Ibid. p.p. 352-40
5. Moody & Martin, *The Course of Irish History*, p.p. 308-9
6. Coogan, *Ireland in the 20th Century, p.p. 651, 657-9, 6002*

7. Feeney, *Sinn Fein, A Hundred Turbulaent Years*, p. 37
8. Coogan, *Ireland in the 20th Century*, p.p. 657-60
9. Moody & Martin, *The Course of Irish History*, p. 311
10. Feeney, *Sinn Fein, A Hundred Turbulaent Years*, p.p. 396-7
11. Duffy, *The Concise History of Ireland*, p. 236
12. Moody & Martin, *The Course of Irish History*, p.p. 310-433
13. Feeney, *Sinn Fein, A Hundred Turbulent Years*, p.p. 398-9
14. Coogan, *Ireland in the 20th Century*, p.663
15. Feeney, *Sinn Fein, A Hundred Turbulent Years*, p.395
16. Ibid.p.p. 392.398, 400-1
17. Coogan, *Ireland in the 20th Century*, p.p.661-2
18. Feeney, *Sinn Fein, A Hundred Turbulent Years*, p.p.395, 406
19. Coogan, *Ireland in the 20th Century*, p. 663, 666-7
20. Feeney, *Sinn Fein, A Hundred Turbulent Years*, p.p. 404-9
21. Coogan, *Ireland in the 20th Century*, p.p. 670-2
22. Moody & Martin, *The Course of Irish History*, p.p. 327-9
23. Bright, (editor) *Let's Go Ireland 2003*, p.65
24. Feeney, *Sinn Fein, A Hundred Turbulent Years*, p.412
25. Moody & Martin, *The Course of Irish History*, p.p. 327-9
26. Coogan, *Ireland in the 20th Century*, p. 673, 676
27. Ibid. p.p. 326-9
28. Ibid. p.p. 676
29. Ibid. p.p. 677
30. Moody & Martin, *The Course of Irish History*, p.p.329-30
31. Coogan, *Ireland in the 20th Century*, p.p.679-80
32. Feeney, *Sinn Fein, A Hundred Turbulent Years*, p. 415
33. Coogan, *Ireland in the 20th Century*, p. 680
34. Moody & Martin, *The Course of Irish History*, p.p. 330-1
35. Coogan, *Ireland in the 20th Century*, p. 681
36. Feeney, *Sinn Fein, A Hundred Turbulaent Years*, p. 417
37. Moody & Martin, *The Course of Irish History*, p. 331
38. Ibid. p.p. 332-3
39. Coogan, *Ireland in the 20th Century*, p. 689
40. Ibid. p.693-6
41. *The Wall Street Irish American*, Aug/Sept 06
42. *The Wall Street Irish America*, Apr/May 07, p.10
43. *The Irish Echo*, Feb. 21-27, 2007
44. *The Irish Echo*, Mar. 7-13, 20 07
45. *The Irish Echo*, Mar. 14-20, 2007
46. *The Irish Echo*, Mar. 14-20, 2007
47. *The Irish Echo*, Feb 28-Mar 6, 2007
48. *The Irish Echo*, Mar. 28-Apr. 3, 2007
49. *The Irish Echo*, May2-8, 2007
50. *The Irish Echo*, May 9-15, 2007

INDEX